COLLECTED ESSAYS IN LAW

# Legal Scholarship and Education

## Collected Essays in Law Series

*General Editor: Tom D. Campbell*

Dispute Processing and Conflict Resolution

*Carrie Menkel-Meadow*

ISBN: 978 0 7546 2305 2

Objectivity in Ethics and Law

*Michael Moore*

ISBN: 978 0 7546 2329 8

Crime, Compliance and Control

*Doreen McBarnet*

ISBN: 978 0 7546 2349 6

Democracy Through Law

*Johan Steyn*

ISBN: 978 0 7546 2404 2

Legal Reasoning, Legal Theory and Rights

*Martin P. Golding*

ISBN: 978 0 7546 2669 5

Meaning, Mind and Law

*Dennis Patterson*

ISBN: 978 0 7546 2749 4

Living Law

*Roger Cotterrell*

ISBN: 978 0 7546 2710 4

Law as Resistance

*Peter Fitzpatrick*

ISBN: 978 0 7546 2685 5

Mark Tushnet

# Legal Scholarship and Education

ASHGATE

Published by
Dartmouth Publishing Company Limited
Gower House
Croft Road
Aldershot
Hampshire GU11 3HR
England

Ashgate Publishing Company
Suite 420
101 Cherry Street
Burlington, VT 05401-4405
USA

Ashgate website: http://www.ashgate.com

**British Library Cataloguing in Publication Data**
Tushnet, Mark V., 1945-
Legal scholarship and education. - (Collected essays in law)
1. Law - Study and teaching - United States 2. Critical legal studies - United States 3. Jurisprudence - Research
I. Title
340'.0711'73

**Library of Congress Cataloging-in-Publication Data**
Tushnet, Mark V., 1945-
Legal scholarship and education / by Mark Tushnet.
p. cm. – (Collected essays in law)
Includes index.
Articles originally published 1979-2005.
ISBN 978-0-7546-2673-2 (alk. paper)
1. Law–Study and teaching–United States. 2. Critical legal studies–United States. 3. Jurisprudence–Research. I. Title.

KF 272.T87 2008
340.071'173–dc22

ISBN 978 0 7546 2673 2

Mixed Sources
Product group from well-managed forests and other controlled sources
www.fsc.org Cert no. SGS-COC-2482
© 1996 Forest Stewardship Council
FSC

Printed and bound in Great Britain by
TJ International Ltd, Padstow, Cornwall

# Contents

# Acknowledgements

The editor and publisher wish to thank the following for permission to use copyrighted material.

Blackwell Publishing for the essays: (1987) Legal Scholarship in the United States: An Overview, *Modern Law Review*, **50**, pp. 804–17; (2005) Survey Article: Critical Legal Theory (without Modifiers) in the United States, *Journal of Political Philosophy*, **13**, pp. 99–112.

Chicago-Kent Law Review for the essays: (1994) The Death of an Author, By Himself, *Chicago-Kent Law Review*, **70**, pp. 111–5; (1996) Interdisciplinary Legal Scholarship: The Case of History-in-Law, *Chicago-Kent Law Review*, **71**, pp. 909–35.

Constitutional Commentary for the essay: (1988) The Future of Constitutional Law Scholarship, *Constitutional Commentary*, **5**, pp. 28–32.

Duke Law Journal for the essay: (1990) Introduction (Symposium on Frontiers of Legal Thought), *Duke Law Journal*, **1990**, pp. 193–200.

Foundation for the Study of Independent Social Ideas for the essay: (1993) Idols of the Right: The "Law-and-Economics" Movement, *Dissent*, **Fall 1993**, pp. 475–82.

George Washington Law Review for the essays: (1984) Introduction, *George Washington Law Review*, **52**, pp. 239–42; Essay on clinical education, *George Washington Law Review*, **52**, pp. 272–9.

Georgetown Journal of Legal Ethics for the essay: (1995) Evaluating Students as Preparation for the Practice of Law, *Georgetown Journal of Legal Ethics*, **8**, pp. 313–25. Reprinted with the permission of the publisher, Georgetown Journal of Legal Ethics © 1995.

Harvard Journal of Law and Public Policy for the essay: (1997) Law, Science, and Law and Economics, *Harvard Journal of Law & Public Policy*, **21**, pp. 47–52, reprinted with permission.

Journal of Legal Education for the essay: (1986) Critical Legal Studies: An Introduction to Its Origins and Underpinnings, *Journal of Legal Education*, **36**, pp. 505–17.

Texas Law Review for the essay: (1979) Truth, Justice, and the American Way: Constitutional Law Scholarship in the Seventies, *Texas Law Review*, **57**, pp. 1307–59. Copyright Texas Law Review Association.

UMKC Law Review for the essay: (1997) An Introduction (to Symposium: Academic Evaluations Focus), *UMKC Law Review*, **65**, pp. 643–6. Reprinted with the permission of the UMKC Law Review.

Wisconsin Law Review for the essays: (1980) Post-Realist Legal Scholarship, *Wisconsin Law Review*, **1980**, pp. 1383–401, copyright 1980 by The Board of Regents of the University of Wisconsin System, reprinted by permission of the Wisconsin Law Review; "Everything Old Is New Again": Early Reflections on the "New Chicago School," *Wisconsin Law Review*, **1998**, pp. 579–90, copyright 1998 by The Board of Regents of the University of Wisconsin System, reprinted by permission of the Wisconsin Law Review.

Yale Law Journal for the essays: (1981) Legal Scholarship: Its Causes and Cure, *Yale Law Journa*l, **90**, pp. 1205–23; (1990) Critical Legal Studies: A Political History, *Yale Law Journal*, **100**, pp. 1515–44.

# Series Editor's Preface

Collected Essays in Law makes available some of the most important work of scholars who have made a major contribution to the study of law. Each volume brings together a selection of writings by a leading authority on a particular subject. The series gives authors an opportunity to present and comment on what they regard as their most important work in a specific area. Within their chosen subject area, the collections aim to give a comprehensive coverage of the authors' research. Care is taken to include essays and articles which are less readily accessible and to give the reader a picture of the development of the authors' work and an indication of research in progress.

**Mark Tushnet**

# Introduction*

The essays collected here discuss legal scholarship and education in the United States in the late twentieth century. They are more concerned with the intellectual structures of legal scholarship and education than with the material conditions of legal education or with the way in which legal education was then organized. In this Introduction I offer comments on how my prior work looks to me from my present location.

Notably, all but one of the essays here dates from the 1980s and 1990s. The reasons for the temporal limitation are simple enough. Legal academics in the United States typically follow one of two career paths into the academy. In the 1970s, when I started my career as a law teacher, most served as judicial law clerks (as I did), engaged in legal practice briefly (as I did not), and then entered the academy. Some then and even more now obtain an advanced degree in an allied discipline – economics, history, political science, for example – and then enter the legal academy, perhaps after serving as a judicial law clerk but rarely having practiced law. Neither career path provides the novice legal academic with an opportunity to grapple with the state of the *legal* discipline, in the way that candidates for advanced degrees in allied disciplines work through the classics in their fields and assess where their own scholarship stands in relation to the field. Many of my early essays were my efforts to come to grips with the state of legal scholarship in the way that a candidate for a doctoral degree does with respect to his or her discipline. Having done so to my satisfaction, I redirected my efforts to contributions to substantive legal scholarship, leaving it to others to relate my substantive work to the history of legal thought.

In addition, my early years in the legal academy coincided with the development of critical legal studies. As the very name suggests, that subdiscipline, or approach to legal scholarship, contained an important element of critique, that is, of assessment and criticism of existing forms of legal scholarship. Once the general outlines of the critique had been developed, there was little to add, other than to apply the critiques to new versions of old forms. (Some of the essays in Part Two are such applications.) Further, the seeming waning of critical legal studies – a matter I address in Essay 5, the only recent article in this collection – pushed my work in a substantive rather than self- or field-reflective direction. Again, it seemed more interesting to me to do scholarship whose predicates were the underlying approaches taken in critical

* I thank Laura Kalman for suggesting that I collect my essays on legal scholarship and legal education, and Tom Campbell for giving me the opportunity to do so.

legal studies than to articulate and defend those approaches in methodological or quasi-philosophical terms.

Taken as a whole, the essays in Part One make several related claims. The first group consists of descriptions of what I understood to be the predicates of critical legal studies. These include the so-called indeterminacy thesis – that, in all interesting cases (a category that itself requires some analysis), the legal materials available to a skilled lawyer in any mature legal system allow the lawyer to make, and a decision-maker to adopt, any position that advances the lawyer's interests (including those of the lawyer's client, of course) or the decision-maker's preferences. They also include the claim that 'law is politics', with the implicit addition 'all the way down'. One version of that claim is that there is no form of *legal* reasoning that is not, on analysis, reducible to political argumentation broadly understood to include arguments predicated on moral theory or, less grandiosely, visions of the good society.

These claims led to additional claims about legal scholarship. The one of most interest to me was that legal scholarship was of necessity a subject for what I tended to call sociological inquiry, and what others associated with critical legal studies called historical inquiry or ideological critique. Because legal arguments were indeterminate and law was politics all the way down, legal arguments, of which legal scholarship was a sub-category, had to be understood as a form of political action. Just as one would analyze why a presidential candidate took a particular position by examining how the candidate might think the position advanced their electoral goals, so one would analyze legal scholarship by examining the politics associated with it. But indeterminacy meant that there was no politics *necessarily* associated with any particular legal account, which meant in turn that one ought to examine how particular arguments figured in legal-political discourse at any historical juncture. As the essays in Part One suggest, the so-called critique of rights associated with critical legal studies, and in particular with my own work, was best understood as that sort of political analysis. It asked how the rhetoric of rights functioned in the period from roughly 1970 to 1980, and did not offer a philosophical analysis of the 'concept' of rights in some trans-historical sense.

My essays on critical legal studies underemphasized, though they did not completely ignore, another strand in the field. That strand supplemented the historical and sociological accounts with which I was most comfortable with more psychologistic accounts, which attempted to explain why – again, at particular moments – specific forms of legal argument actually appealed to people and motivated them to act (or to accept the status quo). Importantly, these accounts were consistent with the prevalent methodological premises of late twentieth century social science – that all successful historical and sociological accounts ultimately had to refer to the motivations *individuals* had for their actions. To the extent that my essays recognized the psychologistic strand in critical legal studies, the essays can be taken to present the field as offering a social scientific account of law that at least in terms of method sought to comport with prevailing methodological standards. To the extent that the essays underemphasized that strand, they misrepresented the field and opened it up to the criticism that the 'law is politics' slogan was mistakenly deterministic because it had no place for individuals and their choices.

Understanding that critical legal studies is, or was, a form of historical and sociological analysis casts some light on its current condition. As Essay 5 argues, the core propositions of critical legal studies are now the conventional wisdom among US legal academics. The indeterminacy thesis, qualified appropriately as it had been in early critical legal studies, is widely accepted, with disagreement arising only with respect to two propositions. The first was never truly made in critical legal studies, that *every* statable legal proposition is indeterminate. The second is the proposition that indeterminacy is resolved by political choice. Here real disagreements do arise, with some legal scholars claiming that indeterminacy can be resolved through distinctively legal techniques. I should note, though, that in my view those claims are made with decreasing force and internal commitment as the scholars' sophistication increases. Put another way, sophisticated legal scholars in the United States today accept both of the core propositions associated with critical legal studies.

At the same time, the widespread acceptance of those propositions does not mean that 'critical legal studies' as a sub-disciplinary field is flourishing. Essay 4 argues that critical legal studies was never really a sub-discipline of law, but was instead what I call a 'political location,' a place – sometimes physical, as in the meetings of the Conference on Critical Legal Studies, and always conceptual – where people sharing roughly similar jurisprudential views (that is, some versions of the core propositions) *and* political views could get together to support each other in their academic careers. As conditions changed inside and outside the legal academy, the need for such a location changed as well. The increasing conservatism of US courts, for example, pushed mainstream liberals somewhat to the left. This meant that people whose views were farther to the left for mainstream liberals to be comfortable with in the 1980s were now not as 'extreme' as they had been, and could find political allies outside the community identified with critical legal studies.

The essays in Part Two shift from critical legal studies as a sub-field to legal scholarship more generally, but most of them look at mainstream legal scholarship from the left perspective I found in critical legal studies. With a couple of exceptions, the essays are united by a single theme: Mainstream legal scholarship consists of a series of attempts, always unsuccessful, to avoid or conceal the political judgments necessary to resolve legal controversies.

The essays fall roughly into three groups. The first deals with legal scholarship through the early 1970s, and focuses primarily on the legal process school. As I interpreted that school's approach, it relied on a combination of informal social scientific descriptions of the distinctive competencies of different law-making institutions with an untheorized account of what constituted good legal judgment to provide what its proponents thought – or at least were taken to have thought – to be non-political answers to legal questions. (In fact, there were at least moments in the works of legal process scholars when one could glimpse rather explicit statements that, in the end, the judgments relied on were politically weighted rather than politically neutral.) Along with others, I argued that legal process scholarship failed in its ambitions. Given my interests I focused on claims about courts' distinctive capacities, and argued, in essence, that with minor exceptions courts could do (and had done) just about everything legislatures could do, and that legislatures could do just about everything courts could do. In addition, I made what I think is the easier argument that the criteria of professional competence on which legal process scholars relied when they referred to 'good judgment' were inevitably political.

The second group of essays deals with law-and-economics as a sub-discipline. Here the critical arguments have become, in my judgment, increasingly credible over time, although their insights were right from the outset. The first generation of scholarship in law and economics made dramatically reductionist assumptions, defended on the ground that theory makes progress only by starting simple and getting complex, and on the additional ground – originally laid out by Milton Friedman – that the reductionist theory generated predictions or descriptions of events that actually fit the real world. But, critics of law-and-economics argued, the predictions and descriptions were not actually that good.

Second and third generation law-and-economics scholarship developed increasingly complex models. These models had two characteristics. First, they showed that any predictions and descriptions about the real world were going to have to take into account a much wider range of facts than had first generation scholarship – and a much wider range than was realistically available. The predictions and descriptions then turned out to rest on *assumptions* about the real world. But it would seem preferable actually to look at the real world directly instead of making assumptions about the world merely to feed into a formal economic model. This point brought to the fore the connection between the critical legal studies' approach to law-and-economics and that taken by the law-and-society movement in the United States and scholars of sociolegal studies elsewhere.

Second, first-generation law-and-economics scholarship dealt with 'big' problems: the justification (or, given its political spin, the criticism) of an interventionist government, the fundamental structure of basic legal concepts in property, contract, and tort, and the like. The more complex models developed later sharply reduced the credibility of univocal claims about these big problems, substituting alternative and sometimes directly contradictory claims. Second and third generation scholars turned increasingly to small problems or puzzles. This is the natural course of normal science after a paradigm shift. But it made law-and-economics a sub-discipline that came to be more and more self-contained and less and less interesting to the wider scholarly community.

Law-and-economics survived, of course, because it was congenial to the conservative political climate in the late twentieth century. Its intellectual vitality could be questioned. Adherents seemed to be engaged in a restless search for new concepts – 'norms' theory (discussed in Essay 11), behavioral law-and-economics, and now neuroscience – that would give law-and-economics a non-political foundation. These moves made transparent what critics had maintained from the outset: Law-and-economics was a modern version of earlier efforts to resolve legal questions without reference to politics. Economics was particularly attractive because it had the aura of science (see Essay 10), but the half-life of conceptual innovations was strikingly short: The 'New Chicago School' and norms scholarship has basically disappeared in less than a decade. The lure of science as law's salvation continues, with left-leaning American legal scholars in the early twenty-first century hoping to find answers to law's problems in contemporary neuroscience, and right-leaning ones placing their hopes in evolutionary biology. I myself would not put a large bet on the possibility that either enterprise will succeed.

The final pair of essays in Part Two moves away from law-and-economics to address interdisciplinary legal scholarship more broadly defined. The essays here are less critical than the prior ones. That may result from the fact that proponents of interdisciplinary scholarship make weak claims about their ability to resolve legal questions in a non-political way, or even no such claims at all. More important, I think, is that I deploy my skepticism about legal scholarship's ambitions in a somewhat more ironic tone – perhaps the result of the shift in my interests noted at the outset of this introduction, from scholarship about scholarship to scholarship itself.

Part Three contains two rather outdated essays on the scholarship on US constitutional law. In the 1970s and 1980s that scholarship was obsessed with questions about the proper methods of constitutional interpretation. I contributed to that literature, which we now understand was produced in response to, or as part of, an effort, largely successful, to reorient constitutional law in a more conservative direction. That reorientation having occurred, the issues of interpretive method have receded from the heart of constitutional scholarship. With power in hand, conservatives now are as willing as liberals were to be eclectic in their interpretive approaches. The political dimensions of constitutional law were always reasonably apparent, which made my efforts to debunk claims for political neutrality something like shooting ducks in a barrel, in contrast to the far more difficult task shouldered by those who sought to make the same demonstration for private law subjects.

I suggested that constitutional law scholarship would become intellectually vibrant only if it abandoned two prevailing modes: the pretense of political neutrality by scholars who were evidently interested in achieving preferred political outcomes, and legal advocacy overtly in the service of political goals. At the highest levels of legal scholarship, those modes have been largely abandoned, although some conservatives regarded as working at the intellectual peaks still use them. The best recent scholarship has moved, as I suggested it should, in the direction of absorbing some of the insights of political science. My own work has drawn on what political scientists have had to say about constitutionalism generally, about the specific institutional forms of US constitutionalism, and about constitutional law in other legal systems. And, I should note, I have been increasingly interested in traditional doctrinal scholarship, although I confess that I find it difficult to reconcile my critical impulses with my doctrinal ones.

The final Part contains several quite brief essays on legal education rather than legal scholarship. In my mind, they are united by two themes perhaps not readily apparent to any readers of the essays. Both themes are loosely connected to ideas associated with critical legal studies. The first, most clearly stated in Essay 17, is that the model of clinical legal education, in which law students provide legal services to clients, usually of low income, who would otherwise find it difficult to obtain representation, offers the *pedagogical* advantage of helping students understand how the law works in the real world, and the *intellectual* advantage of providing students and instructors with factual material that they can use in developing the kind of sociological perspective on the law that, I believe, critical legal studies argued was essential to full comprehension of law in society. In addition, at its inception and even today, though somewhat less so, clinical legal education had political content, because the clients to whom legal services were provided were poor and disadvantaged. This only barely concealed political content helped relegate clinical legal education to the margins of legal education in the United States, even as it made clinical legal education attractive to those who occupied the critical legal studies political location.

The second theme in these essays is also political. I urge teachers to innovate in pedagogic and evaluative techniques that somehow help students work together, to be cooperative learners rather than competitive individualists. There are, I believe, good grounds in pedagogical theory for the use of such techniques, and as Essay 18 argues there are equally good arguments that such techniques prepare students for their experience in legal practice. But my primary interest in these cooperative techniques is that they can model a kind of social action that in my view lies at the heart of politics.

In a sense, then, a single strand unifies all these essays: Politics pervades legal scholarship and legal education, and we have an intellectual and political obligation to make that fact clear.

# Part One

# Critical Legal Studies

# [1]
# Introduction

The critical legal studies movement is hardly unified: any summary must be little more than its author's view of the subject. With that caveat, this introduction will sketch what I believe to be at the heart of the critical legal studies approach.

Examination of critical legal studies reveals two intertwined points. First, critical legal studies is a sustained attack on all types of formalism. Second, that attack is also directed towards liberal political theory because some version of formalism is essential to the coherence of liberal political theory. The attack on formalism makes critical legal studies the heir to legal realism, which itself was an attack on one or two versions of formalism. But the critical legal studies approach is comprehensive in a way that legal realism was not, and its rejection of liberal political theory sharply distinguishes critical legal studies from legal realism.

Formalism, to critical legal theorists, claims that some type of analysis provides a solution to problems of legal choice, policy choice, or social analysis by limiting the range of pure choice within which the analyst — judge, policy-maker, social scientist — operates. The easiest version of the critical approach is the direct descendant, or perhaps only a simple revival of legal realism: the demonstration of the inability of doctrinal analysis to produce results that are independent of the prior predelictions of the judge or academic doing the analysis.

People usually nod in agreement, but then continue to produce large quantities of doctrinal analysis attempting to demonstrate which solution is most consistent with the fundamental structure of torts or contracts or the theory of the Constitution. Alternatively, they attempt to restore nondoctrinal formalism to the legal system by offering what may be called post-realist responses, including the invocation of law and economics to provide normative guidance to the disposition of legal problems, and the invocation of systematic moral philosophy a la Rawls and Nozick.

This introduction cannot provide detailed examples of the different approaches within critical legal studies towards analyzing each of these formalisms. Some people take on law and economics from within; others find the rhetorical modes of modern literary theory — deconstruction, post-stucturalism, and the like — more suitable to the critical task. These modes of analysis first identify the hidden assumptions necessary to make the surface analysis coherent, then demonstrate that those same assumptions would also make the contrary analysis coherent.

The connection between the critique of formalism and the challenge to liberal political theory is that liberal political theory depends on formalism. Liberal political theory centers around the individual, who is conceived of as the locus of sheer preferences. Those preferences are ineradicably individual. The only inherent connection between one individual's preferences and the existence of other people is that other people serve as methods by which the individual's preferences can be achieved. That connection leads to an effort to coordinate action through contract and, notably, the application of coercive power. Coercive power is located in an institution, the state, primarily because we cannot guarantee the success of our contractual enterprises unless there is some coercive power available to enforce sanctions for breaches (assuming roughly equal physical power among contractors and their allies). The state, therefore, serves to promote the achievement of individual preferences and to solve the problem of social order that arises when we try to enforce our own preferences in the absence of sanctioning institutions. But the very fact that the state is an institution creates a new set of problems, which is captured in Hobbes' image of the Leviathan. Those who staff the Leviathan are no different from the rest of us in their view of others as a means to accomplish their ends. Hence, the coercive power we have lodged in them to serve our goals may be used by them to serve theirs. Some method must be developed to control the exercise of the coercive power of the state. Liberal political theorists usually label that method "The Rule of Law." According to the rule of law, those who staff the Leviathan will be constrained to act in our interests rather than in theirs by requiring that they act pursuant to rules announced in advance, that they not sit in judgment on cases in which their personal interests are implicated, and so on through Lon Fuller's list of the characteristics of the rule of law.

The idea of the rule of law is necessarily a version of formalism.

The first formulation to which people are attracted, that the staff must act pursuant to rules announced in advance, is ordinary doctrinal formalism of the sort that the legal realists attacked. The idea of the rule of law is so important to liberal political theory that, since the realists, there have been continual efforts to reestablish the coherence of the idea of the rule of law by inventing new formalisms, such as law and economics, policy science, and sociological determinism.

The critical legal studies approach, if its critiques of all versions of formalism succeed, will render unavailing the solutions liberal political theory offers for the Hobbesian problem of social order. Because the critical legal studies approach aims to critique all versions of formalism, however, its task can never be concluded. Some formalism can always be invented to survive the critiques mounted against the formalisms we have addressed so far. That is inescapable. But the critical legal studies approach has been successful often enough to provide a reasonably solid basis for an inductive generalization, or at least to place the burden on those who defend the rule of law to articulate a coherent version of it.

Critical legal studies does not have a positive program. Of course many things ought to be done in the next few weeks and years, but they are not derived from an overall normative or descriptive theory of the operation of the political system. Rather, they are the result of intensely pragmatic judgments about what appears useful in the present circumstances. In this sense, critical legal studies can simultaneously have no program and yet be committed to particular political positions on specific issues.

One thread running through the various critiques of specific versions of formalism raises another point about the positive program of critical legal studies. Each formalism, in different ways, is undermined by a set of premises that place individualism in the foreground, but perceive the individual as existing in a broader community. The critique gets its bite, not by rejecting the set of premises as a whole, but by reversing the priorities of the items already within the set, by bringing to the foreground the communitarian assumptions that are necessary to comprehend the individualist premises. From this, one could spin out a positive program aimed at reversing the priorities within liberal political theory, not just as a matter of intellectual analysis, but as a positive political program. The idea would be to develop an alternative communitarian political theory in which the social aspects of human life have both analytic and practical priority over the individualist aspects of human life.

Most of the people who have engaged in the theoretical work of the critical legal studies movement have been quite reluctant to develop such a communitarian political theory. Because human life is both social and individual, inevitably, no internally coherent theory of politics will adequately account for both the individualist and social elements of human life. If we tried to develop a communitarian political theory that reversed the priorities of liberal political theory, it would be subject to the same kind of critique that we have leveled against liberal political theory.

Finally, the political action associated with the critical legal studies approach requires that we make pragmatic assessments. But how can one make pragmatic assessments of what ought to be done without having a broader theory? Usually we can make a pragmatic assessment of who will be helped and who will be hurt by particular political actions. The basis for choosing which side we want to be on without a broader theory can be found in making atheoretical choices. By living in the world, we are able to identify pain and suffering in an atheoretical way. Although such perception does not automatically lead to alleviation of pain and suffering, that sort of existential phenomenology can provide the ground for a choice of sides in the absence of a broader theory of social and political life.

# [2]
# Critical Legal Studies: An Introducion to its Origins and Underpinnings

These comments take on the task of explaining why Critical Legal Studies (CLS) forms an appropriate part of a jurisprudence course. Additionally, it provides an overview of what might be included in that part of the course. Material from CLS is already infiltrating the materials used in the first-year curriculum, and at least one prominent British text on jurisprudence has included a brief discussion of CLS in its chapter on American Legal Realism.[2] As that discussion suggests, Legal Realism is one of the intellectual origins of CLS; the other is the progressive tradition in American historiography.

In many ways CLS is a direct descendant of American Legal Realism, which flourished in the 1920s and 1930s and left an important legacy to all legal thought.[3] CLS interprets Legal Realism along the following lines. The Realists offered a critical analysis of law as they saw it. At the time the Realists wrote, many lawyers, judges, and scholars seemed to think that they could draw on a relatively small collection of fairly abstract concepts—CLS has focused on "liberty of contract" and "property rights"—as the basis for decisions in particular cases. Results could either be deduced from the necessary meanings of the concepts or intuited from the social understanding of their meanings. The critical dimension of Legal Realism established that these assumptions were unfounded.[4] The concepts were so abstract that they led to contradictory conclusions, and because of social divisions—between employers and organized labor, for example—there could be no broadly

1. The proximate source of this introduction was a talk given at the Workshop on Jurisprudence sponsored by the AALS on March 20-22, 1986.

2. Lord Lloyd of Hampstead & M.D.A. Freeman, Lloyd's Introduction to Jurisprudence 709–16, 5th ed. (London, 1985).

3. It is a matter of some controversy whether CLS offers anything that the most thorough going Legal Realists did not. See e.g., Robert Gordon, Critical Legal Histories, 36 Stan. L. Rev. 57, 102 n. 102 (1984). Like Gordon, I doubt that much of interest turns on the resolution of that controversy. As I discuss below, I believe that CLS has in some ways deepened the basic insights of Legal Realism, but whether that counts as an innovation seems to me an uninteresting question.

4. Here as elsewhere I use words such as "established" to indicate my view that the arguments offered by the Legal Realists were correct. Those interested in this discussion as an effort to retrieve the intellectual background of CLS may substitute words that do not express such evaluations.

shared social understandings on which intuitions could properly be based.[5]

The second intellectual source of CLS is the progressive tradition in American historiography. Like Legal Realism, progressive historiography flourished in the 1920s and 1930s. The progressive historians, including Charles Beard and Vernon Parrington, argued that the best way to understand the course of American history was to pay attention to the play of interest groups in American society.[6] Much of their work was devoted to debunking the claims of filiopietistic writers that the best way to understand the course of American history was as the working out of the idea of progress within a generally liberal political framework. The progressive historians looked at American policies and politics and saw much more of economic interest at work; for that they were, rather like CLS people today, called Marxists.[7]

In CLS the most important voice for the progressive tradition has been that of Morton Horwitz.[8] Historians found Horwitz's work entirely congenial—so congenial that they awarded his book their most prestigious professional award, the Bancroft Prize—because he told a story with which historians were familiar. He looked at antebellum courts and found that they were making decisions that, as he interpreted them, promoted the advance of American corporate enterprise and industrialization. Historians had heard versions of this story before. In the late 1940s Louis Hartz and Oscar Handlin, for example, had written studies that made the same point.[9] But while Hartz and Handlin had examined legislative policies and found that they promoted industrialization, Horwitz reached the same conclusion after examining judicial decisions.

Unlike the historians, lawyers felt threatened by Horwitz's story, and the reviews by lawyers were much more critical.[10] The reason is that, for lawyers if not for historians, there has to be a difference between judges and legislators;[11] otherwise the distinction between law and politics collapses. The role of the progressive tradition in CLS has been to support the general judgment that there is no tenable distinction between law and politics, just as the

5. See, e.g., Oliver Wendell Holmes, Herbert Spencer: Legislation and Empiricism, 7 Am. L. Rev. 582 (1873).

6. See Richard Hofstadter, The Progressive Historians: Turner, Beard Parrington (New York, 1968).

7. It may be worth noting that "debunking" is just another word for "trashing" or "demystification."

8. See Morton Horwitz, The Transformation of American Law, 1780–1860 (Cambridge, Mass., 1977).

9. Louis Hartz, Economic Policy and Democratic Thought: Pennsylvania, 1776–1860 (Cambridge, Mass., 1948); Oscar & Mary Handlin, Commonwealth, A Study of the Role of Government in the American Economy: Massachusetts, 1774–1861 (New York, 1947).

10. See, e.g., John Reid, Book Review, 55 Tex. L. Rev. 1307 (1977); Peter Teachout, Book Review, 53 NYU L. Rev. 291 (1977); A. B. Simpson, The Horwitz Thesis and the History of Contracts, 46 U. Chi. L. Rev. 533 (1979). Citations to other reviews can be found in Wythe Holt, Morton Horwitz and the Transformation of American Legal History, 23 Wm. & Mary L. Rev. 663, 666 nn. 8–9 (1982).

11. This is not to contend that Horwitz's analysis was unflawed. What is of interest here is the comparison between the lawyers' and the historians' responses, not the accuracy of their respective judgments.

Realists' critique of rules had argued. The general point of both traditions was to emphasize the importance of relations of power in the employment and development of law—what CLS has come to refer to as the importance of illegitimate hierarchy as an ordering institution in our society.

The Realists made another important point, which was constructive rather than critical. They argued that deduction and intuition had to be replaced by explicit and fairly systematic policy analysis. This constructive program had three elements. First, decision-makers, whether judges, legislators, or lawyers advising clients, had to identify those social interests actually at issue in a particular controversy, and had to think about how those interests might be affected by the various courses of action that might be pursued. Understanding the consequences of legal decisions required studying the actual operation of the legal system, drawing on sociology and political science for organizing concepts.[12] This study came to be called policy analysis, and it is now so widely accepted a way of thinking about law that the forms for student evaluation of teaching routinely ask whether the teacher adequately explored policy issues in the course.

Second, according to the Realists, although lawyers should abandon abstract legal concepts as the basis for decision, they should still pay attention to some important but nonetheless abstract social interests, such as promoting human freedom and material well-being. For while people might disagree about *how* those interests should be advanced and *whether* other particular values ought to be promoted, no one would disagree *that* these most fundamental values are important. Thus policy analysis could be grounded on these newly identified and broadly shared social understandings.

The third element in the Realists' constructive program was a method of legal analysis, the method of balancing. Once the precise interests at stake have been identified and their relation to the broad social values understood, decision-makers should balance the interests to arrive at an appropriate decision.

The Realists' constructive program provides the framework for most legal thought today. One need only read a randomly selected law review article or—perhaps a better indicator of what we teach our students—a randomly selected student note or comment to find that the right answer to the question at issue can be found by balancing the interests identified in the appropriate three-part test.

CLS accepts the critical aspect of Legal Realism but challenges its constructive program. Because it does so by using the critical techniques developed by the Realists, CLS is in this sense a true descendant of Realism. The way in which CLS is concerned with the political dimensions of law and domination can be explored by examining the CLS attack on policy analysis, balancing, and shared social values—that is, on the constructive program of Legal Realism.

12. The usual citation for this point is Harold Lasswell & Myres McDougal, Legal Education and Public Policy: Professional Training in the Public Interest, 52 Yale L.J. 203 (1943).

The CLS attack on policy analysis has focused on what is at present the most popular systematic form of policy analysis, law-and-economics. Law-and-economics attempts to identify what the most efficient solution to a legal problem is. That is, suppose we know how wealth is distributed in a particular society and the preferences of its members. Law-and-economics attempts to determine what rule will allow that society to achieve the most of what its members want, given the existing distribution of wealth. Everyone knows that many interesting questions are assumed away when law-and-economics takes the distribution of wealth as a given. But its proponents claim that answers to many questions are insensitive to the distribution of wealth—there could be large changes in that distribution and no changes in the efficient rules—and that, in any event, if you care about wealth distribution, it is pretty silly to worry about tort or contract law rather than, for example, the tax system.[13]

CLS has attacked law-and-economics in a number of ways. I am not competent to evaluate the technical attack, but I can describe it: The legal system, through its rules of property, contract, and tort, creates a set of entitlements. These entitlements constitute the pattern of wealth-holding in the society. If you are trying to figure out what the efficient rule of contract law is, you cannot take the distribution of wealth as given, because the rule you come up with defines the distribution of wealth. A second line of attack is that economic analysis—and by extension policy analysis more generally—necessarily proceeds by making simplifying assumptions about the world. Law-and-economics has increasingly relaxed those assumptions to make the economic models more realistic. But as the realism of the models increases the conclusions that we can draw become weaker and weaker. The most sophisticated economic analyses end up where the Legal Realists began, with a list of things we ought to think about. The third attack on policy analysis is still more general. Legal rules, and the distribution of wealth, do not merely *reflect* individual preferences. To some degree the rules shape those preferences. Decision-makers must therefore ask not only "What can we do to provide what people want" but, "How will what we do affect what people want?"

The Legal Realists' constructive program answered this question by offering its method of balancing. Sensible decision-makers, brought up in their society and sensitive to its present desires and its aspirations, would be able to take into account everything that policy analysis identified and could come up with the right answers. Here CLS makes a simple point. In our society the class of decision-makers is not representative enough to provide the assurance the Realists wanted. Decision-makers are an elite, demographically unrepresentative and socialized into a set of beliefs about society and technology that skew the balance that they reach. The CLS challenge to balancing, then, is the claim that balancing is a social process that needs to be examined sociologically. The concern for sociological analysis of the actual exercise of power is one part of the legacy of progressive historio-

13. See, e.g., A. Mitchell Polinsky, An Introduction to Law and Economics 105–13 (Boston, 1983).

graphy. Sociological analysis inevitably raises political questions. For example, CLS argues that the Realists did not go far enough in demanding a democratization of law and, notably, that neither the New Deal nor the present Democratic Party does so either.

Concern for the politics of legal thought is even more evident in the most fundamental part of the CLS challenge to the Legal Realists' constructive program. The Realists wanted lawyers to worry about how the legal system promoted broadly shared social values. Parts of the CLS argument here are simple applications of the Realists' critical arguments: The social values are described so abstractly that they could justify any decision, and there is some disagreement even about these abstract values—consider the environmentalists' challenge to arguments for increasing a society's material wealth. But the more important part of the CLS argument goes deeper. CLS insists that the social values, on which there may well be agreement, are not valuable in some abstract and timeless sense. They are values because our society is structured to produce in its members just that set of values. But if that is so, the entire constructive enterprise collapses on itself, because you cannot think about altering legal rules to conform to a society's values when those values are constructed partly on the basis of the legal rules themselves.

Taken together, the CLS arguments are bound to be unsettling. If the argument about the social construction of values is correct, people who talk about radical changes in social organization are likely to seem at least weird and off-the-wall.[14] CLS tries to put into question the deepest values of a society: Because there is nothing timeless about those values, we might simply decide to abandon them. CLS might not be able to make much headway with these arguments were it not aided by developments in other disciplines such as philosophy and sociology, whose important thinkers have also argued that social reality is itself socially constructed.

My reference to developments in other disciplines indicates where CLS goes beyond the progressive historians as well. Progressive historians tend to tell a story in which social and political developments were more or less strongly dependent upon or derived from economic developments; that is why they were sometimes called Marxists. In emphasizing economics they relied on the dominant methodological theories of historical knowledge available to them. These theories were quite strongly influenced by the model of the natural sciences and tended in the direction of a fairly strong determinism.

CLS has developed a critique of these versions of social theory which draws on the legacy of Legal Realism. One version of the critique is straightforward. Social theories attempt to provide systematic explanations of many aspects of the social order by drawing on a much smaller list of aspects that the theory identifies as fundamental. Virtually all social theories identify as fundamental some aspects whose definition requires recourse to legal

14. And after all, if their argument is correct, where do *their* values come from? Well, CLS does not argue that contemporary society is hermetically sealed against values that might, for example, be remembered as attractive relics of the past, or might be imagined by appreciating what modern art tells us about ourselves.

concepts. For example, in its classical versions Marxism derives its conclusions from premises that involve statements about ownership of the means of production. Yet if, as Legal Realism showed, the concept of ownership, like all other legal concepts, is empty and meaningless—in the sense that it can have any content and implications whatever—nothing can be derived from it. To the extent that social theories rely on legal concepts, they cannot find the explanations that they seek.

The second version of the critique of social theory goes beyond the perhaps accidental fact that most social theories use legal terms. It applies Legal Realism to the effort of social theorists to provide "law"-like explanations. Stated most abstractly, Legal Realism established that particular conclusions—outcomes in cases—could not be derived from general concepts—rules of law. It did so by showing, in example after example, that however one defined the general concepts, a critic could derive contradictory conclusions by, for instance, exploiting ambiguities in the concepts or drawing on other concepts that could not be kept out of the discussion. These analytic techniques can be used to develop a general critique of the effort to link general concepts to particular results, and that critique undermines social theory. Taken as a whole, the CLS challenge to social theory suggests that the initial effort to provide a general theoretical account of how domination occurred was misguided. At present, CLS takes the position that no such general account is available. All that we can have are examples of how domination occurs in particular settings.

This critique of social theory has a number of consequences that I will discuss presently. For the moment, the point I would like to make is that, just as progressive historiography and Legal Realism fit into the available discourses in other disciplines in the 1930s, so CLS fits into the discourses current today. The critique of rules, and more particularly the critique of social theory, has strong affinities to discussions of method in the philosophy of the social and natural sciences, as well as in various disciplines in the humanities.[15]

I turn now to a description of the current state of CLS. First, however, I must interject a number of qualifications. CLS is a developing body of thought, and it would be unsound to attempt to freeze it with an absolutely precise description. Further, different participants in the effort to push CLS ahead have different opinions, and as one of the participants, I have my own views on matters in controversy.[16]

One issue should be mentioned, only to be put aside. It seems to be a standard line in statements by critics of CLS that CLS has no constructive program. As I will indicate at the conclusion of these remarks, there is a deep sense in which that is correct. But in the superficial sense that these critics appear to intend, their comments are simply wrong. CLS offers many prop-

15. A useful recent overview of these developments, which includes a helpful bibliography, is Quentin Skinner, ed., The Return of Grand Theory in the Human Sciences (New York, 1985).

16. I should probably note my guess that I am in the minority these days on most of the issues I will mention.

osals for alternative programs. These proposals run from the mundane, such as William Simon's suggestion that a random selection of welfare determinations be automatically subjected to review on appeal,[17] to the grandiose, such as Roberto Unger's description of various forms of public control over investment.[18] I suppose that the critics' point is that, though they can *read* these statements about what ought to be done, the cannot quite understand how those practical proposals are related to the critical or theoretical dimension of CLS.

Here I will give the short answer to this criticism and will devote the rest of my paper to explaining that answer. The short answer is that the point of the proposals is to continue the critique of existing society, not to get these particular proposals adopted in the short run. This position is, as I will now try to argue, related to ongoing discussions within CLS.

To illustrate this relation, I will describe what is, or at least what was, probably the central debate within CLS.[19] The early position in CLS was that one could say something systematic about the relation between legal rules and power—for example, we can say, though with many qualifications, that the legal system is tilted in favor of capitalism. So long as it is not bound by too many qualifications, that statement or some variant has a fairly obvious intuitive appeal.

The dominant position responds by identifying—or perhaps more precisely by stressing more strongly than the early position—the difficulties inherent even in heavily qualified versions of the early formulations. Three of its arguments have been particularly effective. The first emphasizes the Legal Realists' skepticism about rules, which made it impossible to say that "the legal system" is tilted in any direction at all: If decision-makers can in principle reach any conclusion they wish within the legal system, "the system" cannot be tilted, though of course the decision-makers might be biased. The second argument is that no one has shown that any particular aspect of the legal system, or even the legal system as a whole, serves the interests of capitalism better than do obvious alternatives, including wholesale rejection of vast bodies of law. For any particular rule in the law of contracts in some state in the United States which might be thought to support capitalism, there is a precisely contrary rule, within an equally capitalist system, that is, in another state. International comparisons demonstrated that capitalist economic systems could be found in countries with widely divergent legal systems. The final argument against tilt is that the legal system in fact has little direct impact on the maintenance of capitalism. It provides a framework within which bargains can be struck, and its rules

17. William Simon, Legality, Bureaucracy, and Class in the Welfare System, 92 Yale L.J. 1198, 1267–68 (1983).

18. Roberto Unger, The Critical Legal Studies Movement, 96 Harv. L. Rev. 561, 596–97 (1983).

19. The labels that have been attached to the polar positions in this debate are "rationalist" and "irrationalist." See, e.g., Clare Dalton, Book Review, 6 Harv. Women's L.J. 229, 231 (1983). I have concluded that these labels are more misleading than helpful in providing an initial orientation to the discussions, and I have decided simply to call one the early position and the other the dominant position.

are a sort of disaster insurance against unforeseen calamities. But it is difficult to see how an institution whose purposes are so limited could have much of systemic impact.

These arguments have forced a reformulation of the early position. Agreeing that tilt could not be found systematically in the rules of the legal system, the reformulation argued that it is located in the construction of the categories used to organize legal thought and in the construction of the operations used to relate those categories.[20] This seems to me the present state of the position: It claims an analytic program, but has not yet made much progress in demonstrating the program's power.

The renunciation of the theoretical dimension of the initial project of CLS helps explain an otherwise curious characteristic of recent critical legal scholarship. Although it devotes a great deal of attention to phenomena that occurred in the past, much of the work is relentlessly ahistorical. It focuses synchronically on particular moments in the past[21] or offers a sort of comparative statics,[22] but never gives a diachronic account of transformation over time. I believe that this ahistoricism is linked to the critique of social theory, because diachronic accounts explicitly or implicitly rely on social theory to give them coherence. One tradition in the philosophy of history holds that narratives must draw on covering laws—the generalizations of social theory—of which sequences of particular events are specific instances based on identified initial conditions. Another tradition is less explicitly theoretical and claims only that historians provide narratives of past events. But the selection of the events that are placed in the narrative's sequence, out of all the possible events that could be used, seems to require some (usually implicit) theoretical account, if only the common sense theories held by well-socialized readers of historical narratives. Having renounced social theory, CLS is barred/precluded from using these standard traditions of historical writing—thus its characteristic ahistoricism.

Alternatively, one could provide a multitude of competing stories about how things changed, while insisting that none of the stories has the sort of epistemological priority that social theories gives to the narratives of the standard traditions. Or one could rely on the critique of social theory as a background against which only one account was offered, demanding that readers abjure the usual expectations they might hold about the epistemological claims implicit in such narratives. Either of these courses—the many stories or the one told with a raised eyebrow—could force readers to consider what might be the basis for the critical legal scholar's choice of stories to tell. And that would bring the politics of CLS directly into the discussion.

20. See, e.g., Gordon, *supra* note 3, at 109-13.

21. See, e.g., Duncan Kennedy, The Structure of Blackstone's Commentaries, 28 Buff. L. Rev. 205 (1979); Mark Tushnet, The American Law of Slavery, 1810-1860: Considerations of Humanity and Interest 9 (Princeton, N.J., 1981) (describing efforts to analyze a "general" law of slavery without regard to variation over time). As the latter example suggests, the "moment" can be extended for a rather long period—fifty years in my book on the law of slavery. But the ahistoricism remains because no change that the study seeks to explain occurs during the extended period.

22. See, e.g., Gary Peller, The Metaphysics of American Law, 73 Cal. L. Rev. 1151 (1985).

The view of historical analysis that I have just sketched is implicit in much recent critical legal scholarship, but I believe that the body of work would be strengthened by explicit discussions of these issues. More often the issues have been taken up in the use of structuralist and deconstructionist methods. These methods lie behind much of the currently dominant practice. As soon as an analyst offers a systematic explanation of something, the dominant strain in CLS decenters the explanation, rearranging the terms and categories used in the explanation to demonstrate that the reorganized explanation is just as good as the original one.[23] This decentering project has no termination.

The use of deconstruction has developed its insistence that general social-theoretical explanations are unavailable into the position that all one can do is provide minutely detailed maps or descriptions of phenomena. At this point the open question for the dominant view arises. In general, though it has abandoned the search for social theory, it has not abandoned the view that social power (illegitimate hierarchy) exists. Somehow the detailed descriptions are to reveal how power actually operates. They do so not by invoking social theory or covering laws, but by educing, in an essentially intuitive way, understanding out of the reader's immersion in details. But we need to ask, how is this understanding supposed to emerge?

One possible answer is that the dominant program does not really aim at understanding in the usual sense. Rather, this view maintains, proponents of the dominant program have made a strategic judgment that in the present circumstances their political goals are more likely to be reached by using deconstructive methods. This view breaks the connection between the analytic program and the politics of critical legal studies.

A second possibility is that understanding emerges because of the essentially literary techniques used by those presenting the detailed descriptions. It might be that these techniques operate in a sphere epistemologically distinct from that in which social theory is thought to operate. If so, the emptiness of social theory need not imply that we cannot gain knowledge via deconstruction.[24]

A third possibility, and the one that I believe many critical legal scholars would prefer to pursue, is that we can analyze the ways in which intuitive understanding emerges from detailed descriptions. The anthropologist Clifford Geertz has argued that all knowledge is this sort of "local knowledge."[25] But neither Geertz nor anyone who has appropriated his terminology has done much to explain the sense in which "local knowledge" is knowledge. The effort to do so seems sensible for two reasons. First, we know that people sometimes have different intuitions about a particular problem, and we ought to be curious about how and why intuitive understandings are sometimes shared and sometimes divergent. Second, the analytic effort may be required by the CLS emphasis on domination and illegitimate hierarchy.

23. See, e.g., David Kennedy, The Turn to Interpretation, 58 S. Cal. L. Rev. 251 (1985).

24. Though I am not competent to evaluate this possibility, I gather that the French post-structuralists have been unable to sustain their similar epistemological claims.

25. Clifford Geertz, Local Knowledge (New York, 1983).

These terms have normative connotations that suggest that any accurate understanding of hierarchial situations would refer to domination. But that judgment plainly needs some sort of defense.

One line of defense, which appears in some works, is to rely on an essentially romantic view of human nature. Joseph Singer, for example, counters hard-nosed views that "what people *really* like is doing horrible things to each other" with the sensible response that they "do not want just to be beastly to each other. . . . [T]hey also want not to harm others."[26] The difficulty is that as Singer pursues his analysis, he forgets the implication of the "not just" and "also"; in other words, he forgets that people do indeed sometimes want to be beastly. What to those on the bottom is an illegitimate hierarchy is to those on the top a perfectly sensible one.[27] The romantic view of human nature denies that anyone could hold the latter belief in good faith, but, in the absence of a fairly elaborate late Sartrean exposition of the concept of bad faith, the denial is unpersuasive.

A second line of defense for judgments about domination can be called strategic silence. Gary Peller's analysis of the reification of consent in the law of rape provides a useful example.[28] In a standard deconstructive analysis, Peller argues that the concept of consent can be applied in particular settings only by "construct[ing] the context which is supposed to provide the ground for representing the event," a course that "promises total circularity."[29] Peller's aim is to demonstrate that the use of consent as a defense in the law of rape projects "the ideological message . . . that consensual sexuality is consistent with male domination in society."[30] But it should be clear that the same analysis could be used to explain what might be called the Maileresque assessment that female domination requires men to engage in sexual behavior that society creates to be coercive. The technique of deconstruction, that is, cannot in itself support the political conclusions implicit in the use of the term "domination" as applied to particular arrangements. Because the political open-endedness of the deconstructive technique is so obvious, the silence about it in the CLS literature should be understood as strategic, designed to place on the table the political judgments implied by any use of language.

But strategic silence only raises the political issues; it does not explain why one ought to adopt the feminist interpretation of consent and reject the Maileresque interpretation of coercion. This fact suggests that the idea of strategic silence could be extended. The extension would hold that there is

26. Joseph Singer, The Player and the Cards: Nihilism and Legal Theory, 94 Yale L.J. 1, 54 (1984).

27. In one sense the topic of my book, *supra* note 21, was the examination of how people could come to have that belief.

28. Peller, *supra* note 22, at 1187-91.

29. *Id.* at 1189-90.

30. *Id.* at 1191.

nothing beyond that silence, that the process of decentering our understandings is indeed interminable. One offers the feminist interpretation of rape because one has made a political judgment that in our society congealed forms of domination are more likely to be broken up by that interpretation than by the Maileresque alternative. But that is an ungrounded political judgment, open to discussion and alteration as times, circumstances, and understandings change.

The critique of social theory thus replaces one form of political analysis with another. Instead of having political positions flow from social theory, the dominant CLS project simply takes political positions. But not just any political positions. The politics of the dominant position is the politics of decentering, disrupting whatever understandings happen to be settled, criticizing the existing order whatever that order is. Some CLS proponents are attracted to small-scale decentralized socialism.[31] But that attraction must be understood as the embodiment of a critique of large-scale centralized capitalism. It cannot set forth a permanent program, the realization of which would be the end of politics.[32] In fact, in a socialist society, the critical legal scholar would criticize socialism as denying the importance of individual achievement, and decentralization as an impediment to material and spiritual achievement. Roberto Unger captured this dimension of the irrationalist project in his description of destablization rights, "claims to the disruption of established institutions . . . that have . . . contributed to the very kind of crystallized plan of social hierarchy and division that the entire constitution wants to avoid."[33]

With all this in hand, we can in conclusion turn to the implications of the critique of social theory for the future of CLS. Of course the Legal Realist analysis of rules will continue to be used; the legal academy's commitment to the coherence of rules is strong enough to require repeated assaults. It might be useful as well to develop detailed analyses of how law and beliefs about law are implicated in practices of domination and liberation, but the institutional impediments to sustained empirical research by legal academics are so substantial that it is unlikely that critical legal scholars will produce much along these lines.

I should mention too that one part of the future of CLS is its continued institutionalization as part of the pluralist intellectual world of the legal academy. It now seems to be a more or less standard practice in symposia and

31. See, e.g., Gerald Frug, The City as a Legal Concept, 93 Harv. L. Rev. 1057 (1980); Mark Tushnet, Federalism and the Traditions of American Political Theory, 19 Ga. L. Rev. 981 (1985).

32. The same point must be made in connection with the assertions that altruism and paternalism should play a more vital role in our law as compared with its present individuals. See, e.g., Duncan Kennedy, Form and Substance in Private Law Adjudication, 89 Harv. L. Rev. 1685 (1976); Duncan Kennedy, Distributive and Paternalist Motives in Contract and Tort Law, with Special Reference to Compulsory Terms and Unequal Bargaining Power, 41 Md. L. Rev. 563 (1982).

33. Unger, *supra* note 18, at 600, 611–15.

workshops to include someone from CLS, or at least to feel bad if you do not manage to round one up (or if you willfully ignore them.)[34]

But the most important implication of the dominant CLS analysis is that any critique of the existing order is consistent with the project of CLS. Statistical studies, casual empiricism, classical social theory, the most old-fashioned doctrinal analysis—all might be critical legal studies so long as three conditions are met. First, the work should not be defended on grounds that suggest that something more enduring than interminable critique might result from following it through. Second, it must be designed as a critique rather than as a defense of the existing order—or of a slightly modified version of the existing order that, once modified, would be the end of politics. Finally, the work should actually operate as a critique.[35]

Perhaps the program of interminable critique swallows itself. If it is widely accepted, people may at first resign themselves to their inability to transcend critique. But they may come to see that that inability is itself transcendent, creating a new form of life in which the terms on which critique must proceed today have become unintelligible.

I would like to close by elaborating this point about interminable critique. I will do so by describing one of the more controversial CLS arguments, which has been called the critique of rights. According to this argument, it would seem that we could abandon such valued rights as the constitutional protections our society gives to free speech and to the antidiscrimination principle. The CLS argument has two parts. The first applies the critique of legal concepts to the concepts embodied in these ideas about rights. Here the critique argues that the rights are defined on too abstract a level to be helpful in resolving the claims presented in particular cases. Nor will recourse to underlying values or to a balancing process help, for reasons I have already reviewed. This aspect of the argument is not unusual or, in itself, particularly bothersome, because it relies on positions for which the Realists were thought to have adequate answers.

One person to whom the critique of rights was described reacted by calling the world that it depicted "Kafkaesque." According to the critique of rights, people cannot know what rights they have, and there are no political methods that guarantee those rights. The term "Kafkaesque" is perfectly appropriate and provides a clue to the justification for the constructive program—or for the program of interminable critique. For by invoking Kafka's vision, the term allows CLS to say that it, like Kafka, is describing the condition of the modern world. Those reared in, or attracted to, premodernist traditions may well find the world so described quite distasteful. But

34. I suspect that CLS is about to become one of the quotas that law schools feel they ought to fill: one trusts-and-estates teacher, one teacher of jurisprudence, one representative of law-and-economics sort, one of CLS. (As with all quotas, of course, the more categories any one person occupies the better—imagine finding someone who wanted to teach trusts and estates, jurisprudence, and law-and-economics.)

35. This final pragmatic criterion may be controversial, for some critical legal scholars may claim that a statistical study or a doctrinal analysis or a social theory of the classical type cannot actually function as a critique in our society as it is presently constituted. I disagree, but will reserve my comments on this issue for another forum.

the point of modernism is precisely that that is just the way things are these days.

CLS is thus the form that modernism takes in legal thought. Like modernism in philosophy and sociology, it displaces settled understandings, insisting that whatever we have is something we create and recreate daily. As a form of modernism, CLS argues that our lives are structured by institutions that we create and sustain, and that our lives have no meaning outside those institutions and the processes by which we create them—and create ourselves. So, in part, the CLS program is justified in the way all modernist programs are: The program consists of shattering congealed forms of life by showing that they have no particular integrity. And whatever makes that demonstration effective—utopian yearnings, close analysis of legal texts, concrete proposals—is part of the program.

Perhaps this analysis could be continued indefinitely. But if the CLS critique is interminable, this article is not.

# [3]
# Introduction (Symposium on Frontiers of Legal Thought)

This collection of articles and essays on the frontiers of legal thought[1] shows the ways in which some aspects of legal thought have developed in the past decade.[2] Building on the insights of the American Legal Realists but rejecting many of their political positions and policy prescriptions as well as their fondness for the "scientifization" of law,[3] scholars associated with critical legal studies began a project that continues to evolve—a project which has been transformed by its interaction with the work of minority and feminist scholars. Many of the themes in this new, "critical/feminist/minority/post-modernist" scholarship[4] are found in the articles and essays here.

At the risk of simplification and distortion, I would suggest that a decade or so ago essays of this sort would have exhibited a number of characteristics, only some of which are represented in this collection. First, there would have been some methodological prescriptions. Legal doctrines would have been described in a way that showed how each doctrine represented a logically unstable solution to problems posed by

---

1. Or at least on some of the frontiers of legal thought; no one would contend that this collection touches exhaustively on the topics or methods of contemporary legal analysis.

2. Many of these essays, along with others, were presented at a conference at the Duke Law School on January 25-27, 1990, sponsored by Duke's Forum for Legal Alternatives (FLA), the *Duke Law Journal*, and about a dozen other university and law school groups. As a participant in the conference, I would like to note my appreciation to the FLA, Tony Taibi, and Dana Lesemann for putting together an exciting event. *Frontiers of Legal Thought* will appear as three consecutive issues of the *Duke Law Journal. Frontiers of Legal Thought II & III* [hereinafter *Frontiers II* and *Frontiers III*] are forthcoming.

3. Though I note that some residue of that affection can be found in the essay by Elizabeth Mensch & Alan Freeman, *Efficiency and Image: Advertising as an Antitrust Issue*, 1990 DUKE L.J. 321, which appears to take some comfort from the fact that "even" some mathematicians have adopted approaches similar to the ones they commend.

4. I use this locution to suggest that, though no single tradition dominates the field, there is an identifiable grouping of legal thought represented here.

the coexistence of competing values all of which deserved protection to the fullest, but none of which could be so protected. In addition, the logical demonstration would have been accompanied by an insistence on the proposition that legal doctrines ought to be understood not as the product of some abstract logic, but rather as a form of life that simultaneously ratified and provided the opportunity for transformation of the status quo.

Second, there would have been a political stance implicit in the topics chosen for analysis, but it would have differed somewhat from the political stance implicit in the selection of topics in this collection. Because critical scholars were attempting to revive the Realist tradition as they understood it, they focused on the terrain most important to the structure of the legal academy—the first-year curriculum. Analyzing the structure of the basic common law subjects and constitutional law was important to establish the significance of the enterprise. Other areas, such as labor law and race discrimination, were addressed because the subjects[5] were thought to be of particular political concern.

The essays in this collection continue along the lines of work I have briefly described above, and they simultaneously shift our attention and deepen our knowledge. All participate in the project of logical deconstruction. Rudolph Peritz's *A Counter-History of Antitrust Law,*[6] as its title indicates, plays competition policy and protection of private property policies against each other in offering an interpretation of the development of antitrust policy that shifts attention from more traditional "consumer welfare vs. populism" analysis. David Millon, in describing *Theories of the Corporation,*[7] examines the history of the ways that corporations have been conceptualized, and he concludes the essay by discussing the Delaware Chancery Court's analysis in the *Time*[8] takeover case. A key to his analysis is the "public/private" distinction in corporation law.

Peritz and Millon continue the project of deconstruction, extending its reach while using now-familiar tools. Yet, their essays and the others in this collection have moved beyond the essential first step of demonstrating the logical inadequacy of the categories typically used to analyze legal problems. If these essays share a single characteristic, I would say it is their insistence that legal doctrines and categories must be histori-

5. In both senses.

6. 1990 DUKE L.J. 263.

7. 1990 DUKE L.J. 201.

8. Paramount Communications, Inc. v. Time, Inc., [1989 Transfer Binder] Fed. Sec. L. Rep. (CCH) ¶ 94,514 (Del. Ch.), *aff'd,* Fed. Sec. L. Rep. (CCH) ¶ 94,938 (Del. 1990).

cized.[9] That is, the logical demonstrations are insufficient because, as we all know, at any particular time lawyers are convinced that the structure of legal thought within which they are implicated is just about as logically coherent as anyone could reasonably expect. The incompatibility between the logical analysis and the experience of lawyers itself needs explanation. For the authors of these essays, the primary form of that explanation is the demonstration of the historical circumstances in which lawyers came to believe that there was no tension between their experience and the logic of the law.

For example, Millon analyzes the various concepts implicated in the construction of a law of corporations which routinely have been thought to go in lock-step with one another. He shows, however, that the actual practice of the legal theory of the corporation is better described as "mix and match": As we examine the history of theories of the corporation we find that individual lawyers, judges, and scholars essentially endorsed all of the possible arrays of concepts at some point or another, even though adherents of each array contend that substituting even one item in the array would be logically ridiculous. Similarly, in their essay *Efficiency and Image: Advertising as an Antitrust Issue,*[10] Elizabeth Mensch and Alan Freeman relate an episode in the evolution of antitrust policy in which the possibility of imposing antitrust liability for certain types of advertising that foreclosed competition was briefly considered, only to be rejected as incompatible with the true economic foundations of antitrust; they too emphasize the historical nature of the categories of economic analysis that many today take as grounded in the science of economics.

The project of historicizing the categories of legal analysis is not, however, without its pitfalls. We are, after all, trained as lawyers and not as historians, and our ability to pull off the historical project is less well developed than our ability to pull off the project of logical deconstruction. I suspect that much of the persuasiveness of the historicizing project will arise from a sort of allusive "culture critique" of the sort introduced by the Freeman-Mensch story about cereal boxes.[11] More extended analyses are likely to prove more difficult.[12]

---

9. I believe that the *program* of treating doctrines and categories historically was both stated in and implied clearly by the critical work of the 1970s to which I have referred, but the essays here are significantly more self-conscious about the necessity of that program.

10. Mensch & Freeman, *supra* note 3.

11. *Id.* at 321-22, 372.

12. For example, I find the Freeman-Mensch discussion of "jeans," *id.* at 365-66, drawing on the work of certain "culture critics," wildly implausible. (I offer this and some other criticisms in this Introduction as a participant in the exploration of the frontiers of legal thought, and to demon-

A second difficulty may reside in the form of the project itself. As Peritz notes in his discussion of the term "genealogy,"[13] these essays deal with structures of legal thought that, for analytic purposes, must in some sense be frozen in time, like the slices of cell tissue preserved for the electron microscope. Two problems, then, are likely to arise. First, if legal thought is dynamic, then constructing structures to analyze the process necessarily distorts the phenomenon even as it allows us to get some grasp on it. Second, and perhaps of greater importance for the historicizing project, by dealing with successive structures—as in Peritz's discussion of "periods"—we may develop a "comparative statics" of legal thought but be unable to develop a truly historical understanding of the dynamics of transformation.

The historization of legal thought is the first characteristic of these essays. A second characteristic is a shift in the topics addressed. Most dramatically, of course, several of the essays deal not with the topics covered in first-year courses, but rather with the topics covered in second- and third-year courses. And the essays on public law issues do not take the topics covered in introductory courses as their direct focus of concern. I take this shift to be a demonstration of the extension of the frontiers of legal thought: The essays explore new domains without, of course, suggesting that we have completely mapped the areas of law that were the focus of earlier work.[14]

In *Encounters on the Frontiers of International Human Rights Law: Redefining the Terms of Indigenous Peoples' Survival in the World,*[15] Robert Williams brings to the discussion of rights the perspective of indigenous peoples throughout the world who have attempted to mobilize the human rights community on their own behalf. Gerald Torres and Kathryn Milun offer an American example of the difficulties of the enterprise in their discussion, *Translating* Yonnondio *by Precedent and Evidence: The Mashpee Indian Case,*[16] which deals with a celebrated lawsuit that raised issues of the "survival" and "continuity" of an indigenous people. In focusing on the problems of "translation," Torres and Milun suggest a new twist on the critical discussion of the language of rights, and thereby complement Williams' essay.

strate that, like every reader of these essays, I must engage with them and not merely appreciate them.)

13. Peritz, *supra* note 6, at 268, 315.

14. Leslie Bender's essay, *Feminist (Re)Torts: Thoughts on the Liability Crisis, Mass Torts, Power, and Responsibilities,* 1990 DUKE L.J. — (forthcoming *Frontiers III),* discussed in more detail later in this Introduction, is a good example of a deepened treatment of a topic covered in first-year courses.

15. 1990 DUKE L.J. — (forthcoming *Frontiers III).*

16. 1990 DUKE L.J. — (forthcoming *Frontiers III).*

Taking the two essays together, I am led to think that I would now augment my presentation of the critique of rights.[17] I would now suggest that the language of rights, as it is used by the international human rights community and by the domestic legal community, is part of the legacy of Eurocentric domination of legal discourse. To the extent that indigenous peoples appeal to the legal system—as they often must—or to principles of legality—as they often will choose to—they may be faced repeatedly with the problem that the language in which they are asked to speak is unsuitable for the topics they wish to address. In a sense, indigenous peoples often will be attempting to translate their experiences into a language constructed by, and out of the experiences of, the Western cultures that were in part the agents causing their difficulties. Translation is not impossible, of course, but it almost certainly distorts the underlying experience, as Torres and Milun show. And to the extent that even successful translations are distortions, appeals by indigenous peoples—and perhaps by peoples whose cultures are not as completely Eurocentric as that of the dominant majority in the United States, as Gary Peller's essay *Race Consciousness*[18] suggests—may perhaps have a self-limiting quality.

The amount of limitation, though, itself can be changed. I am hesitant to believe that people, or cultures, can be truly "bilingual" in a way that makes translation unnecessary. At the same time, however, I do not doubt that people and cultures can influence each other, thus increasing the degree to which each is partially bilingual, and thereby reducing the amount of inaccuracy in translation. Notice, though, that my claim here is about *mutual* influence; neither indigenous people nor invaders will be the same after the contact. Peller's essay suggests that at least as a strategic matter, it might make sense for the black community in the United States to promote a form of internal development that historically has been criticized by many whites and blacks as a bad form of race consciousness.[19] Yet, because of the inevitability of mutual influence, I remain skeptical about the permanent utility of the program suggested in Peller's essay, though less skeptical about its temporary pragmatic political utility.

What is at stake, I think, is the possibility of the transformation of and within the legal tradition of rights. I believe that Peller's essay contains more than a little of what Duncan Kennedy refers to in passing as the sentimentalizing of African-American culture. Yet, Peller's essay provides an appropriate context for Kennedy's discussion, in *A Cultural*

---

17. For my most recent foray, see Tushnet, *Rights: An Essay in Informal Political Theory*, 17 Pol. & Soc'y 403 (1989).

18. 1990 Duke L.J. — (forthcoming *Frontiers III*).

19. *Id.*

*Pluralist Case for Affirmative Action in Legal Academia,*[20] of the ideology of colorblind meritocracy. Much of what Kennedy says is an entirely sensible and quite moderate argument that the legal academy's standards of merit are strikingly narrow, and that much would be gained if the academy adopted a more sensible standard of merit. Kennedy also argues that the reasons for the narrowness of the existing standards are cultural and ideological, and necessarily so. This argument, too, is hardly extreme. One of the many contributions of minority scholars to the legal academy has been to allow these arguments to be made in this form.

Another contribution, this one made by feminist scholars as well, has been to open up discussion of some issues that had been taken as closed by many liberals. The dialogue between Charles Lawrence, in his article *If He Hollers Let Him Go: Regulating Racist Speech on Campus,*[21] and Nadine Strossen in *Regulating Racist Speech on Campus: A Modest Proposal?,*[22] deepens the understanding of the first amendment as it operates in contemporary society. Jack Balkin, in *Some Realism About Pluralism: Legal Realist Approaches to the First Amendment,*[23] provides the jurisprudential and historical context in which current controversies among liberals over the proper interpretation of the first amendment have arisen. Balkin argues that the analytic techniques that liberals have inherited from the Legal Realists make it quite difficult to sustain the kind of first amendment fundamentalism that most of us associate with Justices Hugo Black and William Douglas.

Lawrence's essay works out, in a particularly important practical and doctrinal context, the maneuvers that Balkin identifies in the more abstract context of jurisprudence. This combination of doctrinal and theoretical analysis places much of what Strossen says under rather severe stress—with one, for me, decisive exception. Strossen emphasizes, in a way that Lawrence does not, that regulations of racist speech on campus are to be administered by the very authorities who, if such regulations are adopted, will have been dragged into the regulations kicking and screaming. She is in my view rightly skeptical about the proposition that these people would administer the regulations in a way that Lawrence would find satisfying. I concede that the political struggle that would lead to the adoption of the regulations might transform the sensibilities and inclinations of campus administrators. But, in that political process concessions will inevitably be made to what opponents of regula-

20. 1990 DUKE L.J. — (forthcoming *Frontiers III*).
21. 1990 DUKE L.J. — (forthcoming *Frontiers II*).
22. 1990 DUKE L.J. — (forthcoming *Frontiers II*).
23. 1990 DUKE L.J. — (forthcoming *Frontiers II*).

tion will characterize as first amendment values, as Lawrence himself indicates. Those concessions, I believe, are likely both to limit the impact of the regulations, as Katharine Bartlett and Jean O'Barr suggest in *The Chilly Climate on College Campuses: An Expansion of the "Hate Speech" Debate,*[24] and to reduce the transformative impact of the political struggle on campus administrators.

The debate over regulation of racist speech on campus may not yet have produced dramatic changes in the regulations in place or the atmosphere on campuses, but it has already transformed the academic discussion of the first amendment. Leslie Bender's article, *Feminist (Re)Torts: Thoughts on the Liability Crisis, Mass Torts, Power, and Responsibilities,*[25] offers another perspective on the possibility of change within, and therefore change *of,* the legal tradition of rights. Beginning with the insight that much of the discussion of the so-called tort liability "crisis" has a tone reminiscent of some discussions of rape in which the focus becomes whether the victim should be blamed, Bender expands our understanding of the "crisis" by drawing on feminist theory. A critique of rights, or of what she calls the "ethic of rights," is at the heart of her essay. She contributes to the historicizing project through her analysis of the way the "public/private" distinction works in discussions of the "crisis" of the tort system. In addition, she sketches a program of transformation, based on feminist thought, that would supplement, or perhaps ultimately displace, the tort system's reliance on an ethic of rights and monetary compensation.

From one perspective,[26] the feminist theories on which Bender relies have provided new metaphors, made vital by their connection to a substantial political movement, for ideas about empowerment once associated with movements that have lost vitality.[27] From a more traditional perspective, some of her suggestions may disturb—which is as it should be. Bender's attention to the possibility that tortfeasors should engage in personal service to the injured—or, as has been suggested, that the chairman of the board of Exxon should join the people attempting to cleanse the shoreline of the oil discharged by the *Exxon Valdez*—forces on us a reconsideration of notions of liberty that ignore the connections between

24. 1990 DUKE L.J. — (forthcoming *Frontiers II).*

25. Bender, *supra* note 14.

26. Which, as feminists have shown, may itself be limited.

27. Bender's notion of empowerment is, it seems to me, not all that different from "Power to the People" or even "All Power to the Soviets" (where, as was meant in the initial formulation, "soviet" referred to a collective form of social organization rather than to the Union of Soviet Socialist Republics).

the exercise's of one person's liberty (to dump oil and the like) and the protections others have of their forms of life.[28]

Whether that reconsideration would lead us to adopt a new form of responsibility, however, might be questioned. The situation in Japan is suggestive. There, anecdote has it, officials high in the hierarchy of corporations that damage the environment apologize personally to the individual victims of their companies' torts. Even so, one would not want to offer Japan as an exemplar of a legal system truly committed to protection of the environment or of workers from injuries due to a corporation's pursuit of profit. Bender's suggestion, that is, may not be the best remedy for the difficulties she identifies in our present tort system.

Yet, to conclude in that way would be misleading. For as I have tried to suggest throughout this Introduction, one characteristic of these essays and articles on the frontiers of legal thought is that they all participate in on-going political projects of transformation. By calling them "projects," I mean to point out that they are implicated in a dynamic process of social change, and the dynamics of the process may give meaning (as yet incompletely understood) to the particular suggestions for reform that the authors have devised. That is, we would go wrong if we simply thought about what the tort system would look like if Bender's suggestions about allocation of burdens and personal service were simply inserted into a scheme that was otherwise unchanged. For those suggestions to be adopted, much would already have to have changed in the way we think about torts, and the conceptual changes we would already have undergone would themselves change the way in which we would relate Bender's suggestions to, for example, ideas about liberty.

I conclude by returning to American Legal Realism. After completing their task of logical deconstruction, the initial Realists turned to a sort of common sense social theory, under the label of policy analysis, to replace the logical formalism they had abandoned. The revival of Realism has shown, I think, that small scale or common sense social theory does not offer a satisfactory solution to the intellectual problems Realism posed. As I have tried to suggest, in the end we are driven to large scale social theories that deal with overall social transformation. That, of course, may be the largest frontier of all, and the essays here move us deeper into that territory.

28. Bender, *supra* note 14.

# [4]
# Critical Legal Studies: A Political History

I imagined that an article on critical legal studies in a centennial issue like this one ought to be an exposition of the origins of the ideas of critical legal studies and a description of the lines of inquiry that are open for future work in the field. In light of the content of critical legal studies, I imagined as well that the form of the presentation ought not be the standard expository essay. On reflection, however, I concluded that, though I had to avoid the expected content, I could *not* depart from the standard form.[1] I had to avoid the expected content because critical legal studies is less an intellectual movement in law (though it is that too) than it is a political location.[2] By describing the political location that is critical legal studies, I hope to indicate what its intellectual content is and sketch its possible future. The story of critical legal studies is

---

1. "Could not," because of my concern that departures from the standard form require a degree of technical competence in writing that I lack. I have been uncomfortable with the publication of law review articles in the form of short stories, or short stories in the form of law review articles, because they strike me as yet another manifestation of the "lawyer as astrophysicist" mentality that I have criticized. *See* Tushnet, *Truth, Justice, and the American Way: An Interpretation of Public Law Scholarship in the Seventies*, 57 TEX. L. REV. 1307, 1338 n.140 (1979). This was brought home to me in a conversation with a former roommate, now a professor of literature, in which my wife and I were trying to identify the author of a line of poetry quoted in a newspaper puzzle. My friend immediately began by saying something like, "Well, it couldn't be by *X* because the line is too long for him." I realized then that there is a world of understanding about literature to which I essentially have no access, and I now wonder about the degree to which other law professors do. The cynical version of this point is that if law professors could write short stories, they would be short-story writers rather than law professors. On the other hand, my cynicism is tempered by my recollection of the short stories my father wrote. After he retired from medical practice, he wrote what I think of as Jewish science fiction. He was not a particularly elegant writer, but the novelty of the content was frequently enough to sustain interest in his stories. So too, perhaps, with law review articles in the form of short stories. The appearance of my former roommate and my father in this footnote is not adventitious. *See infra* pp. 1533-34, 1536.

2. I use the word "location" to convey the sense that critical legal studies is a place where people with a wide but not unlimited range of political views can come together for political education, sustenance, and activity. "Place" is of course a metaphor; perhaps more accurate but more verbose would be the suggestion that critical legal studies is a form of self-identification that allows people to recognize each other as basically sympathetic to a broad but not all-encompassing political agenda. That recognition occurs at professional meetings, in law school faculties, and through the reading of the professional literature.

a story of how the legal academy simultaneously tolerates and contains a radical political location.[3]

## I. Present History

From the inside there is something awkward in talking about critical legal studies as a "movement" or "school." As I read articles by and about critical legal studies, I not infrequently find myself puzzled. The authors of the articles provoking this reaction describe what they believe critical legal studies to be, and yet the descriptions do not resonate strongly with what I think about the law. Where the articles are merely descriptive, or are written by critics of cls,[4] I can dismiss my reaction by saying to myself that these critics or outsiders do not understand what cls is. Where the articles are by people whom I regard as co-participants in the enterprise of critical legal studies, however, that response is unavailable to me. So when I find these authors taking as central to their understanding of cls propositions that I find extremely problematic, or dismissing as unimportant propositions that I find central, I have to figure out what is going on. After all, I know that I am supposed to be associated with critical legal studies in some important way.

The most plausible explanation, and the one I explore here, is that critical legal studies is a political location for a group of people on the Left who share the project of supporting and extending the domain of the Left in the legal academy.[5] On this view the project of critical legal studies does not have any essential intellectual component,[6] which is why I cannot readily identify a great

---

3. Initially I had decided not to include reference to specific items of cls in this Article. I was concerned that readers would interpret it as an attempt to adjudicate claims of entitlement to the cls mantle, which would be particularly problematic because I would be doing so after having accepted the invitation of the editors of *The Yale Law Journal* to write it. The editors have persuaded me, however, that the absence of citations would make the Article seem directed solely to insiders to cls, itself a difficulty in light of their invitation, and that the absence would make my points seem to float free. I have responded to that concern by relying, to the greatest extent possible, on work identified as cls by other people. I must note my residual concerns that my citation strategy will fail to identify people and their work which ought to be included in the account, and that it may include people who have good reasons for objecting to their inclusion. For a bibliography of cls work up to 1984, see Kennedy & Klare, *A Bibliography of Critical Legal Studies*, 94 YALE L.J. 461 (1984); a more recent selective bibliography, updated through August 1989, is available from Professor Richard Bauman, Faculty of Law, University of Alberta. R. Bauman, Critical Legal Studies: Selected Bibliography (Aug. 1989) (unpublished manuscript on file with author).

4. In this Article I use "cls" rather than "CLS" because it abbreviates a description of legal studies that are critical, so that the words prefacing "studies" are ordinary adjectives. In addition, I believe that the usual form is "law and economics," not "Law and Economics." The typography may convey a sense of what is ordinary and what is extraordinary in legal studies, and I want to take a position on that question.

5. I do not consider the possibility that cls is coextensive with the Left of the legal academy, because there are obviously some people on the Left who do not consider themselves to be part of cls.

6. In this formulation, "essential" carries a great deal of weight. At any time there will undoubtedly be a substantial number of general propositions on which most people committed to the cls project agree ("law is politics," "law is substantially indeterminate," "law is a form of mystification, among other things," for example). But, first, agreement on the general level says nothing about the particular content people will give to those propositions (itself a cls point), and second, as the political location develops, the propositions on which there is general agreement will change, as they already have.

deal that is common in the intellectual production going under the heading of critical legal studies.[7] There should be nothing surprising about this conclusion, of course, in light of the proposition common to most cls authors that law is politics. For, if law is politics, presumably one might also believe that legal-intellectual positions are politics too. Treating cls as a political location may illuminate the meaning of the claim about law and politics as well. When people associated with cls assert that law is politics, I take them to mean that when one understands the moral, epistemological, and empirical assumptions embedded in any particular legal claim, one will see that those assumptions operate in the particular setting in which the legal claim is made to advance the interests of some identifiable political grouping.[8] Yet people who seek to advance the interests of a single group may make varying underlying assumptions, with the result that some in the "movement" will find themselves disagreeing with the legal claims asserted by others who, they agree, are also in the movement. It is in that sense that critical legal studies can be understood as a political location notwithstanding the disagreements among participants in the movement.[9] At present one might describe the political location of critical legal studies as occupied by certain feminists ("fem-crits"),[10] certain theorists concerned with the role of race in law (critical race theorists),[11] a group influ-

---

7. One strand in cls, labeled below the postmodernist, asserts that the description in the text must be accurate because there are no "essential intellectual components" of any enterprise, but only positions that people take. For reasons I discuss below, I disagree with that strand. (But, of course, what else could I do but take a position? That is, to write a political history of cls in another way would be to demonstrate or embody a commitment to a different strand in cls. For example, one might write a political history that focused on the numerous—in my mind, innumerable—occasions when attempts to develop a formal structure for the movement were beaten back, and on the networks of personal contacts that constitute cls. To do so, however, would be to become a part of cls in a different way from the way in which I have become a part of the movement.)

8. Note that I do not take the claim to be that those assumptions *necessarily* or in *all* settings operate to advance the interests of an identifiable political grouping.

9. The enumeration that follows should not be taken to suggest that the groups have rigid boundaries, such that a person identified by me or others as falling in one group necessarily cannot fall in another. In fact, everyone associated with cls has been influenced to varying degrees by people in each of the groups, though it does seem to me that almost all of us find our centers of gravity closer to only one of the groups. Professor Bauman's bibliography has a section entitled "The Special Role of Roberto Unger," *see* R. Bauman, *supra* note 3, at 2, and in my view Duncan Kennedy has a similar role; they are, more than most, unclassifiable in the categories I use in this Article.

10. For an informal history of the fem-crits, see Menkel-Meadow, *Feminist Legal Theory, Critical Legal Studies, and Legal Education, or, "The Fem-Crits Go to Law School,"* 38 J. LEGAL EDUC. 61, 62-66 (1988). Menkel-Meadow identifies herself, Jeanne Charn, Clare Dalton, Ann Freedman, Mary Joe Frug, Nancy Gertner, Judi Greenberg, Martha Minow, Frances Olsen, Elizabeth Schneider, and Robin West as "fem-crits." (She also identifies others as feminists *tout court*; in light of the critical dimensions of feminist jurisprudence, the classifications here may be particularly inexact and probably should be developed entirely by finding out who identifies herself as a fem-crit.) I use the term "fem-crits" because it is used by many of those who identify themselves as fem-crits. In this Article I have otherwise tried to refrain from using the term "crits" and have used more awkward constructions such as "adherents of critical legal studies" because, for myself, I find the term "crits" marginalizing and when used by adherents of critical legal studies almost an internalization of that marginalization. I am unsure whether the term "fem-crits" operates in the same way.

11. Mari Matsuda, in *Pragmatism Modified and the False Consciousness Problem*, 63 S. CAL. L. REV. 1763, 1763 n.3 (1990), identifies herself, Regina Austin, Derrick Bell, John Calmore, Kimberlé Crenshaw,

enced by recent developments in literary theory (postmodernists),[12] a group of cultural radicals,[13] and a group that stresses the role of the economic structure in setting the conditions for legal decisions (political economists).[14]

Even on this description of the location, however, there do seem to be some common elements to that which is found there. If critical legal studies is the location for people who identify themselves with a particular political project, that project is located in the legal academy. For the people involved in the project, the psychology of self-identification may require that they see themselves as sharing certain intellectual commitments, in order to be a political location in the academy rather than, for example, a political location in electoral politics. And, in general, there does seem to be a sufficient degree of commitment to three propositions about law: that it is in some interesting sense indeterminate; that it can be understood in some interesting way by paying attention to the context in which legal decisions are made; and that in some interesting sense law is politics.[15]

My effort to describe cls as a political location would be distorted were I to attempt to specify in much detail the different ways in which people have developed the implications of these rather vague propositions. In the course of my presentation I will put a little more flesh on the bones, but to do more would be to suggest, erroneously, that in my understanding of the enterprise the intellectual content of various cls positions has a higher priority than cls' functions as a political location. Further, like all political locations, cls has an internal politics, some aspects of which I will discuss, and an external politics, which is my primary concern.[16] The external politics of cls consists of its relations with the settings in which its adherents find themselves. The details of cls positions have played a relatively small role in those external politics—in

---

Harlon Dalton, Richard Delgado, Charles Lawrence, Gerald López, Gerald Torres, Patricia Williams, and Robert Williams as associated with critical race theory.

12. Hunt, *The Big Fear: Law Confronts Post-Modernism*, 35 MCGILL L.J. 507, 512 n.7 (1990), lists the following United States scholars as authors of "some of [the] more interesting manifestations" of postmodernism: Jack Balkin, Drucilla Cornell, Clare Dalton, Gerald Frug, Christine Desan Husson, and Gary Peller.

13. Peter Gabel is the most prominent of this group.

14. As this Article indicates, I associate myself with this last group. Others include Wythe Holt, Morton Horwitz, Karl Klare, and Katherine Stone. Given the aim of this Article to describe the toleration and containment of critical legal studies by the mainstream legal academy, I will not say much about the merits of the contributions made by scholars affiliated with other strands of critical legal studies, except that their work is extremely interesting, has flaws like everything else, and deserves more extended attention than I could give it here.

15. I argue in the next Part that these propositions are related efforts to answer the question, "How does one theorize a leftist stance in law after legal realism and the critique of social theory?"

16. My comments about the internal politics of cls may suggest, erroneously, that there are deeper divisions within the location than actually exist. In fact, discussions within cls indicate that we share far more in our common opposition to a system of illegitimate hierarchy than we disagree among ourselves.

large part, I believe, because those outside the movement have had little inclination to attend to these details.[17]

Critical legal studies has become one of the accepted elements in the pluralistic universe of legal scholarship. Law faculties believe that it is generally a good thing to have one (but not more than one) cls advocate in the building,[18] although, as is usual in the assimilation of a novel approach to law, they frequently find particularized objections to each specific advocate proposed for appointment.[19] One reason for this degree of acceptance lies in the hierarchical politics of the legal academy. There are now enough cls people at leading law schools that some of the authority flowing from hierarchy has attached to cls work.[20]

Another reason lies in the general politics of the country. The intellectual vitality of the Center-Left, which is the location of most legal academics, has quite simply disappeared. In law, people continue to go through the motions of defending center-left substantive positions and center-left jurisprudence, but

17. For example, if people interested in law and economics spent one tenth of the time understanding critical legal studies that cls people spend understanding law and economics, we would all be better off. It is instructive to compare the relative sophistication of the treatment of law and economics in M. KELMAN, A GUIDE TO CRITICAL LEGAL STUDIES (1987), with that of critical legal studies in R. POSNER, PROBLEMS OF JURISPRUDENCE (1990).

18. There is resistance to the appointment of more than one cls advocate because of the entirely unwarranted view that their political commitments dictate that they will not be good colleagues, but will go around stirring up trouble by attempting to indoctrinate students in the classroom (as if the presentation of moderation and balance as the style and content of law is not indoctrination), or voting on hiring decisions with regard solely to politics rather than the merits (as if the definition of "the merits" were so incontestable that only efforts to question the definition are necessarily political). As to the latter point, I think it worth pointing out that I am hard-pressed to identify a leading law faculty that has denied tenure to someone prominently identified as a right-wing law and economics person, and find it absurdly easy to identify faculties that have denied tenure to cls people. (I use "deny tenure" in the accepted sense that includes sending strong messages that it would not be a wise move on the applicant's part to go through the formal tenure process.) One might hypothesize, of course, that it is not politics that leads to the denial of tenure to people identified with the Left, but rather that, because of the political views held by these junior faculty, it is more common for law faculties to misjudge their merits at the appointment stage. To the extent this hypothesis rests on the proposition that law faculties are better at assessing the merits of right-wing people than of left-wing people, it hardly means that law faculties are nonpolitical. (The denial of tenure at Stanford Law School to Richard Markovits, a non-right-wing law and economics scholar, presents some special problems, but my judgment is that this denial is consistent with the hypothesis that faculties systematically misjudge the merits of people with nonstandard political views.)

19. In addition, there appears to be something akin to a "deviance quota" operating in faculty hiring. Deviance can be defined in a variety of ways, incorporating, for example, people interested in law and economics (less so today than in the recent past), people interested in law and literature, people interested in critical legal studies, women, and minorities. A faculty's definition of deviance and the size of its deviance quota may limit the opportunities for any more deviants to be hired, whether they be adherents of critical legal studies, women, or minorities.

20. This authority has simultaneously presented critical legal studies with some internal political problems. It has eased somewhat the task of recruitment to critical legal studies, particularly because many potential law teachers actually attend the high-status schools at which prominent adherents of cls teach. At the same time, the same prominent adherents receive a degree of deference within cls that generates resentment among those who find themselves studying or teaching at schools lower in the status rankings. (This observation is predicated on the fact that not everyone associated with critical legal studies completely lacks aspirations for recognition by institutions able to confer high status, even as we believe that there is no particularly good reason why those institutions should be able to confer such status.)

it has become almost tiresome even to the people doing the work.[21] In addition, the rightward drift of the nation's politics has induced a similar drift in what is regarded as the Center-Left; to be just to the left of the middle of the policy spectrum today, one must be advocating policies that would have been regarded as quite conservative two decades ago.[22] Yet center-left legal academics know they used to believe something else, more like the egalitarian views associated with cls. Though they do not feel themselves to be in bad faith, they tend to recognize in cls the defense of positions they once held and with which they still feel some sympathy.

A third reason for the embedding of cls in the pluralistic universe derives from the proliferation of alternative, but dissident, legal theories by feminist and minority scholars. Here the political story is quite complex.[23] Friendly criticism by these scholars of certain aspects of critical legal studies turns out, somewhat paradoxically, to enhance the role of those aspects. Center-left legal academics have some degree of commitment to increasing the diversity of the academy. I put it in those terms, rather than saying "affirmative action," because the way in which the academy has justified its affirmative action efforts has been to invoke the value of diverse perspectives in enriching our understanding of the law. Yet once faculties articulate the value at stake to be diversity as such, they find it difficult to resist the intellectual pressure to incorporate political diversity as well.[24]

In addition, some feminist and minority scholars who share the cls political location have disagreed with some formulations of the indeterminacy thesis, and in particular with the use of that thesis to challenge the importance of the vindication of rights, especially constitutional rights.[25] Centrist liberals have responded to what they see as two aspects of this criticism of the critique of rights. First, the criticism accepts large portions of cls claims about indetermina-

21. Recent events in central Europe are likely to revitalize the rhetoric of center-left policy and jurisprudence. *See infra* pp. 1537-38. There seems to me a complete cls response, invoking a rather weak form of the indeterminacy thesis, to the claim that those events demonstrate the superiority of capitalist democracy: What sort of savings and loan institutions are entailed by the establishment of capitalist democracy in eastern Europe?

22. Perhaps the best example is the changed discourse about public responsibility for the provision of health care. The present centrist-liberal position is that there should be public provision of health care insurance for those not covered by private insurance systems; the vision of the Great Society, I think, was that there should be public provision of health care, period.

23. I doubt that this footnote will defuse the political problems that my statements in the text may create. However, it seems appropriate even so to say that, in my effort to describe the politics of cls, I will be speaking more of center-left academics and cls scholars as actors in the political process, and less of feminist and minority scholars as such actors.

24. Difficult, but not impossible. My sense is that it is just as difficult these days for a dedicated conservative (at least one who does not specialize in right-wing law and economics) to get a job on many law faculties as it is for a cls person to do so. For a suggestion that this results in part from the fact that there are structural reasons why center-left academics are likely to see conservatives seeking jobs in the legal academy as less "qualified" than cls people, see *infra* text accompanying note 92.

25. A selection from a rich literature may be found in *Minority Critiques of the Critical Legal Studies Movement*, 22 HARV. C.R.-C.L. L. REV. 297 (1987). My most recent contribution to this discussion is Tushnet, *Rights: An Essay in Informal Political Theory*, 17 POL. & SOC'Y 403 (1989).

cy and the alienating quality of appeals to the rule of law, and adds to them more radical feminist and racialist critiques. The premise of the criticism tends to be that the cls critique of rights fails adequately to understand the role that ideologies of rights, understood as such, have played in the historical construction of liberation movements.[26] Second, however, the criticism has an ambivalent tone to it, in part because it results from the critics' attempts to establish a scholarly identity that is independent of prior work and in part because it results from the critics' rejection of the intellectual and academic hierarchy that was part of the reason the critique of rights became influential.

On law faculties, for example in discussions about hiring, some centrist liberals reacted to feminist and minority criticisms of the critique of rights as more of the same radical nonsense. Others, though, amplified the ambivalence present in the critics' works in an effort to domesticate this strand of minority and feminist scholarship, treating it as rejecting (rather than engaging in a political dialogue with) the cls critique of rights. Because of their need to present themselves as politically progressive, they constructed a political position to their left but to the right of cls, into which they placed certain minority and feminist scholars. The existence of a critique of rights within cls allows centrist liberals to treat the minority and feminist responses to that aspect of cls as differentiating feminist and minority scholarship from "real" cls. In this way, the constructed "real" cls serves as a useful negative reference point for centrists and liberals.[27]

At least in the initial stages of the process of expanding the legal academy to include feminist and minority scholars, though, this strategy has beneficial consequences for cls. It creates some opportunities for radical feminist and minority scholars, through the agency of centrist liberals, when those same liberals have been erecting barriers to the advancement of others associated with cls. Yet these radical feminist and minority scholars, precisely because they are engaged in a common project with other cls scholars, see critical legal studies as a project that deserves support. In addition, most feminist and minority scholars, associated with cls or not, recognize that in the internal politics of law schools, cls people are likely to be on their side more often than people on the Center-Left or rightward.[28] Finally, the centrist-liberal strategy will work only if there are enough "real" cls people around to make them a credible negative

---

26. Having participated in the construction of the critique of rights, I take it as a point of personal privilege to note that I disagree with this evaluation of the critique's appreciation of the role of rights-ideologies in liberation movements. For my engagement with this question, see generally M. TUSHNET, THE NAACP'S LEGAL STRATEGY AGAINST SEGREGATED EDUCATION, 1925-1950 (1987).

27. One identified with cls can find this phenomenon a little irritating, though one can live with the irritation in light of the political importance of expanding the academy to include feminist and minority scholars. Indeed, one might characterize a function of cls as prying open some space for those scholars.

28. "Likely" and "more often," not "always on every issue," thus creating a certain degree of tension in the relationship.

reference point.[29] The dynamics of the process, then, are to make cls in all of its versions an acceptable part of the pluralistic universe.[30]

The situation in the legal academy should not be regarded complacently, for there are substantial barriers to the further development of the political location that is critical legal studies. I deal with some of those barriers in Part V, but one deserves attention here. In the early stages of the development of cls, people could be hired without anyone knowing that they were "crits,"[31] either because the movement had not yet come together or because the applicants had not yet undergone the political transformation into critical legal scholars. As a result, discrimination against cls tended to occur at the tenure stage. It was then more visible, and it affected people who had built up friendships among wider groups of the faculties involved, which meant that political discrimination was more difficult than it might have been at an earlier stage. Today, in contrast, such discrimination tends to occur at the point of hiring. Applicants are asked to define their position with respect to cls or, even worse, positions are imputed to applicants based on the courses they took, the people who have supported them for appointment, and the like. At the hiring stage, applicants for positions almost by definition do not have close ties to members of the faculty doing the hiring, so the latter have a smaller investment of the emotions that lead them to fight hard when tenure denials are involved. Discrimination is thus more difficult to discern ("We just didn't *need* someone in your field this year"), and political battles therefore more difficult to wage.

One still hears a certain amount of demonizing of cls, often in the form of genteel redbaiting,[32] and there is enough anti-intellectual Babbitry in the legal academy to suggest that there are limits to the degree to which cls can really become entrenched in the pluralistic universe.[33] For the present, considering

29. In the unlikely event that feminist and minority viewpoints become entrenched in the legal academy, the utility of cls as a negative reference point will diminish. We are not yet near that point.

30. In my view, cls has incurred some costs in the process of transformation, leading it to become somewhat more acceptable. Some of the radical edge is gone from both the rhetoric and the intellectual positions of the people who identify themselves with cls. Although this has occurred in part because of the changing age structure of the group, and is related to questions of recruitment that I discuss in Part V, I should note (or confess) that I have detected some blurring of the edges in my own work. Although I would like to think this results from maturation and reflection, I am not sure that it does; it may just be a sort of Sartrean bad faith on my part. *See also infra* note 53.

31. *See supra* note 10 (discussing significance of term "crits").

32. Sometimes the redbaiting is not so genteel, as when it is suggested that the logical implication of some cls position is identical to the political program of the Khmer Rouge. I would have thought that opponents of cls would understand that, given the indeterminacy thesis, cls adherents would probably not be embarrassed by such an argument. The indeterminacy thesis, in a suitably weak version, is precisely that there are no particular large-scale logical entailments of abstractly stated political prescriptions. If some position attributed to cls implies the political program of the Khmer Rouge, it also implies whatever utopian or practical political program the critic of cls wishes to advance. *See also supra* note 21.

33. For a recent example of this anti-intellectualism, notable only for its venue, see Lasson, *Scholarship Amok: Excesses in the Pursuit of Truth and Tenure*, 103 HARV. L. REV. 926 (1990). It is worth recalling the difficulty law and economics scholars had in getting the legal academy to take their work seriously at the outset, and the continuing anti-intellectual dismissal of the "graphs and numbers" aspects of law and economics work.

the situation overall,[34] though, cls is here to stay. I consider what *that* means in Part V.

## II. THE ENLIGHTENMENT

The origins of critical legal studies as a political location are relatively easy to identify.[35] In early 1976 David Trubek returned from a trip to Cambridge and told me that he had spoken with Duncan Kennedy. They had agreed that there were a number of people doing academic studies of law that seemed to have certain common themes, and that it might be useful to gather these people, and a few others, to see whether that perception was accurate. The themes dealt with questions of ideology in ways that seemed compatible with the traditional focus on "law and society" at the University of Wisconsin Law School, yet concentrated on legal doctrine in ways that seemed compatible with more mainstream approaches to legal scholarship. If that perception were correct, the thought was, some sort of organizational locus for that intellectual work would be useful. Though the work had come to the attention of Kennedy, it was being done by people scattered throughout the country, often with no sense that anyone other than Kennedy might be interested in it or might make helpful comments on it. In addition, of course, there was the possibility (quickly realized once the organization got off the ground) that there were people doing similar work who had not sent it to Kennedy but who would want to affiliate with a group of sympathetic scholars.

I was then serving as Associate Dean at Wisconsin, and had a certain amount of excess energy—and the soul of a bureaucrat—which made it appropriate for me to do most of the organizational work attendant to putting on an academic conference. Even at the start there was some sense that a relatively formal structure was needed to provide the location for the academic activities that Trubek had referred to, and we developed a list of "steering committee" members to put on the letterhead.

The intellectual themes in the work that drew people together have now become standard lines about critical legal studies. Describing the political history of cls requires that those themes be identified at this point, but, as is common in overviews of cls,[36] I must indicate at the outset that I will not be describing "tenets" of cls or dogmas to which one must adhere in order that one's self-identification with cls be accepted by others who similarly self-

34. By which I mean that individuals associated with cls are likely to face rather more trauma in hiring and tenuring than people not so associated, and may end up "underrecognized." For a discussion of this issue, see *infra* text accompanying notes 99-101.

35. I rely here primarily on my own recollection, checked by some conversations with others associated with the early days of cls. I am notorious in my family, however, for not remembering things very well. For another account of the origins of cls, see Schlegel, *Notes Toward an Intimate, Opinionated, and Affectionate History of the Conference on Critical Legal Studies*, 36 STAN. L. REV. 391 (1984).

36. *See, e.g.*, M. KELMAN, A GUIDE TO CRITICAL LEGAL STUDIES 2 (1987).

identify. There are at best family resemblances among various versions of these themes, and, as a matter of intellectual integrity, adherents of each version will criticize other versions for their intellectual shortcomings. Yet it turns out that the existence of the family resemblances may be the most important dimension of the work.

One characteristic of the work to which Kennedy and Trubek referred was the identification, in numerous substantive areas of law, of paired oppositions and standard arguments deploying sets of claims from one side of those oppositions against sets drawn from the other side.[37] Deriving from the work of the legal realists, this technique led, in the first instance, to the development of the "indeterminacy" argument. As it was derived from the analysis of paired oppositions, the indeterminacy argument held that within the standard resources of legal argument were the materials for reaching sharply contrasting results in particular instances. Those results, it appeared, were exactly what people arguing directly over moral or political goals were seeking. Later this technique mutated into philosophically more sophisticated deconstructionist techniques,[38] but adherents of cls continue to hold to the general perception that there is no interesting difference between legal discourse and ordinary moral and political discourse.

As we saw it, the legal realist versions of this technique had led some of the realists to offer a relatively informal descriptive and normative sociology of law.[39] Descriptively, the existence of a community of lawyers, sharing what Llewellyn called a "situation sense," eliminated the possibility that contradictory results, available as a matter of theory, would actually be realized in practice.[40] Normatively, the values of that community, or some other community into which it could be transformed, justified the choices among possible results at which the legal system arrived. The law and society tradition, with which Trubek and I were particularly sympathetic, had attempted to provide a more systematic basis for the realists' informal sociology of law. Some in that tradition, however, were more skeptical of the normative acceptability of the results found acceptable by the community of lawyers. A second theme in the work to which Kennedy and Trubek referred, then, was a critique of the sociology of law that was implicit in the way legal realism had been assimilated in the legal academy.

37. CRITICAL LEGAL STUDIES (A. Hutchinson ed. 1989), described by one reviewer as "easily the best introduction to the 'mainstream' of CLS," Book Note, 100 ETHICS 912, 912 (1990), includes excerpts in this vein from R. UNGER, KNOWLEDGE AND POLITICS (1975), and Kennedy, *Form and Substance in Private Law Adjudication*, 89 HARV. L. REV. 1685 (1976).

38. *See, e.g.*, Balkin, *Deconstructive Practice and Legal Theory*, 96 YALE L.J. 743 (1987); Dalton, *An Essay in the Deconstruction of Contract Doctrine*, 94 YALE L.J. 999 (1985).

39. Other realists moved in the direction of positivist policy science. *See, e.g.*, Lasswell & McDougal, *Legal Education and Public Policy: Professional Training in the Public Interest*, 52 YALE L.J. 203 (1943). Positivism had little influence on the development of critical legal studies, and positivist Marxism rapidly became marginalized within cls.

40. K. LLEWELLYN, THE COMMON LAW TRADITION 260-61 (1960).

The critique drew upon the work of Weber and Marx, and a great deal of the early work associated with critical legal studies involved efforts to make sense of a Marxist-Weberian notion of the relative autonomy of law.[41] There were latent tensions in these efforts. For some, Marxism was attractive because it argued against the inevitability of the permanent triumph of the capitalist system. Yet, while it was in that sense liberating, the strains of historical determinism in Marxist thought were in another sense confining. And of course, Weber's sociology, with its emphasis on the "iron cage" of rationality in bureaucratic societies, had an even more pessimistic message.[42] The cultural-radical strand in cls contributed an additional impetus to the forces emphasizing freedom of choice rather than determinism, while the continuing influence of the Marxist-Weberian tradition allowed cls to incorporate concern for what Unger has called "formative contexts" into the movement's intellectual work.[43] This combination of elements, though, is not tidy, and causes obvious intellectual tensions, if not within individual adherents of cls then within the body of work called critical legal studies as a whole. These tensions, in turn, provide opportunities for critics of cls to challenge the coherence of the movement's intellectualized program.

Another dimension of the tensions within early cls work was that the efforts to develop a notion of relative autonomy repeatedly ran up against what many took to be the epistemological implications of the analysis of legal texts. In part because we were dealing with legal texts, and legal doctrines in particular, and because in dealing with those texts and doctrines we had come to see the existence of paired oppositions as central to the phenomenon being analyzed, the critique of the sociology of law directed attention to problems of ideology and consciousness.[44] Somehow the community of lawyers resolved the contradictions expressed by the paired oppositions in a way that *seemed to them* normatively acceptable.

Once the work focused on normativity as a social phenomenon, it could draw into the domain of critical legal sociology the fact (if it was a fact) that to some people the resolution of the contradictions did not *seem* at all acceptable. The critique of the sociology of law thus led to the issue of alienation from, or as expressed within, the legal system.[45] This critique was reinforced

41. *See, e.g.*, R. UNGER, LAW IN MODERN SOCIETY (1976); Klare, *Law-Making as Praxis*, 40 TELOS 123 (1979).

42. For a discussion of Weber's analysis of rationality in the modern era, see A. MITZMAN, THE IRON CAGE: AN HISTORICAL INTERPRETATION OF MAX WEBER (1970).

43. *See* R. UNGER, SOCIAL THEORY: ITS SITUATION AND ITS TASK 88-89 (1987).

44. My contributions to this discussion were Tushnet, *Perspectives on the Development of American Law: A Critical Review of Friedman's* A History of American Law, 1977 WIS. L. REV. 81; Tushnet, *A Marxist Analysis of American Law*, 1 MARXIST PERSP. 96 (1978).

45. At roughly the same time a communitarian critique of adjudication, in the form of advocacy of alternative dispute resolution mechanisms, became prominent in the law and society community. *See, e.g.*, Menkel-Meadow, *Portia in a Different Voice: Speculations on a Women's Lawyering Process*, 1 BERKELEY WOMEN'S L.J. 39 (1985).

by the cultural-radical strand of cls, which presented the experience of law as oppressive and alienating rather than as a normatively attractive solution to problems of social coordination.[46]

These themes converged in the programmatic statement that law is politics, all the way down. Most people in the legal academy agree, albeit often with some reluctance, that law is politics in the superficial sense that we can talk about identifiably liberal and conservative positions on various issues in the law, ranging from affirmative action to strict liability versus negligence. The indeterminacy argument and the critique of social theory led cls to a different understanding of the proposition that law is politics. We saw law as a form of human activity in which political conflicts were worked out in ways that contributed to the stability of the social order ("legitimation") in part by constituting personality and social institutions in ways that came to seem natural. The legitimating and constitutive operation of law occurred on all levels. Categories of legal analysis that underlay particular doctrines had, as we saw it, both kinds of effects.[47] The concept of "reasonableness" used in tort law is political in the sense that it implicitly and sometimes explicitly relies on images of male behavior to define the norm of reasonableness. The related concept of "rationality" was politically defined to justify the expansion of European states into regions occupied by other peoples. In the end, adherents of cls argue that the entire notion of "the rule of law" and associated distinctions between objectivity and subjectivity incorporated a partial, and therefore political, definition of rational behavior.

Attempting to combine the analysis of paired oppositions in legal doctrine with a critique of the sociology of law led to a number of intellectual and political tensions. First, the sociology of consciousness available within the law and society tradition was severely underdeveloped. Second, any sociology of

46. The cultural-radical strand also influenced the organizational structure of cls, particularly through its emphasis on overcoming alienation through personal contact and its opposition to reified forms of democracy that reproduce the alienation of law as false community. My sense is that the emphasis on personal contact as a medium for organizational growth was particularly attractive to some of the early organizers because it meant that they could engage in a form of intellectual seduction that had powerful sexual overtones. For a literary version of the point, see A. BERNAYS, PROFESSOR ROMEO (1988), which, however, is not quite on point because the sexualization of intellectual seduction is apparent on the surface (and the book is less insightful as a result). For Kennedy's analysis, see Kennedy, *Psycho-Social CLS: A Comment on the Cardozo Symposium*, 6 CARDOZO L. REV. 1013 (1985); for a response, see West, *Deconstructing the CLS-Fem Split*, 2 WIS. WOMEN'S L.J. 85 (1986). Both of these focus on the psychology of male-female relations; my sense is that the intellectual seduction of men combines homoeroticism, projection, and envy as the seduced males imagine themselves in the place of their seducers.

47. The most noteworthy discussions occurred in connection with the distinction between the public sphere and the private sphere. *See The Public/Private Distinction*, 130 U. PA. L. REV. 1289 (1982). The phenomenon occurs, however, on less exalted levels, as when workplace injuries are conceptualized initially on the model of having a hand crushed in a press, then reconceptualized as including environmental harms such as asbestos in the workplace and, later, environmental harms such as sexual and racial harassment in the workplace, but not yet as including the "ordinary" depletion of human capital attendant upon working on an assembly line. For an example drawn from outside the cls literature, see Asch, *Wildlife: Defining the Animals of the Dene Hunt and the Settlement of Aboriginal Rights Claims*, 15 CANADIAN PUB. POL'Y 205 (1989) (analyzing use of terms "wildlife" and "domesticated animals" in treaties and native discourse).

consciousness, when developed beyond the rudiments, was likely to be in some tension with what we took to be the leanings toward determinacy that characterized the main tradition of Marx and Weber.[48] Third, it seemed unlikely at the outset that whatever sociology of consciousness we could develop would describe any serious connection between the legal doctrine that was the focus of the first theme in the work and the concern for consciousness that was the focus of the second theme. Most of the work either stated or suggested that the legal doctrines we studied somehow "legitimated" the legal system, but did not fully explain how. The only mechanism of legitimacy we talked about was a sort of "transmission belt" theory of legitimacy. Under this theory, legal elites articulated fancy theories about why and how the existing system was the only really effective way to advance all sorts of human goods, and then sold those theories to publicists in the mass media, who transmitted suitably watered-down versions to the general public, which accepted the theories as completely sensible. This theory seemed unlikely to be sufficient in the end.[49]

Finally, there was a latent tension between the cultural-radical perception of law as alienating and oppressive and the political location of cls adherents as sometime participants in political activity on the side of the oppressed. The tension, made manifest in the minority and feminist critiques of some presentations of cls positions, was that for many of the oppressed the experience of the law was both alienating and liberating, sometimes simultaneously and sometimes in succession.[50]

More important than these difficulties, however, were what we took to be the implications of the analysis of indeterminacy for social theory itself.[51] Classical social theory had not paid much attention to questions of law, yet legal terms—in particular, "ownership of private property"—played a large role in the fundamental structure of Marxist and, to a lesser extent, Weberian social thought. If those terms were, as we believed them to be, indeterminate, the conclusions of classical social theory regarding the inevitable triumph of the working class or of the "iron cage" of bureaucratic society rested on sand.[52] In short, the indeterminacy thesis threatened the social theory that legal realists had relied on to resolve the normative and descriptive difficulties exposed by their analysis of law. Put a different way, the indeterminacy thesis, developed

48. I use the locution "took to be," and similar ones, to make it clear that I am offering an intellectual history of cls at this point, not an exegesis of classical social theory.

49. Methods of social investigation that were different from those used in the law and society tradition, including introspection and personal narratives, have been used in cls as elsewhere. In my view, however, these methods remain less developed than necessary to provide full support for the central proposition that law legitimates and constitutes society.

50. *See, e.g., Minority Critiques of the Critical Legal Studies Movement, supra* note 25.

51. Here it is easier for me to switch from the language of "paired oppositions" to the language of "indeterminacy," though my sense is that the latter language emerged after the points made in the text became common currency in cls.

52. For some, this line of thought was reinforced by their acquaintance with the work of Karl Polanyi. *See* K. POLANYI, THE GREAT TRANSFORMATION (1944). For me, the most important article was Samuels, *Interrelations Between Legal and Economic Processes*, 14 J.L. & ECON. 435 (1971).

in the specific context of legal doctrine, created an atmosphere in which the deterministic leanings of classical social theory were suspect.[53]

The critique of social theory also had a political dimension. The determinism that we imputed to classical social theory was inconsistent with our understanding of the social movements in the United States for civil rights and against the war in Vietnam, movements in which moralistic consciousness patently played a larger role than we believed classical social theory could account for. The critique of rights, and the criticisms of that critique discussed earlier, are efforts within critical legal studies to develop a sociology of legal consciousness that more adequately accounts for moralistic liberation movements than the "transmission belt" model of legitimation. Further, the determinism we found in classical social theory seemed to us to have a demobilizing effect in the circumstances of the mid-1970's, when the liberal reformist impulses associated in law with the Warren Court appeared to have played themselves out. By bringing questions of consciousness and alienation to the fore, the cls approach might contribute to the development of a social theory that need not be demobilizing in adverse political conditions. At the same time, however, the critique of social theory fit awkwardly with the educated intuitions of many politically active lawyers who associated with cls. They accepted an informal Marxist account of law and society, in which one could explain legal outcomes most of the time by referring to the interests of the ruling class. The critique of social theory threatened that understanding of the legal order, and to the extent that activist lawyers had been able to account for their activity by locating it with reference to that understanding, the critique of social theory called their activities into question.[54]

The combination of the analysis of paired oppositions with the critique of social theory itself created political difficulties for cls. I have described an intellectual program that has a certain degree of coherence, but few people associated with cls at the outset thought that each element in the program was as important as the others, and many who agreed with some parts of the program were uncomfortable with others. The family resemblance among the works that initially identified themselves with cls was their political orientation on the Left. The Left, though, is hardly a narrow terrain itself, and political differences within the Left sometimes were associated with intellectual differ-

53. In this connection, the implications of postmodernism as a critique of all totalizing theories seem particularly important. To the extent that postmodernism supports a form of pluralism—theories that offer local solutions without making grander claims—it seems consistent with the political practice of cls. I remain uneasy about whether a postmodernist can hold a leftist political position, even as I acknowledge that the "can" in that statement itself suggests that I have not fully assimilated the postmodernist lesson.

54. To the best of my recollection, the standard critique of Marxist determinism—that because the engine of history ran in the direction of the triumph of the working class, deliberate action was unnecessary—did not play an important part in early cls thinking.

ences over elements in the cls "program."[55] In particular, the implicit "transmission belt" social theory, which linked our attention to mandarin legal texts[56] with social transformation or legitimacy, was implausible; yet it was associated with the critique of social theory, which might be tainted by the association. People on the Left, that is, could still have an image of a mobilized working class as the vehicle of social transformation, propelled by changes in the technical relations of production.[57] This counter-image of social theory led to tensions within cls about the appropriate form of our organization. Some believed that a left-wing political organization had to make some effort to connect with other political organizations on the Left, and that the theoretical work was basically useless for left-wing politics. Others believed that the theoretical project was interesting enough, and difficult enough, that internal development was more important, and that attempts to expand the scope of the organization were likely to cause even more political difficulties as the degree of internal political homogeneity (already low enough to cause political problems) would inevitably diminish.

The solution turned out to result from what I see as Duncan Kennedy's political judgment and my bureaucratic mentality. For Kennedy, it was more important to sustain cls as a political location for people who found such a self-identification valuable than to adopt a particular organizational stance. Further, he and others in the core group of early cls believed that the political conflicts

---

55. I doubt that there are tight conceptual connections between the political positions and the intellectual ones; indeed, my guess is that the best account of the association would be sociological and psychological. An important element, for example, seems to me a deep ambivalence about the obviously important role that has been played by people who teach at Harvard Law School. The ambivalence is that people either have mentors at Harvard or understand that a strong cls presence there provides some validation for their own efforts, and yet they correctly believe that the position of Harvard in the legal academy is an example of illegitimate hierarchy. This ambivalence affects the degree to which people on the Left differentiate themselves intellectually from others on the Left.

I suppose that a comment about my own position, as I see it, is appropriate at this point. I attended elite institutions, including Yale Law School, and had a prestigious judicial clerkship. But my grades at Yale were not that good, so I did not receive the kind of institutional blessing that attends the "superstars," and I marginalized myself/was marginalized by being identified as a Marxist, by playing a prominent role in the organizational structure of cls, and by being nasty in print to people who, according to the standards of hierarchy, deserved better treatment. Further, when cls got started, I was teaching at the University of Wisconsin Law School, which occupies a peculiar place in the hierarchy of the legal academy, and now teach at Georgetown, which, as far as I can tell, occupies no particular place at all in that hierarchy. My sense is that, as a result of all this, I am what anthropologists call a "liminal" figure, who is allowed to operate between institutions with a certain facility that, according to the anthropologists, may yield deep insights (on the part of the anthropologist, not the liminal figure, I hasten to add) into the operation of the institutions. I should say that I remain somewhat puzzled about my role in the internal politics of cls, particularly because I have not done much more, since the mid-1980's, than write articles. I am reasonably sure—and annoyed—that externally I am seen as a safe ambassador from cls to the mainstream.

56. The phrase is drawn from Gordon, *Critical Legal Histories*, 36 STAN. L. REV. 57, 120 (1984). For what it is worth, my view is that Gordon's response to criticism of attention to these texts is not completely successful.

57. For reasons that I do not understand, the challenge to cls from the traditional Left has not picked up on G.A. Cohen's rehabilitation of classical Marxist theory. *See* G.A. COHEN, KARL MARX'S THEORY OF HISTORY (1978), *discussed (sympathetically) in* Tushnet, Book Review, 68 CORNELL L. REV. 281, 285-86 (1983).

were more apparent than real, and that when people actually got down to the business of doing something they would discover that their common political orientation was more important to them than their political disagreements. For me, being a bureaucrat meant getting the job done: maintaining the mailing list, making sure there were newsletters sent out, helping people who wanted to put on events get on with the job. I do not claim to have thought through the political significance of being a bureaucrat in this context, but it turned out that getting the job done is pretty much what cls needed at that point. For cls as a political location, what mattered was not getting the intellectual line right, though because we were located primarily in the academy we did have to do intellectually interesting work. What mattered was keeping the location available to people who needed it.[58]

In the years after the location was established, it moved like an amoeba over the landscape of the Left in the legal academy. It extended to new constituencies, absorbed some and rejected others after an initial flirtation, and extruded a very few who had initially been associated with cls. In the process the location was transformed, as strands within the location found themselves located somewhat differently with respect to the group as a whole: marginalized or in the center, after having been in the center or on the margins. Through all this, the occupants of the location continued to influence each other, though not without some strain.[59]

## III. THE DARK AGES

In the late 1960's and early 1970's the faculty of Yale Law School fired six professors.[60] The Official Story is that the faculty had decided to raise the standards for granting tenure. The real story is somewhat different.[61]

58. One indication of the role of cls as a political location is the rather rapid falling away of people like George Fletcher who, though interested in the analysis of paired oppositions, did not share the political orientation that characterized cls as a political location.

59. Because my focus in this Article is on the external politics of critical legal studies, I will not examine the largely internal political history of the process by which the location transformed itself.

60. Richard Abel, Lee Albert, John Griffiths, Robert Hudec, Larry Simon, and David Trubek. I know of no other sequence of such concentrated firings. The firings at Harvard Law School of Dan Tarullo and Clare Dalton, coupled with President Derek Bok's refusal to agree to the law faculty's recommendation that David Trubek (again) be appointed to the faculty, have not (yet) reached a similar level of intensity. In 1986-87 four people were fired at the New England School of Law, at least in part because of a perception that they were associated with critical legal studies.

61. Calling what follows the real story can be defended in two ways. The weaselly way is to say that I am recounting the events as they were interpreted within cls, not as they "really" happened. The other way is to begin by noting that the publication records of people promoted from within at Yale in the years after the firings did not materially differ from those of the people who were fired at the time they were fired. The next step is to explain that fact in the face of the Official Story. One possibility is that the number of internal promotions was small, and the publication records lay at the tail of a distribution which, when fully understood, centers around a higher tenure standard. Another is that the faculty, after coming to understand the costs of firing people, simply changed its mind. A third is that the faculty indeed raised the tenure standard in the sense of demanding of itself a much firmer predictive judgment about future scholarship than it had used in the 1960's, and that the post-tenure publication records of internal promotions, while

New Haven at that period was a city in substantial turmoil. Leaders of the Black Panther Party were being prosecuted for murder in a case that attracted national attention. The Yale campus experienced the usual disruptions resulting from protests against the war in Vietnam, made somewhat more prominent perhaps by the presence of William Sloane Coffin at the University.[62] The cultural radicalism of the period led students to engage in flamboyant dress and behavior. The Yale Law School student body was not immune from these influences, even cultural radicalism, which in turn affected the faculty at the Law School.[63] The faculty had invested a great deal in developing a sense of itself as "the best and the brightest" of a generation of policy-oriented legal intellectuals.[64] What seemed to them a flamboyant cultural radicalism constituted a direct rejection of principles to which the faculty were devoted at the core of their being.

The faculty of the Law School meanwhile had undergone a significant expansion at the junior level, and the younger faculty became tainted by the mere presence of students who were only a bit younger. In addition, though few of the junior faculty had radical politics, they were all substantially more sympathetic to the claims being made by students than were many of the senior faculty. The senior faculty took on the air of a beleaguered garrison, defending the ramparts at all costs against the assaults of the barbarians. Those who suggested even in the mildest way that the students might be on to something were politically unreliable. Under the circumstances, any disagreement threatened the institutional stability to which many of the senior faculty were dedicated.

The political disagreements between the junior faculty and the majority of the senior faculty were, in the larger scheme of things, relatively minor. John Griffiths helped set up a legal research seminar on problems arising from the draft, and conducted empirical research on the effectiveness of the *Miranda* warnings[65] given by federal agents investigating draft evasion.[66] Understandably, he did not turn in his draft card. No faculty member, as far as I can recall,

---

thin, are still too recently compiled to disconfirm those judgments. (To pull this one off, though, one would also have to concede that, as to a fair number of those fired, the faculty's predictive judgment about future scholarship was simply dreadful.) My view is that none of these explanations of the similar records of people promoted after the firings and those who were fired comes close to plausibility.

62. Coffin, a minister, was among those indicted for antiwar activities. For an account of the trial, see J. MITFORD, THE TRIAL OF DR. SPOCK (1969).

63. A "commune" was established in the courtyard of the Law School, though by national standards it was a relatively tame affair.

64. I am reasonably confident that I believed the faculty and people like them to be indeed "the best and the brightest," according to the standards developed by their community. Thus, when that phrase was used to describe the generation that got the nation involved in the Vietnam War, as in D. HALBERSTAM, THE BEST AND THE BRIGHTEST (1972), I took it to be a criticism of those standards rather than of the people. That view has, I think, permanently affected my position on questions of meritocracy in law school politics.

65. *See* Miranda v. Arizona, 384 U.S. 436 (1966).

66. *See* Griffiths & Ayres, *A Postscript to the Miranda Project: Interrogation of Draft Protestors*, 77 YALE L.J. 300 (1967).

joined that segment of the student body arguing in favor of terminating the Panther prosecution, though I remember Larry Simon expressing some misgivings about the way the rhetoric of "the rule of law" was being deployed to support the prosecution.[67] Yet these minor political disagreements demonstrated that the junior faculty were "unsound."

To many of the senior faculty, the junior faculty's lack of judgment was demonstrated as well by their scholarship. Richard Abel was positively uninterested in doctrinal scholarship of any sort. Griffiths did a certain type of doctrinal scholarship, but not one that the senior faculty was comfortable with. Griffiths' major work, prior to his firing, amounted to a powerful assault on the prevailing view in criminal law scholarship, developed by Herbert Packer, that society faced a choice between a "due process" model and a "crime control" model.[68] Griffiths argued that Packer had identified only a single model of the criminal process; Griffiths offered instead what he called, necessarily but misleadingly, a "third" model, which today would be viewed as an interesting communitarian-feminist approach to criminal procedure but which then was seen as wildly totalitarian.[69] In many ways the reaction to Griffiths' articles can be understood as a model of the whole process. Not only were they severely critical of what many on the senior faculty regarded as the culmination of a life's work by a major figure in the field; they also had a tone suggesting that Griffiths could not believe that anyone with an ounce of intellectual integrity could take Packer's work seriously, let alone write it. Even worse, they were published almost contemporaneously with the massive stroke that ultimately led Packer to commit suicide.[70] If Griffiths didn't exactly cause the stroke, for the senior faculty his behavior—which his hypercritical tone exemplified—was typical of the sort of thing that led men of their generation to *have* strokes.

Griffiths' scholarship was symptomatic in another way. Most of the senior faculty had absorbed the New Deal understanding of legal realism. In that understanding, symbolized by the work of Myres McDougal, the indeterminacy of formalistic legal rules should be replaced by a form of policy science that drew informally upon the wisdom of the social sciences to inform legal judgment. Social science would be called upon to answer questions that lawyers found interesting as they attempted to resolve conflicts that formalism left unresolved. Taking the standard line at Yale Law School more seriously than

67. For additional discussion, see *infra* text accompanying notes 76-78. I use the examples of Griffiths and Simon precisely because they have not subsequently been closely associated (to put it mildly) with critical legal studies.

68. *See* Packer, *Two Models of the Criminal Process*, 113 U. PA. L. REV. 1 (1964).

69. *See* Griffiths, *Ideology in Criminal Procedure, or a Third "Model" of the Criminal Process*, 79 YALE L.J. 359 (1970); Griffiths, *The Limits of Criminal Law Scholarship*, 79 YALE L.J. 1388 (1970).

70. *See* Seltzer, *Herbert L. Packer*, 26 STAN. L. REV. 997, 999-1000 (1974) (mentioning Packer's stroke in late 1960's and alluding to his suicide in 1972); *see also* Gewirtz, *A Lawyer's Death*, 100 HARV. L. REV. 2053 (1987) (on our inability to confront the fact that people commit suicide).

its purveyors did,[71] the junior faculty went back to the roots of legal realism and found them more radical than legal realism appeared to be in the New Deal understanding. David Trubek co-authored an article with Judge Charles Clark, arguing that Karl Llewellyn's late work betrayed the fundamental insights of earlier legal realism.[72] For them, Llewellyn had reinscribed formalism in law by locating it in the "situation sense" of the lawyering class.[73] If, as I have noted, "situation sense" was a socially constructed phenomenon, it could be investigated by the techniques of social science. Now, however, social science would not be merely instrumental to policymaking; rather, it would be a true science of law as a social phenomenon.

Trubek and Abel in particular turned to classical social theory for their understanding of that phenomenon.[74] In conjunction with a program in law and development generously funded by the Agency for International Development, they instituted a reading group on the philosophy of social science undergirding a social theory of law, in which Duncan Kennedy, Nancy Gertner, Helene Ietswaart, and several others, including myself, participated. This association with student radicals, even a fairly intellectual association with fairly intellectual student radicals, did them no good in the eyes of the senior faculty. And, in some sense, rightly so. For, in the course of these discussions, shaped by the confrontation of legal realism with classical social theory in a climate of political confrontation, the outlines of what became critical legal studies were sketched.[75]

The moralism of the oppositional politics of the Dark Ages also deserves emphasis. Student discontent with the course of public policy led many of us to reject the role that had become central to the image of lawyering at Yale Law School: the well-meaning public servant interested in influencing the course of public policy by providing informed judgments about what marginal changes in policy would advance the goal of social justice. Part of the draft resistance movement, quite strong in the Yale community, was purely moralistic in its rejectionism. With a Yale Law School education, I could not fail to

---

71. *See* R. UNGER, THE CRITICAL LEGAL STUDIES MOVEMENT 119 (1986) ("Having failed to persuade themselves of all but the most equivocal versions of the inherited creed, they nevertheless clung to its implications and brazenly advertised their own failure as the triumph of worldly wisdom over intellectual and political enthusiasm.").

72. Clark & Trubek, *The Creative Role of the Judge: Restraint and Freedom in the Common Law Tradition*, 71 YALE L.J. 255 (1961).

73. *See supra* note 40 and accompanying text.

74. *See, e.g.*, Abel, *Law Books and Books About Law* (Book Review), 26 STAN. L. REV. 175 (1973); Trubek, *Toward a Social Theory of Law: An Essay on the Study of Law and Development*, 82 YALE L.J. 1 (1972).

75. The long-term effect of these events on the intellectual atmosphere of the Yale law faculty deserves a note. Overall, they seem to have led the faculty to adopt a form of self-presentation that, curiously, combines *Star Trek* with *Marathon Man*: asserting that they are boldly going where no one has gone before, all the while looking over their shoulders nervously and asking, "Is it safe?" (The point at which the metaphor breaks down will be clear to those familiar with *Marathon Man*, and explaining to others why it breaks down at that point would compound the difficulty.)

experience substantial cognitive dissonance when my roommate, outraged at the immorality of the war, framed his outrage in legalistic terms. Sharing his outrage, my only course, really, was to reject his legalism.

For a variety of reasons, I was only a peripheral member of the reading group and the law-and-development community at Yale. It took me a long time to grasp the point of legal realism, which eventually came home to me in a seminar on law and psychiatry co-taught by Jan Deutsch and Jay Katz. Having got it, I produced what in retrospect seems to me my first cls argument. Protests over the Panther trial led to a "town hall" meeting of the Law School community. The predominant rhetoric was that the Panthers, having been lawfully indicted on the basis of what all conceded was probable cause, should be subject to the regular process of the law, which should go forward to its regular conclusion: a trial, a verdict, and, if necessary, an appeal. At that meeting I made the following argument, a version, I now think, of the indeterminacy argument. Crucial evidence leading to the indictment of the Panthers had been seized during a full-scale search of a house incident to an arrest. At the time of trial, such a search would have been unconstitutional and the evidence could not have been used against the Panthers.[76] The Supreme Court had recently held, however, that the prohibition against such searches would not be applied retroactively.[77] Thus it would not violate any constitutional rule enforced by the courts to use the illegally seized evidence against the Panthers. Yet, I argued, it would not be inconsistent with the rule of law for a prosecutor to determine, as an exercise of discretion, that it would nonetheless be inappropriate to use that evidence. Thus I concluded that nothing in the rule of law required that the trial go forward to verdict and beyond. Although it needs cleaning up, I still think it's a good argument.[78]

## IV. Prehistory

The standard account of the origins of cls includes a reference to the influence of the civil rights movement and the Warren Court on the motivations of left-leaning lawyers and academics who were attracted to cls.[79] In this account, the experience of the Warren Court and its interaction with the civil

76. *See* Chimel v. California, 395 U.S. 752 (1969).

77. *See* Hill v. California, 401 U.S. 797 (1971); Williams v. United States, 401 U.S. 646 (1971).

78. Today I would stress, in addition to discretion, the possibility that the prosecutor's oath of office required him to arrive at an independent judgment on the constitutionality of using the evidence, as well as the possibility (which cuts both ways) that the prosecutor's duty to enforce the law—the Constitution as well as the law against murder—supports a decision to forgo prosecution based on illegally seized evidence. (The argument, of course, goes to the coherence of the "rule of law" position that was being articulated to justify continuing the Panther trial. It would not be effective against other arguments, most notably that the Panthers were in fact guilty. Still, though I believe that many people did think the Panthers were guilty, almost none of the rhetoric around the trial dealt with that question, perhaps because that would have opened up directly the question of whether the trial was or was not political in the classic sense.)

79. *See, e.g.*, Binder, *On Critical Legal Studies as Guerrilla Warfare*, 76 GEO. L.J. 1, 13-24 (1987); Schlegel, *supra* note 35, at 406-07.

rights movement convinced us that, notwithstanding the skeptical determinism associated with Marxist social theory, it was possible for law to become an autonomous force for progressive social change. In developing the critique of social theory and the indeterminacy thesis, we attempted to provide a theoretical grounding for our political inclinations.

Without minimizing the explanatory power of that account, I think it worth noting another strand that worked its way into cls. A fair number of the first group associated with cls were "red-diaper babies," the children of leftist activists in the 1930's and thereafter.[80] The formative legal experience for this group, I believe, was the law's half-hearted defense of civil liberties against McCarthyism, not the civil rights movement; the paradigmatic judge was Irving Kaufman, not Earl Warren. Yet such an experience and such a paradigm could hardly generate real enthusiasm for the law as an instrument for progressive change.

It is probably best here to work through my understanding of how that experience played itself out for me. When my parents were called to testify before the House Committee on Un-American Activities, the Fifth Amendment became a living thing in our household. I read and was invigorated by Dean Griswold's *The Fifth Amendment Today*.[81] For all its inspirational defense of the privilege against self-incrimination in the McCarthy era, however, the book ultimately rang a little hollow. While the experience was hardly welcome, my parents suffered no legal sanctions, and few social ones, as a result of their appearances.

Later, the legal system imposed more distress on the family. After the worst excesses of the period had ended, a former activist ran for the school board of Newark. The *Newark Star-Ledger* opposed her candidacy, and in an editorial referred to her as "a dope or a dupe" of the Communists. This being the era before *New York Times Co. v. Sullivan*,[82] she sued the paper for libel.[83] My parents and many of their friends were sucked into this lawsuit, which revived all of the tensions that had been associated with McCarthyism. It was as if the law simply reached out to intrude on people's lives, with no good reason. Nor did "the law" appear in a good light when my mother gave her deposition. One issue in the lawsuit was whether the plaintiff should have known that Communists were present at a meeting in our house. The meeting had been held in our living room, and my mother was asked to describe the room, so that inferences

80. From this point on, I speak only of my own understanding and experience, not that of other red-diaper babies associated with cls; without additional evidence readers may find the account that follows too thin to be interesting, but providing additional detail seems to me akin to "outing" (the public identification of prominent gay people who have not chosen so to identify themselves) backed up by none of the political arguments that can be made in favor of outing.

81. E. Griswold, The Fifth Amendment Today (1955).

82. 376 U.S. 254 (1964).

83. For reported opinions of the case, see Nusbaum v. Newark Morning Ledger Co., 33 N.J. 419, 165 A.2d 177 (1960); Nusbaum v. Newark Morning Ledger Co., 86 N.J. Super. 132, 206 A.2d 185 (1965).

could be drawn from the size of the room as to the likelihood that the plaintiff knew all the people there. My mother began by saying that there was a piano in the corner, with an accordion underneath, and continued in great detail until the point of the question was entirely lost.[84]

For me, then, the law was a slightly farcical enterprise.[85] Why, then, was I interested in law? Perhaps the most important dimension is one that seems silly in retrospect. One reason that my family had been able to get through the McCarthy period relatively unscathed was that my father was a self-employed doctor. Such professionals, including lawyers as I saw it, were in a position to survive no matter what. The worst that could happen—and it did—was that a few patients might leave my father. But he was a very good doctor, and they knew it, which meant that they had to give up something valuable in order to implement their political views. Lawyers might be in the same position. In left-wing circles in the 1950's the image of the lawyer as an independent professional might have made enough sense to lead a young person to think it an attractive career. Everyone needed wills and the other kinds of general practice assistance provided by sole practitioners. By the time actual career decisions had to be made, of course, the structure of the profession and, probably more important, my own aspirations, had changed enough to make the image incongruent with my sense of my career. Undoubtedly, though, the image left its residue.

The law was attractive for another reason. If the powers that be are likely to go after dissidents, lawyers can provide some defensive assistance. Prior to the civil rights movement, in fact, Clarence Darrow was the iconic leftist lawyer. Darrow provided what the culture accepted as brilliant criminal defenses to victims of state oppression such as Dr. Ossian Sweet and John Scopes.[86] On a lesser scale, the lawyers with whom my parents consulted provided essential support in a time of trouble.

If my self-understanding is accurate and the experiences that shaped it are typical of the red-diaper babies, our image of law probably was not all that bright. If cls developed a critique of law, it was therefore not entirely the result of disillusionment by the late-1970's defeat of the movement for large-scale social transformation through law—a defeat which was particularly agonizing after the initial successes of the civil rights and welfare rights movements in the 1960's and early 1970's. The red-diaper babies had never expected much

---

84. I remember the room as being quite large, but that may result from the phenomenon described in the folk-tale, "My Mommy Is the Most Beautiful Woman in the World." For a version of the story, see B. REYHER, MY MOTHER IS THE MOST BEAUTIFUL WOMAN IN THE WORLD (1945).

85. Ultimately, I suspect, it is this that linked the red-diaper babies, who typically had rather bourgeois attitudes about the proper forms of self-presentation, to the cultural radicals, who had rather different attitudes, but who articulated the alienation from and oppressiveness of law in a way that made sense to the red-diaper babies.

86. For the presentation of Darrow in popular culture, see I. STONE, CLARENCE DARROW FOR THE DEFENSE (1941).

of the law anyway. Rather, our influence on the development of cls had two elements. Having seen how the law really worked in McCarthyism's impact on daily life, we were skeptical about claims for the efficacy of the law as an instrument of progressive change. In addition, our experience with the law made us sympathetic to the project of the law and society movement. In particular, we were attracted to the informal Marxism that was shared by many other lawyers, and that posed a counterweight to the development of the critique of social theory.[87]

## V. Future History

In imagining the future of critical legal studies, one must be hesitant, if only because the events of 1989 in China and central Europe seem to indicate that nobody knows anything about how societies actually operate.[88] Alternatively, one might conclude that the cls critique of social theory was basically correct: no large-scale generalizations about how societies work are likely to have much to say about actual historical transformations. A standard question about cls, "Is cls more like law and economics or law and psychiatry?," inevitably calls for predictions in which no one can have much confidence.

Law and economics has settled into the legal academy, while law and psychiatry remains a marginal subdiscipline that has no substantial continuing vitality. As a political location, cls resembles the former more than it does the latter, but the political conditions for continuing support of cls may not persist. The new constituents for critical legal studies, conceived of as a political location, may be harder to come by in the future.

Those political conditions can be divided, for present purposes, into the intellectual vitality of cls and the political circumstances in which legal academics are likely to find themselves in the relatively near future.[89] The intellectual program of cls may well have to be refocused, which may drain it of some vitality. In particular, the developments of 1989 rather strongly suggest that a leftist political movement may find it difficult to take comfort in the continuing effort to discredit classical social theory. To the extent that the critique of social theory relied on an image of self-willed action relatively independent of social circumstances, the events of 1989 are likely to generate a straightforward liberal idealist theory of social change rather than a more radical left-wing theory. To

87. It is probably not insignificant that I was one of the red-diaper babies with these inclinations. By holding a position of some visibility within cls, I was able to suggest by my presence that the cls project was not completely idealist (as against materialist).

88. After those events one wonders about the utility of reading articles on the op-ed page. Certainly some commentators got it right, though probably not at a rate greater than one might expect from a group of monkeys at a typewriter. Perhaps one might read such articles, and indeed this one, for the insights they give not into developments in the world, but into the sensibility of their authors. (I, of course, have a vested interest in defending some version of the latter point.)

89. The intellectual vitality of cls is properly considered a political condition because cls is located in the academy and must therefore have a credible intellectual program for it to serve as a political location.

sustain its intellectual and political force, then, cls may have to return to classical social theory, stressing the limits that social circumstances place on the accomplishment of substantial change while acknowledging that people do indeed, at least sometimes, make history with will and consciousness.

Such a return, however justified politically and (in my view) intellectually, may itself limit the intellectual and even the political vitality of cls. For, on one level, all that needs to be done is the rather boring job of establishing that nothing of any interest follows from "the triumph of capitalist democracy." The standard versions of legal realism are sufficient to make that point. And, to the extent that developments in Europe show that there is a large variety of political and economic choices that fit within the definition of "capitalist democracy" (including forms of social democracy that in other times would simply be called socialism), the return to social theory may itself be relatively uninteresting: choice may be somewhat constrained by social circumstances, but not in any particularly dramatic way.

Looking at the domestic situation, the intellectual program of cls may have its own weaknesses. The cls critique of legalism has, in my view, reached a point where it may be difficult to develop substantial political energy from its continuation. The point may be made by imagining that we have developed a measure of the determinacy of a set of legal rules, the "determinile." A completely determinate legal system would measure 100 determiniles, while a completely indeterminate one would measure zero. Cls adherents at present defend the position that the proper measure of legal systems is probably between five and fifteen; that is, no system is completely indeterminate, but the level of determinacy is relatively low. Mainstream legal theorists at present defend the position that the proper measure of well-functioning legal systems like that of the United States is somewhere between forty and sixty; that is, such systems have a substantial amount of indeterminacy, but not nearly as much as the cls position claims.[90] The positions differ, as is suggested by the existence of a gap between the "most determinate" version of the cls position and the "least determinate" one of the mainstream position. In addition, among cls adherents there is disagreement about the primary reason for the degree of determinacy that there is: power relations associated with gender differences, race differences, and class differences are all candidates of some. Yet at this point we are simply arguing over a mere detail, the question of degree. Such arguments are less likely to generate the kind of political heat generated by the more extreme versions of cls and mainstream positions during earlier phases of the discussion, and are less likely to lead left-leaning legal academics to the cls position.

---

90. For a forceful presentation of this position, see A. ALTMAN, CRITICAL LEGAL STUDIES: A LIBERAL CRITIQUE 90-98 (1989).

The assimilation of cls into the academy appears to have led to a general acceptance of a weak version of the position that law is politics, all the way down. For several reasons, the fact that the academy has accepted that version of the position may not lead to further accretions to cls. First, there remains resistance to the general proposition in its strongest form. At present, most of the force of the strong form—the "all the way down" part—is being carried by feminist and minority scholarship, not all of which is associated with cls.

Second, the academy has had difficulty understanding how people could be interested in the law without being interested in influencing policymakers. Yet, in light of the substantive political views associated with cls, that seems to be the case for cls. The concern of law schools with those presently holding power, or likely to do so in the near future, makes the more radical program associated with critical legal studies seem disconnected from the mission of the law school.[91] People associated with cls have a different sense of where the real political action is, and have started to develop forms of legal theorizing and legal practice that orient themselves toward mobilizing communities for more than incremental change. Yet, from the point of view of recruitment to cls, the difficulty is that the legal academy is likely to continue to have a mainstream-liberal tilt. Because the opportunity costs of becoming a legal academic are higher for right-leaning potential academics, the academy is likely to continue to have a bias toward the Left.[92] Yet, exactly what liberal law professors can do in an era in which the political Right dominates policymaking is unclear. The legal realist move toward positivist science has been discredited, for these academics, by attacks on positivism emerging from elsewhere in the academy,[93] and, more important, by the appropriation of positivism by law and economics, with its rightward bias.[94] At the least, the drift to the right in the legal academy is likely to be a bit slower than the move to the right in

91. Symptomatic is the common observation after the failed nomination of Judge Robert Bork to the Supreme Court that one lesson young legal academics might draw from the episode is to refrain from expressing potentially controversial views in their scholarship, lest they be caught up in a future nomination battle in which their writings would play a prominent role. *See, e.g.*, Murray, *Souter: Some Sad Lessons*, NEWSWEEK, Sept. 24, 1990, at 15. A rational assessment of the probability that *any* young legal academic will be in a position to face such difficulties should lead to the conclusion that young academics who consciously alter their scholarship out of concern about its effect on nomination suffer from grandiose thinking of nearly clinical proportions.

92. That bias could be overcome were the values of the academy to change so that substantial consulting activities came to be viewed as positively valuable for the law school as an institution, reducing the gap in salaries between the academy and the kind of corporate practice to which right-leaning lawyers are differentially attracted.

93. The canned footnote here typically begins with T. KUHN, THE STRUCTURE OF SCIENTIFIC REVOLUTIONS (1970), and continues according to the author's taste and reading.

94. I do not deny the existence of a liberal form of law and economics. *See, e.g.*, Rose-Ackerman, *Law and Economics: Paradigm, Politics, or Philosophy*, in LAW AND ECONOMICS 233 (N. Mercuro ed. 1989). That form may be better economics, because it introduces more complexity into the discussion. Yet precisely because it does so, the effort by right-wing law and economics to cloak its policy prescriptions in the mantle of science is unavailable to liberal law and economics. The liberal version of law and economics thereby does not appear to be substantially different from a fancy way of presenting its adherents' political judgments, reached largely independently of the economic analysis.

social policy.[95] As a result, the academy is likely to retain a place for cls, which can fill the vacuum left by the liberal academy's inability to figure out how to do liberal policy science in a conservative era.[96]

One might apply some aspects of the critique of rights to the situation of critical legal studies. The legal academy has accepted our scholarship in a weakened form, and has thereby given us the sense that we are doing work that meets its criteria of merit. Yet in providing us with that degree of legitimacy, the academy simultaneously defuses the political explosiveness of the positions we thought we were taking: it reinforces its definition of merit and gives us a stake in the maintenance of the system as it is. As discussions of the critique of rights have shown, these aspects of legitimacy have some benefits. The academy's standards of merit are not completely worthless, narrow though they may be, and being able to obtain a stake has often seemed to be necessary to sustain the effort to make even larger changes. But these benefits pose political problems for political movements, and it is as yet unclear that cls will be able to work its way around those problems.

For example, the rightward drift of United States politics will inhibit the recruitment of new adherents to cls. Those who enter law teaching will be drawn from a student body for whom the liberal legal reforms of the 1960's are at best old hat, and at worst examples of the overweening ambition of a "new class" of professionals grasping for power. The group may lean in the liberal direction, but the number of those considering themselves other than standard liberals is likely to be smaller than was the case when cls got started.[97] The cultural-radical strand in cls draws on images of social connection often based upon recollections of the 1960's, which are unlikely to be available to new recruits at a high rate.[98]

---

95. Again, the point is suggested by the liberal academy's treatment of Brown v. Board of Education, 347 U.S. 483 (1954), and Goldberg v. Kelly, 397 U.S. 254 (1970), as paradigmatic cases of what courts actually do, rather than as cases to be considered in a course on legal history as representative of an era that, like the era of Lochner v. New York, 198 U.S. 45 (1905), has been over for a while. *See* Tushnet, *Metaprocedure?*, 63 S. CAL. L. REV. 161 (1989).

96. One indication of the mainstream academy's inability to settle on a way of doing policy science is the apotheosizing of the late Robert Cover, who taught at an institution that, as suggested by its hiring practices, appears to believe that one Cover is worth ten economists (which may actually have the multiplier right). The message may be, "Well, we may not have figured out what to do, but the fact that we revere Cover shows that we remain committed to the left of the political spectrum." I should also note my discomfort with the valuation of hierarchy that has attended Cover's entry into the pantheon, based on my belief that one reason Cover has entered the pantheon (while others equally admirable have not) is that he taught at Yale Law School.

97. As a result, it seems unlikely that the amoeba that is critical legal studies would move to occupy some territory, like that of law and literature or law and science, defined primarily with reference to intellectual approaches to the analysis of law. Adherents of those approaches would be available to cls only if they were predisposed to the political position occupied by cls and, I have argued, they are unlikely to be so predisposed.

98. Within cls, the cultural-radical strand causes a particular set of internal political difficulties. Much in that strand draws on what I call the fetishization of imagined connections, a romantic yearning that one's political location be a place of unalienated connectedness. *See supra* note 46. The fetishization draws in part upon a reconstruction of the experience of the 1960's. Yet, as everyone who took part in the New Left knows, the politics of that movement was hardly the politics of a beloved community. People being who

In addition, many cls adherents are likely to be underrecognized, a condition that potential recruits are likely to perceive. By "underrecognized," I mean that a substantial group of cls adherents, the white males, are likely to have positions at institutions lower in the status hierarchy of law schools than their merits entitle them to, as measured by the criteria of merit applied by most law professors and internalized to some degree by many adherents of cls.[99] The reason is simple: recognition depends on perceptions and actions by widening circles of academics. Underrecognition occurs outside the circle of cls, as a result of hiring decisions by mainstream faculties. Men associated with cls and those who might support them for appointment are committed to increasing the numbers of minority and female scholars in the legal academy. Given a choice between a white male cls adherent and a minority or feminist scholar not associated with cls, their votes are likely to go differentially to the latter, wholly apart from whatever political misgivings people might have about cls. In contrast, people on the Right tend to be indifferent to considerations of diversity. At most they are willing to concede, grudgingly, that their traditional notions of merit ought to be changed somewhat, albeit for them, only in the cases of women and minorities. Their tolerance of deviance is likely to be exhausted when a woman or minority faculty member is hired. As the political dynamics in law school faculties play themselves out, the best result cls people can usually hope for is that the faculty will hire a woman or minority before it hires a less-qualified white male centrist or conservative;[100] only in unusual circumstances will a white male adherent of cls displace the centrist or conservative in the hiring competition.[101]

On the whole, then, cls as such may not be a growth field. This analysis of the dynamics of underrecognition, however, brings us back to the more fundamental way of looking at cls: as a political location. That analysis indi-

they are, there were all sorts of personal tensions, competition for attention, and the like. When the reality of cls as a political location occupied by real live people comes up against the fetishization of imagined connections, serious tensions arise. (In my view, this describes the dynamics of every cls summer camp I have attended, and many other cls events.)

99. The phenomenon would be unimportant if every potential adherent of cls were indifferent to considerations of hierarchy. Not all of us are. If it is necessary, I should add that I do not believe that *I* am underrecognized.

100. The analysis in the text indicates that the following priorities will occur in hiring decisions: (1) mainstream white males; (2) "mainstream" women and minorities (the scare quotes indicating that women and minorities are necessarily out of the mainstream in some respects no matter what their scholarship or overt political affiliations); (3) women and minorities who identify with the Left, including those who present themselves as affiliated with cls; (4) white males who identify with the Left, including those who present themselves as affiliated with cls. (Because the criteria by which conservatives are evaluated differ from the ones discussed here, I cannot readily locate them on the scale just presented.) Thus, I do not suggest that of those associated with cls *only* white males are underrecognized, but only that structural reasons are likely to lead to a systematically greater amount of underrecognition of white males associated with cls.

101. I can imagine that a form of "product differentiation" might occur as some people unconsciously attempt to get around the problem of the "deviance quota" by presenting themselves as "not really cls but something else." It is a strategy well-known in legal education. When considering hiring someone "in" international law, for example, faculties are routinely urged to distinguish between public and private international law, and more recently between European and Pacific Rim international and comparative law.

cates the importance of political alliances within the academy as part of the importance of cls.

The law and society influence on cls suggests that one set of allies might be found in the legal clinics at law schools.[102] Live-client clinics almost universally represent the poor, and are therefore engaged in activity consistent with the political commitments of cls adherents. In addition, the clinics are places where students can observe the law-in-action, and learn how the concepts they see in appellate opinions translate into the actions of street-level bureaucrats, housing courts, and the like. Yet cls adherents and clinicians are likely to find themselves uneasy allies on particular issues, and at odds on others. The clinicians have been struggling to establish their legitimacy in the academy. Having gained a foothold but not much more, they reasonably might believe they have more to lose than to gain by linking up with a group itself not entirely welcome in the academy. Further, the focus in most cls work on the intricacies of mandarin legal thought, as expressed in appellate opinions and the writings of noted commentators, coupled with the cls use of out-of-the-ordinary work from other disciplines, does not fit easily with the daily work of clinicians. An alliance of these two out-groups might make sense, but the tensions in constructing such an alliance have so far been sufficient to limit severely the effectiveness of the cls-clinical connection.[103]

Other out-groups in the legal academy are minority and feminist scholars. They resemble cls in working out intellectual positions defined in substantial part by their opposition to mainstream legal thought, though of course the nature of the opposition is different.[104] Many of these scholars, too, have assimilated more of the cls positions into their own work than have mainstream

102. I do not believe that the law and society movement, discussed in Friedman, *The Law and Society Movement*, 38 STAN. L. REV. 763 (1986), is likely to be a major source of new adherents of cls. The law and society movement already includes a significant number of feminists and "political economists" who are associated with cls. Beyond those groups, the "pure" law and society people tend to be less interested in legal doctrine than most cls adherents are, and in any event they are quite marginal to the legal academy, which makes it unlikely that they will find it politically helpful to become associated with cls. On the other hand, the law and society movement, with its origins in efforts to promote progressive legal reform, has been unable to gain more than a toehold in the legal academy. (For example, the editors of the *The Yale Law Journal* did not think it important to invite a contribution to this issue from someone prominently associated with the law and society movement.) This may induce its members to associate themselves with one group of progressive lawyers already part of the pluralistic universe of the legal academy, that is, with critical legal studies.

103. Identifying critical legal studies as a political project associated with the legal academy explains why it has been difficult to attract significant numbers of practicing lawyers into long-term relations with cls. The amoeba that is cls might extend to include significant numbers of practicing lawyers, but the dynamics of recruitment and retention, which seem to me heavily focused on the legal academy, make that unlikely.

104. My formulation should make it clear that I do not regard all feminist and minority scholars as already adherents of, or even as potential adherents of, critical legal studies. I do regard such scholars as necessarily oppositional within the legal academy, though in complex ways. But if, as I have argued, cls is a political location, there is no particular reason to believe that it must necessarily fully occupy the terrain of oppositional politics within the legal academy.

academics.[105] These groups are likely to mix outrage at and acceptance of the status quo in proportions closer to cls than to the legal mainstream. Of course, the overall agendas of these several groups differ, as is true in any political alliance, and the present balance of power in the legal academy is such that the feminist and minority scholars are likely to capture more of the benefits of the association than are white male cls adherents. Even so, the prospect of sustained political connections among these groups seems reasonably good.

Finally, there is the liberal mainstream. For good reason, many liberal academics do not find cls adherents easy to live with. At the same time, they understand that public policy in the United States has moved more substantially to the right than they find really comfortable. They sense, even if they cannot bring themselves to face up to the implications of the fact, that the Warren Court era is now roughly like the *Lochner* era in being an interesting but closed period in the history of the Supreme Court. And they know that they, like their liberal colleagues in other disciplines, have not come up with credible intellectual/policy-science defenses of the social welfare policies to which they are committed. In these circumstances, cls people are, *faute de mieux*, natural political allies for the liberal mainstream.

Taking the intellectual circumstances of cls together with its political environment, then, we may understand why cls is likely to remain one element in the pluralistic universe of the legal academy, but not much more. In one sense, of course, this demonstrates the success of the project of developing a political location to support the Left in the legal academy. One indication of this is the prevalence of statements dismissing cls as "merely legal realism with an unnecessary radical politics, and pointless anyway since 'we are all legal realists now.'" The first point may perhaps be accurate, but the second seems to me not to be. What was taught at Yale Law School in the 1970's and what its faculty writes today may be legitimate successors to legal realism, but critical legal studies managed to revive a view of the law associated with legal realism that had been lost for a generation.

It is not beyond the bounds of possibility, of course, that the opponents of critical legal studies may overplay their hands and drive centrist liberals toward the left. As a story in *The New York Times* revealingly put it:

> One wonders if [Harvard Law School] Dean [Robert] Clark's reaction—his corporate boosterism, his emphasis on ivory-tower excellence, his less than impassioned commitment to the public interest, broadly defined—may not create divisions within the law school that are deeper than the Critical Legal Studies rift. The danger [sic] is that the fault line at Harvard Law School, by shifting rightward, will isolate its adminis-

105. *Compare, e.g.*, West, *Jurisprudence and Gender*, 55 U. CHI. L. REV. 1 (1988) *and* West, *Feminism, Critical Social Theory and Law*, 1989 U. CHI. LEGAL FORUM 59 (both sympathetically critical of cls positions) *with* Fiss, *The Death of the Law?*, 72 CORNELL L. REV. 1 (1986) (critical but not so sympathetic).

tration and leave those professors in the middle on the same side of the chasm as the Crits.[106]

I suspect that, on the whole, administrators of law schools who have a less exalted sense of the importance of their activities are likely to respond more sensibly to the threat they feel from critical legal studies,[107] and will allow critical legal studies to remain part of the pluralistic universe. Who could reasonably have asked for the academy to welcome this disruptive political presence with open arms?

106. Emerson, *When Legal Titans Clash*, N.Y. Times, Apr. 22, 1990, § 6 (Magazine), at 69. Again I should note that I am reluctant to attribute apocalyptic effects even to a complete cls success at Harvard Law School, even given the importance of Harvard Law School in the status hierarchy of legal education.

107. Given the venue of this Article, I think it important to note at least once that the reception of cls at Yale Law School rather strongly suggests that it is not among the law schools responding sensibly to the threat they perceive from critical legal studies.

# [5]
# Survey Article: Critical Legal Theory (without Modifiers) in the United States

THE conventional wisdom in the United States is that, as Duncan Kennedy is said to have put it, critical legal theory is dead, dead, dead.[1] I argue in this article that such a view is more wrong than right. It is obviously, and uninterestingly, right if it is meant to refer to the fact that there is now no organized venue within which everyone who identifies himself or herself as a critical legal scholar can come together. The Conference on Critical Legal Studies, which held meetings from the mid-1970s to the late 1980s, no longer exists. The claim that critical legal studies is dead has some validity, too, if it is meant to refer to what I call critical legal studies without modifiers. Even those who say that critical legal studies is dead acknowledge that there is a persistent flow of works labeling themselves *critical race theory* or *critical feminist theory*.[2] Works self-identified as critical legal studies, full stop—that is, "critical legal theory without modifiers"—are rare. As the contrasts with critical race and critical feminist theory suggest, *critical legal studies* (without modifiers) now refers to work (a) written almost exclusively by white male legal academics on the political left that (b) does not focus on questions of race or multiculturalism.[3]

The claim that critical legal studies (without modifiers) is dead in the United States is nonetheless wrong, for two main reasons. First, those who wrote important articles early in the career of critical legal studies continue to do so, and correctly see their recent work as continuous with their earlier work.[4]

[1]Robert C. Ellickson, "Trends in legal scholarship: a statistical study," *Journal of Legal Studies*, 29 (2000), 517–43 at p. 525, n. 21, referring to a statement by Duncan Kennedy made in 1996.

[2]For recent examples, see Richard Delgado and Jean Stefancic, eds, *Critical Race Theory: The Cutting Edge*, 2nd edn (Philadelphia: Temple University Press, 2000) and Catherine A. MacKinnon, *Sex Equality* (New York: Foundation Press, 2001).

[3]Symptomatic, perhaps, is the collection of what might be called post-modern critical legal essays in Wendy Brown and Janet Halley, eds, *Left Legalism/Left Critique* (Durham, N.C.: Duke University Press, 2002). The editors' introduction stresses their frustration with the difficulties identity politics had posed for leftist critiques of law and legalism, and the essays are simultaneously attempts to grapple with identity politics and transcend it. That is, questions of race, identity and multiculturalism define the terrain on which the post-modern critique is developed. And members of the relevant identity groups have a privileged position in conducting discussions on that terrain.

[4]"Kennedy was one of the founders of the radical school of legal scholarship known as critical legal studies, and he remains its most unrepentant adherent. Even he acknowledges that critical legal studies is finished as a movement, but he believes that it survives as a school of thought"; Richard Posner, "Bad faith," *New Republic* (June 9, 1997), pp. 34–8 at p. 34.

Second, and more importantly, major components of critical legal studies have become the common sense of the legal academy, acknowledged to be accurate by many who would never think of identifying themselves as critical legal scholars. This article first examines the transformation of critical legal studies, full stop, into critical legal studies without modifiers, sketching the political and academic setting in which the transformation occurred. I then take up the continuing influence of critical legal studies in the legal academy, emphasizing those elements of the original critical legal studies position that have become conventional wisdom in the U.S. legal academy.

As is true of many schools of legal thought, we cannot understand critical legal theory as it developed in the United States without understanding the political and social context in which it emerged and grew. The political context was the entry into the legal academy of a group of scholars from the generation of the 1960s. Their understanding of American law and society was shaped by the experience of the movement against the war in Vietnam and by the more radical branches of the civil rights movement. Some elements in the antiwar movement took the war to demonstrate the irredeemable corruption of U.S. politics, but other elements saw it as a betrayal of the ideals they found in U.S. history and politics, which they sought to retrieve by putting U.S. politics on a new and better course. The mainstream of the civil rights movement similarly sought to vindicate what its adherents thought were the nation's ideals, while the more radical elements were skeptical about the possibility of doing so. Those in the generation of the 1960s who became legal academics fused a devotion to something like the ideals of the rule of law they associated with liberal political theory with skepticism about whether those ideals could *ever* be realized, and with near certainty that they could not be realized in the absence of a large-scale transformation of the U.S. political order, which they saw – correctly – as the form taken by a particular version of liberal politics. They therefore believed that a critical stance toward politics entailed a critical stance toward liberalism as well.

The social context was an elite legal academy dominated almost entirely by white males. In 1967, for example, the Yale Law School's entering class of about 165 had only eight women, and fewer African Americans. The number of women attending law schools grew, fueled initially by law schools' concern that the military draft – which applied only to young men – would drain the applicant pool of male applicants and so reduce the schools' tuition revenue. But, when the first U.S. critical legal scholars began their work, the law schools remained largely male and white. In addition, the law schools were training grounds for lawyers. Faculties had been trained as lawyers, and few had advanced degrees in other disciplines. Critical legal studies emerged as an approach to understanding the practice and ideology of legal professionals.

The political and social context changed as those scholars' careers advanced. Politics in the United States succumbed to a resurgence of conservatism, ending decades of liberal dominance. Critiques of liberalism (in the mild social-democratic form of post-New Deal U.S. politics), which had some bite when liberals holding such views were in charge, came to seem irrelevant – to politics if not to the intellectual world – when conservatives seemed to be running the country. This was particularly true for legal scholars, who – in the United States – believed that their vocation required them to participate in the real world of policy-making.[5]

Perhaps more important, the social context of the legal academy changed as well, along several dimensions. Law faculties became more interested in hiring women and racial minorities. The pool of potential legal scholars who could become critical legal scholars without modifiers was always rather small. As law school hiring practices changed, the white men in that pool began to compete, not for all the positions available, but for those positions available for white men. And, the politics of law school hiring meant that, in general, though with some exceptions, the women and racial minorities who were hired were understood to be on the left side of the political spectrum. That, in turn, reduced the number of positions available for prospective white male critical legal scholars, because "liberal" appointments had to be balanced with more conservative ones. The effect of the politics of faculty hiring was to reduce the number of potential critical legal scholars (without modifiers) entering the legal professoriate.

Harvard Law School had a number of highly publicized fights over tenure, which were understood in the legal academy to focus on the intellectual value of critical legal studies. These fights further impaired the possibility that there would be accretions to the group of critical legal scholars. And, as the numbers of new critical legal scholars diminished, the opportunities for networking across law schools – essential to the development of an intellectual community when each law school had only one or two people who were attracted to critical legal studies – diminished as well, although the hiring process did make it possible to develop networks of critical race and critical feminist scholars.[6]

[5]Morton Horwitz's intellectual trajectory might be taken to exemplify the effects of the changed political context. Horwitz's first book argued that changes in judicial doctrine in the early to mid-1800s were best explained by political and economic factors, just as changes in other forms of public policy were. He then turned to intellectual history, examining the ways in which American legal realism undercut the premises of legal formalism. Most recently, he has written a brief celebratory account of the Warren Court: Morton J. Horwitz, *The Warren Court and the Pursuit of Justice* (New York: Hill and Wang, 1998). This is a preliminary to his work-in-progress on that Court as part of the Oliver Wendell Holmes Devise history of the Supreme Court. (Of course, the fact that Horwitz was chosen to write that volume is an indication of the extent to which critical legal studies has been normalized in the U.S. legal academy.)

[6]Early in the development of critical legal studies, its leading scholars rejected the idea of creating a specialized journal. They were concerned about the diversion of energy that establishing such a journal would require, believed that the large number of existing law reviews provided adequate outlets for the publication of critical legal scholarship, and were concerned that publication in a "captive" journal would not help junior scholars in their search for tenure. Those judgments may have been accurate, but the absence of a journal meant that critical legal studies (without modifiers) lacked one node around which a larger network might have been sustained.

Critical legal studies also had to confront the professionalization of legal theory as increasing numbers of legal scholars came to the U.S. legal academy with advanced degrees in other disciplines.[7] Critical legal studies sometimes presented itself as a theory of law.[8] That led professionally trained philosophers to subject critical legal studies to examination with the tools of their trade, resulting in a judgment that, considered as philosophy, much in critical legal studies was amateurish. For example, sometimes critical legal scholars gestured in the direction of Wittgenstein when they talked about the indeterminacy of law, but philosophers who knew Wittgenstein better than the lawyers did also knew that the very most that could be wrung out of Wittgenstein for purposes of the critical legal studies arguments required one to rely on interpretations of Wittgenstein that were, at the least, extremely controversial among professional philosophers.[9]

From within critical legal studies, these professionalist critiques seemed misdirected. Critical legal studies was an account of the ideology of working lawyers, not, I believe, an attempt to develop a systematic jurisprudence.[10] So, for example, Alan Watson's professionalist criticism of Duncan Kennedy's long article, *The Structure of Blackstone's Commentaries*, made the perfectly reasonable historian's points that Kennedy failed to locate Blackstone's work in the tradition of treatise-writing, and that that tradition, more than ideology, explained the structure of Blackstone's work.[11] But, at least to someone interested in critical legal studies rather than legal history, there was something askew in Watson's criticisms, because Kennedy was using Blackstone as a vehicle for exploring the ideology of contemporary lawyers, and was not engaged in the historians' enterprise. Even so, the professionalization of legal theory, coupled with the understandable though mistaken idea that critical legal studies was a set of amateurish efforts to do what the professionals did better, undermined some of critical legal scholars' credibility.

Finally, critical legal theory was persistently challenged to respond to a perceived inconsistency between the theorists' political stance and their class position. The white male law professors who developed critical legal studies were not the kinds of organic intellectuals that Antonio Gramsci modeled for the

[7]Of the early scholars in critical legal studies, Horwitz had a doctorate in political science, and I had a terminal master's degree in history. I believe that that exhausts the list of those with advanced degrees in other disciplines, although perhaps there were others.

[8]One indication is the inclusion of sections on critical legal studies in coursebooks on jurisprudence, and the attention critical legal theory gained from philosophers. See, e.g., Andrew Altman, *Critical Legal Studies: A Liberal Critique* (Princeton, N.J.: Princeton University Press, 1990).

[9]I note, as a matter of personal privilege, that I always resisted direct references to Wittgenstein in my own writing on indeterminacy, and believe that the only citation to Wittgenstein in my articles was inserted at the insistence of a law review editor.

[10]For a brief discussion, including my unsuccessful attempt to provide a label for the enterprise, see Mark Tushnet, "Rights: an essay in informal political theory," *Politics & Society*, 17 (1989), 403–51.

[11]Alan Watson, "The structure of Blackstone's Commentaries," *Yale Law Journal*, 97 (1988), 795–821.

working class in Europe; they were privileged members of the upper middle classes with only occasional contacts – sometimes through their work in law school clinics, but rarely through their work as legal intellectuals – with the working class or America's underclass.[12]

Some of these difficulties might have been worked out, or at least grappled with, in a vibrant organization that could provide social and intellectual support for people scattered around the country. The difficulties became intractable with the evaporation of the Conference on Critical Legal Studies, to the point that there were essentially no new white male law professors who would identify themselves as adherents of a body of thought they would call critical legal studies. Why, then, did the Conference evaporate? In part, it did so because of the changing priorities of those who had been important in keeping the organization alive.[13] And, in part, it did so because of the simple fact of aging and the accompanying loss of energy, which was not, for the reasons I have sketched, replaced by organizational energy from a younger group of critical legal scholars without modifiers.[14]

Critical legal studies without modifiers has therefore become identified with the work of an older generation of scholars. Still, I think it important to emphasize that these scholars remain productive.[15] In 1999, for example, I published *Taking the Constitution Away from the Courts*, a book that developed – and of course modified on the basis of criticism and reflection – my earlier arguments expressing skepticism about judicial review as an instrument for advancing progressive political goals. The book was clearly an extension of my "Essay on Rights,"[16] which is widely cited as a work of critical legal studies.[17]

One might have thought that the publication in 1997 of Duncan Kennedy's *Critique of Adjudication* would also have been taken as a demonstration of the

[12]For the obvious reason that (in the main) they were members of racial minorities or were women, critical race theorists and critical feminist theorists were less vulnerable to the charge of inconsistency.

[13]I began to devote the energy I had for organizational work to the Association of American Law Schools, for example, and Duncan Kennedy shifted his attention from generating a cadre of U.S. legal scholars to developing critical legal scholars out of Harvard Law School's international graduate program. Roberto Unger did so as well, coupling his work in his native Brazil with a modest, and not terribly successful, effort to become a public intellectual in the United States. For the latter, see Roberto Mangebeira Unger and Cornell West, *The Future of American Progressivism: An Initiative for Political and Economic Reform* (Boston: Beacon Press, 1998). I found no reviews of this book in U.S. law reviews.

[14]In contrast, there has been a continual trickle of younger scholars doing what they *are* willing to call critical race theory, and those scholars have provided the organizational energy to sustain a network of critical race scholars.

[15]Decreasing scholarly productivity is associated with aging, pretty much across the board, so the actual output from these scholars might be smaller than it was earlier in their careers. But, in my view, the quantity of the work being produced is commensurate with the scholars' age.

[16]Mark Tushnet, "An essay on rights," *Texas Law Review*, 62 (1984), 1363–1403.

[17]See also Mark Tushnet, *The New Constitutional Order* (Princeton, N.J.: Princeton Univesity Press, 2003), explaining why that more recent book is also continuous with my earlier work in critical legal studies.

vitality of critical legal theory in the United States.[18] Kennedy presented a fully worked out account of adjudication – the practices of judges doing their daily work – fleshing out in great detail the arguments he had been making since the early days of critical legal theory. Kennedy argues that legal materials such as statutes and decided cases often (or sometimes: the amount does not matter in Kennedy's account) provide substantial constraints on the resolution of particular cases.[19] But, they do not *always* do so. Yet, according to Kennedy, the ideology of the rule of law requires that judges present themselves as *always* subject to substantial constraint by the existing legal materials. According to Kennedy, judges and legal theorists have developed a number of strategies to subsume the cases in which they are in fact not constrained under some larger set of constraints. So, for example, judges attempt to describe their (unconstrained) decisions as fitting coherently into a larger structure, or invoke considerations of public policy that they assert place limits on their discretion, or invoke "rights" that are said to provide answers to the contested issues before them. But, Kennedy argues, none of these strategies ultimately succeeds in providing true rule-of-law constraints on those decisions where the existing materials do not actually constrain. Kennedy then describes how the strategies of concealment affect the play of politics by empowering a segment of the intellectual class who are thought to be particularly well suited to making rule-of-law arguments, by toning down basic political disagreements, and by stabilizing the status quo in the face of threats from those who, while disadvantaged by the status quo, nonetheless remain committed to the ideals of the rule of law.

There is much more in Kennedy's book, but this truncated account should make it clear that the book is continuous with his and others' early works in critical legal theory. For example, Kennedy begins with a modified version of the indeterminacy thesis, and then moves to a quasi-sociological account of the effects of the ideology of liberal legalism. This is classic critical legal theory in form, although, as with my own work, Kennedy's further reflections on the problems that preoccupied him throughout his career have led him to modify (and, in his and my view, to strengthen) the fundamental points. Interestingly, though, the book was not received as a contribution to legal theory – understood not as jurisprudence in the traditional sense, but as an examination of the working theory of U.S. judges. With rare exceptions, its publication was treated as an occasion not for discussion of the substantive arguments Kennedy made, but for reflection on the purported death of critical legal studies.[20]

[18]Duncan Kennedy, *A Critique of Adjudication: Fin de Siècle* (Cambridge, Mass.: Harvard University Press, 1997).

[19]This is Kennedy's version of the indeterminacy thesis, to be discussed below.

[20]I have located only one review of Kennedy's book in a U.S. law review (the *Harvard Law Review*, not surprisingly). It was not reviewed in the major book review issue of the *Michigan Law Review*. In contrast, the book was reviewed in two major British law reviews, two major Canadian ones, and two European ones. The major exceptions to the neglect of the substance of Kennedy's

Perhaps one reason for the muted response to Kennedy's work, and that of others continuing to pursue the lines of inquiry they began in the early years of critical legal studies, is that its substance has become the common sense of the U.S. legal professoriate. The important word here is *become*. The view was quite widespread as critical legal studies was being developed in the 1970s that legal reasoning was a distinctive form of reasoning that allowed a pluralistic society to get on with the business of producing goods without people coming to blows over their (merely) political disagreements.[21] At the same time, as the closing of Roberto Unger's article on the critical legal studies movement said, there was an equally widespread sense that the arguments made to defend that view were intellectually inadequate.[22] Critical legal studies provided analyses of the conventional defenses – conventional, that is, among legal professionals, including legal academics – of adjudication and the rule of law that became the conventional wisdom. Over the decades, though, as my discussion of Kennedy's book suggests, the claims associated with critical legal studies became more tempered. Today the conventional wisdom more closely matches what critical legal scholars argued than what their earlier opponents had argued, but changes in the critical legal studies positions themselves responded to sensible challenges that the original claims were overstated.[23]

For convenience I divide the main arguments of U.S. critical legal theory into two branches. The first deals with some more traditionally jurisprudential issues, such as the degree to which adjudication comports with what the analyst describes as the requirements of the rule of law.[24] Here I discuss the argument that "law is politics" and the (related) indeterminacy thesis. The second attempts to account for the way in which existing liberal legal systems embody particular resolutions of those jurisprudential questions by offering a sketchy description of the social and political processes that produce those resolutions.[25] Here I

arguments are some of the essays in "Symposium, Critical Legal Studies (début de siècle): a symposium on Duncan Kennedy's *A Critique of Adjudication*," *Cardozo Law Review*, 22 (2001), 701–1190. See also Posner's review, "Bad faith," which does address Kennedy's substantive arguments, mostly agreeing with them although nibbling around the edges, although Posner, a political and legal conservative, cannot bring himself to say that Kennedy, a political and legal radical, is mostly right.

[21]Critical legal scholars assigned this view (somewhat inaccurately, I now think) to the Harvard "legal process" school.

[22]"When we came, they were like a priesthood that had lost their faith and kept their jobs," writes Roberto Mangebeira Unger, "The Critical Legal Studies movement," *Harvard Law Review*, 96 (1983), 561–675 at p. 675.

[23]Overstated, I suspect, to get people's attention and dislodge them from the nervous complacency to which Unger referred.

[24]Brian Leiter's description of some topics he deals with in his Jurisprudence course encompasses many of the strands of thought I have in mind: "Do legal rules really constrain judicial decision-making? . . . . Where no legal norm controls a case, how ought judges to decide the case? . . . . Are there principles or methods of legal reasoning that constrain judicial decision-making, or is legal reasoning essentially indeterminate, such that a skillful judge can justify more than one outcome for any given dispute? Is judicial decision-making really distinct from political decision-making of the sort that legislators engage in?"

[25]These accounts have never been fully worked out social-political accounts, but only promissory notes indicating what the author thinks a more extended and serious empirical inquiry would disclose.

discuss the argument that legal categories are socially constructed in ways that can be analyzed in social and political terms.

It may have been that in the early years of U.S. critical legal theory its most provocative claim was that "law is politics." That claim was, I think, widely – but perhaps understandably – misunderstood. Focusing on the U.S. Supreme Court's constitutional cases, commentators across the intellectual spectrum acknowledged that a "political" interpretation made sense of much of the Court's work. Influenced by a prior generation of American legal realists and by some political scientists, many scholars of constitutional law believed that a very good way (and often the best way) to understand the Court's decisions was to see them as more or less direct reflections in constitutional law of the justices' pre-legal ("political") preferences. The claim that law was politics was then taken to be a claim that every decision could be accounted for in the same way. The claim, that is, was taken to be about judicial *motivations*. As such, it was vulnerable to refutation by judges who credibly asserted that their experience belied the claim,[26] and by statistical studies that demonstrated some degree of purely legalist, non-political influence on case outcomes.[27]

The "law is politics" claim, as it was generally understood, might be defended against these purported refutations by scaling it back, in the way Kennedy suggested. Not every decision had to be motivated by politics in the usual sense for the "law is politics" claim to be interesting, and strongly critical. It would be enough that *some* decisions were so motivated, and that the ideology of legalism required that *none* were (or at least required that there be a careful account of why the occasional meanly political decision did not undermine the ideology of legalism). As I have argued elsewhere, it is precisely this scaled-back understanding of the "law is politics" claim that seemed to be vindicated by the Supreme Court's decision awarding the U.S. presidency to George W. Bush.[28] The outrage among many legal academics at that decision was sometimes cast in rule-of-law terms by scholars who were somewhat skeptical of traditional rule-of-law arguments.[29] This indicates that the "law is politics" claim has not swept the field in the U.S. legal academy. And yet, the resistance to the "law is politics" claim is patently weaker than it was earlier. That weakening can be seen in the response to *Bush v. Gore* by Jack Balkin and Sanford Levinson, who criticize

[26]See, e.g., Harry T. Edwards, "Public misperceptions concerning the 'politics' of judging: dispelling some myths about the D.C. Circuit," *University of Colorado Law Review*, 56 (1985), 619–46.

[27]See, e.g., Gregory C. Sisk, Michael Heise, and Andrew P. Morris, "Charting the influences on the judicial mind: an empirical study of judicial reasoning," *New York University Law Review*, 73 (1998), 1377–1500.

[28]Mark Tushnet, "Renormalizing *Bush v. Gore*: an anticipatory intellectual history," *Georgetown Law Journal*, 90 (2001), 113–25.

[29]See, e.g., Margaret Jane Radin, "Can the rule of law survive *Bush v. Gore?*" *Bush v. Gore: The Question of Legitimacy*, ed. Bruce Ackerman (New Haven, Conn.: Yale University Press, 2002), pp. 110–28.

the decision in rule-of-law terms and then express their ambivalence about doing so.[30]

There was, however, another response to the prevailing understanding of the "law is politics" claim. The response is that the prevailing understanding is mistaken. For critical legal theorists, "law is politics" means that legal reasoning has a form identical to the forms used in "ordinary" political discussions.[31] Every argument made in court, critical legal theorists said, could be *and was* made in legislatures considering similar issues: Issues of fundamental principle came up in courts and legislatures, arguments about good social policy were deployed in both venues, and so on through the lists describing the forms of legal and political argument. By the 1990s, if not earlier, this claim had become uncontroversial in U.S. legal discourse. The courts might be the forum of principle, as Dworkin put it,[32] but no one thinks that legislatures are *not*.[33] The strongest claim now prevalent in the U.S. legal academy is that courts and legislatures mix arguments of principle and arguments of policy in somewhat different proportions.[34] That claim, however, is not inconsistent with the critical legal theorists' early formulations.

Neither the scaled-back version of the "law is politics" claim nor the more accurate version is controversial in the U.S. legal academy, but neither is regarded as particularly interesting. The usual response to the scaled-back version is the assertion that the domain of meanly political decisions is quite small, and thus does not in fact threaten a general rule-of-law ideology. The usual response to the argument that legal argument is continuous with moral and other forms of political argument is to wonder why anyone would think that noting the continuity has interesting implications for a rule-of-law ideology. Yet, that very indifference about the argument suggests a transformation in the U.S. legal academy occasioned, if only in part, by critical legal studies itself. Indifference to the question of whether legal argument is different from moral or merely political argument ought to raise the questions that a prior generation of scholars tried to answer: How do pluralistic societies sustain themselves in the face of

[30]Jack M. Balkin and Sanford Levinson, "Legal historicism and legal academics: the roles of law professors in the wake of *Bush v. Gore*," *Georgetown Law Journal*, 90 (2001), 173–97.

[31]The claim was sometimes misunderstood to mean that the resolution of conflicts in the legal arena would always be identical to the resolution of the same conflicts in political arenas, and that the processes leading to such results were the same. Some critical legal theorists did believe that these propositions were sometimes true, but they were probably held more strongly by public-choice theorists, not typically associated with critical legal theory.

[32]Ronald Dworkin, "The forum of principle," *New York University Law Review*, 56 (1981), 469–518.

[33]Indeed, an important recent strand in constitutional scholarship develops the argument that forums *other than* courts are locations for a distinctively principled form of *constitutional* law. See, e.g., Larry Kramer, *"The People Themselves": Popular Constitutionalism and Judicial Review* (New York: Oxford University Press, 2004).

[34]Occasionally one can hear – usually in informal comments – that legislatures are driven entirely by unprincipled concerns, mostly for re-election, but those arguments are rarely put forth as accurate descriptive accounts in serious scholarship. Again, they are most common in public-choice influenced scholarship, which – in its most defensible form – provides such accounts as a means of developing formal models that do better at describing reality than do other models, not as accurate descriptions.

deep disagreements? With "by legal reasoning" taken off the table, an answer resting on quasi-sociological accounts of such processes as hegemony seems strongly suggested. And that too is consistent with the critical legal studies perspective, for reasons I now develop.

A second main critical legal studies claim was the so-called indeterminacy thesis. Again drawing on – or perhaps simply reviving for a new generation – insights from American legal realism, critical legal scholars argued, in one doctrinal area after another, that the purely legal materials at hand (statutes, precedents, "policies," whatever) underdetermined results in actual cases. As critical legal studies developed, bold and overstated claims that *all* results were underdetermined were replaced by more defensible ones, to the effect that many results were underdetermined, or that results in many interesting cases were, or – as in Kennedy's version – that enough results were underdetermined to matter.[35] One or another of these revised versions of the indeterminacy argument is, I think, accepted by nearly every serious legal scholar in the United States.

At the same time, though, the academic community, including critical legal scholars, agrees that results even in the restricted domain of the indeterminacy thesis are quite predictable. That predictability is not inconsistent with the indeterminacy thesis itself, which is a claim about the degree to which *legal* materials determine results and says nothing about whether something else fills in the gap between the underdetermination by legal materials and actual predictability of outcomes.

Exploring the question of what *does* fill in the gap is not a matter of pressing concern for most in the U.S. legal academy. To the extent that they focus on the question, they tend to supply the simple answer, "Politics," understood in the ordinary way. Critical legal scholars have been more attentive to figuring out how underdetermination becomes predictability. They believe that the transformation process must be understood in sociological terms, that is, through an examination of the actual social processes that lead some people to act *as if* the legal materials constrained them when, as a matter of *legal* analysis, the materials do not constrain. At this point critical legal theory connects with the scholarship associated in the United States with the Law and Society Association, and particularly with the "interpretive" strand of that scholarship, which became increasingly prominent in law-and-society circles in the 1980s and 1990s.

These sociological accounts can be divided for convenience into two groups. The first deals with the existence of predictability within the class of judges and, more generally, lawyers. Here the accounts deal with the practices within a particular discourse community that make outcomes predictable.[36] The second

[35]For my version of the second of these revised arguments, see Mark Tushnet, "Defending the indeterminacy thesis," *Quinnipiac Law Review*, 16 (1996), 339–56.

[36]I take work in critical legal studies on legal education to be an example of such accounts. See especially Duncan Kennedy, "Legal education as training for hierarchy," *The Politics of Law: A Progressive Critique*, ed. David Kairys (New York: Pantheon Books,1982), pp. 40–61. This is a short version of Kennedy's self-published pamphlet, "Legal education and the reproduction of hierarchy: a polemic against the system" (1983; rev. edn 2004).

deals with the experience of legality in the general public. Critical legal scholars located in law schools attempted to provide accounts of that experience by means of what came to be called narrative jurisprudence. They were hampered by the intertwined facts that, trained as legal scholars, they tended not to be particularly astute observers of the experience of the general public nor to be particularly effective narrative stylists (except within their own discourse communities). Instead, sociologists themselves produced the leading work, carrying out this part of the critical legal studies analytic agenda.[37]

The claim that law is politics and the indeterminacy thesis were developed in both private law and public, particularly constitutional, law. A third claim of critical legal studies – the critique of rights – was associated almost entirely with public law. In many ways the critique of rights was a simple application of critical legal theory's other main claims, but it had a particularly potent political charge in a scholarly universe dominated by the view that the performance of the U.S. Supreme Court under Earl Warren was a triumphant vindication of liberal legalism. The critique of rights was that there was nothing analytically to be gained by presenting a fundamentally political claim as one involving basic human rights. However those rights were described, the description would underdetermine the outcome in any particular setting, and the experiences that were said to vindicate liberal legalism had to be understood as arising out of specific historical circumstances rather than as expressions of unchangeable and unchallengeable rule-of-law commitments. Early presentations of the critique of rights generated what came to be known as the minority critique of the critique of rights, which in its strongest versions was that the critique of rights failed to appreciate the way in which the language of rights – if not "rights" themselves – worked in the political struggles of racial minorities in the United States.[38] I have said elsewhere that I believe the minority critique overlooked the way in which the sociological strand of critical legal theory functioned in the critique of rights as the vehicle for understanding the actual impact of the language of rights.[39]

Within the U.S. legal academy the minority critique of the critique of rights served as a left-leaning challenge to critical legal studies. It also reinforced the rights-rhetoric that the critique of rights had not seriously damaged. The continuing effectiveness of rights-rhetoric was part of a broader rehabilitation of – or an example of the continuing power of – a variety of formalist defenses of the rule-of-law ideology that had been the focus of critical legal scholarship. That rehabilitation, in turn, meant that critical scholarship continued to have targets on which to focus.

[37]See especially Patricia Ewick and Susan S. Silbey, *The Common Place of Law: Stories from Everyday Life* (Chicago: University of Chicago Press, 1998).

[38]The most important articles in the minority critique of the critique of rights are collected in Kimberlé Crenshaw et al., eds., *Critical Race Theory: The Key Writings that Formed the Movement* (New York: New Press, 1995).

[39]Mark Tushnet, "The critique of rights," *Southern Methodist University Law Review*, 47 (1993), 23–34. See also Mark Tushnet, "Rights: an essay in informal political theory," *Politics & Society*, 17 (1989), 403–51.

In reviewing Kennedy's book, Richard Posner described those targets in saying that Kennedy asserted but did not demonstrate that "policy analysis" was as vulnerable to the critical assault as doctrinal formalism was. This overlooked the fact that critical scholarship provided, and continues to provide, substantial arguments against claims that policy analysis, in the form of law-and-economics (mostly in private law) and public choice (mostly in public law), offers a solution to the problem of underdetermination.

Kennedy himself wrote a classic analysis of why law-and-economics could not solve the problem of underdetermination. He took as his topic the subject of a judicially imposed implied warranty of habitability for rental housing. The standard economic critique of such implied warranties is that they are ineffective in protecting low-income renters against inadequate housing, because landlords will simply raise the rent in response to the imposition of a warranty of habitability, thereby limiting the number of units available to the poor. Kennedy demonstrated that this critique was crucially dependent on unstated assumptions about the shape of the demand curve for housing.[40] According to Kennedy, the claim that law-and-economics – and policy analysis more generally – solved the underdetermination problem rested on assumptions about facts in the world, which law-and-economics scholars rarely examined in sufficient detail to justify their claims. The second and third generations of law-and-economics scholarship have reinforced the critical legal scholars' analyses by proliferating increasingly complex formal models aimed at capturing more and more of the real world's features, with the effect of making it clear that law-and-economics reproduces the underdetermination problem within its own confines.

Policy analysis also returned the "law is politics" claim to the forefront. Law-and-economics was notoriously associated with conservative policy positions. To the extent that law-and-economics purported to solve the underdetermination problem, it did so only by making transparent the political dimensions of law. Something similar occurred in the revival of formalism in public law, in defenses of originalism in its various forms.[41] Critical legal scholars and more standard liberals joined in challenging originalism, using familiar doctrinalist tools. What mattered in the response to resurgent formalism was that no one – probably not even its adherents – truly believed that originalism provided a non-political solution to the underdetermination problem. Originalism just *was* contemporary conservative thought in public law. The identification of law with politics was complete.

[40]Duncan Kennedy, "Distributive and paternalist motives in contract and tort law, with special reference to compulsory terms and unequal bargaining power," *Maryland Law Review*, 41 (1983), 563–658. For a confirmation by a mainstream law-and-economics scholar, see Richard Craswell, "Passing on the costs of legal rules: efficiency and distribution in buyer-seller relationships," *Stanford Law Review*, 43 (1991), 361–98.

[41]Originalists have come to distinguish several variants – original understanding, original meaning, original intent – but the distinctions are irrelevant for the broad purposes of this Essay.

The revival of formalisms associated with political conservatism has meant that works that are (functionally) works of critical legal scholarship continue to appear, now produced by younger scholars who do not identify themselves as critical legal theorists. David Barron, for example, provides an analysis of the ways in which localism and regionalism interpenetrate in a discourse of policy and legal analysis of local government law, in an article that a generation ago would have been instantly identified as critical legal scholarship.[42] Samuel Bagenstos' articles on the Americans with Disabilities Act deploy the techniques of critical legal studies as well.[43] Yet neither author identifies himself with, or is identified as working in, a field called critical legal studies.

These references indicate the continuing vitality of the *ideas* associated with critical legal studies even as the label seems to have disappeared. Those ideas are now deployed in a new political and social context. The legal academy has been transformed, with a strong ideology of liberal centrism displaced by an almost equally strong pluralist ideology that tolerates a range of ideas wide enough to encompass those that would have been called critical legal studies at an earlier point. The political context is probably more important. The conservative resurgence in the United States has left liberal legal theorists somewhat at sea. They have not located social movements like the civil rights movement or the anti-Vietnam War movement to provide them external social supports.[44] Their theorizing, such as it is, consists mostly of nostalgia for a past – in public law, for the Supreme Court under Earl Warren – and romanticism about developments in other nations, such as South Africa and the international human rights community. These are, in my view, unlikely to generate much of enduring value.

The inadequacy of merely liberal legal theories in the face of a probably long era of conservative dominance suggests yet another way in which critical legal theory may yet play an important part. Roberto Unger offered what he called "superliberalism" as a program for radicals.[45] Superliberalism takes liberal principles and pushes them to their limits – and, in the view of ordinary liberals, beyond, to the point of utopianism. There is something to be said for utopian theorizing when mere reformism is politically unachievable, though. Neither the utopian reforms nor the modest ones can be realized in the short run. But, the utopian theorist contends, having utopian programs available for consideration when times change will give progressives a better shot at success than if, at every

[42]David Barron, "Reclaiming home rule," *Harvard Law Review*, 116 (2003), 2255–386.

[43]Samuel R. Bagenstos, "The Americans with Disabilities Act as risk regulation," *Columbia Law Review*, 101 (2001), 1479–1513; Samuel R. Bagenstos, "'Rational discrimination,' accommodation, and the politics of (disability) civil rights," *Virginia Law Review*, 89 (2003), 825–927.

[44]The anti-globalization movement has not (yet) gotten much purchase in elite legal circles, in part, I think, because the free-trade arguments for globalization do seem to promise improvements in the material well-being of many in poor countries, at least for the short to intermediate term.

[45]Roberto Mangeibera Unger, *Social Theory: Its Situation and its Task* (Cambridge: Cambridge University Press, 1987), pp. 209–15.

point, they had accommodated themselves to political reality by proposing only modest reforms (which are unlikely to be implemented anyway).

Utopian theorizing is hard under any circumstances, and perhaps particularly so in the absence of a support structure of like-minded thinkers. So, I return to my starting place. Many of the ideas associated with critical legal studies have become the common sense of the U.S. legal academy. But, the possibilities for the retrieval of the full program of critical legal studies might be quite limited without a social network like that once provided by the Conference on Critical Legal Studies.

# Part Two

# Legal Scholarship in General

# [6]
# Post-Realist Legal Scholarship*

In the broadest terms, the general problem of legal scholarship is this: given an event—a judicial opinion, a statute, a choice about invoking the legal process—located within a surrounding field of other events, past and future, what is the best way to understand or account for that event?[1] At present, several modes of understanding compete for attention. There is the classical method of penetrating the logic of the event to see whether there is some group of ideas with which the event is congruent; there is the method of Chicago-style microeconomics, which attempts to describe the event as the produce of invisible-hand mechanisms that coordinate self-interested decisions by individuals; there are the methods of moral philosophy and of sociology. It is generally agreed that none of these methods by itself provides an adequate account of any legal event seen, as such events must be seen, as having complex relations throughout the surrounding field. Thus, to adopt simplifying labels, classical doctrinalism cannot deal with the existence of competing lines of precedent; microeconomics cannot handle the wealth-distributing aspect of legal events; and moral philosophy and sociology founder on problematic claims about social agreement.[2]

Given this situation, it is tempting to adopt a pluralist stance. An anomaly in doctrinal analysis may be explained by microeconomics; the unexplained remainder may be dealt with by moral philosophy; and, as the various methods are superimposed, every connection between the legal event and the surrounding field is covered. I intend in this essay to argue that

---

* An early version of this essay was presented at the annual meeting of the Society of Public Teachers of Law, Coventry, England, September 13-15, 1979, and a revised version, substantially the same as this one, appeared in 15 J. Soc. Pub. Teachers of Law 20 (1980).

1. This essay is the fourth in a connected series developing a critique of contemporary American legal scholarship. The others are *Truth, Justice, and the American Way: Constitutional Law Scholarship in the '70's*, 57 Tex. L. Rev. 1307 (1979); *Darkness at the Edge of Town: The Contribution of John Hart Ely to Constitutional Law Scholarship*, 89 Yale L. J. 1037 (1980); Book Review, 78 Mich L. Rev. 694 (1980).

2. These difficulties are developed in more detail below.

pluralism fails to solve the general problem. The first portion of the essay argues that each method currently in wide use fails to handle one of two kinds of anomalies, which I call the problems of language and of power.

The problem of language is that when lawyers look at a complex system of rules, they find that the rules, and the standard rhetorical devices for manipulating them, can justify any result at all—or, put differently, justify no results. Since controversies are in fact resolved, the problem of language means that the outcomes rest on choices external to the system of rules. Then the problem of power arises: are those external choices anything more than the wilful preferences of those in a position to make their preferences stick? If my argument succeeds, it reduces the pluralist strategy to a binary one, for there would then be only two distinct "grids" overlaid on the field, rather than a multitude of grids. The final part of the essay then suggests that the problems of power and of language are in fact themselves not distinct. That part does not make an analytic argument to reduce the two problems to one, and so I do no more than start down the road to the conclusion that I think, but cannot show, is correct. The final part alludes to material from investigations in fields other than law, where the theoretical basis for assimilating the problems of language and of power is beginning to be laid.

## I. Doctrinalism Old and New

### A. *Legal Realism*

The legal realists laid the basis for the current dilemmas of legal theory. Imperfectly and with varying degrees of clarity, the realists developed a critique of classical legal analysis that led almost inexorably, and in general quite contrary to their own intentions, to what I have elsewhere called legal nihilism.[3] Because of the power of classical analysis, the realists were forced to develop their critique along two lines. Roughly, their argument was as follows. Classical analysis could not adequately account for the manipulability of legal reasoning—the manipulability that allowed judges to create and then select among competing lines of precedent. Judges claimed that, at least in most instances, the results they arrived at were dictated by the precedents.[4] But,

3. *See Truth, Justice, and the American Way*, *supra* note 1.
4. *See* B. Cardozo, The Nature of the Judicial Process (1921).

when the realists looked at the cases, they saw that the precedents were never dispositive. The judges' claims about the binding force of precedent then became facts for sociology rather than for jurisprudence. If legal reasoning alone did not account for judicial choice, something else had to. It is a tribute to the realists' ability to create a unified alternative vision of legal analysis that they turned to questions of power. Thus, in the original conception, the problems of language and of power were addressed within an integrated although poorly elaborated framework.[5] The primary flaw in the framework was an almost astonishingly simple-minded conception of the operation of power. Because that conception of power was coupled with a very sophisticated understanding of the problems of classical analysis, it became possible for scholars to separate the realists' unity of language and power and still think of themselves as the heirs to realism. That way lay nihilism.

The realist critique of rules was simple and deep. The critique held that law—which purported to be a set of rules that determined either behavior or, more narrowly, outcomes in litigated cases—was in fact completely indeterminate. The study of cases showed the realists what is now a commonplace. Given the precedents available, a plausible case—plausible, that is, within the limits of acceptable legal reasoning—could be made for any proposition whatever. The reason was two-fold. First, the precedents actually available to the realists and to us are extremely variegated; and, second, the acceptable techniques of legal reasoning, such as distinguishing on the basis of the facts or analogizing to other areas of law where cognate problems arise, are so flexible that they allow us to assemble diverse precedents as we wish. Thus we have Karl Llewellyn's catalogue of paired and contradictory maxims of interpretation,[6] which presents the flexibility of standard techniques, or the great casebook by Friedrich Kessler and Malcolm Sharp,[7] which is organized precisely around the contradictory substantive elements in contract law and presents the variety available in the existing set of precedents. What remained was the hard fact that certain lines of argument from the precedents were accepted at some times and

5. In order to avoid justified criticism by historians, I must emphasize that what I present here is a construction of realist thought. The premises of the realists, if pursued, led to the positions discussed in the text, but I do not claim that any realist actually held these positions in the form or to the degree I discuss.

6. K. Llewellyn, The Common Law Tradition: Deciding Appeals 521-35 (1960).

7. F. Kessler & M. Sharp, Cases and Materials on Contracts (1953).

places, while others no less inherently acceptable were not. The realist critique of rules showed that such variability could not be explained within the framework of traditional jurisprudence.

At this date, it is impossible to deny the force of the realist critique of rules—although, as I will argue, many attempts have been made to deflect the critique. Everyone who looks at cases knows exactly how to shred *any* case apart, because it manipulates precedent, or ignores relevant contrary cases, or whatever. And, what is worse, we know in our hearts that the problem is not a simple one of skill; we know that even if the best lawyers—that is, ourselves—were writing the opinions, the same kinds of criticisms could justifiably be brought against what we wrote. It is this vision of complete incoherence that guides the nihilists. But I will suggest later that a case can be made for the proposition that nihilism is persuasive only to the extent that we regard diversity of precedent and flexibility of standard legal reasoning as inherent in any well-developed system of rules. A coherent program of inquiry can lead us to explore other paths: easier propositions, that diversity of precedent is linked to certain forms of social change and that it is conceivable that the link can be broken; and a harder one, that the modes of legal reasoning are similarly linked to those forms.

The nihilist response to the problem of language is quite dispiriting and, for both intellectual and political reasons, has not been widely adopted. Nihilism ignored the problem of power, and found ways to postpone a response to the problem. The most attractive tactic was found in the realist program itself, which, as an intermediate step in the argument, forced into the open the implicit policy decisions made in legal doctrine. Thus, for example, the consideration doctrine masks a policy demanding formality when people make serious undertakings, the law of offer and acceptance is structured by efforts to accomodate the perceived commercial needs of traders, and so on. These are, of course, quite specific and simple policies, but the project they define can be as comprehensive as one desires. That project was to transform law into policy analysis. The transformation had the additional advantage, especially in light of the expansion of government after the 1930's, of reassuring lawyers that they did indeed have something to contribute to the process of law-making—or rather, as it then seemed, the process of policy-making.[8]

8. *See* Lasswell & McDougal, *Legal Education and Public Policy: Professional*

The move to policy analysis ultimately failed. Once the blush of New Deal reformism had faded, it became clear that generalization from simple to more comprehensive policy analysis was probably impossible. The field in which a law—or, now, a policy—was located was extremely complex. One could tinker at one point, only to find the difficulties migrating elsewhere.[9] Reforms that called for governmental intervention occurred in the face of adaptable and politically powerful private interests, which placed stringent limits on politically tolerable and therefore achievable policy changes. For roughly the same reasons, reforms directed at government itself were absorbed and trivialized.[10] The effect was to give an increasingly conservative cast to policy analysis, which tended to conclude that nothing works—that reasoned interventions in complex processes are unlikely to have desirable effects. Such conservatism has highlighted the ultimately political context of policy analysis, which had been subordinated because, until recently, most of the serious intellectuals among American legal scholars, as among American academics generally, have aligned themselves with the Progressive-New Deal tradition currently strongest in one wing of the Democratic Party. It is hardly surprising, then, that most of the recommendations of legal scholars as policy analysts have been consistent with the political program of that tradition. But, once it is so starkly phrased, the convenient congruence between the products of rational policy analysis and the platform of the Democratic Party is obviously problematic. Only recently, however, has a credible, although erroneous, conservative critique, based on the perception that a complex society does not readily submit to rational control, undermined the claim that reason supported the Democrats.

Policy analysis has thus become politicized, and the temporary banishment of the problem of power has ended—at least in this branch of contemporary scholarship. This politicizing has been reinforced by related developments. Lawyers' solutions to social problems have seemed increasingly inapt. About all that lawyers can fairly claim is expertise in structuring decision-mak-

---

*Training in the Public Interest*, 52 Yale L. J. 203 (1943).

9. The classic recent discussion deals with the reduction of judicial discretion in sentencing and the likely compensating rise of prosecutorial discretion. Alschuler, *Sentencing Reform and Prosecutorial Power: A Critique of Recent Proposals for "Fixed" and "Presumptive" Sentencing*, 126 U. Pa. L. Rev. 550 (1978).

10. Starr & Esping-Anderson, *Passive Intervention*, 7 Working Papers for a New Society 14 (July-August, 1979).

ing institutions to confront and take account of all the relevant interests. But the proliferation of procedure is precisely one of the defects of American liberalism. Creating procedures is a solution that exacerbates the contradictions of liberal society, because it is in fact one of those contradictions. The resurgence of political conservatism has exposed these problems in policy analysis, and has deprived policy analysis of its fundamental claim to credibility. Policy analysis rests on the proposition that, given agreement on social goals, reason can be used to realize those goals. Now that political liberalism is no longer the sole occupant of the policy terrain, however, the premise of agreement on social goals has disappeared. This is what the realists saw as the problem of power: doctrinal incoherence is rooted in social division. Judges, for political, intellectual and personal reasons, choose to announce doctrines that advance the interests of one or another segment of a fragmented society.

The legacy of realism then has been to destroy the basis for prescriptive legal analysis. Scholars could no longer tell judges or legislators that some rule should be adopted because it would rationalize a sector of the law. By framing the problem of language, realism had established that each legal sector rested on a host of contradictory premises. Scholars could no longer tell judges or legislators that some rule should be adopted because it would promote or embody wise social policy. By framing the problem of power, realism had established that notions of wise policy were fundamentally contested.[11] What is left is the possibility of a positive analysis of law.[12]

### B. *Microeconomics*

The most prominent school of post-realist positive analysis is associated with Chicago-style microeconomics and law. Actually, a substantial degree of ambivalence affects this school. Most of its adherents are standard American political conserva-

11. Of course, though realism demonstrated the intellectual sterility of prescriptive analysis, it is still produced. My impression of the content of law reviews in the United States, for example, is that they are heavily laden with either doctrinal or policy analysis, the latter of an extremely rudimentary sort. These articles do serve a narrow professional purpose by showing how partisans on one side or the other, who may not be as clever as the authors are, can make the plausible arguments that are the meat of their daily work. But the obvious partisanship of the professional enterprise, and the realist perception that prescriptions will be adopted or not for reasons independent of their rational force, deprive such articles of intellectual interest.

12. *Cf.* M. Friedman, Essays in Positive Economics (1953).

tives, and are therefore at least deeply skeptical of, and more frequently very hostile to, governmental intervention in what they define as private affairs. These political attitudes support, and are supported by, a nearly exclusive focus on allocative efficiency as their subject of inquiry. Then, when faced with rules that depart from what their analysis shows would promote allocative efficiency, these scholars find it hard to resist the temptation to urge that the rules be altered. A truly positive analysis would, of course, try to explain why the departures from allocative efficiency occurred. It is useful here to distinguish among liberal, conservative and positive approaches to that problem. But this distinction requires some background. Scholarship in microeconomics and the law attempts to evade the realists' problem of language without having to confront the problem of power. Microeconomics is thus analogous to the nihilist approach. The problem of language arises because of the diversity of precedent. Scholars like Professor Kronman have developed a brilliant strategy to eliminate that diversity. One selects an area of the law and acknowledges the accuracy of the realist perception that traditional doctrine draws lines that classical (linguistic) analysis found impossible to explain. Then one asserts, as a hypothesis guiding the positive approach, that legal rules should promote allocative efficiency.[13] The way to accomplish that, the argument proceeds, is to select that initial position, defined by the rules, that will minimize the costs, across all relevant transactions, of bargaining for departures from that position. Then the rabbit appears from the hat. It turns out that traditional doctrines actually so organize transactions that one cost-minimizing rule applies to one set and another equally cost-minimizing rule applies to another set with relevantly different economic characteristics.[14]

Now if this approach exhausted the field of legal rules, the problem of language would be solved. But its proponents concede that the approach is not exhaustive. Even if a great deal of law can be handled by this strategy, there remain minority rules, aberrant jurisdictions, and statutory intrusions to be explained. Most commonly, these deviations are said to result from social choices about wealth distribution, about which microeconomics has nothing to say. At this point, liberals and conservatives di-

13. I have deliberately used the equivocal "should" in this formulation.

14. *See, e.g.*, Kronman, *Mistake, Disclosure, Information, and the Law of Contracts*, 7 J. Leg. Stud. 1 (1978).

verge. The liberals, represented by Professors Calabresi and Michelman,[15] abandon positive analysis and draw on the revival of substantive jurisprudence symbolized by the work of John Rawls.[16] But this is ultimately unsatisfying. It is hardly accidental that liberal scholars have admired Rawls. His program is happily congruent with liberalism, and can be given readings that make it fit into the political platform of the Democratic Party. Rawls' credentials as a moral philosopher give the program a basis apparently more substantial than the sheer political preferences of legal scholars. Unfortunately for the liberals, this sense of intellectual support from moral philosophy is unwarranted. Rawls himself treats the difference principle, his criterion for distributive justice, as prima facie compatible with possibilities ranging from restricted laissez-faire to restricted socialism.[17] The liberals' reading of Rawls gives the difference principle an unjustified precision of content. Further, Rawls' theory has been widely criticized by other philosophers from both left and right, and cannot provide the sure guidance that liberals seek. Here the problem of power recurs, for the existence of controverted claims about what justice requires demonstrates the political problem of implementing moral truth in a divided society. Thus, the liberals present a program that will convince only those already converted—or rather, that will temporarily make the already converted a little less uneasy about their beliefs. It cannot last.

The conservative approach to wealth distribution is, however, even less satisfying. It simply relegates the issues to silence. I call this a conservative approach because of its political effect. Conservatives structure their argument around the assertion that allocative efficiency is the primary goal of legal rules. When they say nothing about distributive effects, they convey the message that those effects should not play a role in developing legal rules.

Another version of the conservative approach, which does lead to a useful positive analysis, is to assert that courts, and the common law, are concerned with allocative efficiency and that legislatures deal with issues of wealth distribution. By exploring why courts are said to be concerned with allocative efficiency, we

15. For a discussion, *see* Kennedy, *Form and Substance in Private Law Adjudication*, 89 HARV. L. REV. 1685 (1976).

16. For a discussion of the difficulties in using substantive jurisprudence as a guide to positive analysis, *see* Tushnet, Book Review, *supra* note 1.

17. J. RAWLS, A THEORY OF JUSTICE (1971).

can see why the positive analysis put forward by the law and microeconomics school fails in the face of the problem of power. Professor Priest has provided an explanation that has a baroque elegance.[18] Litigation occurs, he argues, when parties motivated by self-interest discover, after a transaction has gone sour, that the legal rules governing their situation provide an opportunity for one party to gain an unbargained-for advantage. Once the allocatively efficient rule has been discovered by the courts, the opportunity for such windfalls disappears and litigation on the issue therefore ceases. Day by day, in every way, the common law system is becoming better and better—that is, more allocatively efficient. Minority rules and aberrant jurisdictions can be found only during the era before judges happen upon the true rule.

This argument is so neat that one desperately wants it to be correct. But the argument is obviously inadequate, both on its own terms and when the field of law is viewed more broadly. Professor Priest argues, in effect, that the common law system works its way toward equilibrium at the position of allocatively efficient rules. In fact, any equilibrium is unstable because of the availability of recourse to the legislature and because of the potential for disruptive litigation after equilibrium appears to have been reached. Consider first the interpenetration of statutory and common law rules. Suppose Free Trader sues Monopolist and, by chance, the court selects the allocatively efficient rule. Because it is in the nature of monopoly to reduce allocative efficiency,[19] Monopolist loses. It may not be sensible for Monopolist to continue to litigate the issue, but it is surely sensible for it to turn to a different arena. For if Monopolist is well-organized and the various Free Traders with whom it deals are dispersed, as they almost certainly will be, then the theory of public choice—the political analogue of microeconomic analysis—gives Monopolist good reason to believe that it will prevail in the legislature.[20] When Professor Priest's argument is coupled with public choice theory, the result is a nice positive account of the

18. Priest, *The Common Law Process and the Selection of Efficient Rules*, 6 J. Leg. Stud. 65 (1977). He has since repudiated this argument; its results disappear once the analysis takes the possibility of settlement into account. *See* Priest, *Selective Characteristics of Litigation*, 9 J. Leg. Stud. 399 (1980).

19. But see the discussion below on the problem of second-best.

20. M. Olson, The Logic of Collective Action (1965); Peltzman, *Toward a More General Theory of Regulation*, 19 J. L. and Econ. 211 (1976).

commonplace that the law has become increasingly statutory,[21] but we have lost the equilibrium that Professor Priest sought.

Even more, the introduction of public choice considerations raises again the question of power. Professor Priest's strategy, after all, is designed to supply an invisible hand mechanism to account for the existence of minority rules—rules which his argument tries to establish are merely transitional. Such a mechanism would resolve the problem of language without having to deal with the problem of power. But the results of public choice analysis emphasize the importance of relative degrees of organization, and degree of organization is highly correlated with independently described measures of social power such as wealth.

The same point has been made within the Chicago school framework. Some theoreticians have explained the observed tendency toward efficient common law rules by differential interest among litigants in the creation of favorable precedent,[22] and others by differential participation in litigation—which may come to the same thing.[23] Such differences too are correlated with power. Yet another analysis has emphasized the importance of strategic behavior by litigants in disrupting the equilibrium sought by Professor Priest.[24] In the terms used by the realists, this is a facet of fact-skepticism, or, in Professor Danzig's terms, of the capability problem.[25] But even a rejection of fact-skepticism will not rescue Professor Priest, who relies on an invisible hand mechanism wholly independent of the rationality of the judicial process and for which there appears to be no analogue in fact-finding.

The microeconomics approach to law thus runs up against the problem of power. The approach cannot give a positive account of the existence of minority rules and diverse precedents without referring to issues of power. If we turn from the abstractions of that approach to the real world, we can begin to understand why diverse precedents exist. First, a crude version: given a preexisting distribution of wealth, allocative efficiency may heighten tensions between haves and have-nots. Judges may be concerned that the bias of allocative efficiency will not be offset but may instead, if public choice theory is right, be enhanced by

21. *See, e.g.*, L. Friedman, Contract Law in America (1965).

22. Rubin, *Why is the Common Law Efficient?*, 6 J.Leg.Stud. 51 (1977).

23. Landes & Posner, *Adjudication as a Private Good*, 8 J.Leg.Stud. 235 (1979).

24. Kooter & Kornhauser, *Can Litigation Improve the Law Without the Help of Judges?*, 9 J.Leg. Stud. 139 (1980).

25. R. Danzig, The Capability Problem in Contract Law (1978).

legislative intervention. If the bias is serious enough, tensions within the society may accumulate dangerously. These tensions can be defused, however, by some modest redistribution through common law rules that are not allocatively efficient. Litigants will keep pressing these rules towards allocative efficiency, subject to the qualifications suggested by fact-skepticism; but judges have politically sound reasons for resisting the pressures. It may not matter that these judicial interventions, such as the doctrine of substantive unconscionability, may only symbolically state a commitment to redistribution at the cost of efficiency,[26] for it may be as important to defuse tensions within the lawyering class as it is to defuse tensions more widely distributed. Minority rules exist where enough judges are self-conscious about the world of politics. This is not, of course, an invisible hand argument like Professor Priest's, but it does invoke characteristics of judges in the real world, such as attempted political sensitivity. One suspects that this argument makes sense of behavior by judges like Roger Traynor and Skelly Wright, about which adherents of the Chicago approach have little positive to say.

Essentially the same point can be made within the microeconomic framework. As the example of the Monopolist-Free Trader case suggests, the microeconomic analysis works in a Pareto-optimal world where the only obstacles to allocative efficiency are transaction costs. But the real world is not Pareto-optimal, and, by the theory of the second best, interventions designed to promote allocative efficiency in a non-optimal world need not succeed.[27] Among other things, the fact that the world is not Pareto-optimal destroys the basis for Professor Priest's confidence that the common law works toward allocative efficiency. It also shows that the simplifying approach in law and microeconomic analysis achieves elegance at the cost of accuracy. If the complexity of the real world is taken into account, the analysis provides neither a full positive description of nor an accurate prescriptive guide to the development of legal rules in all their variety.

The critique so far has operated within the Chicago framework, and has argued that the premises invoked to resolve the

26. The Contracts Group associated with the Conference on Critical Legal Studies, which includes Professors Jay Feinman, Alan Hyde, and Elizabeth Mensch, has begun to elaborate arguments along these lines.

27. Markovits, *A Basic Structure for Microeconomic Policy Analysis in Our Worse-Than-Second-Best World: A Proposal and Related Critique of the Chicago Approach to the Study of Law and Economics*, 1975 Wis. L. Rev. 950.

problem of power are ultimately incomplete. An external critique is also possible. The realist analysis of the problem of language showed that changes in doctrine could not be anticipated in the absence of an analysis of the problem of power. Because the Chicago approach lacks such an analysis it leaves us with a system of doctrine in which change is random. The approach could still be useful if we could work out the ways in which consumers capitalize that randomness by incorporating it into their plans. Individual preferences for risk and individual ability to withstand the vagaries of randomness, if they were constant, would do the job. But tastes and endowments of those kinds are not independent of the legal-economic regime and therefore will shift as randomness occurs, followed by capitalization, followed by changes in taste and endowments, and so on.[28] Once again the Chicago approach fails because of its focus on the problem of language.

It may be useful to recapitulate the critique of the microeconomic analysis of the law. The difficulty is not that the analysis fails to explain certain anomalies;[29] it is powerful enough to be able to absorb such problems by the addition of Ptolemaic epicycles. Rather, the difficulty is that the project of providing invisible hand explanations cannot be fulfilled. The analysis began with an effort to avoid the problem of language and to dissolve the problem of power by disclosing an order behind the apparent disorder of the common law. Invisible hand mechanisms would have satisfied the latter condition. But the mechanisms had to operate on two levels—one invisible hand to produce order in the cases, and another invisible hand to produce the first invisible hand. Allocative efficiency did a reasonable job as the first invisible hand. Professor Priest's argument was designed both to deal with the residue left over by explanations in terms of allocative efficiency and, more important, to provide the second invisible hand. Even Professor Posner, the guru of the school, was dubious about that argument.[30] Yet

28. *See* Heller, *Is the Charitable Exemption from Property Taxation an Easy Case?—General Concerns About Legal Economics and Jurisprudence*, in Essays on the Law and Economics of Local Governments (D. Rubinfeld ed. 1979); Kelman, *Choice and Utility*, 1979 Wis. L. Rev. 769 (on tastes); Samuels, *Normative Premises in Regulatory Theory*, 1 J. Post-Keynesian Econ. 100 (1978) (on endowments).

29. The currently shining example is the absence of an explanation for the common law's refusal to enforce penalty terms in contracts. *See* Posner, *Some Uses and Abuses of Economics in Law*, 46 U. Chi. L. Rev. 281, 290 (1979). *See also* Michelman, *Comment*, 46 U. Chi. L. Rev. 307 (1979).

30. *See* Posner, *supra* note 29, at 292.

something along similar lines to the same end is necessary if the problem of power is to be avoided.

One can never be sure about these things, of course, but it does seem likely that the positive program of the microeconomic analysis of the law will not succeed in solving the problem of language without facing the problem of power. But the contributions of that analysis are important enought to be noted. The analysis has provided a parsimonious set of assumptions that explains a great deal. The real question is whether the abstractions that allow one to simplify complex phenomena accomplish a helpful reduction or a misleading one. The Chicago approach is both: in its more imperialist claims it is misleading; in its more modest claims it is helpful. It has established that over a rather long period of time—not coincidentally, during the era of the consolidation of bourgeois power—the courts adopted rules of law that were consistent with notions of allocative efficiency. Even if the substantive analysis lays claim to more precision than its premises warrant, the insistence on the invisible hand aspects of the process forcefully counters simple instrumentalist ideas about power. Judges may on occasion have thought in terms of promoting power to the bourgeoisie, but they need not have. As it happens, this particular reinvention of the wheel could be important in the present context, at least if the pernicious normative claims so often associated with the positive analysis can be ignored.[31] For insistence on the invisible hand converges quite neatly with sophisticated Marxist analyses of the operation of power. The microeconomic analysis of the law, when it is linked to the operation of power in specific historical settings, opens the way to answers to the problems of power that are complex enough to explain consistencies across structures of thought and activity yet do not invoke simple instrumentalism.

## II. Legal Sociology Old and New

The realists addressed the problem of power by placing law in its context. Some realists, such as Llewellyn, suggested that one who became immersed in the facts of a case, including its entire commercial and social setting, would somehow perceive the proper result. While immersion might help in areas, limited indeed, where all the participants were in basic agreement, it could not be a general strategy to avoid the problem of power.

31. *See* Samuels, *Toward Positive Public Choice Theory*, 38 Rev. Soc. Econ. 55 (1980).

As one moved from a specific case to its commercial setting, one immediately discovered that one had to consider the entire economy and, after that, the whole society. A project of such immensity is probably misconceived. Further, the move from the case to its setting repeatedly revealed one apparently universal fact: the rules of law make almost no difference at all when we consider anything other than the shortest run.[32] All this has supported the conversion of law into sociology.

The realist legacy here has followed two lines. One, explicitly concerned with the problem of power, focused on judicial decisionmaking and seemed completely empty until recently. The other, implicitly concerned with that problem, retains its vigor. Neither line has been comfortably accomodated in American academic law. Academic lawyers have recurrently felt the tug of prescriptive analysis. Legal sociology is also no stranger to prescriptive arguments. But legal sociology has intellectual ties to sociology—a field in which positive analysis has a very strong tradition and in which the aura of scientism has placed positive analysis in the center of the intellectual terrain. The prescriptions of legal sociologists are therefore intellectually problematic. Their prescriptions are also politically problematic. Legal sociology yields very ambiguous recommendations, for the world is complicated, and sociologists, in contrast to economists, cannot ignore its complexity. In addition, sociology in the United States has been until recently about as theoretically impoverished a discipline as can be imagined. Legal academics have shied away from links with a discipline that, even on its own terms, seemed of little value.

The line of descent from realism explicitly concerned with the problem of power began with rule-skepticism. Scholars refused to believe that what a judge said were his reasons for a decision really were the reasons. Judicial reasons were always cast in terms of existing rules and their implications; but the realists knew that the relation between rules and outcomes had to be indeterminate. The question was then to identify the real sources of judicial decision. Here realism's ancestry in Progressive scholarship and the debunking tradition came through. For, after the "what the judge ate for breakfast" cynicism had passed, scholars saw the world as structured in rather straightforward good and bad terms, corresponding to liberal and conservative political platforms. They then attributed judicial deci-

32. *See* Griffiths, *Is Law Important?*, 54 N.Y.U. L. Rev. 339 (1979).

sion to, in what I am embarrassed to call the most sophisticated works, the interplay of responses along several forms of a liberal-conservative categorization. The next move was to look for the origins of these policy preferences in the social origins and political experiences of the judges.[33]

There is of course something to this kind of argument, but it suffers from an unbearable simple-mindedness. Many law professors, and virtually all at the leading institutions, have spent one or two years as a law clerk to a judge. They know from experience that the vote-counters do not describe what really happens when a judge makes a decision and, with the assistance of people like themselves, writes an opinion. Further, the reductionist account may have had a core of truth in it, but it eliminated much of the richness of the system of legal rules and institutions. Even if it was all a silly game, that game was elaborately choreographed in ways that the vote-counters could not understand. It is as if a scene in a ballet were described by saying that the male character moved from left to right while the female character moved upstage. It is true enough—but somehow lacking in flavor.

The second line of descent provides the opportunity to give a more complete answer to the problem of power. Scholars in this line fully contextualized the legal process. They examined the extent to which stated legal rules affect the behavior of police and citizen,[34] and the degree to which stated rules are taken into account in negotiating contracts.[35] As I have said, they discovered that stated legal rules had little effect. Legal sociology then had three courses to follow. One course repudiated the realist heritage, decried the gap between the law on the books and the law in action, and proposed reforms that would close the gap. That, as should be clear by now, would not work.[36] The two remaining courses took off from the perception that the rules were not doing what they had been thought to be doing, and tried to figure out what they were in fact doing.

One direct descendant of such law-in-action studies is the contemporary study of law as one of many mechanisms used to settle disputes. Here too the approach tends to suffer from an unwillingness to face problems of power, though this tendency

---

33. *See, e.g.*, G. Schubert, The Judicial Mind: The Attitudes and Ideologies of Supreme Court Justices, 1946-1963 (1965).

34. *See* A. Reiss, The Police and the Public (1971).

35. Macaulay, *Non-Contractual Relations in Business*, 28 Am. Soc. Rev. 55 (1963).

36. *See also* Abel, *Law Books and Books About Law*, 26 Stan. L. Rev. 175 (1973).

can be combatted. David Engel has argued that there are serious epistemological issues, akin to those raised by nihilism, in assimilating litigated cases, or disputes affected by law, to unlitigated disputes.[37] By taking the definition of "dispute" as given, the sociologist may unjustifiably fail to treat as problematic the entire field of inquiry, even though that field is itself likely to have been structured by the operation of social power. The political setting of contemporary dispute resolution research may amplify these difficulties. Concern for dispute resolution instead of law is linked with the political program of deregulation and reduction of governmental intervention in so-called private affairs. Alternatives to law as a means of dispute resolution are thought to resemble alternatives to law as a means of regulating other forms of behavior, such as selling goods in the marketplace. And yet the disparities of power that led to regulation and law of course persist.

Another course, with a similarly implicit political program, has yielded contextualized studies of law in action. By far the largest portion of these studies deal with plea bargaining, police behavior, and alternative methods of dispute resolution among the citizenry, with a smattering of attention to the behavior of small businesses in their relations with consumers. The concern, that is, is with the impact of certain rather restricted areas of law on the lower class or, at most, the petty bourgeoisie. It is as if law was the mode of handling peripheral problems of capitalist society.[38]

Unlike the problems associated with other positive analyses, those that attend the contextualization of law appear to be contingent rather than inherent in the enterprise. The problems here lie quite close to the surface. Indeed, the effect of a full contextualization of law has been to bring into question the notion of a neutral rule of law and to reopen issues of power on a more sophisticated level. Studies of law in context make it clear that power is at work in ways that are not obvious. In the explanation of the covert operation of power, we may find the problems of language and power reunited.

Here the starting point is nihilism. As a jurisprudence, nihilism established the potential for infinite variation within a le-

37. Engel, Studying Courts and Alternatives: The Persistence of "Cases and Controversies" (paper presented at the 1980 Annual Meeting of the Law and Society Association, June 5-8, 1980).

38. *See* Book Review, *supra* note 1.

gal system. But as a sociology, nihilism was simply wrong. Nihilism correctly pointed out that existing doctrines—such as unconscionability in the field of private law or state action and equal protection in the field of public law—could be used to move our society towards a socialist future. But it hardly bears emphasizing that the technically acceptable arguments toward that end were never made—except occasionally by conservatives, who then treated the arguments as *reductios ad absurdem* establishing that the doctrines were silly.[39] To revert to an earlier metaphor, nihilism showed that the legal ballet could take place all over the stage; but in fact the dancers move in only a few basic patterns, with occasional flourishes and rapid returns to the fundamentals.[40] The restriction on movement, which nihilism established is not inherent in existing rules, posed two problems. First, given the restrictions, what kinds of variations can a talented choreographer develop? A combination of first-level invisible hand mechanisms and conscious instrumentalism seems entirely sufficient to answer this question. Second, and more interesting, why are certain restrictions and not others imposed at any time? In a sense, this is the question raised by the fact that second-level invisible hand mechanisms apparently are unavailable to microeconomic analysis.

The most promising line of investigation into the second question is, I think, opened up by what I fear must be called the unholy trinity of semiology, phenomenology, and Marxism. Recent scholarship in those fields has addressed another version of the same question: in light of available alternatives, why do people think the way they do? The essential contribution of semiology has been to show how complex ways of thinking are—how ways of thinking indeed make totalistic claims on all who share them. The essential contribution of phenomenology has been to show how forms of life work themselves into complex ways of thinking. And the essential contribution of Marxism has been to show that the fundamental forms of life are those implicated in the material social relations of production—and that those relations, because they contain contradictions, allow contradictory ways of thinking to develop. The trinity thus provides a sophisticated unification of the problems of language and power.

Exploring the line opened up by the trinity is, however, ex-

39. A similar tendency has been noted in the field of general sociology. *See* A. GOULDNER, *Whose Side are We On*, in FOR SOCIOLOGY (1973).

40. *See* Kennedy, *supra* note 15.

tremely difficult. Two related strategies seem unsatisfactory. One is a simple appeal to authority. After all, serious intellectuals at the center of contemporary European social thought are attracted to the trinity. It is hard to accuse American legal scholars of taking serious intellectuals too seriously, but there is something to be said for trying to assimilate the body of thought worked out by such people as Lévi-Strauss, Habermas, Lacan, Barthes, and Althusser. The second strategy would be to summarize the theoretical positions staked out by these intellectuals.[41] These two strategies have similar defects. The intellectual traditions from which the trinity derives were developed in both explicit and implicit opposition to the Anglo-American tradition of empiricism. Because the theoretical work is determinedly anti-empiricist, the theory may seem equally anti-empirical and therefore detached from the real world. In addition, for well-grounded theoretical reasons, the general statements in these works are expressed in extraordinarily dense language, whose near-impenetrability makes it easy for hard-nosed lawyers to dismiss the theories. Yet if the language is simplified, it may seem rather banal: the way people live "affects" the way they think, what they think about one thing is "related to" what they think about a lot of other things, and so on.

A third strategy may be more fruitful. One who reads Lévi-Strauss' theoretical works would, I think, be hard-pressed to understand why he is a major figure in social thought. But one who reads a work where the theory is applied to empirical data, such as *The Raw and the Cooked*, must realize that a very powerful approach is being employed. Similarly, the works of Mary Douglas and Basil Bernstein show how these theoretical perspectives can inform studies that satisfy the most rigid demands for empirical grounding. The third strategy, then, is to develop a body of substantive analysis that is guided by the theoretical perspectives afforded by the trinity, whether or not those perspectives are made explicit. The danger is that, when viewed in isolation, each contribution can be assimilated into standard post-realist thought.[42] But as those contributions accumulate, they will be seen as presenting a unified alternative to that body of thought, an alternative that at least addresses, and treats as related, the

---

41. *See, e.g.*, R. Coward & J. Ellis, Language and Materialism (1977); C. Summer, Reading Ideologies (1979).

42. *See, e.g.*, R. Cover & O. Fiss, The Structure of Procedure 74-75 (1979); Michelman, *supra* note 29, at 312 n. 17.

problems of language and power.

One point in conclusion bears emphasizing. The intellectual program sketched here begins with a positive analysis of contemporary law. By linking law, language, and power, the program treats law as in some way constitutive of a society, as one of the ways in which a society defines itself.[43] But the definition offered by law need not be the same as that offered, to choose a non-random example, by the relations of production. Of course, some definitions have privileged status. It may be of interest to specify the limits on variation of legal doctrine imposed by other perhaps more privileged definitions, or perhaps, to investigate the ways in which the legal constitution of a society may transform the other modes in which it is constituted. The latter question calls for careful political investigation, and shows how the positive program I have outlined can be joined to political action in appropriate circumstances. And so, in a way, we return to where we began, with an analysis of the law that has links to prescriptions about the transformation of the society; positive analysis has been only a detour.

43. *See* Klare, *Law-Making as Praxis*, 40 Telos 123 (Summer 1979).

# [7]
# Legal Scholarship: Its Causes and Cure

I suspect that symposia like this one are convened when it seems that something has gone wrong.[1] I sense that the community of legal scholars is afflicted with a vague malaise, sometimes girded about by a pretentious complacency.[2] Perhaps more important, that community has been operating for some years outside the main currents of significant intellectual activity. I cannot imagine, for example, an intellectual history of contemporary America in which legal thought would play an important part. There may of course be an erroneous premise implicit in the view that legal scholarship should be a central element of the serious intellectual discourse in this country. After all, law, like engineering, is an applied rather than pure endeavor, and no one expects engineers to participate in the intellectual life of the community.[3] Yet, in the past, legal thought has been a component of important intellectual movements. Holmes and the Legal Realists played an important part in the story of American intellectual life in the earlier part of the twentieth century.[4] In contrast, few of the various strands of contemporary thought are informed by legal scholarship.[5] Even as prominent a contemporary legal scholar as Alexander Bickel, for example, warrants but two passing mentions in Peter Steinfels's examination of neoconservatism.[6] The intellectual marginality of legal scholarship is all the more striking in light of the immense role that law plays in American society.[7]

My topic is that marginality. I contend that legal scholarship lies at the edges of serious intellectual activity because of the nature of

1. *Cf.* Persons, *The Wingspread Papers*, 7 Rev. Am. Hist. 447 (1979) (similar observation about papers from conference on intellectual history).

2. This impression is supported by such evidence as Professor Gilmore's elegant dyspepsia. G. Gilmore, The Ages of American Law (1977).

3. *But see* D. Hofstadter, Gödel, Escher, Bach: An Eternal Golden Braid (1979); T. Veblen, The Engineers and the Price System (1921).

4. *See* E. Purcell, The Crisis of Democratic Theory 74-76, 208 (1973); M. White, Social Thought in America: The Revolt Against Formalism 59-75 (1949).

5. The exception might be Ronald Dworkin's role in mainline liberal thought. My comments below, *see* note 53 *infra*, suggest that he may be playing that role in his capacity as a philosopher rather than as a legal scholar.

6. P. Steinfels, The Neo-Conservatives 5, 6 (1979).

7. In the manner of Julia, I refrain from the obligatory citation to de Tocqueville.

The Yale Law Journal Vol. 90: 1205, 1981

the legal scholar's enterprise. In part the problem derives from the dilemmas of professional education in an academic setting. Outside the law school, the main currents of twentieth-century intellectual life, encompassing Max Weber's work, phenomenology, structuralism, and much more, have been driven by scholars' efforts to confront and resolve the question of how an assertedly objective intellectual enterprise could be founded on what analysis showed was an unavoidably subjective base.[8] For those who teach lawyers, however, the question is irrelevant. The conflict between objectivity and subjectivity is alien to their enterprise because no one believes that advocates are, or should be, objective. Thus, in their role as teachers of lawyers, legal scholars are not confronted by the most stimulating problem of twentieth-century intellectual life, and the pressures of professional education make it enormously difficult for them to escape from the constraints of that role.

But more than professionalism or the institutional structure of legal education is involved in the failure of the legal scholar's enterprise to confront the relationship between objectivity and subjectivity that has animated discussions outside the law. Legal scholars' professional endeavors may make them aware that legal rules have no objective content. They cannot bring this personal insight into their scholarly work, however, because their acceptance of fundamental principles of liberal political theory requires them to proceed as if legal rules do have objective content.

In its unadorned Hobbesian version, liberal theory begins with the premise that each of us desires as much as he or she can obtain.[9] We are inclined to grasp everything within reach, without regard to the desires or interests of others.[10] Nevertheless, we recognize that our desire for more will generally be thwarted in the war of all against all. Liberal theory proposes that we solve this dilemma by surrendering some of our autonomy to the state in exchange for security in our possessions. That surrender creates the new danger, however, that the state will exercise the power that we give it in ways that reduce both our possessions and our security. The rule of law is our protection against the state. The state must be constrained by rules that are independent of the desires of those charged with applying them in order to protect individual autonomy and prevent the state from

8. *See* H. Hughes, Consciousness and Society 15-17 (1958); H. Hughes, The Obstructed Path 9-15 (1968).

9. *See* C. Macpherson, The Political Theory of Possessive Individualism (1962).

10. Some exception may be made for close relatives.

becoming another weapon for partisans to use in the general war. The acquiescence of individuals to the liberal rule of law depends upon their continued unshakable faith in its objectivity. Thus the conflict between objectivity and subjectivity cannot readily be confronted within the legal sphere without undermining liberal society itself.[11]

The fate of Legal Realism suggests the poignancy of the dilemmas that legal academics face. Most generally, Realism was a simple and unproblematic attack on the idea that the body of legal doctrine provided an objective basis for decisions in specific instances. Some Realists tried to escape this conclusion by emphasizing the law's relation to social policy, but that route only opened the legal system to even more basic challenges. First, policies are more obviously controversial than the apparently purely deductive arguments of case analysis. The appearance of objectivity could be maintained only by invoking policies of an extremely general sort.[12] Second, neither those policies nor indeed any others could be brought to bear on a specific problem to provide a single solution. Policies, like precedents, could always be used to argue for contradictory results. Neither doctrine nor policy proved sufficient to satisfy the liberal premise that human behavior can be governed by rules that have some supra-individual content. As I will argue, legal scholars have ignored or rejected without serious analysis the disturbing implications of the Realist challenge to the objectivity of the rule of law.

I will develop this argument by examining the body of work now accepted as legal scholarship. I rely in part on a survey of law review articles,[13] but my own observations as a member of the aca-

11. *See* R. Unger, Knowledge and Politics (1975).

12. The work of Lasswell and McDougal is the most obvious example.

13. The details of the survey will be provided on request. Briefly, I examined the signed articles published in the two most recently completed volumes of the following law reviews: Columbia, California, Duke, Michigan, New York University, Pennsylvania, Texas, and Virginia. I chose those law reviews because they are published at relatively elite schools in the hierarchy of legal education. I excluded the schools at the top of the hierarchy—Chicago, Harvard, Stanford, and Yale—because, in my judgment, there is a break in the stratification system between the two groups of schools. That judgment could be confirmed by an examination of the circulation of faculty members, which I suspect would show that faculty circulate within each stratum and that the most elite schools accept faculty members from the less elite schools, but faculty from the more elite schools do not move to the less elite schools.

I excluded student work from the analysis because it is so heavily weighted toward what I describe as the first form of scholarship that its inclusion would distort any rough statistical judgments in a highly misleading way. I also note here, but do not analyze, the phenomenon of privileged access to law reviews. Such privileged access has three forms. A scholar at a more elite school can almost automatically get an article published

demic community form a more important basis for the argument. In this inquiry, I treat myself as an informant.[14]

Legal scholarship today has three forms, for which I have been unable to develop non-invidious labels. The first is traditional legal advocacy, the second is advocacy augmented with concepts drawn from nonlegal fields of thought, and the third is the study of law as a phenomenon. The third form of scholarship is qualitatively different from the first two; roughly, the first two are normative enterprises, while the third is a positive one. I will argue that the first two forms seek to establish the proper or best legal rule. In doing so, they make claims to objectivity that are contradicted by their inherent partisanship. The third form attempts to escape this dilemma. If it can be done at all, the third form can be done only at the most elite schools, where professional pressures are weakest. Such schools, however, maintain their elite position in part by their role in the professional enterprise. Under those circumstances, it is not surprising that legal scholars have, except in isolated cases, been unable to connect their work to the basic themes of contemporary intellectual life.

Most of the articles published as legal scholarship constitute what I have called traditional legal advocacy.[15] These articles most starkly reflect the impact of professional demands upon the academy. Practicing lawyers and others who attempt to affect public policy through law are busy people. Law reviews give them some convenient research tools, through articles that present the arguments for one position or another and explain how the arguments for contrary positions can be rebutted. The structure of such articles makes it clear that they contribute little to reducing the marginality of legal scholarship.

The standard traditional advocacy article has two variants: the case analysis and the policy prescription. The case analysis argues that, when one looks at the cases, certain conclusions follow. For example, one recent article deals with the constitutionality of statutes that limit

in a review at a less elite school. Ceremonial addresses in formal lecture series will almost always be published. These forms of privileged access are infrequently used. Much more significant is the fact that law reviews will almost always publish the work of scholars on the faculties at their own schools.

14. I should note that my primary informant, myself, finds himself on the margins of the legal academic world. The Law School at the University of Wisconsin has attempted to take a path that is quite different from those followed by other schools. In addition, my personal sense of marginality, though qualified by such things as my participation in this symposium, is nonetheless real. I observe, however, that with the exception of Professor Posner, who is obviously a special case, I am the only participant presenting a major paper who has not taught at Harvard or Yale (or both).

15. In the survey, between 60% and 70% of the articles were of this form.

Causes and Cure

the ability of a defendant accused of rape to examine aspects of the victim's history.[16] It discusses the Supreme Court's interpretation of the confrontation clause of the Sixth Amendment and concludes that some of the statutory limitations are unconstitutional. The authors treat their conclusions as deductions from the Constitution, but the legacy of Realism makes that impossible for serious readers to accept.[17] Instead, the article must be read, as I suspect it was intended to be read, as a research aid for lawyers who defend persons accused of rape, and for the judges before whom those lawyers appear.[18]

The policy prescription identifies some goal that the author thinks ought to be pursued. It uses common sense and a rough-and-ready folk sociology or economics to sketch how to achieve the objective. Unlike the case analysis, the policy prescription tends to be relatively open about the act of choice inherent in selecting a goal. Like the case analysis, however, the policy prescription places the act of choice in a frame designed to obscure its subjective and essentially arbitrary character. The choice is made under the guise of identifying a problem to be solved. "Everyone knows," for example, that corporations' boards of directors are unresponsive to the interests of some of those whose lives are affected by their decisions. The solution of that "problem" can be discovered by applying common sense notions about representation and responsiveness.[19] The policy prescription usually ends with a suggestion about how the policy could be enacted into law and is therefore the ideal legislative history.

Despite intended appearances to the contrary, both case analysis and policy prescription rely on choices that are not only subjective but controversial. The dialogue they promote is often intellectually

16. Tanford & Bocchino, *Rape Victim Shield Laws and the Sixth Amendment*, 128 U. PA. L. REV. 544 (1980).

17. In this article, I assume that Realism has carried the day to the extent described. I defend that assumption elsewhere. *See* Tushnet, *Post-Realist Legal Scholarship*, 1981 WIS. L. REV. 1383.

18. One variation, case analysis carried to its highest level, lies in the transitional zone between the two forms. Although there are a few examples from other areas, *see e.g.*, Westen, *Confrontation and Compulsory Process: A Unified Theory of Evidence for Criminal Cases*, 91 HARV. L. REV. 567 (1978); Westen & Lehman, *Is There Life for Erie After the Death of Diversity?* 78 MICH. L. REV. 311 (1980), the best example is the scholastic debate among proponents of various types of interest analysis that allegedly elucidate conflicts of law. An outsider to the discussion finds it bizarre that elaborate competing structures of analysis have been erected on the basis of policies so general that, one would have thought, they could not possibly dictate the kinds of results that interest analysts claim for them. *See* Kay, *The Use of Comparative Impairment to Resolve True Conflicts: An Evaluation of the California Experience*, 68 CALIF. L. REV. 577 (1980).

19. *See, e.g.*. C. STONE, WHERE THE LAW ENDS (1975); R. NADER, M. GREEN, & J. SELIGMAN, TAMING THE GIANT CORPORATION (1976).

sterile,[20] because someone else can simply choose another goal and use the same type of analysis to come to the opposite conclusion. An article that goes with the crooks is followed by one that goes with the prosecutors;[21] one that says that corporate responsibility is a problem is answered by one that says that everything is hunky-dory.

The most intriguing question that remains is why a frame of objectivity is placed around the discussions that I have described. Legal Realism produced the insight that case analysis cannot generate objective answers to legal problems. Bringing concerns about policy to the fore, which some lawyers saw as the only way to save the system, has turned out to be equally manipulable. What is puzzling is the insissistence of authors of even the most advocacy-oriented articles that they do have the objective answers. The objective posture may be just another technique of advocacy. "I like it" is not a very good argument, but "the Constitution says so," stated with appropriate emphasis and in a sincere tone, can be persuasive. I will return to the possibility that an objective posture is good advocacy because the norm of objectivity is an essential element of liberal political theory after discussing the other forms of legal scholarship.

The second form of scholarship, advocacy augmented with concepts from other fields, is a reaction to the failings of the first form of scholarship. It accepts the conclusion that solutions to legal problems cannot be found within the framework of what we traditionally had thought of as law, defined here to include both legal reasoning and common sense. Nevertheless, it retains the hope of reaching objectively defensible results by relying on ideas that are drawn from fields in which scholars' partisanship is not as apparent. Unfortunately, the hope is bound to be disappointed because problems of objectivity and subjectivity infect other fields as pervasively as they do law. The ultimate effect is only to conceal the point at which subjective choice is inserted into the analysis. Indeed, one measure of the quality of scholarship of the second form is the cleverness with which that point is obscured.

20. When those who disagree on proximate goals agree on ultimate ends, the sterility of their discussions results from the ability of sophisticated analysis to show how accomplishing either proximate goal will promote the ultimate end. *See* note 24 *infra*.

21. In fact, more articles supporting crooks are written, largely because of the sociology of legal education. With the expansion of clinical programs in law schools, significant numbers of people with academic interests were hired to staff those programs. Whether on tenure tracks or not, the new faculty members were attracted to writing for law reviews and, because the largest group in their clientele consisted of people accused of committing crime, they were attracted to the pro-crook position. The predominance of that approach is enhanced by the general phenomenon that exists in higher education of younger faculty members writing more than older ones.

Causes and Cure

The second form of scholarship has two variants, doctrinal and policy analysis, which parallel the variants found in the first form. Doctrinal analysis of the second form, like traditional case analysis, invokes a very general, allegedly formal, guiding principle and claims to be able to derive determinate solutions to particular legal problems by application of that principle. For case analysis, the frame of reference is the logical and aesthetic requirements of traditional legal reasoning. There are two dominant versions of doctrinal analysis of the second form, and each has its own lodestar. The school of normative law and economics, Chicago style, looks to allocative efficiency. Moral philosophy, meanwhile, looks to conformity with Natural Law.

I will begin with the Chicago School, whose difficulties are twofold. First, the scientistic tendencies of its approach have led its adherents to a hard-line methodological positivism. The Chicago version of positivism makes it clear that scientistic analysis must be sharply distinguished from normative recommendations and that such recommendations depend on a choice that must be made on some nonscientistic basis.[22] The closer an author making recommendations comes to the Chicago paradigm, the more that author must explicitly admit that efficiency is a subjective preference rather than a self-evident formal axiom. That admission, in turn, defeats the goal of looking for objectively defensible results in other fields.

Second, the scientistic pretensions of the Chicago School have led at least its lesser adherents to make claims about the results of their approach that are indefensible even within its own frame of reference. The fact of the matter is that the Chicago approach is infected by the same problem of indeterminacy that the Realists identified in traditional legal scholarship. The Chicago model of economic analysis can explain how any policy can achieve whatever goal we choose to pursue.[23] Warranties of habitability, for example, both do and do not promote efficiency.[24] This apparently curious outcome may be a result of the state of the art or, as I suspect, a result of internal incon-

22. Posner, *Some Uses and Abuses of Economics in Law*, 46 U. CHI. L. REV. 281, 284-87 (1979) (distinguishing positive from normative economics).

23. *See* Heller, *The Importance of Normative Decision-Making: The Limitations of Legal Economics as a Basis for Liberal Jurisprudence—As Illustrated by the Regulation of Vacation Home Development*, 1976 WIS. L. REV. 385.

24. The arguments are summarized in Markovits, *The Distributive Impact, Allocative Efficiency, and Overall Desirability of Ideal Housing Codes: Some Theoretical Clarifications*, 89 HARV. L. REV. 1815 (1976) (describing conditions under which allocative efficiency is promoted by housing codes). Efficiency, in the models relied on, is defined only in terms of a partial equilibrium. They do not analyze general equilibrium implications. *See* Rizzo, *The Mirage of Efficiency*, 8 HOFSTRA L. REV. 641 (1980).

sistencies in the epistemology that underlies the field, but in either case the immediate problem is the use of unsupported abstraction. When the scientistic pretensions of the Chicago approach are greatest, the analyst follows the model of the physical sciences and adopts a large number of simplifying assumptions. The purified system is then analyzed, and predictions and explanations are generated. The real world, however, is necessarily more complex than the purified system. It may be true, for example, that economists can generate apparently interesting conclusions by assuming that corporate managers respond appropriately and exclusively to profit-oriented incentives. Indeed, they may even be able to explain outcomes in the real world by assuming that managers so respond, although that is more troublesome because of severe measurement problems.[25] But the normative claim that legal regulation should try to affect only profit-oriented incentives simply does not follow.[26]

Similar problems beset the attempt to rely on moral philosophy as a source of legal insight. If economics challenges common sense with Science, the brand of moral philosophy now most in vogue elevates common sense, or at least the common sense of the liberal left, to Natural Law. Contemporary moral philosophy has the rhetorical advantage over Chicago School analysis of the chastening of style[27] that ordinary language philosophy has effected. Indeed, moral philosophers tell charming fairy tales about the legal system. These fairy tales, however, like the economists' stories, rest on extraordinarily severe abstractions from reality. Professor Dworkin, for example, invents a superhuman judge he calls Hercules;[28] scholars following his trail are forced to distinguish between situations in which a principle has a relative weight of 51% and those in which its weight is 49%.[29] Another favorite tactic is to hypothesize a legal system that contains only one rule that bears on a problem and then show how contemporary moral

25. For an example of the gap between theoretical simplification and available evidence, see Landes & Posner, *Legal Change, Judicial Behavior, and the Diversity Jurisdiction*, 9 J. Legal Stud. 367 (1980) (available empirical evidence provides limited support for economic theory of judicial behavior).

26. For an exchange that clarified the point, see Harris & Sullivan, *Passing on the Monopoly Overcharge: A Response to Landes and Posner*, 128 U. Pa. L. Rev. 1280 (1980), and Landes & Posner, *The Economics of Passing On: A Reply to Harris and Sullivan*, 128 U. Pa. L. Rev. 1274 (1980).

27. I borrow the phrase from Edmund Wilson. *See* E. Wilson, Patriotic Gore 635-742 (1962) ("The Chastening of American Prose Style").

28. R. Dworkin, Taking Rights Seriously 105-06 (1977).

29. D'Amato, *Judicial Legislation*, 1 Cardozo L. Rev. 63, 82-84 (1979).

Causes and Cure

philosophy yields clear results in that system.[30] As in the case of economic analysis, discussion of these abstractions has some metaphorical force. But real decisionmakers are weaker than Hercules and real legal systems have more than one rule. Moral philosophy, in its present state, can only rely on objective values that are so abstract that they cannot provide normative guidance in real cases. A theory of justice in a world with serious imperfections is undeveloped in the literature and might help. I would bet, however, that a philosopher's theory of second best would establish that moral philosophy alone must remain insufficient.

The failure of moral philosophy to solve real-world problems emphasizes once more the nature of the legal scholar's difficulty. We must keep in mind the reason for recourse to other fields. Realism showed that subjectivity and indeterminacy resulted when analysis was confined to traditional legal discourse. Because the rule of law requires objectivity and determinacy, scholars looked elsewhere to save the rule of law. I need not argue for my purposes that moral philosophy is subjective.[31] The truly pressing, and endemic, difficulty is indeterminacy.[32] The most dramatic example of this difficulty is the one that I believe made moral philosophy seem attractive. The Supreme Court's abortion cases could only be defended on philosophical grounds. Yet the controversy on the issue among professional philosophers is as substantial as that in the political arena. The lawyer's normative problems are left as unresolved by the invocation of moral philosophy as they are by the invocation of economics. Moral philosophers and economists are divided into the same camps that mere lawyers are, and "respect for persons" or "efficiency" turn out to be translations into esoteric language of "my client wants it." The nonlegal disciplines, as I suspect real economists or philosophers could have told us from the start, were as partisan as law and, therefore, could not provide the support that legal scholars sought. Both Chicago School economics and moral philosophy, when they are sub-

30. Richards, *The Theory of Adjudication and the Task of the Great Judge*, 1 CARDOZO L. REV. 171, 199-200 (1979). *But see* Regan, *Rewriting* Roe v. Wade, 77 MICH. L. REV. 1569 (1979) (performing the Herculean task).

31. I do find it somewhat suspicious, though, that the liberal left of the Democratic Party and not, for example, the Swedish Social Democrats, has a near monopoly on Natural Law.

32. There is another difficulty that is linked more directly to the theory of second best. Even if moral philosophers had the ultimate answers, it is not obvious that those answers would be close enough to contemporary American society for us to enact them in the incremental manner characteristic of American lawmaking; nor is it clear that direct moves in the direction of those answers would be the best steps to take in order to reach them. *See* Tushnet, *Dia-Tribe* (Book Review), 78 MICH. L. REV. 694, 708-09 (1980).

jected to critical scrutiny, accomplish little more than a certain intimidation of those of us less versed in particular scholarly fields. Professional incentives that are already operating will readily eliminate even that effect.

As in traditional legal scholarship, policy analysis is the alternative to doctrinal analysis in the second form of legal scholarship. In traditional policy analysis, common sense is used both to select a goal and to determine how to achieve it. The second form of policy analysis does not, at least openly, dispute the goal. Rather, adopting the strategy of expert analysis in other fields, it questions the common sense prescription for achieving that goal. This analysis takes one of two lines. Sometimes it argues that the common sense route may not get us to the goal as effectively as some other route.[33] For example, when greater corporate responsibility is the goal, the analysis draws on economic theory to show that such responsibility is maximized by market, rather than political, processes.[34] Alternatively, it may examine the side-effects of the common-sense route, showing that, in a world as perverse as ours, following that route will produce a conflict, not with the original goal, but with some other desirable objective. Eliminating discrimination based on gender, for example, will require imposing and enforcing limits on the hours that professional men can work.[35] The next step of this line of analysis is to search for a way to reach the original goal, subject to the constraint that in doing so we do not intrude too much on other values. At the end of the line, of course, the policy analyst all too often concludes that, in light of all the constraints, we really cannot reach the original goal at all.

Sophisticated policy analysis of the type I have just described expresses what I call the "life is just a bowl of Jello" point of view.[36] According to that view, the world is so complex that if you push at

33. *See generally* R. POSNER, ECONOMIC ANALYSIS OF LAW (2d ed. 1977) (discussing efficiency of law in numerous fields).

34. *See, e.g.*, Engel, *An Approach to Corporate Social Responsibility*, 32 STAN. L. REV. 1 (1979); Winter, *State Law, Shareholder Protection, and the Theory of the Corporation*, 6 J. LEGAL STUD. 251 (1977).

35. Powers, *Sex Segregation and the Ambivalent Directions of Sex Discrimination Law*, 1979 WIS. L. REV. 55, 105-07.

36. *See, e.g.*, Graetz, *Implementing a Progressive Consumption Tax*, 92 HARV. L. REV. 1575 (1979) (progressive consumption tax provides theoretically meritorious means of assessing tax liability but practical and political costs ensure its unworkability); Kirp & Robyn, *Pregnancy, Justice and the Justices*, 57 TEX. L. REV. 947 (1979) (question of pregnancy benefits must be addressed only after considering costs and benefits to workers and families); Schuck, *The Graying of Civil Rights Law: The Age Discrimination Act of 1975*, 89 YALE L.J. 27 (1979) (congressional failure to specify adequately the objectives of the Age Discrimination Act moves policy debate into court).

Causes and Cure

one point where you perceive a problem, the most that you can accomplish is to cause the problem to migrate to some other area over which, you hope, someone else has jurisdiction.[37] If other approaches to legal scholarship end up losing their power when they are shown to be indeterminate, the bowl-of-Jello approach tries to escape this trap by triumphantly concluding that there are no good answers. This inherently conservative conclusion[38] fails as a significant intellectual achievement, however, because of the same limitations of professional orientation and liberal imagination that plague the other approaches. The evidence it relies upon establishes at most, after all, that incremental reasoned interventions in a complex situation are unlikely to produce satisfactory results, because incremental intervention fails to deal with surrounding areas into which problems will migrate. But more substantial reasoned interventions may work. For example, the resistance of bureaucracies to change is a typical ground for skepticism about intervention. It may be that if we truly desire change, we will have to do away with bureaucracy. The aim of policy analysis, however, is to make recommendations to policymakers. Members of an existing system of government will only take seriously recommendations for incremental change within the limits of liberal politics. The utopian thinking needed to escape from the bowl of Jello is not likely to be done by those whose immediate audience consists of contemporary policymakers, and who are themselves committed to the assumptions of liberal theory.[39]

37. *See, e.g.*, Alschuler, *Sentencing Reform and Prosecutorial Power: A Critique of Recent Proposals for "Fixed" and "Presumptive" Sentencing*, 126 U. PA. L. REV. 550 (1978) (criminal justice is closed system in which discretion can be reallocated but not reduced).

38. The bowl-of-Jello approach proves to be inherently conservative because it leads to the conclusion that, in the absence of good alternatives, the status quo ought to be retained. Another possible conclusion is available, which I call Burkeanism, but it proves to be unavailing. The Burkean says that whatever choice is made by the system is legitimate and may even contain some hidden wisdom. Although Burkeanism is, on this level at least, coherent, it will not help the scholar in the professionally oriented attempt to advise judges and policymakers. The reactionary can at least say that change is bad. The serious Burkean has to say that change is all right if the system changes, but that is not terribly useful when the issue is whether a change should be made.

39. Resistance to utopianism arises in part from the liberal view that links utopian thinking to the social catastrophes of the twentieth century. Aside from overestimating the importance of thought in transforming the world, this view assumes that only pragmatic tinkerers can learn from experience. Utopians concerned about bureaucracy speculate not about perfecting massive, national bureaucracies, for example, but about constructing alliances among small scale, intensely local activities. *See, e.g.*, J. MANSBRIDGE, BEYOND ADVERSARY DEMOCRACY (1980). This perspective is what gives such power to the otherwise quite different visions of Roberto Unger and Robert Nozick. Moreover, as I suggest below, a utopian approach of this type may be the only way to resolve some of the problems inherent in the liberal theory of law and society. *See* p. 1223 *infra*.

I have argued that the marginality of contemporary legal scholarship results from the combined pressures of professionalism, the desire to support the rule of law, and the attempt to escape the implications of Realism. I first appreciated that something was at stake in those pressures when, after I had made what I regarded as rather mild and standard Realist criticisms of a doctrinal proposal,[40] I was called a power-hungry anarchist.[41] I realize, of course, that nobody really likes to be criticized and I might have discounted, although not disavowed, the epithet, except that I began noticing that similar, hostile rejections of the implications of Realism were expressed elsewhere. The mild version is the definitional stop: partisanship is a defining characteristic of the enterprise and that's the end of it.[42] One can hardly argue with definitions. But that particular definition affirms the intellectual marginality of legal scholarship and excludes from the canon some work done by people who have reputations as important legal scholars.

Concern over Realism's legacy seems to recur at generational intervals. The recent expressions echo charges made in the 1940s that Holmes's anticipation of Realism led inexorably to the intellectual defense of totalitarianism.[43] Professor Bickel's discussion in *The Least Dangerous Branch,* twenty years later, remains the most revealing. In a chapter whose first citation is to the article by Professor Gilmore from which I drew my title, Professor Bickel discusses "the Neo-Realists [and the] Nihilists."[44] He argues that the original Realist position of the 1920s and '30s, insofar as it exploded the claim that the text of the Constitution was a self-evident document, was a reasonable and positive contribution. The danger lay in the work of some of the successors to the Realists who, engaging in "overkill,"[45] asserted the impossibility of any principled decisionmaking and became purely result-oriented.[46] For Bickel, the only proper function of judicial review was "to evolve and apply . . . fundamental reasons of principle

40. Tushnet, *The Sociology of Article III: A Response to Professor Brilmayer,* 93 HARV. L. REV. 1698, 1699-705 (1980).

41. Brilmayer, *A Reply,* 93 HARV. L. REV. 1727, 1728-29 n.16, 1729-30 (1980).

42. *See, e.g.,* Monaghan, *Taking Supreme Court Opinions Seriously,* 39 MD. L. REV. 1, 13-14, 25 (1979) (stating that the premises of our system assume that principled opinions are achievable).

43. *See* White, *The Rise and Fall of Justice Holmes,* 39 U. CHI. L. REV. 51 (1971).

44. A. BICKEL, THE LEAST DANGEROUS BRANCH 74 n.1, 75-84 (1962).

45. *Id.* at 75.

46. "The final fruit of neo-realism," he wrote, ". . . is a genial, nihilistic attitude of coexistence with the Court and its work, along with a complete lack of interest in the process by which the work is achieved, or in the proper role of that process in a democratic society." *Id.* at 81.

Causes and Cure

on which to base men's actions, and which should cut across men's uncontrolled instincts and interests."[47] The neo-realist's view that judges did not engage in this principled discourse, but only did "what they like[d]"[48] was pernicious, and was no less so if it was sometimes true.

> [I]f the estimate of reality on which it feeds is in any degree correct, then reality must be changed to exactly that degree. The sin is mortal, because it propagates a self-validating picture of reality. If men are told complacently enough that this is how things are, they will become accustomed to it and accept it. And in the end this is how things will be.[49]

Professor Bickel's strategy for changing the "neo-realists'" reality avoided, if barely, the definitional stop. As Professor Ely has noted, however, Bickel's later work demonstrated his understanding that his initial strategy needed substantial development, probably in directions different from those suggested by the Wechslerian emphasis on principles or the philosophical emphasis on fundamentals.[50] More important, Professor Bickel, like those Realists he admired, thought that problems of subjectivity were merely difficulties encountered in executing a program grounded in the rule of law. Since the Realists wrote, we have come to understand that the problems they described arose from the concept of rules and from the characteristics of language itself.[51]

Professor Bickel's adversaries deserved his criticism that they were expounding "cynicism pure and simple"[52] because they attempted to maintain a defense of the rule of law while simultaneously pushing Realism to its far boundaries. They understood that liberal political theory provided no explanation for why people, upon assuming the role of judge, could suddenly become moved by preferences that transcended the merely personal. They knew as well that the process of judicial decision was as subjective as other more obviously political activities. What left them open to the charge of cynicism was their continued adherence to some tenets of liberal theory coupled with their failure to appreciate that, by translating the subjectivity of pref-

47. *Id.* at 82.
48. *Id.* at 84.
49. *Id.*
50. J. Ely, Democracy and Distrust 71-72 (1980).
51. The fancy citation for this is L. Wittgenstein, Philosophical Investigations (1953).
52. A. Bickel, *supra* note 44, at 84.

erence from the legislative to the judicial context, they had undermined the only defense liberal theory had against tyranny.[53]

There are two possible responses to Professor Bickel's critique. The first is to deny the force of Realism by attempting to confine its analysis of rules, through moves such as the appeal to neutral principles. That attempt, as we have seen, is intellectually dishonest. Bickel's struggle to work out a Burkean approach to law, which all agree he did not completely realize, demonstrates both the depth of his understanding and the inadequacies of the first two forms of scholarship. The second response is to discuss law without assuming that liberalism's reliance on the rule of law solves the problem of subjectivity. Professor Bickel showed the way by counterposing "personal preference and personal power"[54] to "fundamental reasons . . . which should cut across men's uncontrolled instincts and interests."[55] Legal scholars need not assume that twentieth-century American society approximates the ideal liberal state, and though they may agree that the rule of law is a necessary component of such a state, they need not assume that the preconditions of liberalism exist in contemporary society. To the extent it brackets but does not reject liberal political theory, the second response to Bickel's critique should produce a program of research concerning the social conditions necessary for the realization of the rule of law. To the extent that it does reject liberal theory, the second response should produce a program of research on the conditions under which justice, defined in terms other than the rule of law, can be achieved.[56]

The third form of contemporary legal scholarship—the study of law as a phenomenon—comes closest to these programs of research; it brackets liberal theory by treating law as a phenomenon. In adopting that strategy, however, the third form abandons the professional orientation of the other forms of scholarship and places its practitioners under severe pressure. That pressure can be resisted occasionally only at the most elite institutions or elsewhere only under

53. *See* R. Unger, *supra* note 11, at 83-97. Although Bickel addressed the issue of the rule of law in the context of constitutional law and judicial review, it arises in private law as well. *See, e.g.*, Kennedy, *Form and Substance in Private Law Adjudication*, 89 Harv. L. Rev. 1685 (1976).

54. A. Bickel, *supra* note 44, at 80.

55. *Id.* at 82.

56. Realism is a powerful intellectual force, in part, because it produced those research programs directly, though the Realists themselves were far more sophisticated in their analysis of the concept of the rule of law than they were in this branch of their project. For a more extended discussion, see Tushnet, *Post-Realist Legal Scholarship*, 15 J. Soc. Pub. Tchrs. L. 20, 28-30 (1980).

unusual circumstances. The work produced under those conditions is also likely to be seen as marginal to legal scholarship, and thus legal scholarship's own marginality will persist.[57]

Unfortunately, much of the work in the third form of scholarship only extends approaches that are taken in the second form.[58] The dominant strand of positive analysis of law, not surprisingly, is the economics-of-law approach. I need not recapitulate the various critiques of this approach,[59] some of which I suggested in discussing its normative cousin. Positive analysis along Chicago lines has claimed that the classical common law promoted allocative efficiency. One of the explanations offered for why this should be so is that the legal system somehow tends toward a realization of moral truth or, to modify Emile Coue's autosuggestive aphorism, that every day in every way the common law is getting better and better. Professor Priest tried to describe the mechanism through which such Coueism is effected.[60] But when Professor Priest reduced the abstractness of his model by adding a single new variable that took account of the pos-

57. Proselytizers for the third form sometimes argue that it is professionally valuable. The analytic schemes they develop, they say, provide useful ways of organizing a complex body of information, give insights into the kinds of arguments decisionmakers find attractive, and so on. The professionalist defense of the third form of scholarship is probably valid, but in a rather restricted sense. Someone who is able to analyze cases and policies well, as in the first form of scholarship, and who can augment that ability by drawing on work done in other fields, as in the second form, is likely to be a better lawyer for being able, in addition, to step back from the whole enterprise to see it as an event in the world. Unfortunately, few professionals have enough talent to master the first two forms and then study the third. Selectivity in law school admissions means that the third form of scholarship will be professionally valuable to a significant concentration of students only at the most elite institutions. Although there are inevitably a few students at every law school who could profit from the third form's approaches, the absence of a group of sufficient size is likely to create pressures at the less elite schools against following the model used by some scholars at the more elite schools. Although this process may well create the conditions for linking elite scholarship to broader intellectual currents, it also confines such scholarship to elite institutions. Under those circumstances, those who produce scholarship of the third form may be seen less as lawyers than as social theorists, economists, or whatever, and their work may not be seen as "legal" scholarship at all.

58. On the moral philosophy front, Professor Fried recently suggested that we can examine law as a moral science. Fried, *The Laws of Change: The Cunning of Reason in Moral and Legal History*, 9 J. Legal Stud. 335 (1980). I have been told that the suggestion was not made entirely seriously and, in any event, I cannot devote much attention to it because there are no clear examples of the enterprise.

59. *See, e.g.*, An Introduction to Post-Keynesian Economics (A. Eichner ed. 1979); Time, Uncertainty, and Disequilibrium (M. Rizzo ed. 1979); Komesar, *In Search of a General Approach to Legal Analysis: A Comparative Institutional Alternative* (forthcoming Mich. L. Rev. (1981)); Markovits, *A Basic Structure for Microeconomic Policy Analysis in Our Worse-Than-Second-Best World: A Proposal and Related Critique of the Chicago Approach to the Study of Law and Economics*, 1975 Wis. L. Rev. 950.

60. Priest, *The Common Law Process and the Selection of Efficient Rules*, 6 J. Legal Stud. 65 (1977).

sibility that cases could be settled before judgment, his earlier result disappeared.[61]

In any case, what Chicagoans call allocative efficiency can equally well be called capitalist accumulation[62] or the redistribution of wealth from poor to rich or economic development.[63] Perhaps more to the point, the common law can at most be consistent with one construction of allocative efficiency, even within the neoclassical tradition of economics. It might not be consistent with other constructions, and the premises of positive analysis do not provide the basis for choosing between those constructions.

Positive economic analysis of law has generated some useful insights, although I suspect that Chicagoans will take my specification of those insights as a backhanded compliment. A major contribution, for example, is the Chicago School emphasis on invisible hand mechanisms, as opposed to the conscious choices of participants, as a means of explaining activities in the legal system. That contribution has unfortunately been embedded in more specific and less defensible claims, and attacks on the specific claims may discredit the more important general point. In light of all the problems inherent in positive economic analysis of law, I confess to being unable to rid myself of the sense that, although it has drawn attention to the subtle operation of power, we would know more about law had the same energy and intelligence been devoted to understanding *Middlemarch*[64] and *The Executioner's Song*.[65]

The most productive course that the third form of scholarship could take probably would involve social theory. Social theory in the twentieth century has revolved around efforts to resolve what have been conceived of as epistemological problems of social knowledge. The problems arise as claims to objective knowledge are confronted with the reality that knowledge is produced by individuals located inextricably within the arena about which they are said to have knowledge. Marxism, by insisting that all knowledge is a social product and thus that knowledge can have no transcendent validity, generates the central position to which all theories of knowledge respond.

61. Priest, *Selective Characteristics of Litigation*, 9 J. LEGAL STUD. 399, 400-01 (1980). Priest's general conclusion in this article—that the cases most likely to be resolved by judges are those whose decisions are least likely to be predicted by any explanatory theory—only confirms, if in a limited way, the indeterminacy of the rule of law.

62. *See* M. HORWITZ, THE TRANSFORMATION OF AMERICAN LAW xvi (1977).

63. *See* O. HANDLIN & M. HANDLIN, COMMONWEALTH 53-92 (1947).

64. G. ELIOT, MIDDLEMARCH (1871-72).

65. N. MAILER, THE EXECUTIONER'S SONG (1979).

## Causes and Cure

There is a direct line, intellectual and institutional, from Realism to the use of social theory in analyzing law.[66] Such work, however, has never had more than the most tenuous toe-hold in law schools. In part, the reasons are again institutional. The point of entry for the confrontation of objectivity and subjectivity would have been Realism in the 1930s. But the cooptive power of the New Deal in the center and Communist labor-organizing efforts on the left was great enough to channel young lawyers, who, after all, had been trained as professionals, away from the issues with which academics in related fields were concerned. Further, legal academia had fewer positions and, I suspect, was more strictly hierarchical, than other academic fields in which a few unorthodox scholars could find lodging at small liberal arts colleges.[67]

More recent institutional history is also relevant. Perhaps the best example comes from Yale Law School, which has been the leading institution dabbling in the use of social theory in analyzing law since Realism came of age. During the 1960s, a period that Professor Abraham Goldstein has called the "Dark Ages" of Yale,[68] a series of decisions not to grant tenure to certain members of the faculty were made. When the full story is told, these decisions will be linked to complex questions of academic and external politics. But there is a broader point to be made. Yale, as a professional school, is subject to the professional pressures I discussed earlier. Its ability to resist those pressures depends on its maintaining its elite position. A number of strategies are available. Chicago, for example, has achieved its position by the single-minded pursuit of one specialty. Yale's strategy has been more subtle. Its goal has been to keep a few steps—or more mundanely, two to five years—ahead of the pack by having scholars on the faculty who are now doing what many more people will be doing in a few years. This strategy, however, has significant implications for hiring and tenure policies. Tenure can be given only to those who can switch specialties before the trend line changes direction. But learning social theory is a difficult enterprise. Few law stu-

66. *See* J. Schlegel, Institutionalizing the Study of Law and Society: The Law Schools (June 20-28, 1980) (unpublished paper presented at the 1980 Annual Meeting of the Law and Society Association) (on file with *Yale Law Journal*).

67. For a collection of essays that makes this point in a limited, and distinguishable, context, see THE INTELLECTUAL MIGRATION (D. Fleming & B. Bailyn eds. 1969) (effect of European immigrants on American intellectual life). The book's list of "300 Notable Emigres," *id.* at 675-718, includes five scholars with significant affiliations with law schools and reveals the wide range of institutions that initially absorbed the emigres.

68. Without challenging the characterization, I must note that it is less clear to me than it apparently is to Professor Goldstein who were the monks and who the barbarians.

dents can absorb enough social theory to become specialists in it at the same time that they acquire the elite credentials as lawyers or legal scholars who are more than technicians. Those who master social theory are, for emotional and intellectual reasons, less likely than others to be willing or able to convert to other activities should the institutional need arise, and are, therefore, not attractive candidates for tenure. Because the conditions for the integration of social theory and law are even less favorable elsewhere than they are at Yale and other elite institutions, the tenuous position of this type of legal scholarship will certainly continue.

More important than all the institutional forces I have described, however, there are certain intellectual reasons for the failure of social theory to emerge in legal scholarship. Sociologists and historians can raise and face problems of objectivity and subjectivity, difficult as they may be, without threatening the foundations of their enterprises because they can reconstruct their fields from the smallest units of human interaction, as phenomenologists and ethnomethodologists have done.[69] As I have argued, that is not true of legal scholars in a liberal society. Some defects in the Realists' early formulations were also influential. Because the Realists were heirs of the Progressive tradition in historiography, they tended to attribute outcomes in the legal system to the self-conscious and usually self-serving decisions of actors in the system. Although they understood that their analysis of legal rules led inevitably to an analysis of the operation of power, they reduced power to the self-interested actions of a few wilful men or to pure subjectivity. Debunking the pretensions of those who say they are motivated only by the public interest is frequently valuable, but it is almost always an incomplete account of the exercise of power.

The institutional and intellectual barriers to the integration of legal and social theory are substantial enough that it is unlikely that legal scholarship will soon be incorporated into the mainstream of intellectual life. There are several responses to the intellectual marginality of legal scholarship. First, one could simply give up; the rewards accruing to unconventional work and the merits of conventional work are both too small. Second, one might try to overcome the barriers I have mentioned. Abandoning the liberal theory of law, one might deny law its privileged status as a device by which to reconcile subjectivity and objectivity and treat it simply as one way

69. This reconstruction has analogues in the utopian program mentioned above, *see* note 39 *supra*, and would begin to deal with the problem of language to which Wittgenstein directed our attention, *see* p. 1217 *supra*.

among many others to talk about human problems subject to the distortions of communication that characterize all of our activities.[70]

The second course is grounded in the hope, which is shared by many contemporary social theorists, that the contrast between subjectivity and objectivity is only a dilemma within the framework of liberal theory and can be transcended when some other currently ill-defined theory is developed.[71] The odds of that hope being well-founded are greater, I think, than the odds that the problems can be resolved within liberal theory. But the chances that it is well-founded seem less than even. That estimate leads to the final possible responses to the argument I have made. Legal scholars can devote themselves to replaying the Realist line each time someone comes up with some clever but, the chances are, unfounded way around Realism's critique of the rule of law. The work of Professor Leff is my example.[72] Finally, they can continue to do conventional legal scholarship, knowing that its premises are unsupported and indeed insupportable, precisely because it makes no less sense than anything else in the world. There is an intellectual tradition here too. For my purposes I can say that it begins with Kierkegaard.

70. *See, e.g.*, Habermas, *Toward a Theory of Communicative Competence*, in RECENT SOCIOLOGY No. 2, at 114 (H. Dreitzel ed. 1970).

71. *See, e.g.*, A. GIDDENS, CENTRAL PROBLEMS OF SOCIAL THEORY 2-7 (1979); R. UNGER, *supra* note 11, at 236-95.

72. *See* Leff, *Economic Analysis of Law: Some Realism About Nominalism*, 60 VA. L. REV. 451 (1974); Leff, *Unspeakable Ethics, Unnatural Law*, 1979 DUKE L.J. 1229; Leff, *Memorandum* (Book Review), 29 STAN. L. REV. 879 (1977) (review of R. UNGER, *supra* note 11).

# [8]

# Legal Scholarship in the United States: An Overview

A LOOK backward offers the opportunity to gain perspective on the current condition of legal scholarship in the United States. A comparison of the contents of leading law reviews in the mid-1930s and mid-1980s proves quite enlightening.[1] I had expected to find major changes in legal scholarship,[2] but in fact discovered that the differences between then and now, though interesting, are relatively marginal.[3] The first part of this essay describes the works published in two leading law reviews then and now, and offers some explanations for the continuities and the modest degree of change. The second part provides a broader perspective on contemporary legal scholarship in the United States.

Perhaps the best summary description of the law reviews is that the articles of the 1930s are transformed into the student notes of the 1980s. That is, in the 1930s many articles consisted of the analysis of cases, the aim of which was to establish that sensible decisions had to rest on grounds external to the cases.[4] Probably the best example of this genre is Louis Jaffe's wonderful article, "Law Making by Private Groups,"[5] which provides a gently phrased but devastating critique of legal concepts then being deployed in opposition to the New Deal. Analysing those concepts and the cases using them, and referring to non-legal sources, Jaffe converted rigid legal categories into continua. By doing so, he could then argue that contemporary problems should be resolved not by figuring out into which category they should be placed but by identifying their proper location on the continuum, in light of the various policies they implicated. This is now an entirely familiar mode of analysis.[6]

Although the topics have changed, today's student notes have the same critical thrust.[7] Those notes appear to scavenge a bit more systematically in the literature of allied disciplines such as

---

[1] I had intended to compare the 1936–37 and 1985–86 volumes of the *Harvard Law Review* and the *Yale Law Journal*, but the 1936–37 volume of the *Harvard Law Review* was a fifty-year anniversary volume, and therefore had too many "overviews" itself. As a result, I have used the 1937–38 volume of the *Harvard Law Review* for my comparisons. I doubt that this has any consequences for my argument.

[2] *See* Tushnet, "Post-Realist Legal Scholarship in the United States," 15 *Journal of Society of Public Teachers of Law* 20 (1980).

[3] All of the judgments reported here are based on "eyeball" evaluations, not careful statistical or systematic analysis.

[4] See, *e.g.* Casner, "Class Gifts to Others Than to 'Heirs' or 'Next of Kin': Increase in the Class Membership," 51 *Harvard Law Review* 254 (1937).

[5] Jaffe, "Law Making By Private Groups," 51 *Harvard Law Review* 201 (1937).

[6] See, *e.g.* Redish & Marshall, "Adjudicatory Independence and the Values of Procedural Due Process," 95 *Yale Law Journal* 455 (1986).

[7] See, *e.g.* Note, "State and Federal Land Use Regulation: An Application to Ground Water and Nonpoint Source Pollution Control," 95 *Yale Law Journal* 1433 (1986).

economics,[8] but the appearance may be misleading. The articles of the 1930s also referred to those disciplines.[9] Legal scholarship in the United States may simply appropriate from other disciplines what those disciplines have to offer: institutional economics in the 1930s, neo-classical microeconomics today. Alternatively, today's somewhat more systematic reliance on other disciplines may be a symptom of the disappearance of a widely shared legal culture: because today's readers simply have a much narrower range of knowledge, authors cannot assume that off-hand references outside the law will actually communicate anything to their readers.

If reliance on allied disciplines is one continuity, another is the persistence of relatively traditional doctrinal analysis designed, as one article in 1937 put it, to answer "basic questions as to the proper *concept* underlying the term[s]" used in the law.[10] These conceptual articles examine the relevant cases and offer solutions grounded in public policy to the problems they identify.[11] The overall sense of continuity in legal scholarship derives in large measure from the similar analytical methods used in the 1930s and today.

If the articles have become the student notes, what has become of the student work of the 1930s? That work, as well as a significant minority of the articles, tended to present readers with descriptive summaries of recent developments, primarily statutory but, to a lesser extent, case law as well.[12] One has the impression that leading law reviews were, in part, a combination news service and research tool for the profession. If that impression is correct, the disappearance of purely descriptive material can be explained by the increasing availability of other, more timely and more specialised news services and research tools.

Another discontinuity lies in the subject matter of law review articles. Categorisation is not easy, but a rough grouping suggests that articles about private law formed a significant minority of those published in the 1930s, while such articles have essentially disappeared today. Most of the space has been transferred to public law articles, but some has been shifted to jurisprudence, legal history, and similar exotica. Again, though, it is easy to

[8] See, *e.g.* Note, "Rationalizing Antitrust Cluster Markets," 95 *Yale Law Journal* 109 (1985).

[9] See, *e.g.* Graham, "The Undistributed Profits Tax and the Investor," 46 *Yale Law Journal* 1 (1936); Sharfman, "The Interstate Commerce Commission: An Appraisal," 46 *Yale Law Journal* 915 (1937).

[10] Paul, "Ascertainment of 'Earnings or Profits' for the Purpose of Determining the Taxability of Corporate Distributions," 51 *Harvard Law Review* 40 (1937).

[11] See, *e.g.* Field, "Sources of Law: The Scope of Federal Common Law," 99 *Harvard Law Review* 883 (1986); Meltzer, "State Court Forfeitures of Federal Rights," 99 *Harvard Law Review* 1130 (1986).

[12] See, *e.g.* LaPorte, "Changes in Corporate Reorganization Proposed by the Chandler and Lea Bills," 51 *Harvard Law Review* 672 (1938); Ely, "The Conservation of Oil," 51 *Harvard Law Review* 1209 (1938); Neff, "Forms for Registration of Securities Under the Acts of 1933 and 1934," 51 *Harvard Law Review* 1354 (1938); Hendricks, "The Surtax on Undistributed Profits of Corporations," 46 *Yale Law Journal* 19 (1936).

overstate the differences. One article in the *Harvard Law Review* in 1938 described the revised curriculum for the Law School, and noted somewhat apologetically that the new curriculum remained dominated by private law subjects.[13] But even in the 1930s, public law articles were a majority of those published; in my categorisation, the ratio of public to private law articles in the *Harvard Law Review* was 2:1, and in the *Yale Law Journal* it was 4:1.[14] One further aspect of the public/private law division is worth noting. The public law articles of the 1930s, concerned as they were with contemporaneous developments, seem of more transitory interest than the private law ones. In the two volumes I examined, perhaps four articles of permanent value on private law subjects appeared,[15] while a generous count would find three similar public law articles.[16] In the light of the predominance of public law articles overall, this is striking. Perhaps it is too convenient to be significant, but it does seem interesting that Erwin Griswold published two articles in these volumes. One, "Renvoi Revisited," remains an important discussion; the other, "Res Judicata in Federal Tax Cases," seems to have been superseded by later developments.[17]

This brief and informal survey of continuity and change in legal scholarship in the United States provokes several observations. First, and probably most important, by the mid-1930s the transition from legal formalism to Legal Realism had come close to completion. If we put aside the purely descriptive articles and student comments, we are left with law reviews that plainly value Realist analyses over formalist ones. Second, and probably related to the first, public law scholarship had already come to dominate. The regulatory state had grown to a point where it pervasively intruded on legal scholarship, although here it is important to note that some of this resulted from the "news service" aspect of law reviews in the 1930s.

Another aspect of continuity derives from what we could call the sociology of legal scholarship. As in all disciplines, most legal scholarship is produced by young scholars, excited by their exploration of new territory (and, to a degree, concerned about making a reputation by publishing in major law reviews). The authors of the 1930s were then new to the academic profession.[18] They continued to teach until relatively recently, and thereby

[13] Simpson, "The New Curriculum of the Harvard Law School," 51 *Harvard Law Review* 965, 980–81 (1938).

[14] The current ratios are, for the *Harvard Law Review* 16:1, and for the *Yale Law Journal* 5:1.

[15] Fuller & Perdue, "The Reliance Interest in Contract Damages," 46 *Yale Law Journal* 52, 373 (1936); Leach, "Perpetuities in a Nutshell," 51 *Harvard Law Review* 638 (1938); Griswold, "Renvoi Revisited," 51 *Harvard Law Review* 1165 (1938).

[16] Lerner, "Constitution and Court as Symbols," 46 *Yale Law Journal* 1290 (1937); Stern, "Separability and Separability Clauses in the Supreme Court," 51 *Harvard Law Review* 76 (1937); Jaffe, *supra* note 5.

[17] Griswold, *supra* note 15; Griswold, "Res Judicata in Federal Tax Cases," 46 *Yale Law Journal* 1320 (1937).

[18] These scholars include Professors Jaffe, Casner, Griswold, and Leach.

defined what counts as valuable legal scholarship.[19] That may account for the transfer of themes from the articles of the 1930s to the student works of the 1980s.

The preceding material has provided an impressionistic account of legal scholarship in the United States. It may help now to step back and offer an equally impressionistic account of why so little appears to have happened in legal scholarship over that period. We can begin with the observation that public law scholarship appears to have been substantially more ephemeral than private law scholarship, itself not a terribly robust enterprise. That characteristic persists. In recent volumes of the *Harvard Law Review* and the *Yale Law Journal*, substantial numbers of pages are devoted to issues that are almost certain to have disappeared by the turn of the century.[20]

I suggest that the predominance of scholarship concerned with relatively ephemeral issues is connected to the growth of the regulatory-welfare state and the associated rise of American Legal Realism. The pre-regulatory state operated through the common law to ensure the stability of the framework within which private transactions could occur. It did so by intervening when breakdowns occurred, sorting out the problems they produced according to rules designed to provide incentives against the occurrence of future breakdowns. The common-law state thus operated in the background, invisible during the daily conduct of life. Of course this state never existed in a pure form, and the image of invisibility may well have been an ideological construct that attempted to conceal the actual allocative role of the common law. The industrialisation of the United States in the nineteenth century produced both an incipient regulatory-welfare state and a crisis for the ideology of the invisibility of the state. Industrialisation exacerbated the tensions between farmers and railroads, and between laboring people and their employers. These tensions were translated into economic and political conflict, which resulted in a variety of regulatory efforts by state and national governments. Simultaneously, the tensions brought to the fore the allocative aspects of the common-law state. In times of social peace, people may be comfortable with what appears to them to be the natural order of society; when social peace comes under strain, the

[19] More precisely, they taught senior scholars, some of whom teach today's students.

[20] These topics include affirmative action, the exclusionary rule, and alternative dispute resolution. *See* Abram, "Affirmative Action: Fair Shakers and Social Engineers," 99 *Harvard Law Review* 1312 (1986); Edwards, "Alternative Dispute Resolution: Panacea or Anathema?," 99 *Harvard Law Review* 668 (1986); Morrison, "OMB Interference with Agency Rulemaking: The Wrong Way to Write a Regulation," 99 *Harvard Law Review* 1059 (1986); Kennedy, "Persuasion and Distrust: A Comment on the Affirmative Action Debate," 99 *Harvard Law Review* 1327 (1986); DeMuth & Ginsburg, "White House Review of Agency Rulemaking," 99 *Harvard Law Review* 1075 (1986); Dripps, "Living with *Leon*," 95 *Yale Law Journal* 906 (1986); Duke, "Making *Leon* Worse," 95 *Yale Law Journal* 1405 (1986); Kaufman, "Must Every Appeal Run the Gamut? The Civil Appeals Management Plan," 95 *Yale Law Journal* 755 (1986).

discomfort people feel may lead them to question the naturalness of the social order.

To stabilise the social order under these circumstances, some sort of explanation of the new developments' "rightness" is helpful. The explanation generally available for the common law would not work for the new regulatory-welfare state. That explanation invoked "the rule of law," which, for present purposes, meant disposition of individual cases pursuant to rules of general application stated beforehand in the relevant legal materials. The actions of the regulatory-welfare state have come to be much more particularised than can comfortably be accommodated within the "rule of law" model. Ailing and infant industries are aided by quasi-feudal governmental support directed at named firms whose political representatives have sufficient power to extract it;[21] public assistance is provided according to an individualised and highly discretionary assessment of need and merit.[22]

The regulatory-welfare state in the United States developed over the course of a century, in fits and starts. Some of its mechanisms, such as regulatory agencies like the Interstate Commerce Commission, used some of the familiar methods of common law decision making. Yet, even when highly rule-oriented bureaucracies implemented governmental regulations, traditionalists raised questions about the "rule of law." For example, New Deal administrative agencies were attacked for failing to distinguish between adjudication and rule-making, and for uniting in agency hands the functions of prosecution and decision-making, which, it was claimed, should be kept separate.[23] Social welfare bureaucracies adopted an ideology of individualised decisions, in some tension with the rule of law, but they too were subject to the pressures towards rule-oriented regularity inherent in the bureaucratic form.[24]

These developments called for the parallel development of an explanation, or ideology, of the regulatory-welfare state. In many ways legal scholarship in the United States has been devoted to developing that ideology. One course, which seems to have dominated continental social thought, would have been to separate these novel aspects of the regulatory-welfare state from the more traditional concerns of the common law. The law, and therefore the rule of law, would deal only with traditional forms of property and social regulation; the rest would be dealt with under the heading of "administration," to which entirely different justificatory principles were applicable.

The political and legal context in which the regulatory-welfare state developed in the United States made it difficult to follow this

---

21 See, *e.g.* Claus Offe, *Contradictions of the Welfare State* (1984).

22 Simon, "Legality, Bureaucracy, and Class in the Welfare System," 92 *Yale Law Journal* 1198 (1983).

23 See Gellhorn, "The Administrative Procedure Act: The Beginnings," 72 *Virginia Law Review* 219 (1986).

24 Simon, *supra* note 22.

course. The regulatory apparatus was imposed on a business community powerful enough to extract "rule of law" concessions in exchange for substantive regulations.[25] Recipients of public assistance were of course less powerful, but they too had an ally: the Constitution. The earliest forms of public assistance, pensions to veterans, were indeed administered. The 1868 statute creating the system of veterans' benefits limited to $10 the fees lawyers could charge veterans seeking assistance, which soon meant that lawyers were excluded from the system. The statute also severely limited judicial review of decisions under the pension statutes. This system endured for over a century. Then the pressures of the rule of law asserted themselves. Veterans challenged the fee limitation as a denial of due process of law, and, though the Supreme Court rejected their wholesale challenge, it suggested that the fee limitation might deny constitutional rights in complex cases,[26] an issue that is the subject of continuing litigation and legislative concern. In addition, veterans invoked post-1970 statutes which, they claimed, authorised judicial review of denials of benefits in conflict with those statutes.[27]

Recipients of other types of public assistance, such as those receiving income maintenance grants, developed a similar two-fold attack on the exemption of "administration" from the rule of law. They invoked the Constitution to challenge various allegedly discriminatory features of income maintenance programs,[28] and they played the various parts of complex statutory schemes against each other, finding in the conflicts among these provisions the space to argue for expanding the benefits.[29]

Thus, the presence of the Constitution, and the continuing elaboration of the regulatory-welfare state, eliminated the possibility that the aspects of government most characteristic of that state would simply be extruded from the legal system and therefore from the purview of legal scholarship. That alone is probably sufficient to account for the predominance of public law articles in leading law reviews. In the United States, such articles are the vehicles for continuing efforts to reconcile the regulatory-welfare state with the rule of law. Elsewhere in developed Western countries, those efforts have largely been abandoned. That may have occurred because those societies have traditions—religious, socialist, and the like—that can be invoked to explain the "rightness" of the regulatory-welfare state, whereas the United States has only the rule of law tradition to draw upon.

---

[25] Gellhorn, *supra* note 23.

[26] *Walters* v. *National Association of Radiation Survivors*, 473 U.S. 305 (1985).

[27] See *McKelvey* v. *Turnage*, 792 F.2d 194 (DC Cir. 1986), cert. granted March 9, 1987.

[28] See Geoffrey Stone, L. Michael Seidman, Cass Sunstein, and Mark Tushnet, *Constitutional Law* 815–21 (1986).

[29] *King* v. *Smith*, 392 U.S. 309 (1968).

The tension between "administration" and the classical rule of law tradition is real, however. Legal scholarship in the United States thus can be seen as an effort to recast the rule of law tradition. Here the triumph of American Legal Realism seems to play an important role. As I have suggested, Legal Realism was received into legal scholarship in the United States as a prescription that sensible legal decisions necessarily rested on a sensible balance of competing policies. The Realists were taken to have established that the formalisms characteristic of the classical rule of law tradition concealed the actual problems, which always consisted of a clash among various policies, all of which were valuable in the abstract but which could not be simultaneously achieved in real-world situations. The Realist message was that law should openly balance those policies.

Most legal scholarship in the United States has been captivated by the metaphor of balancing, so much so that balancing is now generally seen as expressing the rule of law. In particular, the dominant view of the Constitution is that its proper interpretation produces balancing tests in virtually every area of its application. The canonical statement of what due process requires, taken from an income-maintenance case, is almost a parody of the balancing approach: "Identification of the specific dictates of due process generally requires consideration of three distinct factors: first, the private interest that will be affected by the official action; second, the risk of an erroneous deprivation of such interest through the procedures used, and the probable value, if any, of additional or substitute procedural safeguards; and finally, the Government's interest, including the function involved and the fiscal and administrative burdens that the additional or substitute procedural requirement would entail."[30]

The rule of law was thus reformulated to incorporate the flexibility that was necessary for the administration of the regulatory-welfare state. Parallel to this development, and reinforcing it, the demise of formalism in the common law subjects undermined the foundations of constitutional law, with important effects on legal scholarship. Prior to the growth of the regulatory-welfare state, the social order was maintained by transactions between private property-owners whose entitlements were defined by the common law. There was little public law as such, except insofar as the Constitution was taken to prohibit alterations in common law entitlements.[31] After the domain of public law expanded, it was brought into line with the rule of law ideal by recharacterising the rule of law as itself flexible. Then, however, the flexibility of the rule of law was applied to the private law concepts which formed the background for public law.

[30] *Mathews* v. *Eldridge*, 424 U.S. 319 (1976).

[31] For a modern version of this claim, see Richard Epstein, *Takings: Private Property and the Power of Eminent Domain* (1985).

The process can be illuminated by two important examples. The first is the disintegration of the concept of property—its transformation in legal theory from material goods (at the core of the concept) to the now fabled "bundle of sticks."[32] Notably, in the United States the impetus for this transformation was precisely the confrontation between the regulatory state and the Constitution. People could be deprived of their property by regulation of that property, yet regulation was a practical and political necessity. That in turn made it necessary to provide constitutional justifications for regulation, and legal scholars responded by offering the "bundle of sticks" metaphor. Yet, though that metaphor supplied reasons for finding it permissible to regulate one dimension of a disaggregated concept of property, it provided no stopping point for the process of disaggregation. And without a stopping point, the concept of property dissolved: all property became public, at least whenever the state chose to treat it as public. There could be no common law "background" for public law.

The second example is the "state action" doctrine of American constitutional law. According to that doctrine, the Constitution of its own force restricts only the government; private actors can discriminate on the basis of race or penalise people for their political views, as governments could not, subject only to whatever statutory restrictions that happen to have been adopted. The doctrine appears to preserve a sphere of private autonomy free from state intrusion, yet the proviso about statutory restrictions shows that it does not; it is fundamentally a doctrine about courts, not about regulation. Again, as regulation proliferated, it came to seem odd that some normatively troubling actions, such as certain forms of racial discrimination, escaped public control merely because legislatures had not gotten around to prohibiting them.[33] Even more, the disaggregation of the property concept deprived any particular "stick" of normative weight in the service of autonomy, so that invoking constitutional norms against the holder of the "stick" seemed not to intrude on anything truly valuable. Finally, the state action doctrine came to be seen as a flexible "balancing"-type doctrine, in which the costs of judicially mandated intrusions on autonomy in the name of constitutional values were to be weighed against the social benefits of those values.[34] The flexibility of the doctrine was a form of the flexibility of the revised version of the rule of law ideal.

The property and state action illustrations are important because they show that it is no longer possible in the United States to sustain the distinction between public law and private law; this may

[32] Bruce Ackerman, *Private Property and the Constitution* (1977).

[33] See *Bell* v. *Maryland*, 378 U.S. 226, 259 (1964) (Douglas, J., concurring, treating racially restrictive covenants as a form of zoning).

[34] See Glennon & Nowak, "A Functional Analysis of the Fourteenth Amendment 'State Action' Requirement," 1976 *Supreme Court Review* 221, 231–32.

contribute to the explanation of the predominance of public law articles in the law reviews. The concepts that distinguish the domains—property and government—turn out to be indistinguishable. Yet, as I have suggested, this conclusion is in some tension with some aspects of the general view of the role of law in everyday life held by many Americans. The result has been, not quite a crisis for legal theory in the United States, but a nagging sense that something ought to be done to shore up the theoretical foundations of the legal order.

The demise of formalism has made it impossible to offer elements from within the law as the requisite supports. Articles that confine themselves to legal sources inevitably are driven to claims that the proper balance, in the circumstances, is thus-and-so.[35] Experience with balancing tests makes the response easy: the location of the policy balance is determined by the weights the author places on the competing values, but there is nothing in the law that tells us why those are the proper weights. After all, if there were something in the law that did so, it would be precisely the sort of formalist proposition that, we have been persuaded by the Realists, cannot be defended.

I do not want to defend the proposition that the Realists were right, though I believe that they were. What matters for present purposes is that their position—if not their arguments—carried the day. When Realist scepticism was coupled with the growth of the regulatory-welfare State in a context calling for constitutional defences of the state's actions, it produced a demand that could not be satisfied from within the law. That has led to a persistent search by leading legal scholars in the United States for foundations of the law in other disciplines.[36] As suggested earlier, the search is usually a sort of scavenging, motivated by the lawyer's effort to find something in the discipline that will help solve a predefined problem, rather than by the discipline's own definition of its problems and goals.

The usual result is an unthinking appropriation of apparently helpful results, displaying little awareness that the kinds of results that legal academics seize on are often among the most controversial within the discipline. Until recently, academic lawyers lacked the specialised training in these disciplines that would allow them to understand the bases for the results they wanted to appropriate. Over the past decade, the number of legal scholars in the United States who have received advanced degrees in other disciplines has increased, largely because of the rapid expansion and subsequent contraction of undergraduate education in the United States.[37] The

---

[35] See, *e.g.* Redish & Marshall, *supra* note 6.

[36] This search was also fuelled by the Realists' policy orientation. *See* text accompanying note 30 *infra*.

[37] The expansion of undergraduate education induced people to obtain advanced degrees in the allied disciplines, as they anticipated obtaining teaching jobs in undergraduate schools. The contraction meant that tenure track positions in such institutions were filled, thus driving these people into law schools after they received their graduate degrees.

effects of this growth are ambiguous. Those well trained in the allied field are likely to bring a healthy scepticism to their appropriation of its results. Yet, those who receive the best training in the discipline are rather more likely to pursue their careers in the discipline than those who are somewhat less talented economists, historians, and the like. That is, dual degree holders who become legal academics are likely to be below the top rank of those in both law and their discipline. This may lead them to appropriate the discipline's results *more* aggressively.[38]

In the 1940s and 1950s, sociology seemed to be the way out. Eventually, legal scholars began to look elsewhere. In the 1950s and 1960s, academic lawyers turned to Freudian psychology, only to find themselves deep in epistemological and practical issues about psychoanalytic theory and therapy. Sociology and psychology were initially attractive because, in the United States at least, they were vaguely liberal disciplines, just the places that New Deal liberals might look for answers. The current fashion is to look to neo-classical microeconomics, which is, again, compatible with the more conservative tendency of contemporary United States politics. Predictions about academic fashions are always hazardous, of course, but it seems to me likely that, unless the conservative politics in the United States settles in more stably than it has so far, a reaction to the appropriations of law-and-economics will occur.

My discussion has already begun to shift from general considerations about legal ideology in the United States to aspects of the structure of legal education there. Other aspects of that structure illuminate the continuing search outside the law for its foundations. Perhaps the most important is the most obvious: legal education in the United States consists of educating future members of the practising bar. Academic lawyers almost always practise law before becoming teachers, and many continue to do so while they teach. The examination of allied disciplines is always marginal to the enterprise of education for the bar, however important it is ideologically and in establishing the academic credentials of legal scholars. Enthusiasts often claim that knowledge of other disciplines is useful to the practising lawyers, and is therefore an important part of legal education. They say that a lawyer who understands

[38] Another dimension of this problem is that, in the United States, students evaluate articles submitted for publication in academic legal periodicals. Despite the trend mentioned in the previous note, law students are not likely to be sophisticated in the evaluation of material that relies substantially on allied disciplines. Thus, what is published, and therefore what sets the norm for what people think valuable to be published, is likely to be relatively unsophisticated in its use of the allied disciplines. Recently, some law faculties have sponsored faculty-evaluated law reviews (for example, the *Journal of Legal Studies* at the University of Chicago Law School and the *Yale Journal of Law, Economics, and Organization*). However, these journals have, at least so far, been close to house organs for work by members of the faculties of the sponsoring institutions.

economics will be able to give better advice to clients, to cross-examine experts more effectively, and the like; they say that a lawyer with a sense of history, or facility in the use of the literary critic's tools, will have a better sense of what arguments work well, and why. Certainly there is something to those claims, though they really may be no more than claims that, on the whole, people who are well-educated are more likely to be better lawyers.[39]

Nonetheless, the claims for other disciplines are a bit forced. "Marginal" is the right word, for, though the other disciplines contribute to the improvement of a lawyer's work on the margin, by far the bulk of that work is completely traditional. At the same time, it should be noted that many of these observations could be made about the relevance of Legal Realism's critique of formalism to the education of practising lawyers. There too one might say that, whatever is the case in legal theory, by far the bulk of a practising lawyer's work proceeds on the assumption that the stated legal rules are clear enough to justify a firm prediction about what is likely to happen—which is what practising lawyers worry about. This suggests that the allied disciplines face no insurmountable barriers to expanding their role in law schools, despite their marginal application to legal practice. Even so, one might be sceptical, not so much because of marginality per se, but because the record consists of a restless search moving from one discipline to another, with the desires of academic lawyers remaining unsatisfied. As nothing has worked for very long so far, law schools may be reluctant to commit more than a token investment to the allied disciplines.

I have addressed the role of other disciplines in legal scholarship in the United States by placing it in the context of the ideological effort to justify the regulatory-welfare state. There is a more conventional story, according to which academic lawyers look to other disciplines for guidance in resolving the concrete problems of public policy that, according to the Legal Realists, were always at stake in the law. Sociology, political science, economics, and the like help lawyers understand how social institutions respond to the imposition of legal rules, and thereby allow the lawyers to develop rules that do what they should.

I used to believe that story[40] but no longer do. In part, my disbelief results from my distance from the policy-oriented discussions. The other disciplines are used so selectively, and the insights the academic lawyers appropriate are such banal generalities, that I find it difficult to believe that a community of scholars could seriously think that the other disciplines, presented in that form, could actually help.[41] All one needs to do is place oneself on the

[39] One doubts, for example, that lawyers well-trained in economics are, by that reason alone, likely to be better lawyers than those well-trained in physics or formal logic.

[40] Tushnet, *supra* note 2.

[41] This is not to deny that individual members of that community do believe that work drawn selectively from the allied disciplines will indeed assist policymakers.

other side of the policy debate in which any article engages: if it urges alterations in the distribution of wealth, one asks, "But how might markets respond to make those alterations unnecessary and even harmful?" If it urges withdrawal of state regulation, one asks, "But what would the distributional consequences be?" It quickly becomes clear that the partial appropriation of materials from other disciplines could be countered by an equally partial appropriation of another set of materials from that discipline. In addition, the short half-lives of the favoured disciplines suggest that the claim that they provide policy guidance cannot be sustained: psychiatry had its day; economics is now having its day; one awaits the arrival and departure of sociobiology.

The thought that legal scholars in the United States are recurrently drawn to other disciplines to solve ideological rather than policy problems gains additional support when we consider the role played by what I have earlier called "exotica" in legal scholarship. The most obvious area of ideological disputation is jurisprudence. This consists in the main of discussion of "the concept of law" or the obligation to obey the law, which take as an unstated premise that Anglo-American systems of law are justified on the whole, and then try to explain why that is so, and why people are occasionally—but only occasionally—justified in disobeying some laws. Recent studies that link law and literature similarly blend an apologetic and mildly critical thrust.[42] These works attempt to distance their readers from the law by minimising the coercive element in law, and then implicate the readers in the law by treating law as a literary expression of a community consisting of law's "writers" and its "readers," including the readers of this sort of scholarship. The apologetic element is the claim that this sort of community actually exists and is valuable; the critical one derives from the distance these works place between the reader and the law.

"Law and literature" and jurisprudence scholarship is rather remote from the immediate policy concerns that Legal Realism placed at the centre of law. So too is the most significant work in law and sociology or anthropology. At the outset, the "law and society" scholars believed that their work could inform sensible policy-making of a mildly liberal sort. That turned out to be wrong, in part because legal sociology routinely discovered that the social order was far more resistant to change at the instance of legal rules than had been expected,[43] and in part because the politicians receptive to social reform were less receptive to the suggestions made by the legal sociologists. "Law and society" scholarship has taken on a rather sharp critical edge, as it continues

---

[42] See, *e.g.* James Boyd White, *When Words Lose Their Meanings* (1983); Symposium, "Law and Literature," 60 *Texas Law Review* 373–586 (1982).

[43] See Abel, "Law Books and Books About Law," 26 *Stanford Law Review* 175 (1973).

to reveal the gap between the attractive aspirations of the law and its actual performance, as well as the difficulty we have in closing the gap. One consequence of the fact that "law and society" studies have a critical edge is the relegation of such scholarship to the fringes of the legal academy.[44]

The most recent form of exotica in United States legal scholarship is critical legal studies, with which, it must be noted, I am identified. The intellectual background of critical legal studies includes Legal Realism, neo-Marxism, feminism, structuralism, and various other forms of modernist throught, but it would be misleading to think of critical legal studies as a successor to or version of any of these. Because critical legal studies presents itself as a distinctive type of social and legal analysis, it does not lend itself to evaluation by comparison to those other types of modernism: critical legal scholars are indifferent to arguments that their work departs from neo-Marxism or structuralism, as neo-Marxism and the like have been presented by their adherents.

This essay is not the place to describe critical legal scholarship, as it has not been the place to describe law-and-economics or law-and-society scholarship.[45] Rather, it seems appropriate to attempt to assess the significance of critical legal studies at the present stage of its development and assimilation into the legal academy. Critical legal scholars present themselves as on the political left, interested in long-run programs of wealth equalisation and economic and political decentralisation, and in shorter-run programs of transforming the hierarchical relations within the legal academy. Probably the surest thing one can say about critical legal studies is that it is quite unlikely to succeed in these ambitions. At best, it will remain an irritant within the legal academy, like law-and-society research, in providing constant reminders about the failure of the legal system to achieve its best aspirations and, therefore, about the possibility that those aspirations are not really what the system seeks to realise.

Alternatively, critical legal studies might be domesticated, so to speak. It would then fit into the general category of "exotica." As I have suggested, some forms of scholarship in that category, like jurisprudence and law-and-literature, are largely apologetic. Obviously, critical legal studies is not. Yet perhaps the entire category of exotica is fundamentally apologetic. The mere existence of exotica in legal scholarship connects the legal academy to the university as a whole, and so applies a patina of high culture to the

[44] For a discussion, see Friedman, "The Law and Society Movement," 26 *Stanford Law Review* 763 (1986). Perhaps the best indication of this marginality is the fact that one of the most important law-and-society articles, Galanter, "Why the 'Haves' Come Out Ahead," 9 *Law and Society Review* 95 (1974), was rejected by every major law review. *See* Cramton, "'The Most Remarkable Institution': The American Law Review," 36 *Journal of Legal Education* 1, 8 (1986).

[45] For collections of critical legal studies, see David Kairys, editor, *The Politics of Law* (1982); *Critical Legal Studies: Essays from the Harvard Law Review* (1986).

more mundane orientation of law schools. Jurisprudence connects law to philosophy, law-and-literature connects it to literary studies. Critical legal studies, as exotica, connect law to recent trends in scholarship that cross disciplinary bounds, such as structuralism and feminism. In doing so, it may legitimate, not so much the law, but the legal academy as a place properly attached to a university and not just a professional training ground.

To conclude, it appears that, since the 1930s and the triumph of American Legal Realism, legal scholarship in the United States has recurrently attempted to provide an adequate ideological reconciliation of the regulatory-welfare state to the rule of law ideal. Legal Realism made the solution of formalism unacceptable, yet produced only a "balancing" approach that itself heightened the ideological tension. Legal scholars in the United States have looked to other disciplines for help but, in general, have been disappointed by the search. This is likely to continue.

Mark Tushnet*

* Georgetown University Law Center.

[9]

# Idols of the Right: The 'Law-and-Economics' Movement

For the past two decades conservative legal theorists have propagated two right-wing approaches to law. Most public attention has focused on the theory of "original intent" as a guide to interpreting the Constitution. In the law schools, though, the theory of "Law-and-Economics" has had far greater impact. The law journals are filled with law-and-economics articles, and no law school believes itself respectable until it has at least one advocate of law-and-economics on its faculty.

Law-and-economics became prominent in the law schools in part because its message fit comfortably with the politics of the 1980s. President Reagan's appointment of Richard Posner and Frank Easterbrook, prominent advocates of law-and-economics, to the federal courts symbolizes that fit. But the reasons for its influence go deeper.

Why did law-and-economics become a significant movement in legal thought? The easy answer—a right-wing movement in legal thought accompanied the rise of right-wing politics—has no more than a grain of truth. Law-and-economics began to take hold in the legal academy during the 1970s, before right-wing politics of an equally conservative sort became as prominent in national politics. And, perhaps more important, the legal academy was dominated by centrists when law-and-economics became prominent, and has remained so. Law-and-economics became important, not because its politics were congenial with those of the legal academy and the general public (they were not, being substantially more conservative than either), but because its intellectual program seemed, at least for a while, to solve persistent problems in centrist legal thought.

Contemporary legal thought has been shaped by two experiences: American legal realism and the New Deal transformation of government. The legal realists, whose jurisprudence found its source in Justice Oliver Wendell Holmes's early work, and which displaced all competitors in the 1930s, began by criticizing the legal formalism that predominated when they began writing. Formalists believed that legal rules could be deduced, using ordinary logic, from a relatively small set of fundamental principles. In the early decades of the twentieth century formalists tended to be laissez-faire conservatives, and the principles they placed at the base of law were highly individualist and conservative.

The early realists were political progressives who disagreed with the formalists' conservative principles. Although they attacked those principles, their more enduring challenge was to formalism itself, of any sort. They argued that legal materials were so complex and contradictory that nothing in particular could be deduced by legal logic. In a famous article, for example, Karl Llewellyn, a relatively moderate legal realist, compiled a list of "canons" of statutory interpretation and matched each item on the list with an equally well-supported contradictory canon.

The legal realists' critique of formalism left them with what they thought was a serious problem. If legal logic did not generate the

This article is the first in an occasional series of critiques of current right-wing thought.—EDS.

## The Law-and-Economics Movement

results lawmakers arrived at, what did? One group of legal realists gave an answer: politics. For them, law was nothing other than politics conducted in a special forum.

That answer, however, was troublesome. A great deal of law, even outside the area of constitutional law, was made by judges. Why, in a democratic society, should judges determine the rules dealing with liability for industrial accidents or the rules regulating the duties landlords owed tenants, if law was simply another form of politics? The difficulty was exacerbated by the obvious point that judges and lawyers represented a quite narrow stratum of the social and economic system. If the solutions reached through litigation differed from the solutions reached in legislatures, the "legal" solutions could have little claim on the public.

Beyond differences in outcome, the reduction of law to politics, which legal realism seemed to require, posed a serious problem for liberal ideology. The public rhetoric of liberalism, if not its official theory, made much of the difference between politics, where people simply fought over what they wanted, and law, where people were regulated by principles transcending personal interests. If those principles were merely a fancy way to obscure the interests that the law really promoted, the reason for giving law special authority seemed to disappear.

These difficulties were exacerbated by the massive alteration in government's role accomplished by the New Deal. Legal formalism, for all its defects, forcefully distinguished between the public domain, in which government was authorized to act, and the private one, protected against government intrusion by fundamental rights, including constitutional rights.

But the legal realist critique of formalism established that there was no analytic distinction to be made between the public sphere and the private one. In one decision reflecting realist ideas, for example, the Supreme Court said in effect that the government always made regulatory decisions: Letting the consequences of a "natural" disaster lie where they fell, the Court said, was "none the less a choice" than choosing a rule to "shift" the effects from one group to another.

To use a more contemporary example, realists would argue that choosing to leave the distribution of sexually explicit materials unregulated was as much a choice as regulating that distribution. Nor, according to realists, could anyone seriously contend that society had no choice in the matter because it was constrained by the First Amendment. Their critique of formalism established that interpreting the Constitution was no more determinate than any other exercise in legal logic.

Erasing the analytic distinction between the public and private was troubling enough, for ideological reasons. The growth of government, though, made the elimination of the distinction positively threatening. The New Deal, and its validation by the Supreme Court, showed that there were now no limits on what governments could do, and that governments actually might start doing quite a bit. It was no accident that Justice Felix Frankfurter, the leading proponent of a view of the Constitution that authorized the New Deal, was also a leading proponent of judicial restraint in interpreting the limits the Bill of Rights placed on government authority.

Although some legal realists were willing to live with the demystifying consequences of their jurisprudence, most searched for some way to reestablish the authority of law. Law-and-economics is the heir to one of the products of that search.

The trick was to convert "politics" into "policy." Law, these realists said, promoted the policies society sought to achieve. To distinguish policy from politics, they had to find a way to conduct "policy" inquiries that were more neutral than the sheer clash of preferences that characterized politics. Both steps were accomplished when post–legal realists described law as a "policy science." Law, they argued, should promote the policies to which a democratic society was committed, with those policies described so abstractly that no one could seriously disagree with them: promoting security, enhancing material well-being, ensuring liberty, and the like. But, although politics might be one way to promote those policies, politics was too undisciplined. Rather, the argument went, lawyers could use their technical expertise—the "science" part of policy science—to determine, in a neutral way, what legal rules best promoted the abstractly defined goals.

By defining basic policies so abstractly, these post-realists created the possibility of reestablishing the distinction between law and politics. By speaking of policy science, they reestablished the neutrality of law. In many ways treating law as policy science reverted to formalism: abstractly defined policies took the place that fundamental principles occupied in formalism, and scientific and technical expertise took the place of legal logic.

In the end, "law as policy science" was vulnerable to the basic legal realist challenges, but it took some time for that to become apparent. In the meantime, "law as policy science" became transmuted into law-and-economics. Law-and-economics took law's goal to be promoting "efficiency" or economic well-being. That was, its proponents argued, one of the least controversial abstract goals for policy scientists to promote.

## The Principles of Law-and-Economics

Law-and-economics applies the basic assumption of economics—that people try to get the most out of what they have (are "rational maximizers")—to law. If we make that assumption, proponents of law-and-economics ask, what should be the legal rules about accidents, contracts, crime, procedure, and everything else?

The field of law-and-economics really got its start with two articles, one published in 1960 by Ronald Coase, winner of the Nobel Memorial Prize in Economic Science in 1991, and the other published in 1961 by Guido Calabresi, now dean of Yale Law School. Perhaps surprisingly, Coase and Calabresi showed that, if people could easily make deals with each other, it did not matter what the legal rules were.

Suppose I have a legal right to work under safe conditions, but also have the right to trade that right for higher pay. If some employers find it profitable to use some unhealthy materials, they will offer me more to work for them—say, $5.00 an hour—than employers who find it profitable to use only safe materials, who will offer me only $4.00. If I think that, overall, I will be better off with higher pay, I will exchange my "right" to a safe workplace for the higher pay. I will end up working in unsafe conditions for $5.00; other workers, with different preferences, will work in safe conditions for $4.00.

Now suppose I do not have a right to work under safe conditions. Some employers will offer me safe conditions in exchange for *lower* pay—$4.00. Some workers will think they will be better off with lower pay and safe conditions, while others will work for the higher pay—$5.00—in unsafe conditions. Whether workers have a right to a safe workplace or not, that is, they will end up working for the combination of pay and safety they prefer.

This would make law-and-economics uninteresting, except for the crucial point. Things get sorted out only if people can make deals at no cost to them. If it costs something to make a deal—if there are, as Coase put it, transaction costs (costs associated with engaging in transacting)—then it will matter what the legal rules are. Deals move resources—money and working conditions—to where they are most valued by the people making the deals. If transaction costs are too high, some deals that should be made will not be made, and society is the loser (because resources end up in the wrong hands). And, even if deals occur, the cost of engaging in the deal is basically waste; it adds nothing to social well-being.

The point of law-and-economics then became trying to make sure that people could make the right deals. This had two parts. First, there are some general difficulties in making sure that the right deals are made. If a worker does not know how risky it is to use some exotic chemical, and the employer does, the exchange of unsafe working conditions for a higher wage will not be correct (unless we make some rather strong assumptions about how markets for information work). So, legal

**The Law-and-Economics Movement**

rules might be used to ensure that both sides have the same information. And, when there are a lot of people on one side of a deal, coordinating their demands is quite difficult; after most people have signed on, the rest can hold out for a better deal, or each one might make a deal that seems best for him or her personally, only to discover that they all could have done better if they had coordinated their demands. Legal rules can help solve these coordination problems, for example, by allowing any one person to get an injunction that would block the deal.

Second, law-and-economics tried to keep transaction costs low by reducing the number of times people have to engage in deals. Suppose that we find out that most of the time workers prefer safe working conditions. If they do not have a right to safe working conditions, employers will offer $5.00 and unsafe conditions, and then lots of deals will have to be made before the workers end up with safe conditions and $4.00. The cost of making those deals is wasted. In contrast, if workers *do* have a right to safe working conditions, employers will offer safe conditions and $4.00 from the beginning, which is what most workers want. Only a few deals will have to be made, with those few workers who prefer higher pay and unsafe conditions. By giving the "right" to the people who will end up with it most of the time, transaction costs are kept down.

All this is pretty neat, and it certainly appealed to the scientific urges that were part of the legal realist legacy. Still, it was not completely satisfactory. Figuring out what the true transaction costs were, and how to keep them down, might seem to be a technical exercise, but it was not a simple one. People familiar with law could not be confident that judges or legislators would get it right—reintroducing the problem of lawmaking discretion that post-realists tried to suppress.

More important, the economic assumption at the base of law-and-economics was that people tried to do the best they could with what they had. One legacy of the New Deal, though, was persistent concern in lawmaking for the distribution of wealth—that is, for worrying about what people had when they went into the marketplace to make deals. (If workers are desperately poor, they may "choose" to work for $4.00 in *unsafe* conditions, so giving them a right to safe working conditions will make them better off.)

Law-and-economics theorists had a series of linked moves to respond to the problems of lawmaking discretion and wealth distribution. First, they relegated questions of wealth distribution to the legislature. Then, they argued that legislatures were so ridden with interest-group pressures that they could not do a good job of determining the right distribution of wealth. Finally, they argued that courts actually did not have much discretion. Legislatures, in short, *should* not do very much, and courts *could* not do very much. These moves responded to legal realist concerns and, not coincidentally, lent support to government policies of leaving the distribution of wealth undisturbed and letting people do what they wanted to with the resources they happened to have: the intellectual agenda of post-realist thought pushed the analysis to the right.

The argument that courts did not have much discretion was simple and, in the end, quite unpersuasive. The basic idea was that people bring lawsuits only if the legal rules they face impose inefficient results on them—make it too costly to make the right deal. Once the courts manage to develop the right rule, no one will bring a lawsuit challenging that rule. So, even if judges get the right rule by sheer accident, that rule will become a permanent part of the law. In contrast, as long as a bad rule is part of the law, cases will arise challenging it. Eventually, even a court acting randomly will accidentally get the right rule. Day by day, in every way, the law gets better and better.

This argument is elegant. No one believes it, though. It turns out to be fairly easy to generate economic models in which the law can be persistently bad. And, perhaps more important, the argument predicts that cases ought to come out roughly fifty-fifty for the plaintiff and the defendant. Although some isolated subcategories of cases do come out that way, far more categories are tilted one way or the other. So, it seems, judicial discretion cannot be eliminated. If law-and-economics wants the rule to come out right, judges have to exercise choice.

The legal academy found the claim that issues of distribution of wealth should be left to legislatures largely uncontroversial. The final move, deprecating the ability of legislatures, was harder to make persuasive. It began with the unromantic assumption, widely shared in the legal academy and beyond, that questions about the proper distribution of wealth cannot really be answered through rational discussion. They are, instead, questions about which people have strongly held but essentially nonrational views. That, though, played into another view, that legislatures were places where discussion did not matter but "mere" politics, the play of preferences, did.

Law-and-economics relied on the "public-choice" approach to legislation. According to that approach, we ought to think of legislatures as markets for policies, in which voters demand—and politicians supply. Further, politicians are like entrepreneurs, trying to do the best they can for themselves, which usually means doing what is necessary to ensure reelection.

The key to skepticism about legislation as a response either to failures in economic markets or to problems of wealth distribution is a pair of arguments. First, people who have more wealth in the first place are going to be more influential in the market for public policy, so laws that purport to affect the distribution of wealth are probably not going to be very effective.

Second, concentrated interest groups—business lobbyists and labor unions—are going to win out over the public interest—consumers and taxpayers—because it is much easier to organize (get campaign contributions from) concentrated groups. Legislation, then, is going to be worse than ineffective; it is likely to be positively harmful, taking wealth from the diffuse taxpaying or consuming majority and transferring it to those who already are relatively well-to-do.

Some public-choice theorists have argued that their vision of the political process means that courts should interpret interest-group statutes quite narrowly and, more interestingly, that they should interpret the Constitution to bar legislatures from enacting interest-group statutes. Justice Scalia, for example, has relied on public-choice ideas in explaining (or rationalizing) his opposition to affirmative action programs, which he sees as responses to pressures from concentrated women's interest groups at the expense of men, who fall in no "protected categories" in the law.

Law-and-economics needs arguments to limit the role of legislatures *and* judges to respond to legal realist concerns. Unfortunately for its proponents, the necessary arguments are also unpersuasive. The law-and-economics starting point, the assumption that people are rational maximizers, seems sensible enough, if not carried too far. The public-choice arguments, though, are too cynical about politics: Of course special interests have an important, and perhaps undesirable, part in politics, but somehow legislators do sometimes respond to the demands of the public interest. Public-choice theorists have struggled without much success to explain how "public-interest" statutes like environmental laws manage to get enacted, for example. And the argument that courts cannot do anything is strongly counter-intuitive and, it turns out, inconsistent with a lot of empirical evidence.

Law-and-economics, then, got its start because it addressed real problems in legal thought that were the legacy of legal realism. And it ended up promoting a right-wing political agenda that fit comfortably into the contemporary political scene. It was also supported by material and cultural features of the law school scene.

### The Cultural Setting

Some entrepreneurial law professors, most notably Henry Manne (now dean at the George Mason University Law School), saw law-and-economics as a vehicle for institutional and personal advancement that was compatible with their ideological predispositions. During the late 1960s and early 1970s, Manne exposed a large number of law professors to the simple versions of law-and-economics then available, and encouraged them to take the lessons back to their classrooms.

The conservative John M. Olin Foundation has supported programs in law-and-economics at several law schools. The foundation's funds bring outside law-and-economics speakers to faculties, creating a source of "patronage" for the heads of the programs at each law school. More important, the foundation has funded law students themselves: in exchange for a law-and-economics grant—in effect, a reduction in tuition—students are required to enroll in a law-and-economics seminar, for which they also get law school credit. This is an extraordinary arrangement.

Entrepreneurs and outside financing are just a small part of the cultural setting in which law-and-economics flourished. Unsurprisingly, the legal academy is oriented toward those who hold power. Ronald Reagan's judicial appointments—Richard Posner and Frank Easterbrook to the Chicago appellate court, Antonin Scalia first to the D.C. appellate court and then to the Supreme Court, and others less in the public eye but well known in law schools—made law-and-economics ideas part of "the law," not just the academy. Often these judges seem to write "for the law schools," addressing the issues raised by their cases in ways that make it more likely that their opinions will make their way, if not into the law, at least into the casebooks from which students learn the law.

More broadly still, the legal academy's search for an external foundation for law has made it parasitic on whatever happened to be highly regarded in the general culture at the time. In the late 1950s and early 1960s, for example, there was a flurry of interest in psychology and psychoanalysis, which has left no trace in current legal scholarship. Four prominent economists who addressed legal issues—George Stigler, James Buchanan, Ronald Coase, and Gary Becker—received the Nobel Memorial Prize in Economic Science. This validation of their work—and, by inference, the work of their disciples in law schools—has bolstered the position of law-and-economics in the law schools, even though Stigler and Coase in particular have expressed some skepticism about how legal academics have used economics.

## The Future

During the 1980s it seemed as if law-and-economics might become the law of the future. Now it seems likely to play a smaller role.

The growth of law-and-economics reached its limit primarily for the reasons that made it important in the first place. At the start, law-and-economics offered a simple, reductionist analysis of law and a vision of the good society. Its simplicity promised to solve the intellectual problems of explaining how and why lawyers and judges exercised power. But the simplicity could not be sustained.

Outside the legal academy, Judges Posner and Easterbrook were among only a few judges with some sophistication about economics and law. Their colleagues are, by and large, much more ordinary lawyers, educated in an era when the language of economics was rarely used in law schools. As practicing lawyers, they developed "practical" approaches to legal issues. These judges believe that the world with which law deals is much more complicated than the one depicted by law-and-economics. Observing people who come before them in criminal cases and imposing sentences, they know that the cost-benefit calculations that economists use to model the idea that criminal law is a deterrent are only part of the phenomenon of criminal behavior.

Judges, then, may sometimes use economic metaphors, but on the whole they believe that the traditional language of law captures life's complexity more accurately than the simplifications of law-and-economics. Thus, the occasional judicial forays into law-and-economics are vastly outnumbered by more traditional legal analyses. Outside the legal academy, law-and-economics has been contained by what most practicing lawyers see as the world's complexity.

Law-and-economics might break those bonds if it could become sufficiently complex. Indeed, disciplinary pressures push in that direction. After the simple models have been developed, the only way to advance is to

**The Law-and-Economics Movement**

introduce new variables and greater complexity. What results, however, are increasingly technical articles, which noneconomists find difficult to assimilate into their vision of law. Lawyers could appropriate the simple versions of law-and-economics; they cannot deal well with the more complicated ones that characterize leading work in the field today.

The simple models had another advantage. They generated clear policy recommendations: requiring landlords to maintain their premises was a bad idea because landlords would simply raise the rent and reduce the supply of affordable low-income housing; minimum-wage laws were a bad idea because they reduced employment opportunities for low-skilled, entry-level workers, ordinarily teenagers in inner cities.

More complicated models have more ambiguous policy implications. They may identify situations in which landlords will not be able to raise the rents or employment markets in which minimum-wage laws do not disadvantage entry-level workers. And then the policy recommendations are inextricably intertwined with ambiguous empirical questions: are the markets providing employment opportunities to inner-city teenagers ones where minimum-wage laws really do work?

Simple law-and-economics models were vulnerable in other ways. Everyone conceded from the outset that law-and-economics' normative claims about efficiency had to be separated from questions about distribution of wealth, because, on the technical level, exchanges between people produce efficient outcomes only with respect to the distribution of wealth already in place. If there were a different distribution of wealth, there would be a different set of efficient policies.

Posner attempted to meet this objection by providing a different basis for the normative claims: instead of trying to maximize utility, which he conceded could not provide a sensible guide to policy, we could, Posner argued, try to maximize wealth measured in monetary terms. Virtually no one found this satisfactory, because it made the relation between distribution of wealth and the normative claims both apparent and decidedly unattractive: Why on earth should we find a world in which the wealthy were exceedingly wealthy and the poor grindingly poor more attractive than one in which there was less wealth overall but where the wealthy were merely quite well-to-do and the poor were only moderately poor?

Critics of law-and-economics developed other technical objections. Perhaps the most interesting is the "offer-asking" problem. The simple models depended on claims that voluntary trades between people made both sides better off (otherwise, why would they have traded?). It turns out, though, that whether a trade occurs depends on who is entitled to what in the first place. If I have a nice house, I will rarely sell it for what I would be willing to offer on an equivalent house: I will ask for more than I would offer, simply because I have the house at the start of bargaining.

Economists have tried to minimize the offer-asking problem, saying that it arises only in special situations (primarily, where the asset—like the house—is a significant part of a person's wealth), but casual observation suggests that the difficulty is more pervasive. Probably the most effective example critics have developed involves sexual harassment in the workplace: If the law gives women the right to be free of sexual harassment, they ordinarily will demand much more extra pay to waive that right than they would be willing to give up if they had to purchase the "right" from their employers.

The offer-asking problem is only one among several difficulties that arise in trying to work out the notion that voluntary trades are efficient. But, even if that idea could be worked out, other criticisms are more fundamental. Feminists and others drawing on postmodernist thought have raised questions about the coherence of the idea of "voluntary" action itself. Finding that many women described their choices—to remain in abusive households, to participate in producing pornography—as voluntary when the choices seemed quite constrained, they pointed out that people always made "choices" in social settings that themselves helped define what was a voluntary choice and what a coerced or constrained one.

A worker might "choose" to get a little more pay for working with hazardous chemicals, but it became hard to see that choice as truly voluntary unless it was really possible for the workers to find another job for less pay in a safer workplace.

Historical experience showed that at one time people accepted some working conditions as "natural," not places about which real choices could be made, and therefore "chose" to work under those conditions without raising questions about pay. Yet at other times people treated the same working conditions as changeable and therefore demanded more pay for riskier work.

## Feminist Legal Theory

For feminists and postmodernists, what was a voluntary choice, a free exchange, was actually a socially constructed, historically contingent fact. Law-and-economics could offer no leverage on the problems it purported to address once that understanding spread through the legal academy.

The feminist movement had another effect. Within the legal academy and outside it, feminism provided an increasingly strong liberal counterweight to the conservative politics of law-and-economics. Law-and-economics had gotten its start by filling a vacuum in liberal legal theory created by legal realism. In the 1970s a group of male legal academics, adopting the name "Critical Legal Studies," revitalized the skeptical strands of legal realism and offered a leftist alternative in which law was seen as a complex reflection of politics and culture. Although critical legal studies has influenced mainstream legal thinking, its political perspective was unacceptable, and its insistence on the legal realist insights obviously failed to satisfy the mainstream's demand for an alternative to legal realism.

Leading elements of the legal academy have been associated with the center-left since the late 1940s, in part because of the long-term dominance of the New Deal coalition in American politics, in part because conservatives believed that working in the private sector was more socially valuable than working in the academy, and in part because conservatives who went into the academy gave up more, financially, than liberals who did the same. The mainstream needed a left/liberal alternative to law-and-economics that addressed legal realism's concerns.

For some in the mainstream, some versions of feminism provided that alternative. The first generation of feminist legal theorists sought to extend the principles of liberal equality to encompass women's concerns. They insisted that principles of justice could fill the gaps that legal realism found in law, and their political program was compatible with center-liberal desires. More recent developments in feminist legal theory, which fit together with postmodernist versions of multiculturalism, are less acceptable to the mainstream. But, because postmodernist feminists manage to retain their connection to liberal feminism on many issues, the mainstream in the legal academy continues to see feminism as an alternative to law-and-economics. In some versions, feminism still promises to be more comfortable to the centrists who control the legal academy than do law-and-economics or critical legal studies.

Law-and-economics became more diffuse, its policy implications more ambiguous and more easily assimilable to the centrist inclinations of the legal academy, and it became more isolated as a sub-discipline with an agenda of decreasing interest to those outside the sub-discipline. Once an intellectual force that threatened to disrupt the centrist commitments of the legal academy, it has become tamed, normalized, and compartmentalized within the academy. Its grip outside the academy was always weaker, and with the accession of a Democratic administration the hold of law-and-economics seems likely to weaken further.

In the next decade law-and-economics seems likely to continue to be one of the languages that lawyers and policy-makers speak. For a moment it seemed possible that it would become the leading dialect, dominating the conversation of law; now it seems likely to be only a specialized discourse, to be used or abandoned as seems helpful. In some ways that is a sad commentary on the life of an intellectual movement. □

# [10]
# Law, Science, and Law and Economics

Those familiar with my legal scholarship might expect me to denounce the "law" part of law and economics as right-wing ideological trash. Now, of course there is some right-wing ideological trash in law and economics.[1] But I doubt that the equilibrium level of right-wing ideological trash in law and economics is much different from the level of left-wing or centrist ideological trash: we all have our albatrosses to bear.[2]

Assume that what we are after is some more-or-less general way of understanding what happens in the law that has more generality than the flat statement of black letter rules.[3] It is clear that law and economics offers some people a way of gaining that understanding.

Where law and economics goes wrong, when it does go wrong (which is not to say that it always or even often does), is in claiming to be more than a general way of understanding. So, for example, it goes wrong when its proponents claim that it offers a privileged—in particular, a scientific—take on the law. The claim of privilege is something like this: Economics offers the best way for any reasonable person to get a general understanding of the law.

The reason people sometimes go wrong here is, I think, not hard to see. Proponents of law and economics offer the market as the model for thinking about law. And the difficulty, to put it as a provocation, is that there is no such thing as "the market."

---

1. Out of politeness, I refrain from including specific references.

2. I have toyed with the thought that the level of ideological trash is higher for centrist than for right- or left-wing work, but have concluded, at least for the moment, that the difference is not in the level but in the content: centrist ideological trash is vacuous, whereas its competitors are not.

3. By *understanding*, I mean both explanation and prediction, if one thinks those are different.

Or, to put it less provocatively but more accurately, there are actually two sets of things called "the market."

The first set encompasses all the real markets in the world. These markets are historically constituted and consist of a complex blend of practices, including a fair amount of what is called government regulation and a fair amount of what is called individual choice. And in these real, historically constituted markets, the choices individuals make are themselves historically constituted as well, in the sense that we can offer accounts of why people come to make the choices they do.

One way to think about what happens when we see real markets as historically constituted is to think about how we can understand the effects of some legal intervention—some change in the rules, either the general background rules or some more particular regulatory rule. Of course we can say things like this: "A legal intervention that increases the cost of some course of action is likely to decrease the incidence of that action."[4] But in real, historically constituted markets, there are, as we might say, a large number of margins on which legal interventions work. And whether the intervention will actually decrease the incidence of the action depends on how the intervention works on every real margin. Perhaps the more the margins are purely economic, the better the economic account. But even purely economic matters have some cultural margins.

Consider two examples, one large-scale and the other small-scale. Countries in Central and Eastern Europe are introducing different forms of privatization of property. Suppose we identified one marginal difference between the form of private

4. Professor BeVier offers a "catalogue of human frailty" along these lines. Lillian R. BeVier, *Law, Economics, and the Power of the State*, 21 HARV. J.L. & PUB. POL'Y 5 (1997). I wonder, however, how much analytic bite that catalogue has. In the Nineteenth Century, before the rise of neoclassical economics, judges appreciated the existence of scarcity. I believe that the work even of such a judge as William J. Brennan contains an awareness of the consequences of scarcity and of the fact that rules developed *ex post* create incentives for future action. Consider, for example, the proposition that Justice Brennan's opinion in *Goldberg v. Kelly*, 397 U.S. 254 (1970), rested on a hypothesis about the political dynamics of a rule increasing the costs of depriving people of public assistance—that such a rule would induce bureaucrats and legislators to increase appropriations for public assistance rather than keep appropriations at the same level and decrease the benefits to individuals. That hypothesis might be wrong, but it does not fail to demonstrate awareness of the "catalogue of human frailties." In general, if law and economics is said only to contribute an awareness of such a catalogue to legal decision-makers, judges and legislators have been doing law and economics all the time.

ownership of apartments in Hungary and Slovakia. Someone who knows law and economics will be able to tell us: "In light of this difference, there is going to be a tendency for apartments to be transferred from their present occupants more quickly in Hungary." But someone who knows the politics and cultures of the two countries may be able to tell us that the tendency is going to be quite weak, and that in fact, given the cultures and so on, we might observe quicker transfers in Slovakia. This does not mean that the law-and-conomics take on the issue is wrong, but only that there are other margins whose effects might be greater than the one law and economics helps us identify.

Second, a recent study concludes that counties that require their sheriffs to issue permits to carry concealed weapons have lower rates of murder, rape, and assault—and higher rates of burglary—than counties that do not have these "must issue" laws.[5] A law-and-economics perspective helps explain why: If you are a potential criminal trying to decide what to do, you are going to be more reluctant—on the margin—to confront someone who might have a concealed weapon, and the "must issue" laws increase your uncertainty about whether your potential target is such a person. This result makes sense to me, but it turns out that the result apparently depends quite strongly on results from a single state, Florida. If you take Florida out of the statistics, the results on some of the crimes simply disappear. So, to understand the effects of the "must carry" laws, we probably need to consult someone who knows something about the culture of Florida and the other states studied. Again, the law-and-economics perspective increases our understanding but does not provide the whole story.

I seriously doubt that law and economics gives all of us privileged access to general knowledge about how these interventions work on every margin. I want to be clear that my claim is fairly modest here. It is only that for at least some people there are better ways of understanding how a legal intervention works than the ways law and economics offers. So, for example, some people may get a better understanding of how the intervention works by reading deeply in classic works of

5. John D. Lott & D.B. Mustard, *Crime, Deterrence, and Right-to-Carry Concealed Handguns*, 26 J. LEG. STUD. 1 (1997).

literature, which for them illuminate more of the margins than economics does. Others, of course, may find these works quite barren, and may get a better understanding through the economic way of thinking. For them, the market metaphor illuminates. But it is only a metaphor, with no greater status than other metaphors that illuminate better for other people. So, for example, if you are teaching a class about the legal implications of cloning human beings, you probably will reach more students more quickly by telling them to spend a couple of hours seeing the film *Bladerunner* than by telling them to spend the same amount of time reading Richard Posner.[6]

My guess, unsupported by any evidence other than a sense of the legal academy, is that people sort themselves out pretty well. That is, people who are likely to understand more by thinking in law-and-economics terms tend to gravitate toward law and economics, and people who are likely to understand more by thinking in law-and-literature terms tend to gravitate toward law and literature. If that's right, the only issues are questions of what I would call institutional imperialism or, from the other side, institutional tolerance. If, as I think, neither law and economics nor law and literature, nor anything else, offers privileged access to general ways of understanding the law, it is hard for me to see any ground on which to rest the claim that one or another way of arriving at understanding is generically preferable.[7]

The claim for privileged access for law and economics frequently takes a form that deserves special attention. I am going to unpack it in a particular way, which I think captures the central tendencies in the form. It starts with an assumption about the enterprise with which we began, the effort to come up with some general understanding of the law. The assumption is that the best, or in some versions the only, way of acquiring a reliable general understanding is through science, and that economics is a progressive science in a way that its competitors are not. The inference we are invited to draw is that no matter

6. This would be true even if the assignment were to read an article by Richard Posner on the legal implications of cloning human beings, which I am sure would exist by the time you had to make the assignment.

7. Of course, there are obvious economic, institutional, and personal reasons for deploying the rhetoric of privileged access, but they have no particular intellectual status.

what we might say about the *current* relative position of law and economics and its competitors in generating general insights about the law, in the long run law and economics will produce more or deeper insights than its competitors.

A couple of preliminary points here. First, the notion that science on the model of physics is necessarily the best way of acquiring a general understanding about law seems to me insupportable in light of what serious philosophers of the social sciences have had to say about understanding human behavior. It is not at all clear to them that knowledge about human behavior is actually gained on the model of knowledge about the physical sciences.

Second, even if the claim about reliable knowledge in the long run is true, I doubt that it has much to say about how any person ought to invest his or her time. Because we all live in the short run, retooling is likely to be the wrong investment in any particular person's human capital if the payoff comes only in the long run.[8]

Even if the physical sciences provide the right model, however, we still have to ask how close the analogy is. Law-and-economics literature has an interesting rhetorical trope in connection with the claim of scientific status: the citation of Nobel Prize winners in economics. To see the limits of the scientific analogy on which this trope trades, we need to turn to the second set of markets mentioned earlier. This set actually has only one member: the market as constructed in the mathematically precise formulations of rigorous economic theorizing. Now, *this* market really is subject to scientific analysis, through the mathematical manipulations that real economists do, and awarding Nobel Prizes for work dealing with mathematical markets may make sense.[9]

8. If true, it might have some bearing on institutional planning, decisions about whom to hire and the like.

9. Some points deserve making. (1) I doubt that the claims of science would seem quite as strong if the prize were called the Federal Reserve Bank Prize in Economic Science in Memory of Andrew Carnegie. But the real name of the prize is this: the Bank of Sweden Prize in Economic Science in Memory of Alfred Nobel. (2) In the early years of the prize it was evident that those awarding it were acutely sensitive to political considerations. So, for example, the co-winners in 1974 were Friedrich von Hayek, in political terms a libertarian, and Gunnar Myrdal, a socialist, and in 1975 they were Tjalling Koopmans, a mainstream Western economist, and Leonid Kantorovich, an economist from the then-Soviet Union. I doubt that there is much reason to think that

The problem, however, is this: serious people who have studied the philosophy of modern economics seem to agree that the mathematical market appears to have only the loosest connection to real, historically constituted markets. So, asserting that what happens in real markets follows from what happens in the mathematical market has no scientific warrant. Again, I do not want to overstate here. Sometimes people will get insights into what happens in real markets from looking at what happens in the mathematical market. But, then, some people get insights like that from going to a museum and looking at paintings by Watteau or James Rosenquist.[10]

To conclude, I am a tolerant sort. To put it rather pompously, since the Enlightenment there has been a long conversation about the relationship between science and freedom. Modern law and economics is one contribution to that conversation. There is, I think, no reason to believe that that contribution has brought an end to what that conversation can add to human understanding or that it has definitively resolved questions about the relationship between science and freedom. If law and economics is the church at which you worship, I am hardly going to tell you to stop. But I doubt that there is much reason for people who are not turned on by it to try to learn the catechism.

---

the awarders have lost all political sensitivity since then; rather, the political environment in which they operate has changed. (3) There have been some notable mistakes in awarding the prizes in the real sciences, most dramatically the 1949 award in physiology or medicine to the inventor of the frontal lobotomy as a treatment for mental disorder. We are not so far away from the award of many of the economics prizes to be sure that some of them are not clunkers either. (4) People who win prizes for one accomplishment sometimes do not have much to say beyond their particular accomplishments. Here the most recent example is Kary Mullis, who had one great idea about DNA for which he deservedly won the prize and is otherwise a complete loon, even on matters related to DNA. So too, perhaps, for some of the economics winners when they say things outside the domain of their specialization.

10. When we reach levels of real detail, as in Jonathan Macey's suggestion, raised at The Sixteenth Annual National Student Federalist Society Symposium on Law & Public Policy (1997), that law and economics might offer more guidance than law and literature, or art, on the question of whether we should set a ten- or seventeen-day disclosure period for stick acquisitions, I am truly agnostic. I suspect that economic studies will provide a great deal of inconclusive empirical data, and that in the end, someone will have to make a judgment about what is likely to work better. And perhaps a judgment by someone informed by serious study of art or literature will be just as good as, or better than, the judgment of someone who has studied only economics.

# [11]

# 'Everything Old is New Again': Early Reflections on the 'New Chicago School'

Marc Galanter observed that the legal profession's transformation over the past few decades was both signaled and assisted by the rise of legal newspapers such as the *American Lawyer* and the *Legal Times*.[1] The announcement in the pages of the *New Yorker* of a "new" legal "movement" seeking to compare the influence of law and social norms on people's behavior may be an early hint of a similar transformation of the legal academy.[2] At least it introduces the new Chicago school to an audience unaccustomed to reading law reviews. In turn, I take this opportunity, in response to an invitation from the *Wisconsin Law Review*, to raise some questions about the new Chicago school for a more typical law review readership, albeit one likely to be more attuned to traditional law and society studies than are readers of the *University of Chicago Law Review*.

This "new" school's attention appears to focus on the relation between norms and law, a familiar topic in law and society studies. So, for example, the legal anthropologist Paul Bohannon drew on his field research to identify the "double institutionalization of norms," the process by which values are first institutionalized as social norms, and then institutionalized again as law.[3] This appears to be closely related to one concern in the new Chicago school's work. But, rather than engage in dialogue with law and society studies, the leading works in the new Chicago school primarily engage the old Chicago school of law and economics, at least in the sense that they take the theoretical constructs of

---

I would like to thank Naomi Mezey and David Weisbach for their comments on a draft of this Essay. Reactions by Dan Kahan and Lawrence Lessig led me to tone down the draft of this contribution, but I fear that I may still be demonstrating some tone-deafness.

1. *See* MARC GALANTER & THOMAS PALAY, TOURNAMENT OF LAWYERS 71 (1991).

2. Jeffrey Rosen, *The Social Police*, NEW YORKER, Oct. 20 & 27, 1997, at 170, 172.

3. Paul Bohannon, *The Differing Realms of the Law*, *in* LAW AND WARFARE: STUDIES IN THE ANTHROPOLOGY OF CONFLICT 43, 45-50 (Paul Bohannon ed., 1967).

economics—the rational but constrained decisionmaker, for example—more seriously than they do the theoretical constructs of sociology or anthropology.[4] As I will suggest, the work produced by the new Chicago school would profit intellectually by turning its attention to the law and society tradition associated with Marx, Durkheim, and Weber. But then it would seem rather less new than the *New Yorker* article suggests.[5]

Of course the *New Yorker*'s report may reflect only the exuberance of youth, both the youthful reporter and the academics on whom he was reporting. Sometimes, too, people are induced to say foolish things by the prospect of having their words reported. And sometimes proponents of the new Chicago school present themselves in an ironic self-distancing way,[6] modulating their claims for novelty to reflect an implicit understanding that things that might be new at the University of Chicago Law School might not be quite as new elsewhere, even elsewhere in Hyde Park.[7]

Clearly, however, something is going on in some precincts of the legal academy, primarily the precincts inhabited by those whose universe of theoretical concepts was initially populated by strong adherents of the law and economics vision. One can speculate on the reasons for this development. There seems to be general agreement that the form of law and economics studies propelling the field's development over the past generation has become sterile, or at least that those working in that form are straight-forwardly applying an existing paradigm to new areas in ways

4. The new Chicago school maintains certain links to the old Chicago school for reasons suggested *infra*, which is why I insist on characterizing the new Chicago school as developing an approach to the study of norms that is derived from law and economics.

5. I feel justified in treating work that might seem to a detached observer rather disparate as part of a single school because, after all, that is what the producers of that work claim. *See* Rosen, *supra* note 2, at 174 (quoting Lawrence Lessig's statement that he was outlining a research program for "the New Chicago School").

6. *Compare id.* (quoting Lawrence Lessig's characterization of his program as "playful[]"), *with* Dan Kahan, *Between Economics and Sociology: The New Path of Deterrence*, 95 MICH. L. REV. 2477, 2478 n.5 (1997) ("The emergence of interest in social norms within the legal academy can be traced to Ellickson."). For a more restrained statement, see Randal C. Picker, *Simple Games in a Complex World: A Generative Approach to the Adoption of Norms*, 64 U. CHI. L. REV. 1225, 1286 (1997) ("The recent interest in norms and law almost certainly dates from Bob Ellickson's important work on Shasta County."), although even this fails to note that the interest is recent only among a certain community.

7. The University of Chicago was, after all, the site at which an earlier Chicago School—of sociology—developed, and paid attention to the norms associated with urban life.

that no longer yield dramatic or interesting insights.[8] A recent symposium on law and economics repeatedly refers to the field's "cloudy future."[9] Ambitious younger scholars, of whom there is rarely an undersupply, have obvious incentives to discover some novel approach. In general, however, the legal academy's reward structure requires that novel approaches be ones that the younger scholars' elders can appreciate as continuing a tradition with which the elders are associated.[10]

The new Chicago school can be understood, I think, in these terms. Put most generally, the new Chicago school appears to have two components. The first directs attention to the ways in which (1) non-legal norms sometimes substitute for legal ones, as when a social system uses sanctions like disapproval to induce people to act as the system wants them to, and (2) the legal system can incorporate or rely on non-legal norms, for example by developing methods of encouraging people to employ such sanctions. In old Chicago school terms, the first component of the new Chicago school is interested in non-material incentives for compliance with legal rules. The second component involves efforts to provide an account based in rational choice considerations of how non-legal norms take root among people.

In what follows I offer some preliminary comments on these components. The new Chicago school is at its earliest stages, and I do not want to be taken as arguing that the research program it proposes is

---

8. The generous formulation of this is the assertion that the field of law and economics has matured, requiring its practitioners to work with more complex models than were prevalent in the field's early stages. And yet, precisely because the models have become more complex, their marginal contribution to understanding law, relative to the contributions available from alternative methods of inquiry, has sharply decreased. (I am unqualified to assess the marginal contributions of these more complex models to economics.)

9. Symposium, *The Future of Law and Economics: Looking Forward*, 64 U. CHI. L. REV. 1129, 1129-1224 (1997); *see, e.g.*, Richard A. Epstein, *Law and Economics: Its Glorious Past and Cloudy Future*, 64 U. CHI. L. REV. 1167, 1167 (1997).

10. The most obvious exception to this generalization is that a young person who is understood to be really, really smart can strike out on a truly novel course. My candidates for that role are Richard Posner with law and economics and Duncan Kennedy for critical legal studies. In both cases, however, the exceptional quality is qualified: Posner began in the academic heartland of antitrust law, where economics was obviously relevant, and Kennedy's project could be understood as an extension of the project of American legal realism, with which some elders in the academy were still associated when he began his work. The cases of feminist legal theory and critical race theory are more complicated. My account of the first would begin with the observation that "equality" feminists articulated theories that made sense to established liberal male law professors; my account of the second, with the argument that the existence in the academy of those scholars sympathetic to critical legal studies was a precondition to the firm establishment of critical race theory.

not worth pursuing, even though I mostly raise questions about the depth of the insights provided by its work so far. People who have found traditional law and economics a dead end think there is something to be learned by going down this new path, and they may end up being right. But at least so far there are reasons to think that there are better ways to study norms than to force them into a mold derived from a law and economics approach, or at least that there are literatures other than law and economics with which a dialogue on the level of theory would be productive.[11]

The new Chicago school's first component, dealing with non-material incentives, is consistent with the old Chicago school's economic paradigm in which people seek to maximize their satisfaction, whatever the sources of satisfaction happen to be for them. For expository convenience and sometimes for reasons associated with the desire to manipulate mathematical formulas, economists may describe the sources of satisfaction as solely material. They may, for example, measure satisfaction by examining income or wealth. But the approval of one's peers may be a source of satisfaction to which the economists' paradigm would of course give the same analytic treatment as it would to income when *it* is a source of satisfaction.

Two points deserve notice about what is novel about non-material incentives in the law and economics approach, or in the new Chicago school. Consider first social disapproval as an incentive. Plainly, a person will respond appropriately, from the new Chicago school's point of view, to such disapproval only if he believes that he will suffer—that his satisfaction will decrease—as a result of such disapproval. He may not have to believe that his actual behavior warrants disapproval, but he must believe that those who do disapprove of it can in fact decrease his satisfaction. This is quite familiar to sociologists. The disapprovers must be a "reference group" for the actor. The fact that early in the protests against the war in Vietnam the *New York Times* expressed disapproval of draft resistance hardly mattered to draft protestors who saw the editorialists as part of the elite against whom they were protesting. The new Chicago school appears to have rediscovered the idea of reference groups and re-labeled it "social meaning." The interesting question, of course, is how people come to see other people either as a reference

11. Some of the initial new Chicago school works do delve into the sociological and anthropological literature, but, it seems to me, more to rummage around for examples to support theoretical constructs developed independently than to confront the theoretical claims made in that literature. For a parallel comment drawn from another field, see Lawrence Stone, *The Revival of Narrative: Reflections on a New Old History*, 85 PAST & PRESENT 3, 6 (1979), describing Michel Foucault's work as "works . . . of moral philosophy with examples drawn from history."

group whose disapproval matters to them, as irrelevant to their satisfaction, or as something sociologists call a negative reference group, that is, a group whose disapproval actually *increases* a person's satisfaction. Some classics in sociology and cultural studies deal with *this* question.[12]

Consider an example commonly offered to explain the attractions of the new Chicago school's approach. In the early nineteenth century lawmakers wanted to discourage dueling. They first simply outlawed it. But dueling satisfied the interests of a segment of the population that sought to maintain its honor. Dueling promoted honor, and the people who engaged in dueling did not believe that being charged with criminal activity for doing so impaired a person's honor. Put in the terms I have been using, the people who disapproved of dueling, and therefore thought being charged *dis*honorable, were not a relevant reference group for the people who did duel. Lawmakers then adopted another strategy, which turned out to be successful: they barred people who engaged in dueling from public office. This worked because holding public office was a badge of honor to the very people who engaged in dueling.

This analysis is quite ingenious and produced novel insights. But surely it operates only slightly below the surface of the phenomena of dueling and honor. What we need to know, I would think, is why the concept of honor was constructed in ways that made both dueling and holding public office badges of honor.[13] Distinguished historians have examined the Southern culture of honor in ways which would illuminate

---

12. *See, e.g.*, DICK HEBDIGE, SUBCULTURE: THE MEANING OF STYLE (1979); WILLIAM FOOTE WHYTE, STREET CORNER SOCIETY: THE SOCIAL STRUCTURE OF AN ITALIAN SLUM (2d ed. 1955). A comment by Martin S. Flaherty, *Relearning Founding Lessons: The Removal Power and Joint Accountability*, 47 CASE W. RES. L. REV. 1563 (1997), suggests one source of legal academics' claims for novelty as they explore and appropriate material from other disciplines:

> Typically, a graduate student of history will spend years taking courses to acquire both research skills and a general background, mastering the secondary literature in a chosen speciality, and then pouring over archival and other primary source materials—all for a topic that can be as narrow as a single specific event. By contrast, a lawyer, judge, even a law professor will, at most, commonly spend a few weeks constructing a historical account, and then usually proceed directly to certain readily available sources (or their indices) with little or no effort to set the evidence in any context.

*Id.* at 1573.

13. And, perhaps, why the relevant community's response to being barred from public office for dueling was to abandon dueling rather than to abandon public office (on the theory, perhaps, that holding public office was hardly a badge of honor in a society so dominated by lower-class sorts as to elect legislators who outlawed dueling).

the new Chicago school's analysis,[14] but which go unaddressed; indeed, as far as I have been able to determine through a computer search, they go uncited in new Chicago school articles.[15]

More destabilizing possibilities open up once the question of social meaning is on the table. The new Chicago school incorporates non-material incentives as a supplement to the standard treatment of material incentives such as fines or the deprivation of liberty through imprisonment, which is generally thought to reduce one's ability to secure material rewards from one's activities. But once we understand that non-material incentives work only because they have a social meaning to the actor and her reference group, we have to begin thinking about the ways in which *material* incentives are meaningful only because of social meaning as well.[16] Material incentives, that is, are embedded in a particular culture. Consider here what one would have to do to affect the behavior of certain religious ascetics. Fining them for socially disapproved behavior is unlikely to have much impact, because their utility functions, so to speak, place a value of zero on material well-being.[17]

This branch of the new Chicago school can lead to some interesting questions: how do people go about identifying their reference groups, and how does a culture of materialism become important to enough people that a legal system can assume that people typically respond to material incentives? However, those inquiries call for a kind of cultural investigation that seems foreign to the new Chicago school, and that would surely be better conducted through engagement with sociological and anthropological studies and theory. The emerging literature associated with the new Chicago school seems to be looking in the wrong direction, or at least at the wrong literature, for answers. My guess is that older traditions in sociology and anthropology—Marx, Weber,

---

14. *See* BERTRAM WYATT-BROWN, SOUTHERN HONOR: ETHICS AND BEHAVIOR IN THE OLD SOUTH (1982); Kenneth S. Greenberg, *The Nose, the Lie, and the Duel in the Antebellum South*, 95 AM. HIST. REV. 57 (1990).

15. A WESTLAW search in the JLR database on April 9, 1998, located 24 citations to Wyatt-Brown and four to Greenberg, none in articles by authors associated with the new Chicago school. In contrast, it located six citations in the new Chicago school literature to Warren F. Schwartz et al., *The Duel: Can These Gentlemen Be Acting Efficiently?*, 13 J. LEGAL STUD. 321 (1984), written by a law and economics law professor and his students.

16. There are hints of this point in the observation that sometimes, as the experience of imprisonment becomes widespread within a social group, the loss of liberty may become understood as a source of non-material satisfaction, a badge of honor, that offsets the material losses associated with imprisonment.

17. Attempting to shame them is unlikely to work either, because the sources of disapproval are not among their reference groups.

Durkheim—have more to say about the questions that seem worth exploring than the old Chicago school does.[18] I would guess as well that there are a slew of really good novels that provide more insight into those questions than the literature that has become associated with the new Chicago school.

Drawing on such sources would obviously not satisfy the scientistic urges prevalent at the University of Chicago's law school.[19] Those urges drive the second main strand of the new Chicago school as well. This strand is a direct descendant of traditional law and economics because it proposes to provide accounts of the development and entrenchment of norms in rational choice terms. That is, having identified a norm that does not on its face seem to advance the narrowly defined self-interest of those who adhere to it, the new Chicago school proposes to explain how such a norm might emerge and become widespread among people who individually seek to advance their self-interest narrowly defined.

Doing things that give you a deserved reputation for fair dealing, for example, allows people to engage in transactions with you without worrying about whether you will adopt fair interpretations of ambiguous contract terms, and therefore allows contracts to be concluded and performed without adding on expensive mechanisms for monitoring your behavior. Adhering to the norm of fair behavior as defined by the relevant community, then, is in everyone's interest, because it creates a situation in which a larger number of productive contracts can be entered into.

Or so it might seem. Jon Elster, who is clearly sympathetic to rational-choice accounts, has identified a real difficulty with this sort of account. I simplify Elster's exposition without, I hope, losing its sophistication. Suppose I see two potential contracting partners, each of whom has a deserved reputation for fair dealing based on their prior behavior. One of them is *strategically* fair, in the sense that she has figured out that developing a reputation for fair dealing is in her long-term self-interest for the reasons I have suggested. When dealing with a person who has become fair for strategic reasons, I still have to worry that she may not be fair in dealing with *me*. After all, I know from the fact that she is strategically fair that she is a rational calculator, and I have to worry that she will calculate that screwing me in this transaction

18. Pierre Bourdieu does appear in Lawrence Lessig's work. But Bourdieu stands at the (present) end of a longer tradition, and I doubt that his work can be appropriated effectively without engaging with the tradition from which it emerges.

19. *But see* DONALD BLACK, THE BEHAVIOR OF LAW (1976); JACK D. DOUGLAS, THE SOCIAL MEANINGS OF SUICIDE (1967), for appropriately scientific works in the Durkheimian tradition.

will maximize her overall well-being: behaving unfairly may not hurt her reputation much,[20] or—the same point put differently—the large gains from screwing me may be worth the effects on her long-term prospects.

I want to deal with a person who is non-strategically or *sincerely* fair. But the rational choice account runs into two problems at this point. The less important is that I have no way of distinguishing between the strategically and the sincerely fair potential partner, and I therefore (rationally) have to make my choice based on some calculation of the prevalence of strategically and sincerely fair people. This is a classic market for lemons,[21] and it is not going to be one in which the norm of fair dealing is robust. The second problem is more interesting. How can someone rationally set about to become sincerely fair? Elster strongly suggests that it cannot be done. Sincere fairness is a character trait that in Elster's terms may well be a state that is essentially a by-product of *other* conduct, not rationally directed at becoming sincerely fair.[22]

Beyond all this there is a far more serious problem. As any purportedly scientific enterprise, the new Chicago school offers simplified models of norms and their operation, often with "just so" stories that assertedly explain in rational choice terms why norms operate as they do. The problem with this is that norms are really complicated things. Indeed, they are hardly "things" at all. They are unstable, subject to constant renegotiation and redefinition through processes of interaction that lead the new Chicago school to develop models. But modeling requires abstraction, and abstracting from norms is quite likely to generate either models that have essentially nothing to do with the real world of norms, or entirely formal results. Moreover, to the extent that one is interested in real norms in the real world, one would have to do a fair amount of empirical investigation. Aficionados of law and society studies know that legal academics are not well-trained to do such research and, even more, that the legal academy's reward structure actively discourages it.[23] This may account for the fact, as it seems to me, that articles associated with the new Chicago school have a rather high ratio of

---

20. Maybe I don't have such a great reputation in the relevant community, and people won't care much that I have been screwed.

21. *See* GEORGE AKERLOF, AN ECONOMIC THEORIST'S BOOK OF TALES 7 (1984).

22. *See* JON ELSTER, SOUR GRAPES: STUDIES IN THE SUBVERSION OF RATIONALITY ch. 2 (1983).

23. The standard time-to-tenure in law school is shorter than the time needed to design and complete a serious empirical investigation, which means that to the extent that legal academics are drawn to empirical research, they are channeled into producing a quick-and-dirty piece of research early in their careers. This induces sloppy research habits that persist even after tenure (I refer here to tendencies, of course, not to a universal phenomenon).

programmatic statements and illustrative (and short) anecdotes to actual investigations of real norms in real social settings.[24]

My favorite example here is the work of Randal Picker, who has generated some really pretty pictures, which I urge all readers to look at.[25] Picker develops models in which people look around and see how their neighbors are behaving. Based on what they learn, they calculate what they ought to do to maximize their personal returns. For Picker, norms are what a good chunk of a person's neighbors do. Picker's models show how the norm shared by a bunch of people might spread to other people who do not initially share it.

Picker is appropriately modest about his results.[26] For example, he notes that they rest on the assumption that people "do not contest the choice of norm," and that he has no "baseline of change, either through replacement of players or spontaneous mutation or experimentation."[27] But Picker's analysis provides an appropriate transition to my final observations about the new Chicago school. As law professors, the members of the new Chicago school are driven to derive policy prescriptions from their social analysis. And, according to the *New Yorker*, when they do, some observers begin to worry about totalitarianism. Why?

Consider the policy instruments available to someone who has taken the new Chicago school's lessons to heart. The policymaker can attempt to point out to the target population that its *existing* reference groups actually disapprove of the population's behavior; or the policy maker can attempt to *change* the population's reference groups.[28] Alternatively, the policy maker can try to improve the information-processing capacities of the population, so that the population actually gets its calculations of self-interest right, which the policy maker hopes will lead the population to act as the policy maker wants.

Social meaning, I have argued, is essentially a question of culture, and there are many reasons to think that culture is rather resistant to

---

24. New intellectual movements often produce programmatic statements, but my sense is that there is usually a somewhat thicker base of substantive studies for such statements that we have as yet from the new Chicago school.

25. The printed version is Picker, *supra* note 6, but to see the pictures in their full glory you have to visit Picker's Web site. *See* Randal C. Picker, *Home Page for Randal C. Picker:Norms* <http://www.law.uchicago.edu/Picker/AWorkingPapers/norms.html>.

26. He points out, for example, that all he has done is articulate with respect to norms what evolutionary biologists have done with their models of competition between species.

27. Picker, *supra* note 6, at 1287.

28. Picker calls these strategies of attempting to manipulate "the information available to the players" and "the scope of local connectedness (my payoff neighborhoods)," respectively. *Id.* at 1286.

conscious manipulation, particularly by law. *Resistance* does not mean *intractability*, of course, but at least to the extent that lawyers have an interest in developing policies that affect culture, we ought to worry about what exactly we can accomplish: how much change in culture is likely to result from an incremental change in law? And, for obvious reasons, lawyers have an interest in exaggerating the amount of change we can produce, relative to the amount produced by features of the culture over which lawyers do not have control, and which may not be subject to much conscious control at all.

Again the classics in social theory have something to say about this issue. Culture's resistance to law can occur even when the law takes its most modest form, which some new Chicagoans have called *expressive* law. As I understand it, an expressive law is one that simply states the enacting majority's view of what good behavior is; it need not even attach consequences to bad behavior. Expressive laws may accomplish something even so, if they effectively communicate the group's norms to people who might be misunderstanding what those norms are. But culture's resistance to law may impair this communication. Consider here the classic advertisement associated with the 1980s campaign against teenage drug use: The voice-over, "This is your brain," accompanies a picture of an egg, while the voice-over, "This is your brain on drugs," accompanies a picture of an egg being fried. I take it that the strategy here is to get teenagers to calculate their self-interest correctly. But, as I understand it, this ad became something of a joke among teenagers.[29]

This is an example of how expressive laws can fail.[30] There is an additional difficulty, related to my earlier observation that norms are more complex than the models developed in the evolutionary account of norms allow. Ordinarily laws have a lot of details too, and those details may either undermine the law's expressive message or embed more coercion in the law than the pacific notion of law as expressive—and efficacious

29. I am told, for example, that there is a version of the ad in which the words are, "This is your brain on drugs with a side of bacon."

30. Advocates of the efficacy of expressive laws use cultural changes associated with the disapproval of workplace sexual harassment as an important example. I have no strong views on the question of the contribution *law* made to these cultural changes, but do note that the question of causality seems to me more difficult. As I have suggested, lawyers have an understandable tendency to exaggerate law's efficacy, and I would like to see a study from a sociologist that sorted out the possible causal factors more carefully than lawyers do. It might be, for example, that norms against workplace sexual harassment became widespread after the percentage of women in the workplace, or in particular strategic workplaces, exceeded some "tipping point," and that the academic interest in characterizing workplace sexual harassment as illegal arose when that tipping point had been reached, or was approaching.

precisely because it is only expressive—suggests.[31] If culture resists conscious manipulation, and if policymakers find it impossible to enact laws that are merely expressive, we might be worried that they will become frustrated and escalate their efforts. The threat of such escalation may underlie some of the concerns expressed about the totalitarian tendencies of the new Chicago school's theoretical approach.[32]

There are, however, deeper reasons for concern. Classic liberal policies are typically concerned with how people behave, not with how they think. You can think you are the messiah, and liberal policy does not care as long as you do not hurt anyone else when acting on your beliefs.[33] And if you do hurt someone, liberal policy will lock you up, without caring whether you continue to think that you are the messiah while you are in prison.[34] Some of the new Chicago school's policy instruments, in contrast, are directed at what you think. This may not be true of policies aimed at revealing to people what their existing reference groups actually think, at least to the extent that the target population accepts the messages as accurate and as being issued in good faith. But policies aimed at changing a person's reference groups do try to change what people think, and policies attempting to rectify the information-processing defects identified in the work of Aaron Twersky and Daniel Kahneman try to change how people think.

One can of course say that these policies are no different from the processes of public education that modern liberalism has little difficulty accepting.[35] But there is a crucial difference between liberal public education and more general strategies of influencing the way people think: at least in principle you can always opt out of the education decreed by

31. For a discussion applying this argument to specific laws, see Mark Tushnet & Larry Yackle, *Symbolic Statutes and Real Laws: The Pathologies of the Antiterrorism and Effective Death Penalty Act and the Prison Litigation Reform Act*, 47 DUKE L.J. 1 (1997).

32. Of course this formulation implies nothing whatever about the motivations of those associated with the new Chicago school.

33. This is an obvious overstatement. Liberal criminal law, for example, makes one's intentions relevant in determining the degree to which one will be held liable, and at the extreme (the insanity defense) relieves a person of culpability because of what's inside his or her head. At the same time, I think it worth noting that lots of people begin to have their doubts about policy's consistency with liberal premises at precisely these points.

34. Sometimes social policy *has* been concerned that people think they are the messiah while locked up. But it is precisely at such points that liberals have raised questions about the policies being implemented. For an interesting study bearing on these questions, see MILTON ROKEACH, THE THREE CHRISTS OF YPSILANTI (1964).

35. For a defense of public education from a liberal point of view, see AMY GUTMANN, DEMOCRATIC EDUCATION (1987).

public authorities,[36] whereas you cannot escape the mind-influencing messages associated with the new Chicago school's policy instruments (although, thankfully, you can ignore them). The fear of totalitarianism, then, is not that these instruments will produce too much coercion, but that they succeed, when they do, in the wrong kind of way from a liberal point of view.

Of course the term *totalitarian* is misplaced when applied to the actual policies advocated by those associated with the new Chicago school. The term refers to the intellectual tendency of the ideas. Both the mild policies and the troubling tendency remind me of a broader social and intellectual movement, in which manipulation replaces coercion as the preferred method of social control. This broader movement is represented, for example, in managerial interest in redesigning the workplace in the name of promoting "quality of worklife," and in the substitution of a national conversation about race for national policies about race.[37] Recently some sociologists have started to write about the formation of a professional-managerial class, with distinctive interests in advancing its class interests through the extraction of consent rather than through coercion. Although he roots the phenomenon in a different set of class interests, Jurgen Habermas has referred to the process as the colonization of the life-world. The new Chicago school may represent the new imperialism of those of the professional-managerial class who are located in law schools.

36. And public education is most problematic from a liberal point of view precisely at the point when you cannot opt out, as when public authorities prescribe mandatory curricula for private schools.

37. I understand that the latter may be less a matter of principle than an expedient political choice forced on people who actually do have policies they want to advance but find themselves in a political climate where actually doing so is quite difficult. Still, I would have thought that political leaders in the past would have tried to persuade the public that the policies they favored were good ones, rather than engaging in a nominally undirected conversation with the public about race generally.

[12]

# The Death of an Author, By Himself

Legal scholars have heard literary critics proclaim the death of the author. Yet, as this Symposium shows, it is one thing to hear the death of some generalized author announced, quite another to be an author reading his or her own obituary. Authors seem inevitably drawn to the Romantic vision of their task, in which the product of their pens is somehow an expression of their very own individuality. To be told that texts "are"—or at the very least will become—what readers make of them is to deprive Romantic authors of something they believe to be at the core of their activity.

When we think of ourselves as commentators on the legal work of others,[1] we are not troubled in asserting that what an opinion means, for example, is what it is taken to mean by its readers.[2] One line of inquiry developing from this assertion would explore the ways in which particular phrasings affect the meanings readers give an opinion. Obviously, readers who see the words, "Affirmative action programs are subject to strict scrutiny and are permissible only under the most compelling circumstances," are likely to take the words to mean something different from, "Affirmative action programs are permissible when they are reasonable means suitably adapted to rectifying a legacy of discrimination."[3] At the least, readers are likely to think it more difficult to justify affirmative action programs after reading the first phrase than they would after reading the second.

This suggests that the editorial process, in which an author's words are subjected to revision by a first set of readers, may affect what the words that are ultimately published mean. I want to suggest, however, that the effects of this first transformation are likely to be significantly smaller than the already-in-place routines that the larger

1. I acknowledge immediately the problem in this statement, which implicitly purports to distinguish between our "commentary"—taken to be something that exists outside the critical enterprise described by the phrase, "the death of the author"—and that which we comment on, which is the object of—and therefore in some sense subordinate to—our commentary.

2. And not, in particular, what the opinion's author "meant" it to mean.

3. Or maybe not so obviously. On one (controversial) interpretation of the "death of the author" theory, the proposition is obvious only because readers are already socialized into an understanding of the distinction between "strict scrutiny" and "reasonableness."

audience of readers uses in reading the ultimate product.[4] The meaning of a sentence in the passive voice, to use the conventional example, is indeed different from the meaning of a sentence in the active voice, but the margin is, I believe, quite small compared to the differences in meanings that arise from discrepancies between an author's routine and those deployed by readers.

My observations here result from my reflections on recent experiences with an article I wrote. The experience can be summarized in this way: The article I thought I wrote is not the one readers appear to have read, although the words in the article I thought I wrote are the words in the article readers read.

For the past few years I have been playing around with the idea that literary style has something to do with the ability of judicial opinions to become authoritative.[5] Roughly put, the idea is that the "better written" an opinion is, the more likely it is to become an authoritative precedent. In pursuing that idea, I have tried to explore two lines of inquiry that I suspect are linked.

First, and obviously connected to the theme of this comment, literary style is a social construction. So, for example, I have tried to think through propositions like, "Justice Robert Jackson's reputation as a literary stylist is founded primarily on his ability to get off quotable lines rather than his ability to develop a sustained argument, and the ability to get off quotable lines is given a positive value in a setting in which the principal means of communication about law is the short newspaper story."

Second, and more problematic, I have been intrigued by the thought that there may be some connection between the judicial virtue of integrity and literary style. Here I have worried that I may be misled by the fact that we can use the word *integrity* to refer both to the artistic integrity of a literary production, which is itself a virtue in that context, and to a personal characteristic.

One article in the group I have written examined three topics: the literary style of some Supreme Court opinions, the personal characteristics revealed in a hearing on the confirmation of a Supreme

4. Such as it is for law review articles.

5. Mark Tushnet, *The Degradation of Constitutional Discourse*, 81 GEO. L.J. 251 (1992) [hereinafter Tushnet, *Degradation*]; Mark Tushnet, *Style and The Supreme Court's Educational Role in Government*, 11 CONST. COMMENTARY 215 (1994); Mark Tushnet, *Constitutional Interpretation, Character and Experience*, 72 B.U. L. REV. 747 (1992); Mark Tushnet, *Character as Argument*, 14 LAW & SOC. INQUIRY 539 (1989) (reviewing HARRY KALVEN, JR., A WORTHY TRADITION: FREEDOM OF SPEECH IN AMERICA (Jamie Kalven ed., 1988)).

Court nominee, and the literary style of important recent work in the field of jurisprudence.[6] The principal opinion I discussed was Justice Blackmun's separate opinion in *DeShaney v. Winnebago County Department of Social Services*.[7] His opinion contains the widely noted phrase, "Poor Joshua."[8] Although many commentators take the opinion, and the phrase, to show how a judge's empathy can be expressed in his opinions,[9] I found it to be bathetic instead. I contrasted Justice Blackmun's personalization in his *DeShaney* opinion with what I believed to be the more effective personalization in Justice Brennan's dissent in *McCleskey v. Kemp*,[10] and I tried to explain why I believed Justice Brennan's rhetoric was more effective than Justice Blackmun's. This discussion of the opinions' literary integrity was coupled with a discussion of some problems I encountered in reading some passages in several prominent works of narrative jurisprudence. I argued that those passages displayed problems of literary integrity paralleling those in Justice Blackmun's opinion. These discussions of literary integrity bracketed a discussion devoted to establishing as carefully as I could that Clarence Thomas had lied before the Senate Judiciary Committee, which raised the question of judicial integrity.

I think it fair to say that essentially no one saw the article as I did. It has generally been taken as a vicious attack on narrative jurisprudence, and on the work of Patricia Williams in particular; the rest of the article has been ignored.[11] Some of the criticisms articulate inter-

6. Tushnet, *Degradation*, *supra* note 5.

7. 489 U.S. 189 (1989).

8. *Id.* at 213.

9. *See, e.g.*, Martha Minow, *Words and the Door to the Land of Change: Law, Language, and Family Violence*, 43 VAND. L. REV. 1665, 1675 (1990).

10. 481 U.S. 279 (1987).

11. The term *vicious* has been used in conversations. I have collected citations to the article, and quote parenthetically the descriptions to which the citations are attached: Jane B. Baron, *Resistance to Stories*, 67 S. CAL. L. REV. 255, 255 (1994) ("at pains to point up the limitations of the storytelling genre"); Richard Delgado, *The Inward Turn in Outsider Jurisprudence*, 34 WM. & MARY L. REV. 741, 752 n.90 (1993) ("discussing stylistic flaws in certain influential narratives which undermine the format's effectiveness as legal scholarship"); Robert E. Scott, *Chaos Theory and the Justice Paradox*, 35 WM. & MARY L. REV. 329, 345-46 n.85 (1993) ("Mark Tushnet has suggested analogous views" to those expressed in articles constituting a "counter-reaction which questioned the uniqueness of a black voice, and asked if minorities promoted their best interests by demanding to be judged by a standard different from the meritocratic norm purportedly used by white America"); David A. Skeel, Jr., *Practicing Poetry, Teaching Law*, 92 MICH. L. REV. 1754, 1769 n.55 (1994) (reviewing LAWRENCE JOSEPH, BEFORE OUR EYES (1993)) ("Legal storytellers have recently come under attack by commentators questioning the accuracy of the storytellers' 'real-life' accounts"). For the record, my view is that Delgado's characterization is the most accurate among those critical of the article, and that other even more qualified characterizations are even more accurate. *See, e.g.*, Larry Alexander, *What We Do, and Why We Do It*, 45 STAN. L. REV. 1885, 1896 n.43 (1993) ("criticizing *certain* feminist and critical race narratives") (emphasis added); Daniel A. Farber & Suzanna Sherry, *Telling Stories*

esting analyses, actually congruent with my interest in the social construction of standards of style.[12] As an author, my reaction to these comments has ranged from a bemused, "Some of these things are interesting comments on a certain view of narrative jurisprudence in general, but they have little to do with what *I* wrote," to a sterner annoyance at the "mis"-characterization of my views.[13]

On reflection, however, both reactions reflect the Romantic view of authorship that, in my critical writings, I reject. For, in any relevant sense, the article now "is"—and therefore is (without scare quotes)—an attack on narrative jurisprudence, because that is how it has been read by the relevant community of readers.

Some comments on this "transformation" seem worth making.[14] First, we might think that there were some limits to the process. Perhaps it is not worth worrying too much about whether law review editors insert too many passive voice constructions into an otherwise elegantly written article, although I will comment on that issue in a moment. We might think, though, that certainly an article cannot come to mean the opposite of what it "says." That, we might think, would be as if the community of readers inserted the word *not* in a sentence like, "Justice Marshall has argued that the death penalty was unconstitutional under all circumstances," to make it either, "Justice Marshall has not argued . . .," or "Justice Marshall has argued that the death penalty was not unconstitutional under all circumstances." My experience suggests that the limits are rather broad. My article said the following: "I find it largely uninteresting to ask whether the Benetton or Au Coton stories 'actually happened,' because events like those certainly have happened."[15] The critics of my article regularly assert that I do not believe Williams's account of the events.[16]

*Out of School: An Essay on Legal Narratives*, 45 STAN. L. REV. 807, 807 n.3 (1993) ("Mark Tushnet critiques *some aspects* of legal storytelling") (emphasis added).

12. Especially the first and most detailed, Gary Peller, *The Discourse of Constitutional Degradation*, 81 GEO. L.J. 313 (1992).

13. In particular, at the transformation of a critique of selected passages into a criticism of narrative jurisprudence in general.

14. Again, the scare quotes are necessary.

15. Tushnet, *Degradation*, *supra* note 5, at 273 n.101.

16. The incompleteness of my statement was justified by the issue I was discussing. A more complete statement would have been that it was both uninteresting and irrelevant to ask whether the events had actually happened, because Williams's work presents itself as on the contested border between imaginative literature and historical reconstruction (and is designed in part to raise questions about that distinction itself). In one sense, then, the events could not have happened (did Hamlet "actually" kill Polonius?), and in another sense they must have (of course Hamlet "actually" killed Polonius). The events Williams describes exist—for her readers—only within the text itself.

Second, we might explore how the transformation came about. Again, this would commit us to a controversial view of how meaning is constructed. One reason the transformation occurred, I believe, is that it was published along with a severely critical response. What happened was the not uncommon phenomenon of the dissenting opinion defining the scope of the majority opinion.[17] I certainly have occasionally read the response to an article to find a summary of the original's argument, only then turning to the "original," but of course with my view of the article already affected by the response I have read.

Here I invoke what I am inclined to call a socio-political analysis of how readers read. So, for example, I would ask, "What is it about the sociology and politics of the contemporary legal academy that led a community of readers to take my article as it did?"[18] This suggests, however, that authors might properly be concerned about the insertion of too many passive voice constructions, if they are concerned about their works' reception. For, it could be—although we would actually need to do some socio-political analysis to be sure—that readers systematically attach less value to articles with many passive voice constructions than they do to articles with few such constructions. They might do so, for example, if they were regularly told that articles with many passive voice constructions were, for that reason alone, worse than other articles.

Authors, then, might not be completely moribund. They might retain some control over what their works mean, if they understand the sociology and politics of the community of readers.[19] This is not the full-blown Romantic account of authorship, but it may be all that we have.

And yet, at the end of the day, sometimes I certainly want to say, "But that's not what my article says, and it's not what I meant."

17. I owe this observation to my colleague Daniel Ernst.

18. I developed that analysis in my reply to Peller, and need not elaborate it here. Mark Tushnet, *Reply to Peller*, 81 GEO. L.J. 343 (1992).

19. I should note one difficulty that I have elided to this point. Authors confront not a single community of readers, but multiple communities, each with its own socio-politics. An author might therefore be able to exert some control over a work's meaning within one community of readers and simultaneously, because of the very strategies used to exert that control *there*, lose control completely within another community.

# [13]

# Interdisciplinary Legal Scholarship: The Case of 'History-in-Law'

Holmes, it appears, was right. The legal scholar of the late twentieth century, if not the lawyer, is "the man of statistics and the master of economics."[1] Of course, just as we must now read the word *man* more inclusively, so we must read *statistics* and *economics*. Legal scholarship has become broadly interdisciplinary, to illuminate what Holmes called the process of "weighing considerations of social advantage,"[2] that he believed essential to—or even definitional of—law. The most-cited law review article is by an economist; Justice Rehnquist called the third most-cited "in the area of political science, rather than of constitutional law."[3] Other articles high on the list are even more obviously interdisciplinary than Gunther's.

Is this appearance of interdisciplinarity accurate? Not entirely. First, a high proportion of the most-cited articles are doctrinal in the classic sense despite the criticisms Judge Edwards has made of a legal scholarship that fails to engage the doctrinal concerns of the legal profession.[4] Although Herbert Wechsler did sometimes develop arguments that could fairly be called *political science*,[5] his most-cited article is purely doctrinal, devoted to an examination of the logical implications of Supreme Court opinions. So too with the classic Tuss-

* Carmack Waterhouse Professor of Constitutional Law, Georgetown University Law Center. I have benefited from conversations with Mike Seidman and Jack Balkin in framing my argument. Balkin, Martin Flaherty, Robert Gordon, Michael Klarman, and Brian Leiter gave me helpful comments on a draft. They led me to make my position, bizarre as it seemed to them—as Leiter put it, "an odd position, though not an unintelligible one by any means"—more explicit. Every one of them argued that I was too tolerant of bad philosophy and bad history in law, and are therefore particularly not to be associated with my argument except to be put in the camp of those who disagree with it.

1. Oliver Wendell Holmes, Jr., *The Path of the Law*, *in* 3 Collected Works of Justice Holmes 391, 399 (Sheldon M. Novick ed., 1995).

2. *Id.* at 398.

3. Rehnquist's article was cited in Mark Tushnet, *Justice Lewis F. Powell and the Jurisprudence of Centrism*, 93 Mich. L. Rev. 1854, 1860 (1995) (book review).

4. Harry Edwards, *The Growing Disjunction Between Legal Education and the Legal Profession*, 91 Mich. L. Rev. 34 (1992).

5. See, e.g., Herbert Wechsler, *The Political Safeguards of Federalism: The Role of the States in the Composition and Selection of the National Government*, 54 Colum. L.Rev. 543 (1954), which appears at number 69 on the list in this Symposium, Fred R. Shapiro, *The Most-Cited Law Review Articles Revisted*, 71 Chi.-Kent L. Rev. 751, 770 (1996)).

man and tenBroek article on the concept of equal protection,[6] despite the fact that Tussman is a professional philosopher.

Second, and perhaps more important, legal scholarship that displays the form of interdisciplinarity (to use a barbarism) may not be truly *inter*disciplinary. In this Article I use the example of how history is used in legal scholarship to examine whether such scholarship ought to be called interdisciplinary.[7] I focus on that subcategory of legal scholarship even though it appears infrequently on the list of most-cited law review articles, for two reasons. As a part-time historian I am more familiar with the questions of disciplinarity that arise in the use of history in legal scholarship than I am with the parallel questions about economics and philosophy. In addition, to the extent that I am familiar with those parallel questions, they seem to me to resemble the ones I discuss here.[8]

## I. Introduction: Intellectual Voyeurism and Decoration in Legal Genres

I take as my initial text an article by Brian Leiter whose title conveys its thesis: "Intellectual Voyeurism in Legal Scholarship."[9] Trained as a philosopher and as a lawyer, Leiter argues that some interdisciplinary work is "sub-standard," containing "superficial and ill-informed treatment of serious ideas, apparently done for intellectual 'titillation' or to advertise, in a pretentious way, the 'sophistication' of the writer."[10] Leiter uses an article by Gerald Frug as his foil.[11] According to Leiter, Frug drops citations to Nietzsche into his article

6. Tussman & tenBroek, *The Equal Protection of the Laws*, 37 CAL. L. REV. 341 (1949).

7. Some readers might fairly ask, "Who cares?" That is, does anything turn on whether legal scholarship can be fairly called interdisciplinary? Perhaps not much. I believe, however, that asking the questions illuminates the practice of legal scholarship. For a discussion of what, if anything, can be gained from efforts to police the boundaries of disciplines, see *infra* text accompanying notes 89-103 (concluding that the policing effort in itself is unlikely to be productive).

8. For example, on the rare occasions that practitioners of law and economics attempt to offer more than the most superficial reasons why economics has something to say to law, they tend to rely almost entirely on Milton Friedman's famous essay on the methodology of positive economics, without acknowledging that Friedman's account of economic methodology is highly contested among philosophers of economics. *See, e.g.*, DANIEL M. HAUSMAN, THE INEXACT AND SEPARATE SCIENCE OF ECONOMICS 162-69 (1992); DONALD N. MCCLOSKEY, THE RHETORIC OF ECONOMICS (1985). This is not to take a position on the question here; I am hardly qualified to offer an opinion that anyone ought to take seriously. Rather, it is to suggest only that the arguments I make in this Article about the use of history in law may well be available to those who might want to argue about the use of economics (and philosophy) in law.

9. Brian Leiter, *Intellectual Voyeurism in Legal Scholarship*, 4 YALE J.L. & HUMAN. 79 (1992). For a similar argument, see Charles W. Collier, *Interdisciplinary Legal Scholarship in Search of a Paradigm*, 42 Duke L.J. 840 (1993).

10. Leiter, *supra* note 9, at 80.

11. Gerald Frug, *Argument as Character*, 40 STAN. L. REV. 869 (1988).

without acknowledging that Nietzsche's position, when fully understood, does not support the limited points for which Frug cites Nietzsche,[12] and that Frug's appropriation of Nietzsche, while sometimes superficially consistent with the body of Nietzsche's work, offers claims that are highly contested among scholars more familiar with that work.[13]

I am in no position to say whether Leiter's criticisms of Frug are accurate.[14] Assume they are, in the sense that philosophers familiar with Nietzsche would agree with Leiter. Why should it make any difference *to legal scholarship* that Frug merely displays the name of Nietzsche in his article? One reason might be that Frug could be asking his readers to accept his arguments *on the ground that* Nietzsche made them. Here Nietzsche would be an authority whose word carries weight. That would be a peculiar use of philosophy in law. Lawyers must know that few philosophers examine what their predecessors have said as a source of authority in the way a Supreme Court decision is a source of authority in constitutional law. Philosophers pay attention to Nietzsche's arguments, or Aristotle's, because—and to the degree that—the arguments carry rational force.

One can imagine that Frug relies on Nietzsche to provide him with lemmas along the way to his own conclusion.[15] Frug would be assuming both that Nietzsche's conclusions are themselves well-supported—lemmas that Frug need not argue for because Nietzsche proved them—and that they do indeed support Frug's conclusion. And perhaps he is wrong about that. Or perhaps the fact that Frug appears to believe—if he does so appear—that Nietzsche's arguments support his own arguments itself demonstrates a fundamental failure of reasoning ability: It is circumstantial evidence of Frug's inability to make good arguments, which casts doubt on the arguments he does make. Or, finally, Frug's failure to appreciate difficulties with his view of Nietzsche may indicate that he has not understood the true difficulty of the issues with which he is concerned: Frug may make hard questions seem easy, and had he truly grappled with Nietzsche's work he would have seen how hard the questions are. But in none of these cases is the true criticism that Frug's use of Nietzsche is superficial or ill-informed.

12. *See, e.g.*, Leiter, *supra* note 9, at 83-85.

13. *See, e.g.*, *id.* at 88-90.

14. For what it is worth, they do have the ring of accuracy to my ears.

15. Instead of asserting, "Because Nietzsche said X, we should conclude Y," Frug might be asserting, "As Nietzsche demonstrated, X, from which I conclude Y."

For all that, Leiter is surely on to something. Here I think it helpful to introduce a distinction between philosophy$_1$ and philosophy$_2$. Philosophy$_1$ is what people regarded as philosophers do. Some, for example, offer reasons that any reasonable person should find rationally compelling for the positions they assert on matters of philosophical interest. Others, in James Tully's words, seek to "dissolv[e] philosophical problems, not by presenting yet another solution, but by a survey which brings to critical light the unexamined conventions that govern the language games in which both the problem and the range of solutions arise."[16] And there surely are other philosophers' practices. Philosophy$_2$ is different. For present purposes, philosophy$_2$ is the practice engaged in by lawyers using philosophy: philosophy-in-law rather than legal philosophy.

The distinction matters because the practices of legal academics and philosophers differ. Like philosophers, legal academics are interested in determining the truth and establishing the conditions of justice. Like philosophers, legal academics are interested in getting tenure and building a secure reputation. And like philosophers (and lawyers), legal academics are interested in making a case that persuades their audiences. Although reasons that reasonable people would find rationally compelling form one part of such a case, legal arguments are, I believe, more highly rhetorical than philosophical ones.[17] A good legal argument has many components. The authority of the person making the argument itself has weight,[18] for example, in a way that may not happen in philosophy.[19] A good legal argument quite often is one that is simple enough to encapsulate in the obligatory parenthetical when it is cited, even though arguments that are rationally compelling may be quite complicated. And, finally, good legal arguments often have a certain rhetorical flair.

16. James Tully, Strange Multiplicity 35 (1995).

17. Of course I would not want to push the distinction too hard, for I am sure that philosophical practices are also rhetorical.

18. This may be part of the reason for the heavy predominance of people teaching at the highest ranked law schools on the list of most highly cited articles. That conclusion must be qualified, however. For understandable reasons, people teaching at such schools have readier access to the law reviews published at their home law schools. Until recently, those reviews were more readily available for others to consult and then cite. It will be interesting to see what will happen as more law reviews are easily available in computer-accessible data bases.

19. There may be a presumption, in any scholarly field, that it is worth paying attention to arguments made by a person who has written interesting and persuasive things in the past. Yet, I would think that philosophers would not give weight to the mere fact that John Rawls made an argument in the way the legal academy gives weight to the mere fact that a celebrated law professor has made a new argument. (People in both fields might, of course, come to the new contributions with a strong principle of charity in interpretation.)

Often legal scholars provide citations to fancy philosophers as a form of decoration for their arguments. I use the term *decoration* for a reason: According to one of his law clerks, Justice Abe Fortas handed over a draft opinion to the law clerk with the instruction, "Decorate it," meaning, "Come up with the citations to support what I wrote."[20] For Fortas, to work in the genre *judicial opinion* meant that one had to offer case authority to support conclusions arrived at for other reasons and justified on other grounds.[21]

So too with philosophy$_2$. To do it well the author must decorate it with citations to fancy philosophers. Leiter suggests that these citations are designed to "titillate" or perhaps intimidate readers.[22] Alternatively, they simply satisfy the genre's demands: "Nice move," a reader might say, on seeing a citation to Nietzsche or—my favorite—Alfarabi.[23] The citation shows the author to be a Serious Person, but within the genre of philosophy$_2$ it is not taken as a serious effort to use philosophical authority to support the author's conclusion. In this sense something that is quite bad philosophy$_1$ may be effective philosophy$_2$—unless the conventions of philosophy$_2$ are that citations to philosophers are rhetorically effective only if they are good philosophy$_1$.[24]

Is the use of history in legal scholarship different? The answer might be yes if we focus on original intent theorists of constitutional interpretation.[25] For them, the very fact that the Framers and ratifiers of the Constitution and its amendments understood the document's provisions in a specified way is authoritative. They need no reasons for the constitutional positions they take; it is sufficient that the Framers and ratifiers understood the Constitution as they did.

20. LAURA KALMAN, ABE FORTAS 272 (1990).

21. This is not a necessary implication of Fortas's instruction. He could have believed that case authority was the only justification for his decision, and the only reason for arriving at it, and could have known that such authority existed without being able to locate it himself. The saying, "He has forgotten more law than you will ever know," suggests this position, at least to the extent that it implies, as I believe it often does, that the subject has not truly forgotten the law, but merely cannot retrieve it at the moment. I have argued elsewhere that Fortas's instruction is not best understood in this way, although a similar injunction issued by William O. Douglas would best be so understood. Mark Tushnet, *Themes in Warren Court Biographies*, 70 N.Y.U. L. REV. 748, 755 (1995).

22. Leiter, *supra* note 9, at 80, 91.

23. *See, e.g.*, THOMAS L. PANGLE, THE ENNOBLING OF DEMOCRACY 6 (1992). A citation to Alfarabi demonstrates that the author is a student and probably a disciple of Leo Strauss. The citation comes early in Pangle's book, and Alfarabi is never cited again.

24. Despite the criticisms I have received from those who commented on an early version of this Article, I remain convinced that philosophy$_2$ does not have such a convention.

25. As will appear, I use the term *original intent theorists* quite broadly, to encompass all legal scholars who use historical evidence to support interpretations of law in the present day.

There are of course standard objections to originalism, the most potent of which is that it is, quite literally, irrational.[26] Here I want to focus on a different point. Originalist law review articles constitute their own genre of scholarship, which I call history-in-law (instead of history$_2$).[27] I believe that history functions in that genre as decoration rather than authority. To support that assertion, I must first describe the genre of historical writing.

## II. The Tropes of Historical Discourse

Few practicing historians think that all they do is dig up facts no one knew before. Historians realize that in one way or another, they are all storytellers. And as storytellers they operate with a few well-established story lines, under the constraint that a historian can use a particular story line only when it has some—often minimal—support in the sources.[28] Here I sketch four that I believe are quite common in modern historical scholarship.[29]

The first and probably oldest is the story of progressive development, which has garnered the pejorative label *Whig history*. According to this story, today's institutions and ideas are the outgrowth of institutions and ideas in the past. To some extent today's ideas and institutions are really the same as those in the past: a story of continuity. To some extent they are different, but only because we have come to understand better what those ideas mean and what those institutions are designed to accomplish.

26. There may be reasons for adopting originalism as a theory of interpretation, but there can be no reason outside of originalism for adopting a particular originalist interpretation. Originalists must take the mere fact that the Framers took a particular position as dispositive, and they depart from originalism when they explain why the Framers' position was sensible, sound, wise, or anything else—when, in short, they offer reasons to justify the Framers' position. Originalists have done quite badly in explaining why people today should be bound to decisions made in the past solely on the ground that the Framers made those decisions. Or, as Shakespeare put it, "What's Hecuba to him, or he to Hecuba, That he should weep for her?" William Shakespeare, Hamlet, act 2, sc. 2. It is an equally standard response to arguments like this to assert that originalism, whatever its defects—including its irrationality—is better than alternative modes of constitutional interpretation, particularly in constraining judicial interpretation. I doubt it, and the arguments I made to support my doubts apparently led enough people to cite my work for me to be included on the list in this Symposium, Shapiro, *supra* note 5, at 769.

27. In what follows I specifically exempt those working in the genre *legal history*, who I would identify roughly as legal academics who are members of the American Society of Legal History and who participate regularly in the Society's activities. (Obviously this distinction itself is a form of boundary-drawing, and the concerns I raise in § IV *infra* about who polices the boundaries are relevant here as well.)

28. The basic sources here are Hayden White, Metahistory (1973), and Hayden White, Tropics of Discourse (1978).

29. I focus on tropes commonly used in intellectual and institutional history, which are the closest analogues to the tropes using history in law.

The historian explains how those old institutions and ideas held the germ for (or were the seeds of—the metaphors vary) today's institutions and ideas, and demonstrates their gradual unfolding. That which we today find unpalatable in the past is presented as incompatible with the fundamental commitments of the past itself: As people gradually became more aware of their true commitments, they discarded the rest.

The story-line of *decline and fall* is the obverse of Whig history. Here the historian describes how institutions degenerated. This story has its own variants. Sometimes the historian celebrates the demise of an institution that deserved to die. Sometimes the historian regrets the decline, to the point of writing a jeremiad celebrating the past in contrast to the degenerate present. And sometimes the historian sees the features that caused the decline as inherent flaws, so that the institution was eaten away by its own commitments.

A third common story-line is *irony*, of which the last variant of the story of decline and fall may be an example as well. The historian shows what people in the past intentionally set out to do, and demonstrates how things turned out quite differently. In some versions this story-line resembles Whig history. To the Whig historian, the best in today's society is the residue of the past's wisdom, and we can be encouraged in confronting today's injustices by the thought that this too shall pass. To the complacent ironist, we stand apart from the past. We look bemusedly on their illusions, and are comforted because we know they were deluded. The complacent ironist, that is, elevates his or her present knowledge above what appeared to be knowledge but was actually mere prejudice.

A more self-conscious ironist understands that just as things turned out differently from the way people in the past thought they would, so things might—indeed, are likely to—turn out differently from the way we think they will. This stance, too, might lead to complacency: Whatever you think is the best thing to do is likely to have ironic consequences, so why bother to do anything?[30]

A final story-line is *complexity and contradiction*. Here the historian demonstrates that the past is a foreign country where people managed to think that things we find inconsistent were entirely compatible, indeed sometimes entailed by each other. The historian

30. There is a third type of ironist, who thoroughly deconstructs the narrative of irony itself, turning it into one of many tropes available to historians without having any special epistemological status itself.

shows how complicated yesterday's ideas and institutions were. The simple fact that people in the past used words we use today does not mean that those words meant to them what they mean to us. For example, the Fourteenth Amendment's framers clearly wanted to protect what they called civil rights, but the scope of that class was substantially narrower than what today is encompassed within the term.[31] Historians can trace how words that used to mean one thing came to mean something else,[32] with the effect of estranging us from the past—that is, making it stranger than it seemed at first.[33]

Even more troubling, historians can do the same with institutions as well as concepts. For example, a historian of the death penalty can show that the social meaning of death and punishment in the late eighteenth century was so different from the social meaning of death and punishment in the world of AIDS that the institution of capital punishment is simply a different institution today. Or, a historian of Congress can show that the House of Representatives in the early twentieth century was inserted into a political and cultural system unique to that time, so that the institution we call the House today is historically continuous with, but dramatically different from the one that met in the same building in 1905.

An odd alliance of cultural conservatives and cultural radicals supports the search for a usable past. The conservatives wish to find a past to celebrate as a model for today, and the radicals look for elements in the past that they think offer hope of radical transformation. Mostly, however, historians try to emphasize the pastness of the past. They take up particular events, ideas, and institutions as they were in the past, and situate them in as full a context as they can. By doing so, they hope to dissolve any illusions that we can easily learn lessons from the past, or identify straight-line connections between single ideas or institutions in the past and today's ideas and institutions, or even between small-scale complexes of ideas and institutions then and now. Precisely because the whole world was different then, particular ideas and institutions were different.

These and other story-lines, not the discovery and mere presentation of facts, constitute the practice of history. Once we understand

31. Most notably, today we think that people have claims against private entities for denials of civil rights, a concept that would have baffled the Fourteenth Amendment's framers.

32. *See, e.g.*, RAYMOND WILLIAMS, KEYWORDS (1976); DANIEL RODGERS, CONTESTED TRUTHS (1987).

33. Historian Robert Darnton writes of "the unfathomable strangeness of life among the dead." ROBERT DARNTON, THE KISS OF LAMOURETTE at xiv (1990).

that history is a practice, a new set of questions arises. What constitutes a good performance within that practice? Who determines what constitutes good historical practice? These questions return us to my discussion of Leiter's criticism of intellectual voyeurism. There I suggested that Leiter's criticisms were misplaced because he misunderstood the practice he was criticizing: He thought it was philosophy and applied philosophers' standards, but it actually was philosophy-in-law, which must be assessed by other standards.

Similarly, seeing history as a practice, we might wonder whether the criteria for good performance have much bearing on other practices. In particular, the criteria for determining whether someone has done well at the practice of history-in-law may be different from those for determining whether someone has done well at the practice of history, and they may be developed and applied by lawyers and legal academics rather than historians.

## III. The Tropes of History-in-Law

### A. *Law-Office History and Whig History*

Thirty years ago constitutional historian Alfred Kelly, who had assisted the National Association for the Advancement of Colored People's legal team in developing a brief on the Fourteenth Amendment's historical background,[34] criticized what he called law-office history.[35] To Kelly, law-office history was characterized by "the selection of data favorable to the position being advanced without regard to or concern for contradictory data or proper evaluation of the relevance of the data proffered."[36] Law-office history was, Kelly asserted, often "very bad history indeed."[37] "It fails to stand up under the most superficial scrutiny by a scholar possessing some knowledge of American constitutional development."[38]

One difficulty with Kelly's definition of law-office history is that law-office history that disregards contrary evidence and the like is not very good advocacy. As Jefferson Powell puts it, "[S]ystematic anachronism and quotation out of context is *unconvincing advocacy* and unacceptable scholarship."[39] Truly effective law-office history

34. *See* MARK TUSHNET, MAKING CIVIL RIGHTS LAW 197-99 (1994).
35. *See* Alfred H. Kelly, *Clio and the Court: An Illicit Love Affair*, 1965 SUP. CT. REV. 119.
36. *Id.* at 122 n.13.
37. *Id.* at 126.
38. *Id.* at 132.
39. H. Jefferson Powell, *Rules for Originalists*, 73 VA. L. REV. 659, 675 (1987) (emphasis added).

acknowledges the contradictory data and explains them away. Michael McConnell's originalist scholarship is law-office history of the highest quality, as one might expect from an advocate of McConnell's talents. By examining it, we may obtain a greater understanding of one aspect of the practice of history-in-law.

Recently McConnell offered a revisionist interpretation of the original understanding of the Fourteenth Amendment with respect to school segregation.[40] The conventional wisdom is that in its framers' and ratifiers' understanding, the Amendment did not make school segregation unconstitutional. Without recapitulating the supporting evidence in detail, I can summarize it in a few sentences. The Amendment's framers and ratifiers distinguished among civil, political, and social rights, and believed that the Amendment protected civil rights alone. There was some uncertainty about the contours of each category, but when opponents asserted that the Amendment would require school desegregation, supporters responded that it would not, because school attendance involved a social rather than a civil right.[41] In addition, the Congress that sent the Amendment to the states for ratification itself enforced school segregation in the District of Columbia.

McConnell makes an ingenious argument against the conventional wisdom. McConnell's argument has several important elements. As an originalist he seeks the original understanding of the Amendment's framers and ratifiers. Unfortunately, direct evidence of the ratifiers' understanding of the Amendment's implications for school segregation is hard to come by.[42] Popular opposition to school desegregation was admittedly widespread in the North, but the Amendment was adopted in extraordinary times, "when a political minority . . . imposed constitutional change on the Nation . . . with little regard for popular opinion."[43] Congress' acceptance of segrega-

40. *See* Michael McConnell, *Originalism and the Desegregation Decisions*, 81 VA. L. REV. 947 (1995).

41. The evidence supporting this aspect of the conventional wisdom is summarized by McConnell. *See id.* at 959-60.

42. The evidence, though hard to locate, is actually more extensive than McConnell acknowledges. *See* Michael McConnell, *The Originalist Justification for Brown: A Reply to Professor Klarman*, 81 VA. L. REV. 1937, 1944 (1995) ("Although in theory, evidence of the understanding of the state legislatures at the precise time of ratification would be a superior basis for interpretation, it does not exist."). It does exist, for example, in reports in local newspapers at the time of ratification. The NAACP had several volunteer lawyers examine such evidence in preparation for the reargument in Brown v. Board of Education, 347 U.S. 483 (1954). *See* TUSHNET, *supra* note 34, at 196-97. The results are available in the NAACP Papers (on file with the Library of Congress, Manuscript Division, box II-B-141).

43. McConnell, *supra* note 42, at 1939.

tion in the District of Columbia may have reflected the constraints of contemporary politics rather than a principled understanding of the Fourteenth Amendment's implications. Or, it may have reflected the fact even its framers did not fully understand the implications of the principles to which they were committed. They were, however, committed to the protection of civil rights. When the Amendment was adopted, it might have been reasonable to think that access to education was not a civil right, because it was then "in a fledgling and uncertain state."[44] By 1900, and certainly by 1954, "[c]ommon schools had become the 'pillars of the republic.'"[45] Thus, given the framers' own understanding of the concept *civil rights*, by 1900 or 1954, access to education without regard to race was a civil right protected by the Fourteenth Amendment.

McConnell's argument about the concept of civil rights is not entirely original. It can be found in embryonic form in *Brown* itself, with Chief Justice Earl Warren's statement that "we cannot turn the clock back to 1868," but "must consider public education in the light of its full development and its present place in American life throughout the Nation."[46] I developed it in slightly greater detail for anti-originalist purposes.[47]

More original is McConnell's quite ingenious argument about the Civil Rights Act of 1875. A cynic might say that McConnell argues that Congress' failure to outlaw school segregation in 1875 demonstrates that the Fourteenth Amendment's framers and ratifiers understood in 1868-69 that school segregation would become unconstitutional upon the Amendment's adoption. McConnell demonstrates that a majority in each house of Congress at separate times voted to outlaw school segregation in the course of considering the 1875 Civil Rights Act. Congress did not enact the prohibition, however, because of some procedural obstacles that made it impossible for both houses to agree on the provision at the same time.

44. *Id.* at 1951.
45. *Id.*
46. Brown v. Board of Education, 347 U.S. 483, 492-93 (1954). McConnell quotes and criticizes the first of these statements, but does not quote the second. McConnell, *supra* note 40, at 1132 & n.859.
47. Mark Tushnet, *Following the Rules Laid Down: A Critique of Interpretivism and Neutral Principles*, 96 HARV. L. REV. 781, 800-01 (1983) (developing analogy between right to contract, treated as a civil right in 1868, and right to access to education in modern United States). Against the claim that this sort of analogizing demonstrates the "indeterminacy of originalism," McConnell asserts that this sort of analogizing is "not a matter of mere conclusory labelling or assertion, but of reasoned legal argument, which we can understand and evaluate." McConnell, *supra* note 42, at 1951-52. He actually addresses only half of the argument against originalism, which claims that *other* analogies are just as well-supported by reasoned legal argument.

How does the debate over the 1875 Civil Rights Act illuminate the original understanding of the Fourteenth Amendment? Not, of course, because the Amendment's adopters believed that Congress had some authority to interpret the Amendment.[48] Congress has to act to exercise such authority. The procedural obstacles McConnell discusses are just as much a part of the process by which Congress exercises its interpretive authority as the substantive provisions it enacts. Nor does McConnell contend that constitutional super-majorities in Congress supported desegregation, but only that majorities did.[49]

Once McConnell's argument is unpacked, we see that the votes in Congress are far less decisive than the scores of pages McConnell devotes to them make them seem. The question is what the Amendment's adopters understood it to mean. One way to find that out is to examine what they thought the Amendment meant after it was adopted. So, for example, when one of its supporters argued in 1874 in favor of a statutory ban on school segregation on the ground that the Fourteenth Amendment made segregation unconstitutional, we can infer, albeit with some qualifications,[50] that the supporter had that same understanding in 1868-69. McConnell demonstrates that a large majority of members of Congress in 1874 who had been in Congress in 1868 and who supported the Amendment then argued against school segregation on constitutional grounds. He infers that those who supported the Amendment in 1869 (when it was ratified) probably understood it to enact a principle against school segregation.

Nothing whatever in this argument turns on the fact that both houses of Congress voted to prohibit school segregation. McConnell uses positions asserted in the 1874 debates to determine what the Amendment's supporters in 1868 understood it to mean. Members of the 1874 Congress are simply a convenient sample of the 1868 supporters.

How might a constitutional historian address McConnell's argument? First, and perhaps most obvious, a constitutional historian, understanding the argument's logic, would ask for more evidence: What

48. I have no idea whether the Amendment's adopters did understand the Amendment in this way, but as I show next, such an understanding is irrelevant anyway.

49. *See* McConnell, *supra* note 40, at 953 ("In a large number of votes over a three and one half year period, between one-half and two-thirds of both houses of Congress voted in favor of school desegregation and against the principle of separate but equal.").

50. The supporter's views may have changed, or he might be strategically or rhetorically casting his argument in terms of constitutional principle when he simply believed segregation to be unwise policy.

reason is there to believe that the congressional sample is representative of the Amendment's supporters in 1868? One might think that the congressional sample consisted of the most persistent and dedicated political activists, whose views might have been more radical than those who served and retired. What did the Amendment's supporters who were *not* in Congress in 1874 think? A historian would try to track representatives and senators from 1868 who left Congress to see what they believed. Did they write private letters discussing the proposed ban on school segregation?[51]

Second, and more interesting, what might a historian say about McConnell's argument about the concept of civil rights? A historian might attempt to embed the concept of civil rights in a larger intellectual, political, social, cultural, and religious universe.[52] A historian would ask most narrowly, How did people connect the concept of civil rights to their understanding of the proper roles of legislatures and courts in a democratic United States? Although today we think that courts automatically enforce most principles embedded in the Constitution, perhaps the Fourteenth Amendment's adopters had a different view. They might have thought that, at least in some dimensions, the question of school segregation presented what we would now call a political question. The Constitution, they might have thought, enacted a principle condemning school segregation, but that principle was to be enforced solely through legislative action.

A historian would also want to know whether the concept of civil rights was bound up with broader concepts about the well-ordered society. If it was, as I suspect, it might help to understand the religious framework within which the adopters operated, because their concept of civil rights would ultimately be connected to their religious views, through their vision of the well-ordered society. More specifically, a historian would want to know how the 1868 concept of civil rights was connected to the 1868 vision of the public role in providing education, not in the sense of whether people in 1868 thought of access to education as a civil right but in the sense of whether their vision of the

51. A standard argument against using private letters from congressional supporters of a proposed constitutional amendment as evidence of the ratifiers' understanding is that those letters were unavailable to the public when it considered the amendment's adoption. For a version of the argument, see McConnell, *supra* note 40, at 954 ("Constitutional interpretation by its nature depends on public statements and public acts. . . . [W]hat matters is their public position on what the Constitution means."). Post-ratification evidence like McConnell's is subject to the same objection, which—as I indicate in the text—I do not believe to be a serious one.

52. *Cf.* Powell, *supra* note 39, at 674 ("The founders' comments on constitutional issues always are parts of a larger historical and intellectual whole.").

public role in providing education affected the way they defined civil rights.

As the horizon of inquiry broadens, the historian would become increasingly nervous about McConnell's mode of argument. That mode holds the concept of civil rights constant and inserts new facts about education. But if the facts about education are complexly bound up with the definition of the concept of civil rights, it is not obvious that one can fairly insert new facts without adjusting the concept of civil rights itself. The rhetoric of the conventional wisdom captures this point as follows: Someone who concludes that inserting new facts into old concepts leads to conclusions that we know the adopters rejected probably doesn't have a real grasp on what those old concepts were. Perhaps if we recalled a Republican senator who served in 1868 from the grave and taught him about the place of education in 1954, he would tell us that of course access to education was a civil right under those new circumstances. But perhaps he would tell us instead that he would structure his concept of civil rights to guarantee that it would not encompass access to education under those new circumstances.[53]

McConnell's is, I emphasize, exceptional law-office history. His rhetorical skill allows him to lead readers to think that the votes in 1874 were in themselves important.[54] He is extraordinarily talented at accounting for contradictory data. In discussing segregation in the District of Columbia, for example, McConnell forthrightly points out that proposals to desegregate the schools were defended, even by the adamantly anti-slavery Senator Charles Sumner, on policy rather than constitutional grounds.[55] But, McConnell points out that "the Fourteenth Amendment did not apply to congressional legislation," with the consequence that "senators were free to vote in accordance with their assessments of practical impact . . . rather than according to the perceived dictates of the Constitution."[56] True enough, but perhaps a

53. Similarly, the senator might say that his substantive concept of civil rights indeed encompassed education under the new circumstances, but might point out that the complex of ideas he held about civil rights included an understanding that courts would not enforce all constitutional rights; in a legal universe where courts do enforce all constitutional rights, he would not include education within the complex procedural-substantive concept of civil rights. We misunderstand the concept of civil rights that he himself held in 1868, although he now knows that he expressed himself inartfully, because he could not know what was going to happen with respect to public education or the judiciary as social institutions.

54. On the rhetorical level, McConnell accomplishes this by devoting as many pages as he does to those votes, thereby inducing readers to believe that the votes are in themselves significant.

55. McConnell, *supra* note 40, at 977-80.

56. *Id.* at 980.

bit too cute: A historian might note that congressional Republicans were the political heirs of those who had made abolition of the slave trade in the District of Columbia the centerpiece of their efforts to attack slavery within the ante bellum constitutional framework. They might wonder how those politicians, having won the war and proposed a highly principled rejection of segregation in schools everywhere else in the nation, somehow were merely practical in considering desegregation in Washington.

McConnell says that to read Congress' actions "as proof that the Congress of the day viewed segregation as constitutionally legitimate is to overread the evidence."[57] As "proof," surely. But how about "strong evidence"? And, after all, McConnell is asserting that "the Congress of the day viewed segregation as constitutionally illegitimate."[58] It is hardly overreading the evidence regarding segregation in the District of Columbia to think that it provides no support whatever for *that* proposition. McConnell is adept at using the rhetorical strategy of overstating his opponents' claims without appearing to do so, and then reasonably rejecting the overstated claims.

Perhaps the most dramatic example of McConnell's rhetorical ability is found in his discussion of post-1869 cases in which courts were asked to rule on the legality of school segregation. According to McConnell, from 1868 to 1883, nine Northern supreme courts considered the constitutionality of school segregation: Five—a majority—found that school segregation did not violate the Fourteenth Amendment. Four others invalidated school segregation.[59] McConnell acknowledges that the courts striking segregation down relied on state law, although sometimes the state law used equality language that, McConnell asserts, allows us to "infer that the court would have given the Fourteenth Amendment a similar construction had it reached the federal constitutional issue."[60] In one interesting move, McConnell discounts decisions by the California and Indiana supreme courts on the ground that "California had not ratified the Fourteenth Amendment, Indiana was notoriously the most racist of the Northern states, and both courts were dominated by Democrats, the party hostile to

57. *Id.*

58. His precise words are, "[S]chool segregation was understood during Reconstruction to violate the principles of equality of the Fourteenth Amendment." *Id.* at 1140. Note the equivocation on "during Reconstruction" here.

59. *Id.* at 971-75.

60. *Id.* at 972.

Reconstruction."[61] Courts upholding segregation, readers are invited to infer, were motivated by mean political considerations, while those striking it down were motivated by deep constitutional principle.

McConnell concludes:

> The experience in the Northern states during the fifteen year period after ratification of the Fourteenth Amendment thus falls short of proving that school segregation was understood to violate the Amendment, but it is also inconsistent with the equally extreme view that the Amendment had no bearing on the issue.[62]

This is a classic rhetorical move, describing two extreme positions and implicitly asking readers to take a position in the middle, here that the Fourteenth Amendment had some bearing on the question of school desegregation. Along the way, readers may lose sight of two propositions. McConnell's originalist argument is precisely one of the extreme views, that the Fourteenth Amendment's adopters understood it to make school segregation unconstitutional. And, perhaps more interesting, McConnell's evidence is actually this: With the exception of one unappealed lower court decision, not a single post-1868 court held that school segregation violated the Fourteenth Amendment, and every court but one to consider the question held that it did not.

It is important to emphasize that I am analyzing McConnell's rhetoric here, treating his work as history-in-law rather than as history. If my arguments have any bite, they do so because they identify places where even as talented a rhetorician as McConnell slipped. So, for example, he might have done better to avoid the rhetorical strategy of describing two extreme positions when his is one of them. And yet even that suggestion must be qualified. With respect to what audience would McConnell "have done better"? Not, I think, with respect to his primary audience. Consider the likely citation patterns for McConnell's article.[63] The standard parenthetical is likely to be "(arguing that original understanding supported holding segregation unconstitutional)." It will be followed by something like: "*Contra* Klarman, Response." It is unlikely that the criticisms contained in this

61. *Id.* at 974. I particularly like the reference to California's failure to ratify the Fourteenth Amendment. McConnell carefully does not claim that California's supreme court was thereby relieved of its obligation to enforce the Amendment. *Cf. id.* at 972 (discussing an 1868 Iowa Supreme Court case invalidating segregation before Fourteenth Amendment was legally binding).

62. *Id.* at 977.

63. Concurring in Missouri v. Jenkins, Justice Thomas cited the article to support the following proposition: "*Brown I* itself did not need to rely upon any psychological or social-science research in order to announce the simple, yet fundamental truth that the Govenrment cannot discriminate among its citizens on the basis of race." Missouri v. Jenkins, 115 S. Ct. 2038, 2065 (1995) (Thomas, J., concurring).

Article will be picked up at all. This Article is in a Symposium on legal scholarship, not on segregation or originalism, and its title does not suggest that somewhere embedded in the article is a criticism of McConnell's argument.[64] The criticisms I have offered are therefore unlikely to impair the enduring rhetorical effectiveness of McConnell's article. Why, then, should he bother to improve on an already highly effective product?

A historian reading McConnell's work might be tempted to echo a comment made about the Charge of the Light Brigade: "C'est magnifique, mais ce n'est pas l'histoire."[65] The historian would be wrong, and not only because one can translate "histoire" as "story." McConnell tells a compelling story within the genre of law-office history, which is history-in-law, not history as done by historians. The criteria for evaluating how well he performs are drawn from law rather than history. And, indeed, McConnell himself may think so. Responding to a critic who argues that constitutional history should consider "historical forces—political, social, economic, ideological, cultural,"[66] McConnell writes that, when offered as a reason to avoid attempting to justify or criticize Supreme Court decisions, "this is not just an attack on originalism. It is an attack on the traditional enterprise of constitutional law, in which the meaning of the Constitution is seen to be a legitimate question for historical and interpretive inquiry."[67] He was engaged in a legal inquiry, not a historical one.

### B. *History Lite and the Search for a Usable Past*

The past decades have seen the invention of two major constructs in the intellectual history of United States law: civic republicanism and classical legal thought. I use the words *invention* and *construct* advisedly. Martin Flaherty describes much of the literature on civic republicanism as history "lite."[68] Having scavenged the secondary historical

64. As a result, even computer-assisted research techniques may not make a difference here: The first move in the research strategy may be to locate citations to McConnell's article; the second is to look at the list of titles; the third is to discard those whose titles do not suggest that they contain substantive comments on McConnell's article. In light of my emphasis on the role authority plays in legal scholarship, it may be worth noting that occasionally this Article will survive the third step because my name appears as its author.

65. Pierre Bosquet, quoted in OXFORD DICTIONARY OF QUOTATIONS 136 (Angela Partington ed., 4th ed. 1992) ("C'est magnifique, mais ce n'est pas la guerre.").

66. Michael J. Klarman, *A Response to Professor McConnell*, 81 VA. L. REV. 1881, 1934 (1995).

67. McConnell, *supra* note 42, at 1955.

68. Martin S. Flaherty, *History "Lite" in Modern American Constitutionalism*, 95 COLUM. L. REV. 523 (1995).

literature,[69] legal scholars found something that seemed attractive, and then pursued original sources to discover snippets that could be quoted in support of their contemporary positions. They then created a body of thought they called civic republicanism. Historical material is almost exactly described as decoration in this literature.

Civic republicanism was attractive to the center-left in the legal academic spectrum. A similar construction occurred, I believe, further to the left, as Duncan Kennedy and Morton Horwitz invented what they called classical legal thought or liberal legalism. In both cases the constructs serve the legal academy well, but are problematic from a historian's point of view.

### 1. Civic Republicanism and the National Identity

The difficulties with the civic republicanism construct, treated as history, are well-known, and I merely sketch them here.[70] I have already outlined one set of problems. Civic republicanism is a term that describes one part of a complex intellectual universe in the founding era. As historians have shown, it existed in uneasy tension with ideas about religion and commerce. What the ideas of civic republicanism mean in a nation with far greater religious pluralism than existed at the founding, and where commerce is global, is quite unclear. Just as the post-Civil War concept of civil rights had the meaning it did because it was part of a larger complex of ideas, so did civic republicanism. Taking "it" out of its context makes it into something else. What it becomes may be interesting or normatively attractive, but it has little relation to the ideas actually held at the founding.

Then too the ideas actually held at the founding may not be all that attractive. Some of its contemporary advocates are attracted to civic republicanism because it provides an account of public citizenship that contrasts with the intense privatization of concerns republicanism's advocates attribute to liberalism.[71] Their critics responded that civic republicanism as it actually was had unattractive aspects—militarism, anti-feminism, and elitism—that make it an unappealing

69. The term "scavenge" is drawn from Kathryn Abrams, *Law's Republicanism*, 97 YALE L.J. 1591, 1591 (1988).

70. Descriptions of civic republicanism appear at numbers 47 and 93 on the list in this Symposium, Shapiro, *supra* note 5, at 769, 771.

71. It may be appropriate to note here that while I am sometimes linked to contemporary civic republicans, *see, e.g.*, Richard H. Fallon, Jr., *What is Republicanism, and Is It Worth Reviving?*, 102 HARV. L. REV. 1695 (1989), my endorsement of the concept was heavily qualified. *See, e.g.*, MARK TUSHNET, RED, WHITE, AND BLUE 17 (1988) ("Republicanism made sense only in a specific social setting").

model for contemporary constitutional thinking. Stripping civic republicanism of those elements, while normatively attractive, converts it into a body of thought actually held by no one in the past. Notably, modern civic republicanism tends to treat slavery in classic Whig fashion: as an excrescence fundamentally incompatible with the founders' deepest commitments.

As Martin Flaherty notes, lawyers' appropriation of civic republicanism is more sophisticated than other originalist scholarship, but it nonetheless drains the founders' intellectual universe of its real complexity.[72] I believe the reason is that modern civic republicans are not truly interested in history as such. Again, Flaherty makes the point well. Cass Sunstein, according to Flaherty, does not "invoke[ ] the Founders solely as one might cite Antonio Gramsci or Michel Foucault, that is, on the strength of the usefulness of ideas put forward by thinkers who otherwise have no direct connection to our constitutional culture." Rather, he "invokes [them] for . . . the authority that springs from their historical connection with a document and the culture it continues to shape."[73]

Modern civic republicanism offers a Whig interpretation of our present national identity.[74] The people of the United States are constituted not by ethnicity or religion, but by our shared commitment to the Constitution.[75] That commitment is reproduced by creation-narratives that describe our origins in the Constitution and by tales of development that connect the creation to the present. To modern civic republicans, their vision of civic republicanism at the founding provides a more attractive national identity than the narrative that describes the founding as liberal through and through.

The claim might well be correct in that comparative version. Consider, however, an alternative creation-narrative that acknowledged the historical complexity of the founders' intellectual universe. Such a narrative would connect us to a world in which liberal and republican elements were both available, where republicanism included militarism and elitism as well as public-mindedness, and where liberalism included pure selfishness and the power of self-making that Crevecoeur celebrated. I confess that I find the identity constituted

72. Flaherty, *supra* note 68, at 571-74.

73. *Id.* at 574.

74. The following draws on Mark Tushnet, *Living in a Constitutional Moment?: Lopez and Constitutional Theory*, 46 CASE W. RES. L. REV. 845 (1996).

75. The underlying normative claim, I believe, is two-fold: that commitment to some supra-individual identity is a human good, and that one important supra-individual identity is national. I find the first element compelling, the second far more problematic.

by that narrative far more interesting and normatively attractive than the identity constituted by Whig civic republicanism. For one thing, it acknowledges on the national and historical levels complexities in national identity that parallel the complexities of personal identity that introspection reveals.

In some sense, then, better history would give us a better narrative of national identity. That, however, is plainly a nonhistorical argument. History "lite" is satisfactory as a form of history-in-law to the extent that one finds the national identity it constitutes more attractive than the alternative that historians' history would constitute.

### 2. Classical Legal Thought and the Puzzle of Critical Legal Histories

The second great invention of recent studies of the intellectual history of legal thought is classical legal thought. Here too the work is so familiar that I will not describe it in detail.[76] Briefly, classical legal thought is said to be a body of thought characteristic of the late nineteenth century. It relied on highly abstract distinctions, for example between the state and the market, that generated legal conclusions across the entire range of law.

The narrative of classical legal thought combines two historians' story-lines: decline and fall, and irony. As Robert Gordon put it in an early assessment, the story describes "how the construct was purified of its preliberal elements and elaborated to its highest pitch in the late nineteenth century; and how, at the moment of its perfection, it started to decay under attacks from without and the pressure of its own internal contradictions."[77] And, according to Gordon, we still are "living in its ruins, no longer believing in its . . . powers, and clinging to it still because we have found nothing to replace it. . . ."[78]

Gordon calls liberal legalism a construct, which "arose and developed its own characteristic set of mediating devices" in the nineteenth century.[79] In his usage, as elsewhere in the literature on classical legal thought, the body of thought was constructed by people in the past. On closer examination, however, it appears that classical legal thought

76. The only work specifically about classical legal thought on the list in this Symposium, Shapiro, *supra* note 5, at 767, appears at number 42, but others—*e.g.*, numbers 80 and 83 (Olsen)—are strongly influenced by the construct.

77. Robert Gordon, *Critical Legal Histories*, 36 STAN. L. REV. 57, 115 (1984).

78. *Id.*

79. *Id.* at 114.

was constructed in the late twentieth century rather than the late nineteenth.

A signal of the difficulty with the construct is that "it" seems to be a living—though decaying—historical subject. The actual people who adhered to classical legal thought rarely appear in scholarship discussing it.[80] And for good reason. As constructed in recent scholarship, classical legal thought is a highly rationalized body of thought that seemed for a moment to resolve all contradictions. It decayed because it did not. I am not a specialist in late nineteenth century legal thought, but I have looked closely enough at works by people I would have thought associated with classical legal thought—Christopher Tiedemann, James Bradley Thayer, and George Ticknor Curtis—to know that what they actually believed was more complex than the story of classical legal thought allows.[81] Indeed, precisely because classical legal thought is a construct created in the late twentieth century, we can be reasonably confident that no one ever adhered to it.[82]

Why, then, pay attention to classical legal thought? Kennedy and Horwitz did identify some interesting things in late nineteenth century legal thought, which earlier scholars had not seen. They then drew the strands they identified together into the construct *classical legal thought*. That construct may function in some ways as an ideal type. People familiar with the construct are able to read the sources differently, seeing in each source one or another of the themes that form the construct.

Scholars who see classical legal thought as an ideal type may be misled in ways that Gordon's argument suggests. In usages drawn from Max Weber's confrontation with Marxism, the term *ideal type* is connected to a sense that ideal types do more than draw diverse

80. For a criticism along these lines, see Daniel R. Ernst, *The Critical Tradition in the Writing of American Legal History*, 102 YALE L.J. 1019 (1993) (reviewing MORTON J. HORWITZ, THE TRANSFORMATION OF AMERICAN LAW, 1870-1960 (1992)).

81. For a discussion of Tiedemann and Thayer, see Mark Tushnet, *Thayer's Target: Judicial Review or Democracy?*, 88 NW. U. L. REV. 9 (1993), and, for a discussion of Curtis, see Mark Tushnet, *George Ticknor Curtis, in* AMERICAN NATIONAL BIOGRAPHY (forthcoming 1998).

For example, Curtis, who died in 1894, was a Unionist Democrat whose concerns about law and order led him to strongly oppose the New York draft riots. After the War Curtis became a leading patent lawyer, representing Cyrus McCormick and Samuel F.B. Morse. Shortly before he retired from the active practice of law, Curtis took up the cause of Utah's Mormons, of all people, represented Mormon interests in the Supreme Court, and wrote powerful pamphlets defending their right to religious liberty. Curtis's thinking about law cannot be captured by the simplifications of classic legal thought. For an elaborate demonstration of the complexity of legal thought in this era, see Thomas A. Green, *Freedom and Responsibility in the Age of Pound: An Essay on Criminal Justice*, 93 MICH. L. REV. 1915 (1995).

82. For an exemplary study of how one lawyer actually thought about law, see DANIEL R. ERNST, LAWYERS AGAINST LABOR 24-48 (1995).

strands together.[83] Ideal types also have an associated dynamic. Intellectual history, of the sort represented by Kennedy and Horwitz, deals with ideas. The analogue of the dynamic of an ideal type in intellectual history is the connection among ideas. How, then, were the ideas of classical legal thought connected to each other? Not, according to Horwitz at least, because one followed inexorably from another.[84] Indeed, Horwitz's work is designed to show that ideas people believed to be connected rationally were in fact not so connected. To make this argument, however, it is essential to show that some people actually did think the ideas were connected. Drawing together strands that appear in the work of different people—creating an ideal type—will not do.[85]

As a form of critical legal history, classical legal thought is said to be connected to our current way of thinking about law. Again, the metaphors vary: Residues of classical legal thought can be found in ours; classical legal thought has left us a legacy on which we still live; our thought is genetically connected to classical legal thought; the construct *classical legal thought* helps us identify continuities between legal thought then and now. But, because no one actually adhered to classical legal thought, these claims are puzzling.

As with modern civic republicanism, contemporary creators of classical legal thought may have noticed statements made in the nineteenth century that somehow resemble statements made today, and assert connections. At the same time, they insist that classical legal thought was a highly interconnected body of thought: If a person adhered to one element of classical legal thought, he was quite likely to adhere to a great many others. At this point, the relation between classical legal thought and the present becomes quite obscure. In their best work, the modern creators of classical legal thought succeed in the historians' enterprise of emphasizing the pastness of the past. They make classical legal thought quite strange by describing how its adherents managed to think that many concepts, which we today see as quite unrelated, were actually tightly bound together.

Its creators offer classical legal thought as a critical enterprise. The more strange it is, however, the more puzzling is the claim that it

83. *See* MAX WEBER, MAX WEBER ON LAW IN ECONOMY AND SOCIETY 213, 352 (Max Rheinstein ed., 1954).

84. *See* HORWITZ, *supra* note 80, at 33-63.

85. I do not doubt that some people actually did believe that some of the strands were rationally connected, and that in the universe of late nineteenth century legal thinkers we can find a network of connections drawn by one or another thinker that actually covers the entire construct of classical legal thought.

offers a critical perspective on modern legal thought. If one thought that classical legal thought combined elements that were logically mutually entailed, one would have some critical leverage. Suppose a critic thought that some people adhered to one element of classical legal thought that the critic found unattractive, and thought as well that people rejected other elements on the ground that they found those elements unattractive. If the elements of classical legal thought were mutually entailed, the critic could then chastise them for logical inconsistency, and hope that they would abandon the critic's disfavored element rather than embrace the elements they currently reject.

Unfortunately, that is not how the literature on classical legal thought reads. It emphasizes internal contradiction rather than insisting on logical entailments. Although its adherents are presented as believing that classical legal thought constituted a logically integrated whole, they were wrong. Actually, according to today's scholars of classical legal thought, classical legal thought was nothing more than an ensemble of disparate elements, bricolage in Levi-Strauss's terms.[86]

This way of presenting classical legal thought has some critical bite, but not much. Consider again the critic who finds some aspect of today's legal thought unattractive. If the critic's targets believe that legal thought consists of logical entailments, they may believe that some logical necessity compels them to accept some things they dislike in order to get other things they like more. Critics may combat a false necessitarian strain in today's thinking by demonstrating that classical legal thought was bricolage even though its adherents thought it consisted of logical entailments.[87] The critic might thereby induce readers to discard a rule if they initially believed it to be an unfortunate but necessary consequence of other, more fundamental rules.

If all legal thought is bricolage, however, the idea of genetic connections between past legal thought and today's, and the ideas of legacies and residues, become quite hard to understand. Consider, for example, a concept like *patriarchy*. Legal scholars surely can identify elements of legal thought in the nineteenth century properly denominated patriarchal, and they can do so as well with elements in contemporary legal thought. But, precisely because the earlier elements were part of an ensemble of ideas strikingly different from today's, the con-

86. Claude Levi-Strauss, The Savage Mind 17 (1966).

87. I believe that this is the dominant theme in Gordon, *supra* note 77.

cept *patriarchy* cannot mean the same thing when applied both to older and to contemporary ideas.[88]

The construction of classical legal thought looks like history, but it is not history as historians would do it. It overlooks too much complexity in the way people in the late nineteenth century actually thought about law, and it fails to connect their legal thought to anything other than a vaguely described economic system and a badly specified conservatism. That said, classical legal thought is perfectly fine history-in-law. Its creators, like the modern civic republicans, have substantially affected the way we think about law, whether or not they have taught us much about the past.

## IV. Policing the Boundaries

One might think that some historians' standards could be relevant to assessing the use of history in legal scholarship even if history-in-law is a genre of legal scholarship rather than a version of historical scholarship.[89] That would be true to the extent that those who engage in one practice take seriously the comments and criticisms made by people who engage in another. It might be part of the practice of history-in-law, for example, that criticisms levelled by historians count against the persuasiveness of a history-in-law argument. Most notably, one might think that legal scholars using history in law would perform badly if they got the facts wrong.[90]

One might think that, but one would be wrong.[91] In 1992, the *Yale Law Journal* published an article by two well-regarded scholars in which they made a number of elementary factual errors.[92] One is particularly striking: The authors asserted that Robert Morris made cer-

88. See Reva Siegel, *"The Rule of Love": Wife Beating as Prerogative and Privacy*, 105 Yale L.J. 2117 (1996), for an interesting though undertheorized effort to establish a genetic connection through a process Siegel calls "preservation-through-transformation in the structure of a status regime," *id.* at 2178.

89. Flaherty, *supra* note 68, at 551-52, argues for invoking standards that "come from the discipline of history itself" because historians "commonly resolve what is historically convincing," and because it makes sense to defer to specialists.

90. *See id.* at 552 ("Perhaps the most basic [criterion] is simply getting elementary facts straight.").

91. Historians have other standards as well, but they seem to me as much standards of effective argument, such as "Do not disregard contrary evidence" and "Do not quote out of context," as they are standards of good historical practice.

92. David A. Strauss & Cass R. Sunstein, *The Senate, the Constitution, and the Confirmation Process*, 101 Yale L.J. 1491 (1992), with errors identified in John O. McGinnis, *The President, the Senate, the Constitution, and the Confirmation Process: A Reply to Professors Strauss and Sunstein*, 71 Tex. L. Rev. 633, 634-35 n.7 (1993).

tain statements at the Constitutional Convention.[93] In fact, Gouverneur Morris made them.[94] A historian would find this a significant mistake. To understand what the speaker meant, an intellectual historian would say we have to understand how those statements fit into the speaker's overall intellectual universe. The historian would try to relate the speaker's statements about the President's power to nominate to the speaker's views about popular democracy, aristocracy, the well-ordered government, religion, and much else. A historian would at least worry that a set of words uttered by Gouverneur Morris really meant something quite different from the same set of words uttered by Robert Morris.[95] If one misidentifies the speaker, that effort at real understanding simply cannot get off the ground.

Of course even historians make mistakes. Sometimes the mistakes may be irrelevant to the historian's argument.[96] Or sometimes a historian may have sufficient authority, based on his or her prior work or the power of the argument elsewhere in the piece where the mistake occurred, for historians to treat a mistake as harmless. Neither response seems to me available here.[97]

As we have seen, history-in-law does not really try to explain what people in the past thought. A misidentification is therefore not terribly significant. Indeed, the critic who pointed out the identification error did not regard it as a scholarly failure. He concluded, instead, that "The *Yale Law Journal* must share responsibility for many of the[ ] errors."[98] And the authors responded, "We are grateful to [the critic] for correcting some errors in identifying the first names of certain delegates. We do not believe, however, that these errors are relevant to the correctness of the propositions discussed in our essay."[99] That is nicely put: The error lay in providing the wrong first name, not in naming the wrong person. Of course even these scholars

93. Strauss & Sunstein, *supra* note 92, at 1498.

94. *See* McGinnis *supra* note 92, at 639 n.29 (citing THE RECORDS OF THE FEDERAL CONVENTION OF 1789, at 539 (Max Farrand ed., 1966)).

95. McGinnis, *id.* at 639-40, does briefly describe Gouverneur Morris's broader views.

96. I am embarrassed to note that in TUSHNET, *supra* note 34, at 176-77, I located Topeka in Oklahoma, as part of a transition between one discussion and another. But I *am* embarrassed. (I also note that I am invoking my authority *qua* historian here.)

97. One can, just barely, construct an interpretive theory according to which the mere fact that some founder—no matter who—uttered certain words has some bearing on how the Constitution should be interpreted. If originalism in its best forms is questionable, this bastardized originalism seems completely implausible. (Jack Balkin suggested the possibility of such an interpretive theory to me, without endorsing it.)

98. McGinnis, *supra* note 92, at 635 n.7.

99. David A. Strauss & Cass R. Sunstein, *On Truisms and Constitutional Obligations: A Response*, 71 TEX. L. REV. 669, 672 n.17 (1993).

would undoubtedly have preferred to get at least the names right,[100] although they appear unconcerned about the relation between a person's particular statements and the overall context of thought that can deepen our understanding of those statements.

This is only one example, but surely it is suggestive. Getting the facts right did not matter much to these authors or even to their critic. Yet it would seem that the least demanding requirement a historian would impose on a legal scholar's use of history is that the legal scholar get the facts right. The practice of history-in-law apparently can go on even when that requirement is not met.[101]

Readers of a draft of this Article sounded Jefferson Powell's theme.[102] Bad history, they urged, was bad advocacy and *therefore* was bad history-in-law, just as Leiter believes that bad $philosophy_1$ is bad $philosophy_2$. I may be too cynical, or I may have read more widely in the literature that constitutes history-in-law, but my understanding of the practice is that the connection between the standards of $discipline_1$ and those of the legal academy is much looser than that.[103] Asking legal scholars to satisfy even the most basic criteria drawn from the practice of history misunderstands the practice of history-in-law.

## V. Conclusion

Law-office history has a bad name, at least among historians. It shouldn't.[104] Law-office history is a legal practice, not a historical one. The criteria for evaluating it, for determining what is a successful per-

100. Similarly, practitioners of history-in-law undoubtedly think they are writing history, just as practitioners of $philosophy_2$ may well think they are doing $philosophy_1$. The connection between engaging in a particular practice and thinking that you are engaging in a different one is quite complex. I find Stanley Fish, *Dennis Martinez and the Uses of Theory*, 96 Yale L.J. 1773 (1987), the most helpful introduction.

101. This would not be true if the article or its authors lost credibility because of its sloppiness with respect to historical detail. It is not my impression that this has happened, although I have been told that some scholars "think that even this mistake was indicative of a general insouciance about history that robs the argument of much of the force it sought by invoking history in the first place." (I regard the source of the information as confidential.)

102. *See supra* text accompanying note 39.

103. Martin Flaherty pointed out to me that this may change as more scholars with formal training in other disciplines become law professors. I confess to some skepticism. Although a full-scale defense of my position is out of place here, I simply assert the following: The politically motivated resurgence of originalism as a theory of constitutional interpretation has generated what is now a very large body of legal scholarship—history-in-law—that is (a) quite bad according to historians' standards, and (b) published in the most prestigious law reviews.

104. Having gone back and forth in my mind over including this footnote, I decided to point out that this Article is written in the trope of *irony*. My ambivalence about including this footnote reflects my concern that I have failed if the footnote is necessary.

formance, must be drawn from legal practice rather than from historical practice.[105] I believe the same conclusion can be drawn about interdisciplinary legal scholarship generally. In this sense, lists like the one that opens this Symposium are extremely helpful in identifying the legal academy's criteria for good performance.[106]

105. I have refrained from describing those criteria, in large part because the material discussed in § IV *supra* shakes my confidence in my ability to do so. That is, my first candidate for doing history-in-law well probably would have been that it helps to get the facts right. With that off the list, I am puzzled about what comes next.

106. A cynic might say that the list indicates that the two main criteria are that a good performer have a job at a top-ranked law school and write articles that students at top-ranked law schools regard as worth publishing. As a colleague and I have argued elsewhere, however, this cynical view fails to appreciate that the causal arrow may run from "having high potential as a good performer" to "having a job at a top-ranked law school" rather than, as the cynic would have it, the other way. Mark Tushnet & Timothy Lynch, *The Project of the Harvard Forewords: A Social and Intellectual Inquiry*, 11 CONST. COMMENTARY 463, 468-69 (1994-95).

# Part Three

# Constitutional Law Scholarship

# [14]

# Truth, Justice, and the American Way: An Interpretation of Public Law Scholarship in the Seventies

*What do the decisions of courts in general and of the United States Supreme Court in particular represent? In this Article, Professor Tushnet draws eclectically from the inadequacies of prior jurisprudential responses, the current state of public law scholarship, legal nihilism, and Marxist thought to support an answer, earlier suggested by Holmes, that is as disquieting as it is compelling.*

In 1873 Oliver Wendell Holmes, Jr., wrote a comment on scholarly response in England to a decision that upheld the convictions of labor strikers for criminal conspiracy to interfere with their employer's business.[1] The English commentary criticized the decision because it demonstrated that the law, which should be neutral, actually favored one class over another. Holmes in turn criticized the commentators' assumption that law could be neutrally derived. To him, their arguments "presuppose[d] an identity of interest between the different parts of a community which [did] not exist in fact."[2] Holmes challenged the presupposition of the critics on two levels. He first demonstrated that no single, unifying theory explained the development of the common law or, by implication, the law as a whole.[3] He further claimed, in his

A shorter version of this Article was presented at the Second National Conference on Critical Legal Studies, Nov. 10-12, 1978, in Madison, Wisconsin. As always, I must acknowledge the help of Elizabeth Alexander. In addition, Robert Gordon, Arthur Leff, David Trubek, and Bill Whitford made useful comments. I also owe a debt to the faculty of the Law School of the University of Texas.

1. Comment, *The Gas-Stoker's Strike*, 7 AM. L. REV. 582 (1873). For a discussion of Holmes' comment, see Tushnet, *The Logic of Experience: Oliver Wendell Holmes on the Supreme Judicial Court*, 63 VA. L. REV. 975, 1029-31 (1977).

2. Comment, *supra* note 1, at 583.

3. *See id.*

Texas Law Review Vol. 57:1307, 1979

deeper moments, that the multiplicity on the intellectual level resulted from a lack of unity on the social level.[4]

Both assertions pose immediate and related problems. If there is in fact no unity to the law, what do the decisions of the courts represent? The obvious answer had been given long before by Thrasymachus:[5] the interest of the stronger. For several centuries the liberal theory of the rule of law, with its assumption that general rules, applied even-handedly, would produce effects that benefited all, had been thought an adequate response to Thrasymachus. But Holmes' second claim, if true, would discredit the liberal theory, not for its philosophical inadequacy, but because the social basis upon which its acceptance must rest could not exist in a class-divided society. At the same time, however, the description of judicial behavior implicit in Thrasymachus' answer is obviously far too simple. When a judge selects a doctrine, he or she may be exercising power, but it rarely feels like that. Nor is there an obvious connection in many areas of the law between doctrine and power: the fellow-servant rule is one thing, but what of the doctrine of supervening cause to which it is related? The weakness of the answer is particularly apparent in constitutional law, whose function is precisely to displace decisions made by a majority, in a sense by the stronger, in favor of the interests of the minority. The claim that constitutional law is a simple expression of class power rings especially hollow.

Because I believe that Holmes was fundamentally correct even about constitutional law, I will explore his challenges in this Article. The first two sections illustrate that the problems Holmes addressed have plagued American public law, and the associated scholarship, from its beginning. The first section presents a historical overview of public law scholarship through the 1970s and demonstrates that the problems in this scholarship are so persistent that they provide inductive support for Holmes' claim that they are rooted in a class-divided society. The second section examines several areas of contemporary scholarship and argues that the prevailing approach also fails to answer Holmes' challenge. These two sections are designed both to show that the challenge retains the ring of truth and to establish that, if constitutional law scholarship is to be intellectually respectable, prevailing conceptions of the scholar's role must be altered.

The third section examines legal nihilism, the most powerful an-

4. *See id.*
5. *See* PLATO, THE REPUBLIC, Book I, 338.

swer to Holmes and to the general problems of legal scholarship. Nihilism gains its power precisely because it agrees with Holmes that there is no overall coherence to the law. The nihilists sometimes also agree that the incoherence is based upon social division, but tend to accept division as an immutable fact of life and the use of law in aid of power as either random, or if systematically applied in favor of one or several groups, unalterable. The final section develops a post-nihilist approach to public law scholarship. Drawing upon Marxist thought, I argue that legal doctrine can be understood as a complex expression of power in a class-divided society and that a Marxist approach can begin to explain why nihilism properly rejects synthetic analyses of law in contemporary American society. The Marxist approach, however, also provides reasons for rejecting nihilism itself as incorrectly generalizing from law in class-divided societies to the idea of law in general. I must confess, however, that my suggestions for post-nihilist scholarship are offered with a great deal of skepticism and some sheer hope.

## I. The Course of Constitutional Law Scholarship

American constitutional law scholarship can be viewed as a continuing dialogue between natural law and institutionalist perspectives. Both assume that the constitutional design should guarantee the conditions of a just society, but differ in the assignment of the courts' role in that order. The natural law jurist believes that the Constitution embodies principles of justice and that courts should therefore give content to those principles in particular cases. The institutionalists, because they are either moral relativists or skeptics, or because they see majoritarianism as fundamental to justice, treat the Constitution as specifying only an institutional design and concomitantly question judicial displacement of legislative choice.

### *A. The Background*

The dialogue began at least as early as *Marbury v. Madison*,[6] in which the Supreme Court asserted its power to overturn legislative decisions when necessary to protect individual rights. The Court's concern for rights could have rested on either substantive or procedural grounds. Rights could have been given substantive content, by referring to a supportable theory of justice or to a widely shared view of what constituted a good society, or they could have been validated by the process by which the rights were developed. Professor Duncan

6. 1 U.S. (1 Cranch) 137 (1803).

Texas Law Review Vol. 57:1307, 1979

Kennedy has shown that legal thought in the era of Marshall and beyond was unintegrated, containing both substantive and procedural strains.[7] In public law the dominant strain, as displayed in early Supreme Court opinions, was one of process; John Marshall believed, for example, that the evolutionary process by which common law rights developed was itself sufficient to entitle them to respect.[8] In addition, an important theme of the liberal social theory on which the Nation was founded made process validation philosophically necessary. That theory found value judgments to be necessarily subjective, a condition that rendered impossible the establishment of a stable political order on any group of objectively derived substantive values.[9] Liberal theory adapted to this difficulty by focusing on process:[10] judges were not to center on subjective notions, but on what seemed objective aspects of the general lawmaking process.[11] Process validation also appears to reconcile majoritarianism and judicial review, since it does not challenge the propriety of well-considered decisions made by an organ truly representative of majority will. Instead, this approach points to blockages in the representative process and acts either to remove them or to supplant substantive decisions pending the improvement of the process.

Process validation was extremely popular within the legal community, but its appeal outside that circle was limited.[12] It was simply too difficult to articulate and to integrate with developing themes in other aspects of intellectual life, at least when the relevant process was common law adjudication, to gain mass acceptance. The common law process was, as its defenders made as plain as they could, unsystematic and inductive, moving from particular cases to general rules and back again. But the enlightenment of American society was inducing a general trend toward the deductive approach to ideas. The obscurity of common law reasoning further frustrated the defenders of the method

7. D. Kennedy, The Rise of Classical Legal Thought II-64A-6 (1978) (unpublished manuscript).

8. *See generally* R. Faulkner, The Jurisprudence of John Marshall 67-79 (1968).

9. *See generally* R. Unger, Knowledge & Politics (1975).

10. Religion would have been an alternative adaptation, but one that implicitly rejected liberal premises. However, the secularism and religious pluralism of American society were so entrenched by 1800 that direct appeal to religious values would not have been consistent with other structures of society, the second requirement for an acceptable constitutional theory. Appeal to rights justified in secular terms could, nevertheless, still draw support from sectors in which religious values remained important.

11. *See generally* Nelson, *The Eighteenth-Century Background of John Marshall's Jurisprudence*, 76 Mich. L. Rev. 893 (1978).

12. *See* P. Miller, The Life of the Mind in America (1965).

Truth, Justice, and the American Way

in an era when democratic control over significant social institutions was a primary political issue.

The antislavery movement, with its strong religious components, provided a social base in which natural law theories could take root.[13] In a sequence to be repeated, the abolitionists saw that slavery was accepted as the result of existing processes, rejected not just those particular processes but the whole idea that outcomes could be validated by process, and developed transcendent theories of substantive justice that demonstrated the legal unacceptability of slavery. These theories have rightly been regarded as deviant, for although the impulse that generated the theories had a permanent effect, their substantive components never settled into constitutional law. That impulse, however, led scholars to base their adherence to natural law views on the argument that the rights protected by the Constitution were those generally thought deserving of protection. By this maneuver natural law scholars attempted to avoid the charge that judges were writing their personal and therefore subjective values into the Constitution; they could concede that values were subjective while maintaining that courts could decide, by an essentially empirical inquiry, which subjective values were widely shared.

Once this legerdemain was effected, however, the institutionalist challenge was obvious: How can a court protect an interest on the ground that it is generally thought deserving of protection in the face of a determination by the representatives of the people that the interest should not be protected? Of course, truly aberrational statutes might be struck down, but as long as a statute met minimum standards of rationality, the institutionalist challenge was hard to answer.[14] The challenge lost its vitality, however, not because a solid rebuttal was formulated, but because during this period the Supreme Court considered mainly issues of institutional design and reached results that authorized action in aid of what were then regarded as important elements of the human personality. The Court's approach, in other words, was consistent with the dominant "release of energy" principle, which itself was rooted in normative conceptions and which was so widely shared that it formed a solid basis for consensus validation.[15] Substantive bases for

13. *See generally* R. Cover, Justice Accused: Antislavery and the Judicial Process (1975); W. Wiecek, The Sources of Antislavery Constitutionalism in America, 1760-1848 (1977).

14. For a powerful early statement of this challenge, see Eakin v. Raub, 12 Serg. & Rawl. 330 (Pa. 1825) (Gibson, J., dissenting).

15. *See generally* J. Hurst, Law and the Conditions of Freedom in the Nineteenth-Century United States 3-32 (1956).

constitutional law were thus found in consensus, not in coherent theories of justice.

By the 1870s and 1880s, however, consensus validation had become extremely weak. The Civil War and its constitutional ramifications had shaken the belief in norms shared throughout society. Attempts to restore that belief took several forms. Some consititutional theorists claimed that the extension of rights to blacks merely carried out the plan implicit in widely shared values, even though pressures of the moment and influences from social position impeded the overt expression of that plan.[16] Others, arguing that the constitutional changes after the Civil War only made clear that existing common law rights were shared by black men too, reverted to the process-validation approach.[17] Neither attempt was wholly persuasive, largely because they both once again required a degree of sophistication in expression that made widespread acceptance difficult. Just as earlier theorists had abandoned process validation because they found it easier to support their positions on less recondite grounds, so later theorists found it difficult to appeal to intellectualistic theories of either process or what we would now call "reflective equilibrium."[18] Even apart from the strains of the Civil War, consensus was evidently breaking down. The precise context of Holmes' observations,[19] a labor dispute, illustrates the point well enough, and developments in legislation further showed that the social basis for consensus validation was disappearing; social legislation in aid of workers and farmers was enacted, bringing legal challenges that shaped the jurisprudential response to the breakdown of consensus. Defenders of the consensus-validation approach constructed elaborate theories to justify overturning such statutes,[20] but though the synthesis of common law rights with consensual validation dominated the Supreme Court for many years, its internal weaknesses were apparent from the moment of its creation: a philosophical defense of judicial intervention in aid of rights was too subtle to be effective, and the basis for consensus had been eroded.

Holmes' challenge, further elaborated in his influential lectures on the common law,[21] set the framework for serious public law scholarship to the present. Of course, theorists devoted time to elaborating the

16. *See, e.g.*, H. BELZ, A NEW BIRTH OF FREEDOM 54-57 (1976).
17. *See, e.g.*, J. TENBROECK, EQUAL UNDER LAW 66-91 (rev. ed. 1965).
18. *See* J. RAWLS, A THEORY OF JUSTICE 19-21 (1971).
19. *See* note 1 *supra* & accompanying text.
20. *See generally* A. PAUL, CONSERVATIVE CRISIS AND THE RULE OF LAW (1960).
21. Holmes, *Law in Science and Science in Law*, 12 HARV. L. REV. 443 (1899); Holmes, *The Path of the Law*, 10 HARV. L. REV. 457 (1897).

process-consensus synthesis, but the synthesis could not answer Holmes' challenge because developments in the political economy made it the bulwark of a retreating social order. However, it was difficult indeed to come up with an alternative that acknowledged the fragmentation of American society while maintaining the connection between law and justice. Holmes' articulated position, that of neutral observer of a partisan struggle, is hard to sustain among professionals, like law teachers, who aspire to public influence. Holmes himself occasionally slipped from the detached role, though he engaged in an extended effort to develop a theory of judging that could be used by an observer wearing judicial robes.[22]

Roscoe Pound developed the first substantial response to Holmes, which culminated in the theory of sociological jurisprudence.[23] Sociological jurisprudence called for a delicate adjustment of law to actual conditions, an adjustment that would be based upon careful inquiry into the facts of social life that law was to regulate and upon considered choices among alternative legal solutions to social problems that would reflect the actual operation of legal institutions. Inquiry and ultimately choice, however, must have some basis. One might be sheer partisanship. But although the institutional position of the sociological jurisprudes was reasonably secure, their intellectual position would have been undermined had they become overt partisans. If they simply chose sides in an essentially political struggle, they would have had to explain why they concentrated their efforts in the upper reaches of academic life, and they would have found such an explanation hard to come by. Instead, the sociological jurisprudes reverted to consensual validation. The Supreme Court's problems, they ultimately concluded, arose from the Court's assumption that there was societal agreement with its premises. In fact, they claimed, the Court properly searched for consensual validation but found the wrong consensus: the Court relied on a nonexistent agreement, but could be rescued if it returned to the real consensus.[24]

Thus, sociological jurisprudence responded to Holmes' challenge by denying the thrust of his second perception, that all law is partisan.[25]

22. *See* Tushnet, *supra* note 1, at 1041-44.

23. *See generally* White, *From Sociological Jurisprudence to Realism: Jurisprudence and Social Change in Early Twentieth-Century America*, 58 VA. L. REV. 999 (1972).

24. *See* Pound, *The Theory of Judicial Decision* (pts. 1-3), 36 HARV. L. REV. 641, 802, 940 (1923-1924).

25. As I argue in section IV of this Article, that perception was itself derived from a perfectly accurate view that the advance of capitalist industrialization had fragmented the social unity needed to support a belief in enduring neutral principles of law.

Texas Law Review Vol. 57:1307, 1979

The legal realists, however, shared the vision of Holmes and once again raised his challenge.[26] Responding in part to the increasing importance of mediating institutions such as labor unions, the legal realists acknowledged the partial fragmentation of bourgeois society. Some took the fragmentation to be complete and argued that no legal decision had a necessary relation to any other, or to any enduring scheme of values.[27] But this vision proved too bleak. More commonly, the legal realists revived the process-validation approach to the law. Because the various sectoral interests asserted themselves in the legislative process, it yielded acceptable results, not because the results were consistent with principles of justice, but because they were produced by an acceptable process. The realists were also pressed to adopt this position by attacks on realism as amoral in a world threatened by the moral anarchy of totalitarianism.[28] Thus, legal realism embodied the full revival of institutional concerns and, by replacing a morality of results with a morality of process, sought to incorporate natural law approaches into the institutionalist framework.[29]

The realist synthesis, which reached its fullest expression in the school of "reasoned elaboration"[30] of the late 1950s and early 1960s, ultimately proved unacceptable. Scholars could tolerate this solution only as long as they were willing to accept the outcomes of process as generally just. But the civil rights and antiwar movements forced these realists to acknowledge the tension between their approach to morality and the perceived requirements of a just society. Their response, as typified by a pamphlet written by Justice Abe Fortas,[31] was to try to domesticate the substantive challenges. Thus, civil disobedience, according to Justice Fortas, was acceptable when dissenters challenged statutes as unconstitutional, but unacceptable when they challenged

26. It is important here to emphasize that the transitions from laissez-faire public policy to Progressivism to New Deal policy supported these intellectual developments. See Purcell, *American Jurisprudence Between the Wars: Legal Realism and the Crisis of Democratic Theory*, 75 AM. HIST. REV. 424 (1969); White, *supra* note 23. My main concern, however, is with intellectual weaknesses of the various forms of constitutional theorizing in American society, since the inability of intelligent people to develop a theory that has any staying power suggests that the social basis for such a theory is lacking.

27. Wesley Sturges is named as an example of this kind of advocate in G. GILMORE, THE AGES OF AMERICAN LAW 81 (1977).

28. *See* White, *The Evolution of Reasoned Elaboration: Jurisprudential Criticism and Social Change*, 59 VA. L. REV. 279 (1973).

29. Institutionalism was only one strand of realist thought; another strand yielded scientistic approaches, treating law as policy science. *See* Lasswell & McDougall, *Legal Education and Policy: Professional Training in the Public Interest*, 52 YALE L.J. 203 (1943). One descendant of this strand of realist thought is the law and economics school, which has had little influence on constitutional law scholarship. *See* notes 156-160 *infra* & accompanying text.

30. *See* White, *supra* note 28, at 279 n.2.

31. A. FORTAS, CONCERNING DISSENT AND CIVIL DISOBEDIENCE (1968).

them as evil, regardless of their constitutionality.[32]

Although this approach was sensible within the terms of the realist synthesis, it failed to capture the experience of even those civil rights activists whose actions it sought to justify. Further, the civil rights movement brought into sharp relief the failures of the pluralistic legislative process upon which the realist synthesis relied for its morality of process. The responses to the civil rights movement took several forms. One group of scholars, acknowledging the distinction between law and justice, concluded that the latter could be achieved through political action that only tactically relied on legal action. This group developed parts of the theory of public interest law,[33] but in the nature of the enterprise was largely uninterested in the details of traditional constitutional law scholarship. Another group placed the civil rights movement in a modified institutionalist framework, arguing that it was possible to identify those general situations in which pluralism was likely to fail and thus to justify judicial intervention in those situations either to restore pluralism[34] or to correct the substantive results of the distorted process.[35] The branch of equal protection law concerned with suspect classifications and part of the branch concerned with fundamental interests are the products of this revised institutionalism.[36] A final group transformed institutionalism into natural law, by first insisting on the relevance of substantive theories of justice to constitutional law and then expanding the notion of the institutional competence of courts.[37]

The realist synthesis also failed to answer the Holmesian challenge; it simply shifted the locus of difficulty. Holmes had said that law could not be seen as the product or embodiment of neutral principles of justice because the fragmentation of society precluded agreement. The realist synthesis responded by propounding that process was all. But the absence of the social conditions for agreement on substance was simultaneously an absence of the conditions for agreement on process. Furthermore, the bleakest realists, whose views were not

32. *Id.* at 51-57, 63.

33. *See, e.g.,* Cahn & Cahn, *Power to the People or the Profession?—The Public Interest in Public Interest Law*, 79 YALE L.J. 1005 (1970).

34. *See, e.g.,* Baker v. Carr, 369 U.S. 186 (1962).

35. *See, e.g.,* Frontiero v. Richardson, 411 U.S. 677 (1973).

36. Stewart, *The Reformation of American Administrative Law*, 88 HARV. L. REV. 1667 (1976), is an interesting synthesis of the public interest and reconstructed institutionalist approaches. The leading contemporary scholar who holds this view is John Hart Ely. *See, e.g.,* Ely, *Toward a Representation-Reinforcing Mode of Judicial Review*, 37 MD. L. REV. 451 (1978).

37. The logical sequence would be the reverse, but the major works in the expansion of the notion of institutional competence were not drawn together until 1977. *See* R. DWORKIN, TAKING RIGHTS SERIOUSLY (1977); notes 64-68 *infra* & accompanying text.

accepted into the realist synthesis, had accurately described the extent of fragmentation in bourgeois society. The sectoral interests to which adherents of the synthesis attached themselves as partisans existed as constructs but not as real social forces. Thus, the realists' attempt to achieve justice through partisan activity in politics while bracketing that activity from their analysis of the law led to artificiality in both spheres: the divorce of law and substantive principles of justice could not be sustained by injecting those principles into a political arena that was perceptibly unresponsive to claims of right. By the 1960s the failure of the realist synthesis was generally apparent; institutionalism had had its day and had been superseded.

### *B. The Current State of Constitutional Scholarship*

Attempts to reinfuse constitutional law with principles of justice persisted into and throughout the 1970s. The attempt to recast constitutional law as natural law has faced a recurring challenge that recapitulates, on a somewhat different level, the natural law/institutionalist dialectic of the preceding half-century.

Dissents from the realist synthesis in the 1960s failed to make much headway because they relied on substantive moral positions that, while heart-warming, seemed rooted only in the authors' evident good will.[38] Professor Frank Michelman made the first significant effort to develop rules of constitutional law that had an apparently more objective basis.[39] He drew on the work of his colleague at Harvard, John Rawls, who had completed but had not yet published his major reconstruction of political theory. When Rawls' book[40] appeared, it was greeted with enormous enthusiasm in the law reviews.[41] Because I am concerned here with intellectual history, I need not rehearse the critiques of Rawls produced in these and other articles. It is enough to note that critics generally perceived Rawls as presenting a serious but

38. *See, e.g.*, Black, *The Supreme Court, 1966 Term—Foreword: "State Action," Equal Protection, and California's Proposition 14*, 81 HARV. L. REV. 69 (1967); Black, *The Lawfulness of the Segregation Decisions*, 69 YALE L.J. 421 (1960); Pollak, *Racial Discrimination and Judicial Integrity: A Reply to Professor Wechsler*, 108 U. PA. L. REV. 1 (1959).

39. Michelman, *The Supreme Court, 1968 Term—Foreword: On Protecting the Poor Through the Fourteenth Amendment*, 83 HARV. L. REV. 7 (1969).

40. J. RAWLS, *supra* note 18.

41. *See, e.g.*, *Symposium: John Rawls's* A Theory of Justice, 40 U. CHI. L. REV. 486 (1973); Bentley, *John Rawls: A Theory of Justice*, 121 U. PA. L. REV. 1070 (1973); Michelman, *In Pursuit of Constitutional Welfare Rights: One View of Rawls' Theory of Justice*, 121 U. PA. L. REV. 962 (1973); Scanlon, *Rawls' Theory of Justice*, 121 U. PA. L. REV. 1020 (1973). It is of some interest that *A Theory of Justice* is the only law-related work on the list of the 100 books cited most often by social scientists. Garfield, *The 100 Books Most Cited by Social Scientists, 1969-1977*, CURRENT CONTENTS, Sept. 11, 1978, at 5, 16.

flawed effort to demonstrate the moral basis of substantive principles of justice. Nevertheless, Rawls' effort was just what was needed to combat the realist synthesis—a theory predicated on the view that substantive principles were unavailable because they were necessarily subjective. Rawls made it at least respectable to argue that substantive principles could be developed objectively from reasoned reflection about the postions "we" took on concrete issues. Although some have attempted to apply his principles to specific problems of constitutional law,[42] the importance of his work lies not in the principles it proposed, but in the validation it gave to the enterprise of reconciling law and justice.

The Supreme Court's original abortion decisions[43] augmented the attraction of natural law reasoning. Reformulated institutionalism might have dealt with many of the Warren Court's liberal decisions, but it was immediately apparent that the abortion decisions could not possibly rest on institutionalist grounds;[44] only a philosophical defense[45] of the decisions had even a modest chance of success. Constitutional law scholars thus sought guidance from the philosophers. Rawlsian approaches slid into legal discussion because Rawls' Kantianism was virtually the only game in town; it alone developed principles palatable to the liberalism of legal academics.[46]

The several difficulties that attend this development are best exemplified in what must be regarded as the major synthetic effort of recent years, Professor Laurence Tribe's treatise on constitutional law,[47] which at various points makes its Rawlsian heritage clear.[48] The first difficulty is one that may be inherent in the enterprise of structuring a treatise around decided cases: there is no reason to think that cases decided by the Supreme Court even approximate the results that we would reach in applying a coherent moral theory to constitutional law, and little reason to think that the cases in general pose serious moral issues.[49] Nevertheless, Professor Tribe seeks to develop a philo-

42. *See, e.g.*, D. RICHARDS, THE MORAL CRITICISM OF LAW (1977).

43. Doe v. Bolton, 410 U.S. 179 (1973); Roe v. Wade, 410 U.S. 113 (1973).

44. *See, e.g.*, Ely, *Constitutional Interpretivism: Its Allure and Impossibility*, 53 IND. L.J. 399 (1978).

45. For a useful collection of philosophical struggles with the abortion issue, see THE RIGHTS AND WRONGS OF ABORTION (M. Cohen, T. Nagel & T. Scanlon eds. 1974).

46. The contrast to Robert Nozick is evident. It was not until 1978 that any law review published a symposium issue on Nozick's *Anarchy, State, and Utopia*. *See Symposium—Robert Nozick's* Anarchy, State, and Utopia, 19 ARIZ. L. REV. 1 (1977).

47. L. TRIBE, AMERICAN CONSTITUTIONAL LAW (1978).

48. For example, Professor Tribe relies on Michelman, *supra* note 39, for his discussion of poverty. L. TRIBE, *supra* note 47, § 16-33, at 1098-99 n.4.

49. In Richards, *Taking "Taking Rights Seriously" Seriously: Reflections on Dworkin and the*

sophically acceptable body of substantive rules by ordering and explaining existing case law. Needless to say, this method has a deeply conservative effect, since its implicit premise is that existing law need only be tinkered with to make it consistent with philosophically valid principles of justice.

Two examples will illustrate the difficulties that concentration on Supreme Court cases can create for a moral theory of constitutional law. *Smith v. Organization of Foster Families*[50] was a challenge to a New York statute regulating the process by which an authorized placement agency could remove foster children from their foster families. Because of recent developments in constitutional law, a preliminary issue arose about whether the foster parents or the children had a property or a liberty interest in the continuation of their relationship. After a struggle within the Court that left marks on the opinion, the majority concluded that although both had a liberty interest with "its source . . . in intrinsic human rights," the New York scheme adequately protected that interest.[51] Professor Tribe, at first diffidently but then more firmly, used this statement to support his natural law views,[52] as indeed it does. But the Court's struggle with the conclusion is apparent, and a sensitive reading of the case indicates that this portion of it is unlikely to be followed.[53]

The second example shows a similar overreading of a case. Introducing a section on the government's power to shape the mind, Professor Tribe stated his premises:

> Whatever the combination of paths the mind's contents might have traveled to their destination in a particular individual's consciousness, it is beyond dispute that those inner thoughts and feelings cannot themselves subject a person to any governmental deprivation of rights or privileges. "The fantasies of a drug addict are his own, and beyond the reach of the state."[54]

The internal quotation is from Chief Justice Burger, writing to uphold

*American Revival of Natural Law*, 52 N.Y.U. L. Rev. 1265 (1977), the author argues, as he did in D. Richards, *supra* note 41, for what he calls a "methodological natural law" constitutional theory, which claims not that law and morality are inextricably intertwined, but only that as a matter of observed fact, moral concepts are used in American legal discourse. From there, the argument runs rapidly to Rawls. The analogue to consensus validation should be apparent.

50. 431 U.S. 816 (1977).

51. *Id.* at 845.

52. *See* L. Tribe, *supra* note 47, § 10-8, at 508 n.13; § 15-3, at 894 n.16.

53. *See, e.g.*, Drummond v. Fulton County Dep't of Family Servs., 563 F.2d 1200 (5th Cir. 1977).

54. L. Tribe, *supra* note 47, § 15-7, at 905. *See also id.* § 15-5, at 899 ("The Court has insisted that the activities going on within the head are absolutely beyond the power of government to control.").

the power of government to regulate sexually explicit material.[55] In context, the statement is not one of principle, as Professor Tribe would have it, but one of regrettable fact. Yet on the basis of that statement, Professor Tribe argues that existing constitutional law establishes the rationale for barring state criminalization of marijuana use,[56] an outcome that, I am certain, Chief Justice Burger did not have in mind.

The structure of Professor Tribe's book reveals a second and more serious problem with adapting Rawls to existing constitutional law. Rawls' theory of justice has two components: a principle of individual liberty and a principle of distributive justice (the difference principle).[57] Although the former is "lexically prior" to the latter in his theory,[58] Rawls obviously believed, and correctly so, that his major contribution was the development of his principles of distributive justice. In Professor Tribe's treatise the emphasis is reversed.[59] We have a very elaborate presentation of the constitutional law that protects individual liberty, involving discussions of drug-taking, the right to run risks, and the like, and a discussion of distributive justice that occupies roughly one-third the space devoted to the individual liberty issues. Yet Tribe offers no explanation in terms of principles of justice or in terms of the institutional characteristics of American law for the relative lack of emphasis on issues of distribution.[60] One senses that Professor Tribe refrains from extensive discussion of distributive justice because, whatever one might say about existing law and personal liberty, very little in present constitutional law would provide any cornerstone for the application of Rawlsian principles to questions of distribution. The substantive content of constitutional law regarding distributive justice is almost nonexistent; there are certainly no serious echoes of Rawls' difference principle to be heard. Professor Tribe is of course justifiably

55. Paris Adult Theater I v. Slaton, 413 U.S. 49, 67 (1973) (The quotation from the Chief Justice, erroneously transcribed by Professor Tribe, accurately reads, "The fantasies of a drug addict are his own, and beyond the reach of government.").

56. L. TRIBE, *supra* note 47, § 15-7, at 908-10.

57. J. RAWLS, *supra* note 18, at 60-61.

58. *Id.* at 42-43, 60-61.

59. *Cf.* Book Note, 126 U. PA. L. REV. 1447, 1451 (1978) (noting a similar inversion in D. RICHARDS, *supra* note 41).

60. Raising institutional concerns on this issue, as Richards does, *see* note 42 *supra*, at 54-56, is a trap for the unwary. If the institutionalist point is made that determining the precise distribution of wealth that would result from the application of Rawls' difference principle is difficult and should be left to the legislature, the institutionalist can ask why determining the precise contours of liberty is any easier. Nor can the legal Rawlsian respond that liberty is a matter of right while the difference principle is not, for both, in the Rawlsian scheme, have equal status as rights. It is of some interest that Richards defends equalization of financing for education, a proposal that on its face deals with distributional issues, on the theory that education is a basic good that people must have equal opportunity to obtain. *See id.* at 145-47.

critical of recent decisions as lacking "imaginative compassion for the plight of the poor,"[61] but he recommends little more than an infusion of that compassion into present law. As a guide to decision, "be nice to poor people" is better than "kick the cat," but it does not really pour substantive moral content into constitutional law.

The Rawlsian strategy, though, even when well executed, is the primary source of the difficulties with this level of scholarship. Legal realism views ethical norms as subjective; the realist synthesis agrees that substantive values are subjective, but argues that there is an objective morality of process.[62] Rawls transposed the equation by identifying a process, the method of reflective equilibrium, that yields interesting substantive results. Thus, Rawls' arguments overcome the ethical relativism of realism to the extent that that relativism is based on either psychological or epistemological grounds. For many adherents of realism, these grounds are exhaustive and the Rawlsian response conclusive. But the more dedicated realists better understood the legacy of Holmes. Holmes' challenge, I have argued, was not only epistemological or psychological. It did not matter whether there were objective values that could be discovered by the exercise of reason, because the challenge was social as well. No society could be well ordered, Holmes argued, if its internal divisions led to the existence of competing claims to truth, even if an observer were able to show that one claim was correct and the others were false. The results of the Rawlsian process of reflective equilibrium are persuasive only to the extent that they capture something about the moral fiber of our intuitions, but the fragmentation of American society makes it impossible to support the view that a single set of intuitions is pervasively shared or consistently realized in a specific institutional setting.

Rawls' solution, then, leaves constitutional law with the same need to develop objective principles of justice because of political circumstances, but provides no way to specify what those principles are except by vague references to the liberal presuppositions of constitutional scholars.[63] The maneuver executed by the propounders of the realist synthesis to escape the amoralism of strict realism has recently been repeated by Ronald Dworkin, who in effect acknowledges that there is no state of reflective equilibrium for questions of substantive justice,

61. L. TRIBE, *supra* note 47, § 16-33, at 1099.

62. A classic expression is Fuller, *The Forms and Limits of Adjudication*, 92 HARV. L. REV. 353 (1978).

63. For a similar, though more detailed, criticism of Rawls, see Clark & Gintis, *Rawlsian Justice and Economic Systems*, 7 PHIL. & PUB. AFF. 302 (1978).

but who shifts the level of inquiry.[64] Although we do not share a conception of justice, Dworkin argues, we do share a concept of the function of courts. From this shared concept of courts as the organs for the protection of rights, Dworkin derives a range of substantive rights. Although the arguments have the air of a magician pulling a rabbit from a hat, I need not evaluate the deduction of substance from our idea of courts.[65] What matters is the precise parallel between Dworkin's shift from substance to institutions and the shift of the realist synthesis from a morality of results to a morality of process. The realist synthesis failed for two reasons: It was not responsive to the substantive concerns that emerged in the 1970s, and it relied on agreement about the morality of process. Dworkin's position is not susceptible to the first challenge. But it does rely, at least in his initial presentations, on a sharp distinction between the rights-orientation of courts, as we understand the idea of courts, and the utilitarian orientation of legislatures. The distinction has given way under pressure; various critics have shown that certain theories of rights lead to substantive conclusions different from Dworkin's, and Dworkin, in order to maintain his sole reliance on the concept of courts as rights-oriented, reformulated his position to the point where it no longer yielded the interesting substantive results that were the goal of the analysis.[66] Further, Dworkin's fundamental distinction between courts and legislatures is flawed in the same way the realist synthesis was; just as there is no shared understanding of substance, so too there is no shared understanding of the difference between courts and legislatures.[67] Some of us may believe that courts are rights-oriented, but others of us, even after achieving reflective equilibrium, do not. In the absence of that agreement, Dworkin's aims cannot be realized.[68]

64. *See* R. DWORKIN, *supra* note 37.

65. For a survey of objections, see *Jurisprudence Symposium*, 11 GA. L. REV. 968 (1977); Levinson, *Taking Law Seriously: Reflections on "Thinking Like a Lawyer,"* 30 STAN. L. REV. 1071, 1082 (1978).

66. *See* Dworkin, *Seven Critics*, 11 GA. L. REV. 1201 (1977).

67. For a more elaborate presentation of these points, see Levinson, *supra* note 65.

68. A number of recent efforts to rehabilitate natural law approaches to constitutional law attempt to place them in traditional frameworks; they can be seen as elaborations of H.L.A. Hart's observation that the Constitution uses terms that have moral content. H.L.A. HART, THE CONCEPT OF LAW 70-76 (1961). For example, Ely, on the basis of an examination of the issues presented to the Court, *see* note 44 *supra*, and Grey, on the basis of the political theory shared by the framers, *see* Grey, *Origins of the Unwritten Constitution: Fundamental Law in American Revolutionary Thought*, 30 STAN. L. REV. 843 (1978), conclude that as a matter of fact, the Constitution refers to norms not stated within the corners of the document. Neither, however, describes the content of those norms. Richards calls this position "methodological natural law" and argues that while there may be no necessary connection between law and morals, there is such a connection in the Constitution. He then gives Rawlsian content to morality. *See* notes 42 & 49 *supra*. Richards' course suggests the reasons for Dworkin's abandonment of the original observation: once one

Texas Law Review Vol. 57:1307, 1979

## II. Contemporary Scholarship: Some Case Studies

I have argued that the vacillations in constitutional theory between natural-law and institutionalist approaches support Holmes' perception that no unified theory of law is possible. If a large number of people have gone round in circles and have not come up with a theory that can gain acceptance over time, there is reason to think that the problems derive, not from deficiencies in the particular theories scholars propound, but from the enterprise itself. To gain acceptance, a theory must satisfy two requirements. First, it must describe and interpret the lawyer's experience in a way that strikes a responsive chord, or more precisely, it must seem that the theory, if flawed, could be corrected with no more than minor adjustments. Second, to be acceptable over an extended period, the theory must be consistent with the array of social, economic, and cultural structures with which constitutional law is intertwined. The preceding section dealt with the difficulties constitutional theories have encountered in solving the second problem, although I have only alluded to the source of those difficulties. In this section I will advance the argument by examining several areas of recent scholarship in what might be called applied constitutional theory. Each area is characterized by some synthetic effort, and each effort is unpersuasive because both experience and the cases provide us with law that is manipulable and fragmented to the point of anarchy. With that established, we can turn in the next section to the nihilist vision.

The typical constitutional law article today has a standard form. The author identifies a doctrine developed in recent Supreme Court cases, notes some difficulties in the internal logic of the doctrine, indicates that the doctrine seems incompatible with the results of other cases, suggests minor modifications in the doctrine to make it consistent with those cases, and concludes that the doctrine as modified—almost uniformly into a balancing test—provides a sensible way of achieving results without going too far. As we will see, there are some variations on this form; for example, authors can adapt it to a vigorous rejection of Supreme Court decisions. But the standard form and its variants all end at the same place: Supreme Court decisions ordinarily are, and in any event can easily become, embodiments of principles of justice, defined as the standard political principles of the moderate-left of the Democratic Party. In the end, the balancing tests to which standard

adopts a "methodological natural law" point of view, one may be committed to the untenable proposition that some particular set of values is widely shared.

form articles are driven reintroduce the very flexibility that allows courts to disagree with those principles.

When the Supreme Court's decisions were generally in accord with liberal principles, the standard form posed no difficulties; anyone with a modicum of competence could engage in the legal academic's equivalent of the pianist's finger exercises. Since 1970, however, the Court's decisions have been in tension with liberal principles, and even when the results seem satisfactory, there is a pervasive sense that we have been brought back by luck from the edge of the precipice. Under these circumstances, the standard form article seems increasingly removed from reality. We no longer have reason to think that there is a necessary connection between Supreme Court decisions and principles of justice, and yet legal academics continue to churn out articles that assume such a connection.

I will use three areas to illustrate both the fundamental problem for mainline scholarship and the pervasive confusion about whether the function of constitutional scholarship is to explain the cases or to develop principles of justice. In the first area, the Supreme Court has adopted a doctrine, the conclusive presumption doctrine, that all commentators agree is lunatic, even as they attempt at great length to squeeze it into the standard form article. The second involves the principle proscribing only intentionally discriminatory actions. Here the difficulty lies in the failure of the principle to respond to the perceived urgency of alleviating divisive racial problems, despite its ability to capture some important liberal assumptions. Finally, I examine the commentary on cases restricting federal judicial intervention in state court proceedings, most of which has been critical because of the assumed connection between constitutional law and justice.

### *A. The Supreme Court as Keystone Kops*

In 1973 the Supreme Court rediscovered that the Constitution prohibits the state from employing irrebuttable or conclusive presumptions.[69] The Court invalidated Connecticut's structure of tuition at its state university, which forced a person who applied for admission while a nonresident to pay higher fees than resident applicants, even if the nonresident became a Connecticut resident while a student. The Court argued that Connecticut conclusively presumed that the nonresident applicant would not become a state resident entitled to lower fees and

69. Vlandis v. Kline, 412 U.S. 441 (1973). The doctrine had made an earlier appearance in Schlesinger v. Wisconsin, 270 U.S. 230 (1926), but had disappeared after Heiner v. Donnan, 285 U.S. 312 (1932).

held that this conclusive presumption, because it was not universally true, could not be employed.[70]

From the moment of the doctrine's reemergence, it was clear that the Court's reliance on it was seriously misplaced. As every commentator has noted,[71] and as Justice Marshall stated in a concurring opinion delivered at the outset of the new development,[72] conclusive presumption analysis cannot be independent of the analysis of the fairness of statutory classifications, since every classification embodies a conclusive presumption. For example, one classic case upheld a statute that barred opticians from fitting duplicate lenses without a prescription from an optometrist.[73] The statute classified eyeglass fitters into two groups, opticians and fitters of ready-to-wear glasses, and embodied the conclusive presumption, certainly not universally true, that opticians cannot competently fit glasses. The conclusive presumption was identical to the classification. Thus, merely noting that a statute embodies a conclusive presumption does not advance equal protection analysis; the conclusive presumption doctrine makes sense solely as the way to identify a remedy for a constitutional violation established on the basis of equal protection analysis. Ordinarily, a state will respond to a decision invalidating a classification by redrawing the lines defining the classes. Thus, Connecticut could have redefined residency to include persons with Connecticut drivers' licenses, bank accounts, and similar indicia of permanency. The new definition, though perhaps still imperfect because some true residents may not satisfy the reformed criteria, might then be sufficient to support the differential tuition payments. Conclusive presumption analysis gives the state an alternative to redrawing its lines; Connecticut instead could provide each nonresident applicant an opportunity to prove actual residency some time after admission.[74] Thus, conclusive presumption analysis points to individu-

70. 412 U.S. at 452. Several later cases also invoked the doctrine. *See, e.g.*, Cleveland Bd. of Educ. v. LaFleur, 414 U.S. 632 (1974); United States Dep't of Agriculture v. Murry, 413 U.S. 508 (1973).

71. *See, e.g.*, Ackerman, *The Conclusive Presumption Shuffle*, 125 U. PA. L. REV. 761 (1977); Gordon & Tenenbaum, *Conclusive Presumption Analysis: The Principle of Individual Opportunity*, 71 NW. U.L. REV. 579, 582 n.26 (1976) (citing other comments); Simson, *The Conclusive Presumption Cases: The Search for a Newer Equal Protection Continues*, 24 CATH. U.L. REV. 217 (1975).

72. United States Dep't of Agriculture v. Murry, 413 U.S. 508, 517-19 (1973) (Marshall, J., concurring).

73. Williamson v. Lee Optical Co., 348 U.S. 483 (1955).

74. However, this alternative, when implemented, resembles the remedy of redrawing lines. In a bureaucratic institution like a state university, the individualized determination will ordinarily be made on the basis of some sort of checklist, and the outcomes will express a more refined set of categories. A truly individualized decision will be made only in a few residual cases.

alized determinations rather than to redefined categories as remedies for improper classifications.

All this is entirely unexceptionable and obvious. The conclusive presumption cases rest on the implicit decision that the classification employed violated the equal protection clause, and develop an interesting scheme for remedying those antecedent violations. Under the explicit equal protection doctrine adhered to by a majority of the present Court, however, it would have been virtually impossible to argue persuasively that the classifications in these cases violated the equal protection clause. But this did not present a serious problem for the authors of standard form articles who were eager to superimpose a facade of rationality on the Court's decisions. One article suggested that the Court was actually relying on an implicit model of equal protection analysis that had "much to commend it."[75] Another formulated an "individual opportunity principle" that was consistent with the conclusive presumption cases, but that did not "threaten many rules that would otherwise be valid."[76] A third argued that the doctrine "properly can be confined to cases involving unfair adjudicatory practices."[77] These three articles, all published in major law reviews, occupy over 110 pages. Yet all fail to take account of what a detached observer reading the opinions would immediately see: The Court's defenses of the doctrine are flatly inconsistent with what the Court has said when facing equal protection claims squarely.[78]

The Court's behavior, then, is strange, but that of the commentators, who after all have no responsibility for showing that the Court has done something sensible, is even stranger. Each commentator attempted to make sense of the conclusive presumption doctrine, believing that it is connected with general principles of fairness; each accepted the general framework of equal protection law adopted by the Court, believing that it too is connected with the same principles; and each tinkered with applicable doctrine to make the two parts appear to fit together. There is a partial explanation for the commentators' approach: The results of the conclusive presumption cases are generally quite acceptable from a liberal's viewpoint (though one might question in distributive terms the wisdom of the decision to overturn Connecticut's preference for long-term, less mobile students), while the results of the Court's explicit equal protection cases seem at best erratic with a

75. Simson, *supra* note 71, at 241.
76. Gordon & Tenenbaum, *supra* note 71, at 616.
77. Ackerman, *supra* note 71, at 808.
78. *See, e.g.,* Simson, *supra* note 71, at 219-29.

strong tinge of the "bad" about them.[79] The authors' tinkering may be an attempt to demonstrate that even bad equal protection doctrine can be meshed with good results. But as a political strategy it seems odd to proceed from the assumption that one must accept the bad equal protection doctrine. A direct attack on the doctrine would seem more likely to be effective in the long-run, while manipulation of the rules seems unlikely to be effective even in the short-run. Moreover, the audience for this demonstration is obscure. The conservatives on the Court will not, of course, be persuaded to accept the doctrine on the ground that it leads to liberal results, and the liberals do not need persuading.

There is a simple explanation for the reemergence of conclusive presumption analysis. Each case relying on the doctrine was decided by a narrow margin, and each reached a reasonably liberal result contrary to the tendencies of the present Court. A fair interpretation of the process is that Justice Stewart mounted a peculiar hobbyhorse in *Vlandis v. Kline*[80] and the liberal justices went along for the ride to the result they favored. Unfortunately for the liberals, the inconsistency between the conclusive presumption and the general equal protection doctrines made it impossible for the former to become an established mode of analysis, and within a short time the rule was substantially undermined.[81] The conclusive presumption cases may be understood, then, in the way the kremlinologists interpret obscure actions of the Soviet Union.

But kremlinological explanations of Supreme Court action are disfavored in mainstream constitutional scholarship, which prefers to assume that Supreme Court opinions individually attempt to express principles of justice and collectively do so in a reasonably coherent way. When a line of cases establishes a doctrine and a new decision raises questions about the prior doctrine, the commentators interpret or modify both to bring them into alignment. Thus, most scholars rest on the easy assumption that rationally articulable principles of justice exist and oddly enough rely on the Supreme Court to point the way.

### *B. The Supreme Court as Flawed Moralist*

Recent decisions firmly restate the rule that only intentionally dis-

79. *See* Gunther, *The Supreme Court, 1971 Term—Foreword: In Search of Evolving Doctrine on a Changing Court: A Model for a Newer Equal Protection*, 86 HARV. L. REV. 1 (1972).
80. 412 U.S. 441 (1973); *see* note 70 *supra*.
81. *See* Weinberger v. Salfi, 422 U.S. 749 (1975).

criminatory conduct by state actors is unconstitutional.[82] These decisions, unlike the conclusive presumption cases, are not obviously flawed and indeed have a firm base in both precedent and aspects of the individualism of American society.[83] These decisions were uneasily received by the commentators, however, since they threatened the accomplishment of important political goals sought by liberal scholars. The tone of the articles in response to these cases is, once again, one of acceptance with minor modification. And as with the earlier responses, the articles, while of impressive bulk, fail to appreciate that modifications regarded as minor by the authors lead to results clearly disfavored by the Court. Once more, the belief that Supreme Court decisions are vehicles for the articulation of principles of justice contradicts what we know as citizens but sometimes ignore as scholars.

One 135-page monograph[84] urges re-analysis of cases like *Washington v. Davis*[85] in which a plaintiff claims that some apparently neutral policy has a racially disproportionate impact. Instead of making intent dispositive and disproportionate impact merely evidence of intent, the author proposed a "causation principle":[86] "the equal protection clause requires special scrutiny of governmental acts resulting in disproportionate impact whenever such impact is reasonably attributable to race."[87] One should be puzzled by the suggestion that the causation principle is analytically distinct from the Court's requirement of intent. First, the causation principle by definition requires that we attribute an impact to race. The only serious candidate for that attribution is the governmental decisionmaker, and we can attribute an impact to race when we reasonably believe that the decisionmaker had race in mind. The causation principle modifies the Court's present position by allowing a "reasonable" attribution,[88] thus permitting a court to find a constitutional violation in the absence of direct evidence that the decisionmaker was racially motivated. The Court, however, has already acknowledged that an inference of intent can be drawn without direct evidence by relying upon, for example, a disproportionate impact cou-

82. Village of Arlington Heights v. Metropolitan Hous. Dev. Corp., 429 U.S. 252 (1977); Washington v. Davis, 426 U.S. 229 (1976).

83. *See generally* Freeman, *Legitimizing Racial Discrimination Through Antidiscrimination Law: A Critical Review of Supreme Court Doctrine*, 62 MINN. L. REV. 1049 (1978).

84. Eisenberg, *Disproportionate Impact and Illicit Motive: Theories of Constitutional Adjudication*, 52 N.Y.U. L. REV. 36 (1977).

85. 426 U.S. 229 (1976).

86. Eisenberg, *supra* note 84, at 58-83.

87. *Id.* at 40.

88. *Id.* at 73-79.

pled with deviations from traditional policies.[89] The causation principle would simply remove the need for additional evidence in those instances "that fairly beg for invalidation."[90] But what the author regards as a case begging for invalidation, the Supreme Court may not.

Second, the causation principle is said to rely on principles of tort law. In particular, invalidation would occur only when the causal connection between race and disproportionate impact is proximate. This suggests that proximity is a logical or scientific-factual relationship. But as every first-year law student is taught, we determine proximate causation by making an implicit judgment that the defendant ought to be held liable. Thus, this attempt to carve an alternative to the Court's approach also proves inadequate, since even if the Court adopted the causation principle, it could easily find the causal connection between race and disproportionate impact too tenuous in those cases that the inventor of the principle thought "begged" for invalidation. Causation requirements mask but do not eliminate the policy choices that the Court must make, and they cannot dictate results inconsistent with those choices the Court would make if forced to do so openly.[91]

Although the massive effort to lay out the causation principle seems a bit odd, the author did provide an enumeration of his reasons that reveals his assumptions about constitutional law. The principle, it is said, avoids results that the courts "found unpalatable."[92] It requires "only slight changes in the Court's approach to equal protection cases,"[93] and might possibly be "the minimum principled change in the Court's views that will accommodate the pressure . . . to expand the scope of the equal protection clause."[94] It also leaves room to expand the categories of invalid actions if "traditional views of what constitutes a race-dependent decision"[95] change, and it "squares well with an intuitive notion of what the equal protection clause is or should be about."[96] For present purposes, it is irrelevant that all this could be said about the Court's requirement of intentional discrimination. The important point is the author's identification of constitutional law with

89. *See* Village of Arlington Heights v. Metropolitan Hous. Dev. Corp., 429 U.S. 252, 266-67 (1977).

90. Eisenberg, *supra* note 84, at 48.

91. For an analysis of causation requirements in another area, see Tushnet, *The New Law of Standing: A Plea for Abandonment*, 62 CORNELL L. REV. 663 (1977).

92. Eisenberg, *supra* note 84, at 79.

93. *Id.* at 80.

94. *Id.*

95. *Id.*

96. *Id.* at 81.

the "ideal of equality"[97]—principles of justice—and his suggestion that the ideal can be accommodated with the results the Court refuses to reach, since the principles are almost consistent with existing doctrine.[98]

The schizophrenia of this analysis is apparent. The Court is thought to be gravely wrong in refusing to find some actions impermissibly infected by racism, and yet minor modifications of existing doctrine will lead it to acceptable results. This conclusion is made even stranger by the obvious fact that both existing doctrines and proposed alternatives can be readily manipulated: if constitutional tests are flexible, almost by definition they cannot dictate results.

The same problem is evident in another critique of the Court's decisions in this area.[99] Here the author explicitly linked constitutional judgments to assessments of moral responsibility and proposed a "flexible standard of review"[100] to determine whether the disproportionate impact is justified. In this scheme courts would consider "(1) the degree of disproportion in the impact; (2) the private interest disadvantaged; (3) the efficiency of the challenged law in achieving its objectives and the availability of alternative means having a less disproportionate impact; and (4) the governmental objective sought to be advanced."[101] The author's concern for preserving a judicial role "in ameliorating racial inequities"[102] is, it should go without saying, entirely admirable, and the passion for justice that motivates the analysis is evident. But despite obvious concern about the correctness of the Court's decisions, an important section of the article discusses the flexibility of the theory in order to show that distasteful results would not follow from its adoption and that some existing decisions would be preserved anyway. Thus, the theory is applied to *Jefferson v. Hackney*,[103] which upheld a Texas program of funding aid to the aged, blind, and disabled at substantially higher rates than aid to families with dependent children. The author argued that his theory would yield the same result because "the state's interest plainly outweighed the interest of the AFDC recipients."[104] And yet I wonder. The "welfare mess" is, as a matter of practical politics, an AFDC problem, and the image of the AFDC recipient

97. *Id.*
98. *Id.* at 80.
99. Perry, *The Disproportionate Impact Theory of Racial Discrimination*, 125 U. PA. L. REV. 540 (1977).
100. *Id.* at 541.
101. *Id.* at 559-60.
102. *Id.* at 588.
103. 406 U.S. 535 (1972).
104. Perry, *supra* note 99, at 565.

Texas Law Review Vol. 57:1307, 1979

is that of the black or brown mother. It is not at all plain, at least to me, that disparities between aid to the aged, blind, or disabled and to AFDC recipients have no significant racial component.

The two articles examined here represent a broad class of recent constitutional law scholarship, much of it focusing on the Court's rules for examining nonracial classifications.[105] The authors are troubled by recent decisions, but they accept Supreme Court opinions as the framework within which principles of justice should be developed and, more strikingly, believe that many existing doctrines are consistent with those principles. Yet when the authors develop their alternatives to current doctrine, they infuse them with a flexibility that vitiates the endeavor of guiding the law to justice. Balancing tests do not guarantee results, and it is reasonably clear that a Court which refuses to find intentional discrimination in a case like *Washington v. Davis* would also find, using an alternative test, that the balance tipped in favor of the state.

This malleability or subjectivity of doctrine is not peculiar to this particular context. The one consistent element in the substantive analysis of the standard form article is the ultimate recommendation that the Court adopt a balancing test. When the authors criticize the Court's decisions, the substance of their analyses poses a problem, not for the lawyer, but for the observer of the enterprise of legal scholarship. There seems to be a great deal of effort to no apparent end, since the product churned out will not do what its makers want it to do. It will be useful to examine a final topic before attempting to explain what the enterprise actually is.

### C. *The Supreme Court as Institutional Monitor*

The Supreme Court devotes a significant portion of its time to constitutional cases that address the structure of government and do not directly implicate general principles of justice. It decides, for example, that some state legislation unreasonably interferes with interstate commerce,[106] or it allows the national government to impose a tax on helicopters owned by the state police.[107] These cases could easily be accommodated with the constitutional law scholarship of the 1950s and early 1960s when concern focused on the appropriate allocation of

105. *See, e.g.,* Gunther, *supra* note 78; Karst, *The Supreme Court, 1976 Term—Foreword: Equal Citizenship Under the Fourteenth Amendment*, 91 HARV. L. REV. 1 (1977); Perry, *Constitutional "Fairness": Notes on Equal Protection and Due Process*, 63 VA. L. REV. 383 (1977); Simson, *A Method for Analyzing Discriminatory Effects Under the Equal Protection Clause*, 29 STAN. L. REV. 663 (1977).

106. *See* Raymond Motor Transp., Inc. v. Rice, 434 U.S. 429 (1978).

107. *See* Massachusetts v. United States, 435 U.S. 444 (1978).

decisionmaking authority between state and nation, legislature and court. But that interest was replaced by the natural law concern, and a portion of the Supreme Court's work became increasingly anomalous to the commentators. Their difficulty was compounded by the Court's own increasing concern for institutional design, particularly for issues of federalism. It became apparent, in view of the types of issues decided by the Court and without regard for the content of the decisions, that the assumption of concinnity between Supreme Court decisions and principles of justice was indeed doubtful.

Two strategies have developed to vindicate the assumption. The first takes the Court's concerns over design seriously and attempts to demonstrate that the form of government in the United States is essential to the achievement of justice. This strategy, though widely bruited about in conversations among constitutional law scholars, has only rarely been committed to print. The reasons are plain: when two eminent scholars[108] wrote such articles, the failure of their arguments was so obvious that it discouraged imitation. The second strategy rejects the results of the Court's decisions, arguing that true sensitivity to concerns over design would lead to a system in which justice would be achieved. One variant of this strategy is the King Canute approach: as each apparently regressive decision is rendered, the commentator tries to redraw the line there, only to be betrayed by the next round of decisions. Another variant criticizes the internal logic of the Court's decisions. This variant also fails because of its inconsistencies. If the fundamental issue is the achievement of justice, the only relevant questions should be substantive: no matter how we get there, are the results just? Yet rejection of the Court's decisions on internal grounds still assumes that design questions have some bearing on the issue of justice.

Professor Charles Black was the first to attempt to integrate design and natural law perspectives by developing what he called a "structural" approach to constitutional law.[109] Black argues that by examining the arrangement of institutions of government, we will discover that they are designed to promote justice. But precisely how the structures do that and how particular controversial decisions can be developed from perceptions of structural arrangement is unexplained, and few scholars have that grace of expression infused with obvious concern for

108. Michelman, *States' Rights and States' Roles: Permutations of "Sovereignty" in* National League of Cities v. Usery, 86 YALE L.J. 1165 (1977); Tribe, *Unraveling* National League of Cities: *The New Federalism and Affirmative Rights to Essential Government Services*, 90 HARV. L. REV. 1065 (1977).

109. C. BLACK, STRUCTURE AND RELATIONSHIP IN CONSTITUTIONAL LAW (1969).

justice that makes the reader nod in agreement with Professor Black.[110]

Professors Laurence Tribe and Frank Michelman made a second major effort to link design with justice.[111] They examined the Supreme Court's decision in *National League of Cities v. Usery*,[112] which held unconstitutional Congress' requirement that state and local governments pay their employees the national minimum wage. They argued that the decision could be justified on the ground that imposition of the minimum wage would impair the ability of some governments to deliver essential services, such as police and fire protection or local public assistance schemes, to which citizens are entitled pursuant to principles of justice. But *League of Cities* is a patently reactionary decision rife with references to standard conservative arguments against the wisdom of minimum wage legislation generally. Although I detect some diffidence in the presentation of a liberal defense of the decision, I regrettably fail to perceive the twinkle of satire. The Tribe-Michelman argument fails to show how particular institutional designs contribute to justice. If citizens are entitled to receive essential services and Congress impairs the ability of local governments to deliver those services, one remedy would be to require that Congress provide them.[113]

The Supreme Court has given most of its federalism-based attention to developing rules governing federal court injunction of state court proceedings. Those rules do not determine what principles of constitutional law should be applied; they merely determine whether state or federal courts will, in the first instance, decide the cases. Thus, the rules must be connected to principles of justice by arguments about the different abilities of state and federal courts. In a series of cases the Supreme Court has indicated that it would not fulfill expectations gen-

110. The separation of powers in the Constitution provides an example. One aspect of that structural device is the restriction of judicial review to "cases or controversies." In the early 1960s, Alexander Bickel demonstrated that the court had used the "case or controversy" requirement and its various subsidiary rules—standing, mootness, and the like—to avoid deciding sensitive cases. A. BICKEL, THE LEAST DANGEROUS BRANCH 115-27 (1962). Gerald Gunther soon responded with an equally powerful demonstration that the Court's behavior, as Bickel described it, was lawless. Gunther, *The Subtle Vices of the "Passive Virtues"—A Comment on Principle and Expediency in Judicial Review*, 64 COLUM. L. REV. 1 (1964). Few commentators have subsequently attempted to reconcile the disparity between behavior and principle in this area despite the general assumption that behavior and principle are closely related. With Dworkin's emphasis on our understanding of what a court is, *see* notes 64-68 *supra* & accompanying text, have come a few somewhat labored efforts in that direction. *See* Brilmayer, *Judicial Review, Justiciability, and the Limits of the Common Law Method*, 57 B.U.L. REV. 807 (1977); Note, *Filling the Void: Judicial Power and Jurisdictional Attacks on Judgments*, 87 YALE L.J. 164 (1977); Note, *The Concept of Law-Tied Pendent Jurisdiction:* Gibbs *and* Aldinger *Reconsidered*, 87 YALE L.J. 627 (1978).

111. *See* note 108 *supra*.

112. 426 U.S. 833 (1976).

113. I have presented a more detailed criticism of *League of Cities* in Tushnet, *Constitutional and Statutory Analyses in the Law of Federal Jurisdiction*, 25 U.C.L.A. L. REV. 1301 (1978).

Truth, Justice, and the American Way

erated by the Warren Court that federal judicial intervention would be welcomed. The literature in response to the restrictive cases is, as Professor Charles Alan Wright put it, "immense,"[114] burgeoning, and, I must add, largely uninteresting. The cases strain the standard form article because they are inconsistent with the views of a prior, liberal Court and because they take seriously precisely those design concerns that do not easily fit into a natural-law framework.

A typical article generated by these decisions accepts their apparent premises and tries to show that those premises lead no farther than the Court had actually gone.[115] For example, the Court began by following the reasonably well-established rule that the federal courts will not act to halt state criminal prosecutions after they have commenced.[116] It then applied the rule to noncriminal proceedings "akin to a criminal prosecution," such as an action brought by a state prosecutor to close as a public nuisance a theater that showed sexually explicit films.[117] One commentator responded with an elaborate, five-stage inquiry to determine whether federal action should be allowed to halt other types of noncriminal actions.[118] Not surprisingly, the Court ignored this well-intended advice when confronted with the problem and held that the federal courts could not stop any action initiated by the state in its sovereign capacity.[119] The result was not surprising because the Court naturally rejected advice coming from an author essentially out of tune with the Court's premises; what is surprising is the effort embodied in the article.

Another form of response to the Court's decisions is an extended criticism of the illogic of the Court's rules. The best of these argues in great detail that the Court formulated its original position on the basis of precedents incorporating the flexibility of traditional courts of equity, but abandoned this flexibility almost from the start in favor of rules that rest solely on "personal opinions" regarding the operation of state and federal courts.[120] This response, too, is puzzling. The form of the criticism is as follows: The Court said that it was relying on principles of equity and federalism; the cases involving equity on which it

114. C. Wright, Handbook of the Law of Federal Courts § 52A, at 229 n.1 (3d ed. 1976).

115. *See, e.g.*, Soifer & Macgill, *The* Younger *Doctrine: Reconstructing Reconstruction*, 55 Texas L. Rev. 1141 (1977), which is extremely critical of the Court's recent decisions.

116. Younger v. Harris, 401 U.S. 37 (1971).

117. Huffman v. Pursue, Ltd., 420 U.S. 592, 604 (1975).

118. Bartels, *Avoiding a Comity of Errors: A Model for Adjudicating Federal Civil Rights Suits that "Interfere" with State Civil Proceedings*, 29 Stan. L. Rev. 27 (1976).

119. Trainor v. Hernandez, 431 U.S. 434 (1977).

120. Soifer & Macgill, *supra* note 115.

relied had a flexibility that the Court rejected; therefore, the rules rest only on federalism. But this is no criticism at all unless the Court has misinterpreted federalism. Here the authors recite their reasons for preferring that constitutional issues be decided in federal courts.[121] But the Court responds that state courts are just as good as federal courts.[122] Thus, the criticism of internal logic advances the issue nowhere, unless one accepts the authors' views of what federalism in fact requires. The best that can be done is to refer to traditional conceptions of the relation between state and federal courts, and it is easy enough for the Court to say that times have changed enough to warrant the abandonment of prior flexibility.

Another criticism of the cases emphasizes the difficulty in constructing "a coherent account of the policy" underlying them.[123] Yet the cases may not embody so much a policy as a mood. To the extent that the criticism proceeds from the assumption that "judicial enlightenment," like truth, "can emerge from error, but not from confusion,"[124] it is misplaced, for the mood of the cases is clear enough.

The authors of these articles share a concern that pervades their commentary; the concern, however, is not about the Court's craftsmanship: "This view of 'comity and federalism' reflects an obsessive concern with conflict between the state and national sovereigns. It addresses problems of the structure of the Republic, not the rights of people who live in it."[125] Exactly, and just because it does so, views on rights or justice can yield no conclusions about the structural issues that occupy the Court's attention. In the end, the Court is criticized for structural decisions that are "mean-spirited" when the authors have conceded that structure and rights are independent.[126] The analysis of decided cases is incisive but ultimately futile. The authors can appeal finally only to the "generosity and compassion"[127] of their readers, since the Court's views on the matter are so obviously different.

### *D. Constitutional Scholarship and the Sociology of Legal Education*

I must emphasize that the works discussed in preceding sections are examples of what most observers regard as competent, even distin-

121. *Id.* at 1187-91.

122. *See, e.g.,* Stone v. Powell, 428 U.S. 465, 493 n.35 (1976); Huffman v. Pursue, Ltd., 420 U.S. 592, 611 (1975).

123. Soifer & Macgill, *supra* note 115, at 1213.

124. *Id.* at 1215.

125. *Id.* at 1185-86.

126. *Id.* at 1215.

127. *Id.*

guished, contemporary scholarship. Within the terms of that scholarship, the works are good indeed. Regarded from the outside, as an intellectual phenomenon, however, they pose a problem. Faced with decisions by an obviously conservative Court, liberal constitutional law scholars have responded in a curious way. Across all the areas I have discussed, and in others not mentioned,[128] articles share several characteristics: they are inordinately long; they are strongly attracted to the use of doctrines that promote flexibility; they concentrate on Supreme Court decisions; and they attempt to develop law in light of principles of justice that are rarely articulated but uniformly liberal. These symbiotic characteristics derive from elements of legal education, the topic of this section, and from the intellectual history of constitutional law scholarship discussed earlier.[129] The difficulty with standard approaches to constitutional law lies in the tension between the liberal assumptions of those approaches and the conservatism of the present Court. This tension throws the intellectual history of the field into striking relief.

A clear relationship exists between the length of articles and their use of balancing tests.[130] An author can take up a great deal of space enumerating the factors to be placed in the balance and can illustrate the operation of the proposed test by drawing upon decided cases.[131] But decided cases are not treated as merely illustrative. They are presented to show the proper weight to be given each factor on the assumption that the Court has approximated the author's standards of justice. At most, the cases are criticized for giving too much weight to one factor and not enough to another, but because balancing tests describe only a process and do not dictate a result, these criticisms are ultimately unpersuasive.

The length of the average law review article has increased over the past fifty years,[132] which suggests that length does not result from the inherent truth of balancing tests. Rather, length seems to be the result of uncertainty about the intellectual merit and academic status of standard legal analysis. Historically, law schools have promoted teachers to tenure on far weaker publication records than are required else-

128. *See, e.g.*, Perry, *Abortion, The Public Morals, and the Police Power: The Ethical Function of Substantive Due Process*, 23 U.C.L.A. L. REV. 689 (1976); Wilkinson & White, *Constitutional Protection for Personal Lifestyles*, 62 CORNELL L. REV. 563 (1977); articles cited note 105 *supra*.

129. *See* text accompanying notes 1-37 *supra*.

130. At this point, I nervously checked the last page number of the prior draft of this essay and continued.

131. *See, e.g.*, Simson, *supra* note 105.

132. I draw here upon unpublished calculations by my colleague John Kidwell.

where in the university; for example, not until 1969 did the Harvard Law School require even a single article before promotion,[133] and similarly lax standards still prevail in many law schools. Before law schools were integrated into their universities, this disparity in promotion standards was not as troubling. Influenced by legal realism and affected by the increasing bureaucratization of higher education, however, law schools found that they wished (or were forced) to have ties with other departments. These ties could not be maintained if law school scholarship remained as flimsy as it had been; the sociologists, economists, and political scientists would have resented collaboration with, or promotion of, professors who did not write. At the same time, market pressures on law schools, which necessarily pay their faculty members far less than they could earn in other legal endeavors, made it impossible to reduce substantially the nonmonetary attractions, such as lax tenure requirements, of teaching law as a profession.

The law schools' response to this dilemma is embodied in the norm for publication: one article will do, but it must be the last word on the subject.[134] Another standard of publication also derives from the uncertain academic status of legal study and contributes to the length of publications: every article must be self-contained. Authors are encouraged to assume, not altogether unreasonably, that their readers rarely pick up law reviews and that they must, therefore, be provided with the full background of a problem and with detailed summaries of the relevant cases. The presumption seems to be that every reader of one article in a law review is a potential reader of every other. Thus, although constitutional law articles would not have to recite the history of the problem if they were directed only at those interested in constitutional law, they must be self-contained if those interested in corporate law, for example, are to read them profitably.[135]

Because there are a large number of both law schools with untenured teachers seeking promotion and law reviews with unfilled pages, it is not uncommon for two or three long articles on the same

133. J. Seligman, The High Citadel: The Influence of Harvard Law School 126 (1978).

134. These tenure-related considerations have established length as a standard for publication such that articles editors are uneasy about publishing short articles. Thus, even professors with tenure and practitioners who write articles adhere to the standard.

135. The method of beginning at the very beginning and recounting all prior development, a method which assumes that readers have no acquaintance with the problem to be addressed and will not take steps to familiarize themselves with it beyond reading the article, is also related to the lawyer's need to inform generalist judges about specialized problems and to the student editor's belief that training in that method of communication is useful. The method characterizes no other form of scholarly writing of which I am aware.

topic to appear almost simultaneously, a phenomenon that naturally undermines the last-word claim of any article. Moreover, legal realism spawned a cynicism about the stability of law that reduces claims of finality to wishful thinking.

I have mentioned how concentration on decided cases is related to the prevalence of balancing tests and the assumption of justice. It also derives from aspects of legal education. Law students are for the most part concerned not with perpetuating an academic tradition, but with acquiring skills that will be useful in law practice. For peculiar historical reasons, law faculty believe that those skills are best acquired by reading and analyzing cases. Case analysis, however, has become an obsession shared by their students as well. Thus, law teachers spend most of their teaching time paying attention to cases, and it is efficient from their point of view to transform their classroom case analysis into legal scholarship. Even in constitutional law courses, in which most students realize that the subject has very little to do with what they will be doing as practitioners and in which they are thus more tolerant of abstract discussions, law teachers still structure their courses around case analysis.[136] Furthermore, the academic lawyer is affected by the desire to write articles that are relevant to important questions of policy, for the relation between law and policy has been emphasized in legal education since the 1930s. In constitutional law, the policymaking theater is the Supreme Court; to affect policy the writer must speak to the Court. As a result, one cannot be too critical without risking that one's voice will be ignored; most articles, therefore, treat the Court's recent decisions as, on the whole, correct. But such deference is incompatible with the view, held simultaneously by the authors, that the Court should decide cases in accordance with principles of justice, unless some theory were provided to explain why the Court actually does decide cases in that way. But no such theory has been forthcoming. Finally, case analysis serves an implicit ideological goal. In its primary use, case analysis conveys the message that one may extract a rational core from existing law and that anomalies occur only at the periphery. In addition, by looking backward, case analysis suggests the importance of continuity with an era in which the law exhibited, or judges assumed, its coherence. As I will argue,[137] however, legal nihilists have

136. For example, the most innovative recent set of materials for teaching constitutional law, P. Brest, Processes of Constitutional Decision-Making (1976), still retains the focus on Supreme Court cases.

137. *See* text accompanying notes 143-48 *infra*.

Texas Law Review Vol. 57:1307, 1979

transformed the use of case analysis so that, in their hands, the cases display incoherence instead.

Certain characteristics of constitutional law scholarship are, I have argued, inconsistent with some basic beliefs held by its scholars. Although case analysis predominates and writing the "last word" is a chief standard for promotion-oriented publications, at the same time it is generally believed both that constitutional law courses provide more freedom from the case approach because the professional value of the subject is slight, and that scholarship is easily outpaced by rapid and haphazard developments in the field. These inconsistencies are related as well to the increasing attractiveness of using principles of justice as constitutional standards. Such principles might provide stability in the field and thereby justify the practice of attempting to write the last word on a topic. Once one is attracted to justice as a criterion, however, the attention to decided cases may appear misplaced. Were justice a criterion, Supreme Court decisions would at most provide examples of problems that principles of justice might address, and only rarely would they do even this. Consider, for example, that even the two topics that have been the basis for some of the most extensive philosophic discussion of legal matters, abortion and so-called reverse discrimination, were considered by the Supreme Court in cases that either were stripped of factual background,[138] or had exceedingly peculiar factual records.[139] The cases could add nothing to the philosophical discussions, which often focus on the common fact patterns in which the problems arise.[140]

Standard constitutional law scholarship, then, shows scholars in the dual role of expounders of norms and rationalizers of cases and

138. Plaintiffs in abortion cases are usually anonymous. *See, e.g.,* Roe v. Wade, 410 U.S. 113 (1973).

139. *See, e.g.,* Regents of the Univ. of Cal. v. Bakke, 438 U.S. 265 (1978).

140. Indeed, some of the major law review articles defending the Supreme Court's basic holding on the abortion issue betray no awareness of the relevant, and quite interesting, philosophical literature. *See, e.g.,* Heymann & Barzelay, *The Forest and the Trees:* Roe v. Wade *and Its Critics,* 53 B.U.L. REV. 765 (1973); Perry, *supra* note 128. Neither article contains citation to the philosophers' discussions. An awareness of those discussions might have dampened the assertions that easy answers were available to the moral problems posed by the issue and would have made institutionalist criticisms significantly more potent. *See, e.g.,* Ely, *The Wages of Crying Wolf: A Comment on* Roe v. Wade, 82 YALE L.J. 920 (1973). For one astute commentator's passage from assurance to doubt, compare Tribe, *The Supreme Court, 1972 Term—Foreword: Toward a Model of Roles in the Due Process of Life and Law,* 87 HARV. L. REV. 1 (1973), with L. TRIBE, *supra* note 47, § 15-10, at 928.

To some extent, the inattention to philosophy results from what has been called the "lawyer as astrophysicist" assumption, namely that the generalist training of lawyers allows any lawyer to read a text on astrophysics over the weekend and launch a rocket on Monday. There is very little recognition on the first level of scholarship that philosophy is a technical discipline.

produces an essentially natural-law approach to the subject. The first two sections of this essay have established, I believe, the inadequacies of both the role and the approach.

## III. A New Course for Public Law Scholarship

The difficulties of contemporary constitutional law scholarship have occurred because scholars, for understandable intellectual, social, and educational reasons, responded to only part of the Holmesian challenge. Holmes concluded that the logic of liberal law led to a state of legal fragmentation, in which no one's claims had any greater relationship to truth than those of anyone else. The main course of constitutional law scholarship has been a response to the idea that values are purely subjective, attempting to demonstrate that there are some unifying themes or doctrines. But Holmes' challenge has another component, to which no response has been made. The fragmentation, or radical pluralism, of law was both intellectual, in its use of individualist conceptions, and social, in the relation between competing ideas and competing social groups. The social fragmentation against which liberal law must be articulated, and which purely intellectual analysis cannot overcome, has repeatedly confounded constitutional law scholarship.

Holmes' vision, of course, was available for later scholars, and their decision to ignore rather than to challenge parts of what he said reveals significant characteristics of legal scholarship. On the level of ideas, Holmes' vision is exceedingly bleak; one who shares it must often wonder why he or she is a lawyer. It is not surprising that scholars treat that vision with great care; indeed, as we will see,[141] even scholars who understand and agree with Holmes occasionally shy away from the implications of their views. On the level of action, Holmes' position leads to the denial of a necessary connection between law and justice, and even between law and wise policy. In his comment on the gas-stokers' strike, to which I have referred,[142] Holmes advised lawmakers to be prescient and a bit Machiavellian; they could not, as he saw it, be wise. However, lawyers have played a large role in American policymaking, and it is very hard for a legal academic to renounce influence on policy when so many of his or her students will be making it. One might attempt to be influential and at the same time acknowledge that one's claims to policy insight have no foundation whatsoever in one's legal

141. *See* text accompanying notes 149-54 *infra*.
142. *See* text accompanying note 1 *supra*.

ability. Not surprisingly, this rarely occurs. Thus, Holmes' views have led a subterranean existence, primarily providing the backdrop against which efforts to avoid their implications have been played out. Some scholars, however, have adopted Holmes' views, and recently their work has posed a serious alternative to the main course of public law scholarship.

### A. *The Nihilist Challenge*

The direct legacy of Holmes can be found in the work of Professors Grant Gilmore, Arthur Leff, and Jan Deutsch. Professors Gilmore and Leff, while developing their nihilism as private law scholars, have made it clear that they see law as no more than an accumulation of cases decided one by one, and Professor Deutsch has made the point in the public law context. Professor Gilmore savagely and brilliantly attacked the idea that there is a unifying thread to law in his lectures, *The Ages of American Law*.[143] According to Professor Gilmore, American jurisprudence from the early nineteenth century to the present has been guided by a noble but fundamentally mistaken Classicism, which seeks to reduce the inherent confusion of law to a set of relatively austere principles. Classicism has looked to morals, science, or something unique in the law itself as a source of these principles. Professor Gilmore contrasted this American Classicism with British Romanticism, which considered cases as they came and decided them without attempting to build an integrated body of law. To Professor Gilmore, the Classicist effort, propelled by a deep human need for order, is admirable but can never be more than a noble dream.

Professor Gilmore's lectures, while elegant, do not provide the factual basis for his nihilism. He tells a story that is acceptable because of his ability to capture a sense of the law shared by academic lawyers, without describing how this sense corresponds to jurisprudential reality. Professor Leff's strategy is different. He is perhaps an even more entertaining writer than Professor Gilmore, but he has relied on explicit analysis to support his nihilism. Thus, he examined the work of the law and economics school and, after criticizing it from within its own presuppositions, concluded that analysis of the law is no more than one of many equally valid ways of perceiving law with no greater claim of having recognized something fundamental.[144]

143. G. GILMORE, *supra* note 27. For a somewhat more extended comment, see Tushnet, Book Review, 1 AM. J. LEGAL HIST. 373 (1977).

144. Leff, *Economic Analysis of the Law: Some Realism About Nominalism*, 60 VA. L. REV. 451 (1974).

More recently, in a tribute to Professor Gilmore, Professor Leff developed a theory of American law as a game, to illustrate that it could as easily be viewed as a cultural artifact as a repository of economic rationality. But that it can be seen both ways is, to Professor Leff, merely interesting, for it can be seen in an infinite number of other ways as well.[145] Professor Leff treats the subject matter of legal study as a map of a territory: economic analysis of the law covers the territory with strips that run from east to west; legal anthropology covers the territory as exhaustively with strips that run from north to south; and so on, so that even Willistonian conceptualism is as valid as modern ways of thinking about law. Travellers might see a few sights from new angles after they change routes, but they will reach the same basic understanding of the territory no matter which path they take.

An important and vastly underrated article by Professor Deutsch similarly rejects the claim of unifying consistency in constitutional law.[146] He examined a very technical case dealing with federal court procedure and the power of states to regulate interstate commerce. By dissecting the case and rearranging its paragraphs, Professor Deutsch showed that the case cannot be understood either as the product of controlling precedent or as a sensible attempt to guide further developments. In other words, there are no certain antecedents to or descendants of the case; we can in general only consider each case as it arises, since courts construct their decisions from choices among a large number of plausible interpretations of past decisions, with only an existential hope that their choices will work out.

Professors Leff and Deutsch reach their conclusions by different paths. For Professor Leff, there are an infinite number of ways to understand a case or a group of cases, and none has any greater claim to validity than any other. It is, therefore, pointless to attempt to discover "the" meaning of a case; a case is the decision of a court and nothing more. Professor Deutsch, in contrast, revels in demonstrating that any single case is related to every other case. His technique is to juxtapose apparently unrelated cases in an effort to force his readers to work out the connections that he discerns. To Professor Leff, no case is related to any other; to Professor Deutsch, each case is related to every

145. Leff, *Law and*, 87 YALE L.J. 989 (1978).

146. Deutsch, *Precedent and Adjudication*, 83 YALE L.J. 1553 (1974). The extent to which this article has been misunderstood can be seen in the incredible citation of it in G. GUNTHER, CASES AND MATERIALS ON CONSTITUTIONAL LAW 366 n.* (9th ed. 1975), in connection with the substantive claim in the case Professor Deutsch used as the focus of his article.

other.[147] Although these positions appear to be polar opposites, they are fundamentally the same: both authors conclude that we cannot understand the law because any attempted explanation is necessarily incomplete.

For the nihilists, then, there is only one case after another. As Professor Leff eloquently concluded:

> [A]ll we can understand, and that not very well, are the games we ourselves generate and eventually, but predictably, lose. Ultimately, the law is not something that we know, but something that we do.
>
> All right, all right, amen. But at least there is this: on the way to those final defeats, there are, at least for some, some beautiful innings.[148]

Nihilism leads to a massive scaling down of the enterprise, from "games" to "innings" and, I suppose, ultimately to "pitches." This transformation of the scope of legal analysis will provide, in the next section, a guide to post-nihilist scholarship.

### *B. Scholarship After Nihilism*

Nihilism is, even to its adherents, fairly disheartening. Professor Leff, for example, says that it is a position "that I hate a lot, and I do not hate less just because it is almost certainly true."[149] Almost in the nature of things, nihilism cannot become the dominant approach to public law scholarship. Even apart from academics' desires to influence policy, which nihilism might force them to abandon, nihilism as a purely intellectual proposition creates serious strains on the role of the legal academic. Sometimes this strain—Professor Leff's "hatred"—leads nihilists to assert, albeit half-heartedly, positions that are fundamentally inconsistent with their basic philosophy. Although these inconsistencies can be found in the works of Professors Gilmore[150] and Leff,[151] the best examples come from Professor Deutsch's recent collaborative work.[152] These articles combine his peculiar technique of juxta-

147. *See, e.g.*, J. DEUTSCH, SELLING THE PEOPLE'S CADILLAC: THE EDSEL AND CORPORATE RESPONSIBILITY (1976).

148. Leff, *supra* note 145, at 1011 (footnote omitted).

149. *Id.* at 1010.

150. *See* G. GILMORE, *supra* note 27, at 89 (hinting that the problem with the sociological approach to law is that the sociologists have not advanced their inquiries far enough for lawyers to rely on them).

151. *See* Leff, *supra* note 144, at 463 (suggesting that anthropology of law is a superior alternative to economic analysis).

152. Deutsch & LaRue, *Federalism and the Law of Securities Regulation: The Legacy of* Brown v. Board of Education, 34 WASH. & LEE L. REV. 799 (1977); Hoeflich & Deutsch, *Judicial Legitimacy and the Disinterested Judge*, 6 HOFSTRA L. REV. 749 (1978).

position with rather bland assertions of legal or sociological generalizations. It is clear from the format of the articles that Professor Deutsch's collaborators contributed the generalizations,[153] but he has been willing to associate himself with such assertions. If role strain leads to difficulties for scholars as astute as the leading nihilists, it is impossible for most others to bear; put crudely, what could an untenured nihilist write in order to get tenure?[154]

We can, of course, expect scholars to continue to grind out the applied constitutional theory articles; they are easy to produce and hard to relinquish. But this work is likely to be intellectually uninteresting, since the contours of the theory have been set and the content of particular analysis is rather predictable. The contours of post-nihilist scholarship, in contrast, are as yet difficult to discern, but some intimations are available. One possibility, to which Professors Leff and Robert Gordon are attracted, is to move back from the analysis of law to the analysis of how law is analyzed. Professor Gordon's move is into historiography, although I assume that a committed nihilist would suggest that, history being just one damn thing after another,[155] his move will prove unavailing.

Professor Gilmore's metaphors of Classicism and Romanticism suggest a related course. Post-nihilist scholarship could become something like the aesthetics of law. In this context, I must advert to an active area of scholarship, the law and economics school, that has not yet been discussed.[156] This school's work can now, I think, be seen as subject to aesthetic but not to traditional rationalistic analysis. There are subdivisions in the school, but the Posnerians, committed to the primacy of allocative efficiency as the basis for evaluating the behavior of courts,[157] are dominant, and for my purposes are therefore the most

153. In Deutsch & LaRue, *supra* note 152, at 799 n.*, responsibility is explicitly divided.

154. I think it is significant in this connection that Professor Leff is engaged in writing a legal dictionary, perhaps the ultimate expression, short of total silence, of nihilism.

155. *See* Tushnet, *supra* note 143.

156. Very little constitutional law scholarship employs Posnerian terminology. *But see* Scott, *Standing in the Supreme Court—A Functional Analysis*, 86 HARV. L. REV. 645 (1973). This is in part because Posnerians do not purport to address the distributional issues that have been of most interest in recent constitutional law. *But see* note 157 *infra*. In part, however, the disregard of Posnerian approaches has resulted from the incompatibility of their outcomes with the standard liberalism of most constitutional law scholars. *See also* note 158 *supra*.

157. Despite their pretensions of providing a purely positive analysis, the Posnerians find it hard to resist making prescriptions. They argue that courts are structured to promote allocative efficiency and that legislatures are not. This is institutionalism in another guise, but the Posnerians typically criticize, and do not simply characterize, legislative decisions as allocatively inefficient. Their institutionalism leads them to treat distributional issues as those for the legislature; their economics does not speak to distributional issues; people want to know about what legislatures do; and so the temptation to criticize on efficiency terms overcomes the positive analysis.

Texas Law Review Vol. 57:1307, 1979

interesting subdivision.[158] A sensitive reader of Posnerian articles cannot resist purely aesthetic responses: "Professor Kronman did a nice pirouette on page 724," for example, or, "Professor Posner's grand jete was flawed by a disastrous landing."[159] But if one is not committed in advance to the primacy of allocative efficiency, response is limited to the token acknowledgement that the analysis has brought to one's attention interesting but ultimately irrelevant points.[160]

Another possibility for post-nihilist scholarship is suggested at the conclusion of Professor Kennedy's article on "Form and Substance in Private Law Adjudication."[161] The main portion of the article describes two competing structures of private law concepts, which Professor Kennedy labels "altruism" and "individualism."[162] In the conclusion, Professor Kennedy, acknowledging some hesitancy, casts his lot with the altruists. But he does not establish, as the new natural lawyers would want, that altruism is either true or consistent with justice. On its surface at least, Professor Kennedy's analysis is purely descriptive. His ultimate choice for altruism remains, in the terms set by the article, an existential leap.[163] One who makes a choice such as

158. Another subdivision is represented by Professor Richard Markovits. *See, e.g.*, Markovits, *A Basic Structure for Microeconomic Policy Analysis in Our Worse-Than-Second-Best World: A Proposal and Related Critique of the Chicago Approach to the Study of Law and Economics*, 1975 WIS. L. REV. 950, which argues that even on the neoclassical terms used by the Posnerians, problems of second-best so complicate the economic analysis of law that it can contribute very little that is novel—only a checklist of things that intelligent analysts worried about before under different labels—to our understanding. That seems to be the import of Professor Calabresi's work as well. A similar move expands the number and types of externalities and related transaction costs that, on Posnerian terms, justify displacement of market results. For a critique, see Duncan Kennedy, "Two Phases of the Fetishism of Commodities," delivered at the Second National Conference on Critical Legal Studies, in Madison, Wisconsin (Nov. 10-12, 1978).

159. *See, e.g.*, Kronman, *Mistake, Disclosure, Information, and the Law of Contracts*, 7 J. LEGAL STUD. 1 (1978); Posner, *The Right of Privacy*, 12 GA. L. REV. 393 (1978).

160. The sentence in the text is a somewhat generous synopsis of the comments on Posner contained in Bloustein, *Privacy Is Dear at Any Price: A Response to Professor Posner's Economics Theory*, 12 GA. L. REV. 429 (1978); Fried, *Privacy: Economics and Ethics*, 12 GA. L. REV. 423 (1978).

Aesthetic responses also seem appropriate to the third subdivision of law and economics, which, after talking about allocative efficiency, reverts to distributional issues. This work is less interesting than pure Posnerian scholarship, whose power lies in its ability to provide concrete answers in a normless world; the third group's analysis of distribution eliminates the answers and reintroduces the flexibility that law and economics analysis was designed to eliminate. *See, e.g.*, Schwartz, *Contributory and Comparative Negligence: A Reappraisal*, 87 YALE L.J. 697 (1978).

161. 89 HARV. L. REV. 1685 (1976).

162. Individualism requires that one sharply distinguish one's interests from those of others. A preference in conduct for one's own interests is legitimate as long as this preference does not make it impossible to coexist with others. Individualists are preoccupied with justifying restrictions on liberty. *Id.* at 1713.

Altruism competes with individualism through its emphasis on sharing and sacrifice as typified in the "love thy neighbor as thyself" ideal. Unlike individualism, altruism does not require reciprocity from its sharing ideals. *Id.* at 1717.

163. Roberto Unger makes, I believe, the same leap in *Knowledge and Politics, supra* note 9.

Kennedy suggests would write articles that resemble applied theory supporting the "good guys"—the Skelly Wrights and Thurgood Marshalls—and making fun of the "bad guys"—the Warren Burgers and William Rehnquists.[164] But there is an important difference between ordinary applied theory and post-nihilist articles that superficially resemble such work. Although I am not fond of extended metaphors, one seems helpful here: Contemporary constitutional theory is developed by people who see that the emperor has no clothes, who say so in oblique ways, but who are uncomfortable enough with their perception to search for new emperors; theory is applied by people who seek to be the emperor's tailors; post-nihilist scholarship of the sort considered here would be done by people who regarded their work as a political lever to assist in the overthrow of the empire. There are suggestions in Professor Kennedy's article that his conclusion is of this political sort, but given his talent and the nature of the enterprise, a consumer can never be quite sure.

## IV. Non-Nihilist Scholarship After Nihilism

The nihilist vision gains its power from the accuracy of its description of law as radically fragmented. Post-nihilist scholarship, if it is to be intellectually respectable, must accept that description. Nihilism has immediate implications for the definition of the scholar's role. Most scholars of public law write what can be called prescriptive articles: they attempt to prescribe appropriate courses of action for the courts. But the nihilist description destroys the credibility of prescriptive efforts, for it shows that one can fit any result into a structure that satisfies the requirements of legal analysis. Because one recommendation is, within the terms of legal analysis, as good as another, prescription is bound to be unavailing and ultimately unintelligible.

Despite the costs in claims to influence on public policy, then, the post-nihilist legal scholar must stand apart from the legal system and must attempt to work with legal materials in some other way. This too is a legacy of realism, for if realism's destructive program led to nihilism, its constructive one emphasized various forms of interdisciplinary study. However, those who brought interdisciplinary perspectives to bear on the legal system focused, not surprisingly, on those aspects that resembled parts of other social systems. As Professor Deutsch has put

164. Depending on the direction of one's leap, of course, these characterizations could be reversed, but I know of few post-nihilist political conservatives. *But see* Fergenson, *The Sin of Omission: Inaction as Action Under Section 102(2)(c) of the National Environmental Policy Act of 1969*, 53 Ind. L.J. 497 (1978).

Texas Law Review Vol. 57:1307, 1979

it, they produced works about political science, not about law.[165] One task of post-nihilist scholarship, then, is to restore peculiarly legal phenomena to their rightful place in the study of law in society.

Here we can return to Professor Kennedy's article,[166] which takes legal doctrine as its focus. The article need not be read as part of the prescriptive school, although as I have suggested it may be so read, but as the start of a post-nihilist analysis. Nihilism understands that the set of rules and cases, when considered as a whole or in any of the usual divisions, is incoherent. Kennedy argues that the incoherence is patterned: the overall randomness results from laying one pattern over another. If he is right, we can accept the nihilist conclusion that the system as a whole cannot be understood and nevertheless attempt to explain the patterns that give rise to the appearance of incoherence.[167]

In this section, I will suggest how the patterns revealed in some aspects of American public law can be understood in Marxist terms. In doing so, I return to the Thrasymachean position that law is the expression of class power. But the connection between law and class power is indirect and complex. My thesis is that law in a class society is one form of the incomplete hegemony of the ruling class. Although the term "hegemony" has received its widest use in Marxist discussion, its basic meaning has been invoked far more broadly. Professor Deutsch, for example, in discussing criticisms of pluralist accounts of political power, noted that certain items were never even thought of as part of the political agenda.[168] The idea behind the term "hegemony," then, is that certain ideas tend to set the framework for discussion and to impose limits on what can be treated as serious proposals. When attached to a class analysis, hegemony refers to the dominance of ideas that are linked to the class in power.

I will explore the nature of this linkage in a moment, but it may be useful to describe what is perhaps the most dramatic example of the role of hegemony in public law and its scholarship. Professor Tribe, whose intentions are clearly of the best, has written:

> The time will come when constitutional law will answer the scholar's question, Why education and not golf? with the only

165. Deutsch, *Law as Metaphor: A Structural Analysis of Legal Process*, 66 GEO. L.J. 1339, 1339-40 (1978).

166. *See* note 161 *supra*.

167. On initial reading, I had thought that B. ACKERMAN, PRIVATE PROPERTY AND THE CONSTITUTION (1977), was an example of this sort of scholarship. But the reviews, particularly Epstein, *The Next Generation of Legal Scholarship?*, 30 STAN. L. REV. 635 (1978), have shaken my confidence in that reading.

168. Deutsch, *Neutrality, Legitimacy, and the Supreme Court: Some Intersections Between Law and Political Science*, 20 STAN. L. REV. 169, 251-57 (1967).

> reply that makes human sense—"Because education is more important"—and when this answer, however odd it will seem to some lawyers, will seem convincing to those who take their lessons from life itself.[169]

But it is not the answer that seems odd; it is the question. One who took his or her lessons from life itself surely would think (unless "life itself" means "life in the United States") that the relevant question is "Why education and not money or wealth?" But socialism is not on the agenda of contemporary public law scholarship, even though, it bears emphasizing, one could draw on the same cases that support Professor Tribe's answer to provide constitutional underpinnings for an argument for socialism, even though Rawls concedes that his theory is compatible with socialism,[170] and even though contemporary scholarship has developed all the right countermoves—appeals, for example, to concepts rather than to conceptions—to the obvious objections to the constitutional argument for socialism.

A Marxist analysis of law as a form of incomplete hegemony has two elements: a social psychology and a political economy of ideology.[171] The former begins with the idea that people interpret the material conditions of their existence in ways that make their experience coherent[172] and adds that the primary, though not exclusive, material conditions shaping those interpretations are the social relations of production, the relations between people, and the manner in which they guarantee their reproduction.[173] For a Marxist, the defining characteristic of capitalist society is the exchange of labor power for a wage, in which money is used as a homogeneous measure of the varying forms and quality of individual labor.[174] By eliminating individuality in production, capitalist social relations force people to interpret an experience that consists of partial relations, based solely on each person's possession of some quantum of undifferentiated labor power in the productive process. An interpretation of the world shaped by these relations has historically taken the form of an ideology of individualism.

169. L. TRIBE, *supra* note 47, § 11-4, at 574 (footnotes omitted).
170. J. RAWLS, *supra* note 18, at 265-74.
171. For a preliminary effort to develop these ideas, see Tushnet, *A Marxist Analysis of American Law*, 1 MARXIST PERSPECTIVES 96 (1978).
172. This idea is widely shared among phenomenological sociologists. For a collection of materials, see PHENOMENOLOGY AND SOCIOLOGY (Penguin ed. 1978).
173. *See generally* Gabel, *Intention and Structure in Contractual Conditions: Outline of a Method for Critical Legal Theory*, 61 MINN. L. REV. 601 (1977).
174. For a bourgeois philosophical defense of the cash nexus, see C. FRIED, RIGHT AND WRONG 124-26 (1978). This entire work is a fascinating defense of bourgeois individualism because its ideological components are displayed so close to the surface.

Texas Law Review Vol. 57:1307, 1979

The details of this ideology need not be delineated here,[175] for it is individualism and obviously associated ideas, such as the limited reach of law, that I will use in this sketch.

A Marxist social psychology of ideology also recognizes the internal contradictions of capitalism. Although market relations define capitalist society, they do not completely occupy its terrain. Capitalist production in advanced societies is social: workers can see that their individual sale of labor power masks the collective employment of that power. The social aspects of capitalist production generate ideas of wholeness and solidarity that are incompatible with the partial and fragmented aspects of market society. The mechanism by which material conditions generate ideas can here be left unspecified, as a black box that produces two sets of ideas—in Kennedy's terms, the individualist and the altruist.[176] Furthermore, traditional ties to families, religious associations, and neighborhoods persist, albeit in weakened form, even after market relations become dominant.[177] Thus, while the fragmented nature of capitalism supports individualism, the social aspects of capitalist production and the persistence of traditional group ties strengthen altruism. The hegemony of the ruling class is incomplete, therefore, because of internal contradictions in the system of production and because the political conditions of the class struggle can force into the arena issues and ideas that are not derived from the social relations of capitalist production. Indeed, when a Marxist analyzes a particular event or, in the present context, specific doctrines, he or she must not pretend that the structural determinants of a dominant ideology operate directly to produce those doctrines. Rather, transient political forces, the influences of intermediary groups, and the need, discussed below,[178] to present law as a neutral force, all intervene to produce what has come to be called a specific conjuncture inserted into the general structure of capitalist society.

The second component of a Marxist analysis of law is its political economy or, more precisely, its explanation of the role of the state in the realm of ideology. The state should guarantee that existing capital-

175. *See generally* C.B. MACPHERSON, THE POLITICAL PHILOSOPHY OF POSSESSIVE INDIVIDUALISM (1962).

176. *See* note 161 *supra*. It should be clear how Kennedy's analysis of altruism and individualism fits into this social psychology. My primary caveat is that Kennedy too readily assimilates statements from different historical periods into a single structure. Altruism based on pre-bourgeois social relations is different from, although historically related to, altruism based on the internal contradictions of capitalism.

177. *See, e.g.,* C. LASCH, HAVENS IN A HEARTLESS WORLD (1977) (an overstated analysis of the socialization of the family).

178. *See* text accompanying notes 181-85 *infra*.

ist relations of production are reproduced. This understanding of the state simply translates into new terms the liberal argument that the state must act to prevent the breakdown of a society in which each person is authorized, and to some extent encouraged, to consult only individual interest before acting. For our purposes, there are two means by which the capitalist state ensures the reproduction of capitalism: on the level of ideology, by presenting itself as an institution detached from parochial interests, serving as the neutral arbiter of disputes; on the level of material welfare, by accommodating class pressures through guarantees that minimally acceptable amounts of material goods are available to all.[179]

Both the ideological and material levels of the political economy of ideology cut across the operations of the capitalist state.[180] First, the institutions of the state provide opportunities for sectors within the capitalist class to manipulate state power in the service of parochial goals. The capitalist class considered as a whole thus has an interest in structuring the state so as to insulate its institutions from narrow interest manipulation.[181] Historically, the structure that has served this purpose is a state bureaucracy that adheres to the norms of impersonality and neutrality implied by the theory of the rule of law.[182] That theory looks in other directions as well. Precisely because the state bureaucracy is structured to reduce the threat of control by narrow sectors of the ruling class, it may begin to act in support of the interests of the bureaucrats, which need not coincide with those of the capitalist class as a whole. In addition, the universalistic norms of the neutral state, though developed to avoid conflict within the capitalist class, provide intellectual and political levers that the dominated class can employ. Thus, the state, again depending on the conjunctural situation, may invoke general norms to advance the interests of the capitalist class, the state bureaucracy, or the dominated classes. Marxists, however, treat the long-range interests of the capitalist class as determining the limits

179. For a classic formulation of the hegemony of dominant class ideology, see N. POULANTZAS, POLITICAL POWER AND SOCIAL CLASSES 190-94 (1973).

180. In a sketch such as this, inevitable problems of terminology arise. For example, it is almost impossible to avoid using terms suggesting that the capitalist state has a necessary function, but a full explication would not make this suggestion. For a careful presentation of appropriate vocabulary, see E.O. WRIGHT, CLASS, CRISIS, AND THE STATE 15-29 (1978).

181. *See* N. POULANTZAS, *supra* note 179, at 275-95. *See also* Offe, *"Crises of Crisis Management": Elements of a Political Crisis Theory*, 6 INT'L J. POL. 29, 48 (1976).

182. Of course, this does not imply that sectoral interests never capture the state apparatus; analysis of specific settings would have to take account of the political processes by which neutrality is sustained or overcome.

upon the use of neutrality and universalism in aid of the bureaucracy or the dominated classes.

Furthermore, the theory of the rule of law, I have argued, expresses a vision of equality and individualism that is consistent with social relations within the dominated classes. Through its role as an arbiter whose neutrality is ordinarily apparent and frequently real, the state provides an ideological expression of the fragmentation of the dominated classes: if injustice occurs, recourse can be had to the neutral state and thus alternative institutions premised on ideas of solidarity may be avoided.

The theory of the rule of law thus separates justice, the subject matter of law, from politics. But the neutral state does yield, of course, to political pressure even from the dominated classes, most notably in the growth of the welfare state as a complex response to the crisis of the 1930s. The welfare state, the third aspect of the state to which Marxists attend, is not governed by the fundamental principles that underlie the theory of the rule of law. The welfare bureaucracy applies a principle of administration, involving direct distribution of benefits to various constituencies, rather than a principle of neutral exchange within a framework of private transfers. The ideological problem posed by the development of a welfare bureaucracy is, then, the problem of reconciling the regulatory and dependency-oriented processes of administration with the theory of the neutral rule of law.[183] The resolution of the problem has been accomplished by developing legal doctrines—part of the rule of law—that explicitly endorse and thus rationalize the exercise of informed administrative discretion. However, although the observation that the courts defer to administrative discretion is commonplace in some contexts,[184] such deference is hard to fit into traditional doctrines of constitutional law.[185]

Kennedy has shown that sets of private law doctrines can be grouped into structures of thought with internal coherence.[186] Similar structures can be found in constitutional law and, more important, can be linked to the elements of the Marxist analysis of law. I will identify here only two components of these structures and will illustrate how

183. *See* Offe, *supra* note 181, at 42-48.

184. For a dramatic expression, see Vermont Yankee Nuclear Power Corp. v. Natural Resources Defense Council, 435 U.S. 519 (1978).

185. *See, e.g.,* Bell v. Wolfish, 441 U.S. 520, 562 (1979). The Court, obviously aware of difficulties in calling jailkeepers "experts," invoked the rhetoric of deference to expertise while shifting the framework from one of expertise to one of separation of powers. It is not immediately apparent, however, why a jailkeeper's decision to require body-cavity searches is the same, once expertise is put aside, as Congress' decision to enact a statute or even to appropriate money for a jail.

186. *See* note 161 *supra.*

they appear in constitutional doctrine. The dominant structure associates individualism and bureaucracy; it is the ideological expression of the individualistic social psychology and the welfare state of American capitalism. The deviant structure associates group activity and political action; it is the ideological expression of the contradictions within American capitalism. The associations within both deviant and dominant structures are not purely logical, although one can develop theories that are consistent with the premises of each structure and that unify each from within. Furthermore, while the general role of the state in reproducing capitalist relations of production induces the courts to disfavor interests that are disfavored in other contexts, the inducement can be resisted in specific contexts where it is not an essential element in the dominant structure of constitutional law.

The two components of the structure erected here in turn generate two basic propositions: in all contexts, the more highly rationalized the bureaucracy, the more deference its decisions will receive; in all contexts, the more an activity is associated with political action by organized groups, the less protection it will receive. Thus, to use the polar example, when a rationalized bureaucracy denies rights to a politically active group, its action will be upheld more readily than when a political decisionmaker denies rights to individuals. These propositions derive from both an analysis of contemporary constitutional law and a Marxist interpretation of the capitalist state. As to the latter, the defining relations of capitalist society implicate notions of exchange and individualism that fit uncomfortably with the welfare state in which benefits are distributed on the basis of generic characteristics. Yet political and ideological reality—the capitalist state's accommodation to the class struggle—require that welfare state activities be not only carried on, but articulately explained, at least in the legal sphere. Deference to administrative bureaucracies allows courts to conceal the divergence between the individualistic premises of the rules they apply and the collectivistic premises of the rules welfare bureaucracies apply. The dominant structure thus provides ideological support for capitalist state activities with the least impairment of the support given to the defining relations of society.

The deviant structure is, in a sense, secreted in the interstices of the dominant one, since it is impossible for courts, composed of people with varying political perspectives, to obscure completely the collectivism of the welfare state. Given the norm that judges articulate their reasoning, judges who seek to increase the benefits provided by the state, either because they believe that a greater accommodation of the demands of the subordinate classes is needed or because they wish to become allies of those classes, may seize on the occasions when nonindividualistic premises come close to the surface and then articulate in some detail the logic of the deviant premises.

The clearest expressions of deviant premises in recent law come from the incoherence, discussed above, of the new law of race discrimination. Race discrimination involves, almost by definition, class or group oriented action, but American constitutional law has responded to claims based on violations of group-defined interests by forcing them into the mold of intentional discrimination, in a way fully consistent with the individualistic premises of capitalist law.[187] At the same time, intellectual pressure to handle collective problems in a sensible way and political pressure to accommodate demands from the black community led to the flowering of the law of remedies. Thus, when it was difficult to identify an individual wrongdoer, as in freedom of choice plans in desegregation suits which produced precisely the same distribution of children to schools that had existed before the lawsuit, courts mandated rough racial proportions as an appropriate remedy, not for a constitutional violation in the freedom of choice plan, but for the antecedent statutory segregation. As commentators noted,[188] the flourishing remedies grew increasingly remote from the violations that purportedly justified them and induced suggestions that effects mattered more than intent.[189] Once again, intellectual and political elements contributed to the vigorous reassertion of the individualist principle requiring discriminatory intent. The implications of transforming the remedy cases by redefining the violation in group-oriented ways were unsettling,[190] and the political context in which the Court operated allowed it to return to the individualist viewpoint from which it had never openly departed.[191] Race discrimination law can thus fit into a dichotomized structure in which "individualism" and "violation" are related, as are "group-orientation" and "remedy." These pairs are in turn related in fairly obvious ways to the competing inter-

187. The best studies are Freeman, *supra* note 83, and LaRue, *A Jury of One's Peers*, 33 WASH. & LEE L. REV. 842 (1976). *See also* Klare, *Judicial Deradicalization of the Wagner Act, and the Origins of Modern Legal Consciousness, 1937-1941*, 62 MINN. L. REV. 265, 295 (1978).

188. *See, e.g.*, Brest, *The Supreme Court, 1975 Term—Foreword: In Defense of the Antidiscrimination Principle*, 90 HARV. L. REV. 1 (1976); Yudof, *Equal Educational Opportunity and the Courts*, 51 TEXAS L. REV. 411 (1973).

189. *See, e.g.*, Keyes v. School Dist. No. 1, 413 U.S. 189, 201 (1973).

190. *See, e.g.*, Washington v. Davis, 426 U.S. 229, 245-46 (1976).

191. *See* Dayton Bd. of Educ. v. Brinkman, 433 U.S. 406, 417 (1977) (explicitly tying remedy to violation in a coherent way).

pretations of the world generated by capitalist social relations.[192]

Another aspect of race discrimination law connects with the political economy of ideology and its emphasis on the state as bureaucratic administrator. By emphasizing individual discriminatory intent at the stage of violation,[193] the Court explicitly committed a great deal of the law to the informed discretion of the trial judge, who would make inferences of "fact" that appellate courts would find difficult to control,[194] thereby insulating significant portions of the law both from review and from integration into a coherent body of law. At the same time, the trial judge received substantial discretion in the choice of remedies,[195] which had the effect of transforming the judge into school administrator, prison manager, and general policymaker.

The relationship between bureaucracy and individualism can be developed further by examining other areas of recent constitutional decision. A series of cases in the 1940s seemed to establish that the Constitution required areas generally open to the public to be available for first amendment activity, such as speeches or parades.[196] The civil rights and antiwar movements raised public forum questions anew, and even as the Court struck down restrictions on the use of places like libraries[197] and schools,[198] it developed a new doctrine: a public forum was to be open to first amendment activity only when that activity did not interfere with the primary use of the area.[199] It thus became crucial to decide who had authority to determine the question of interference. The Court has consistently committed that decision to the administrators—military officials assessing the need for discipline and for main-

192. Again I must note the radical simplification of the analysis in the text. A more complete analysis would pay close attention to the rhetoric of the cases, to their political context, and perhaps most important, to the remaining contradictions in the present accommodations of violation and remedy. For example, Dayton Bd. of Educ. v. Brinkman, 433 U.S. 406, 417 (1977), seemed to require a reasonably close relationship between violation and remedy, but Milliken v. Bradley, 433 U.S. 267, 285-88 (1977), authorized a broad remedial order requiring extensive special reading programs when the connection between intentional segregation and reading impairment was, to put it generously, highly speculative. Clearly, a full explanation would note that *Dayton* involved busing children, while *Milliken* involved only transporting dollars.

193. *See* Dayton Bd. of Educ. v. Brinkman, 433 U.S. 406, 413 (1977).

194. *See id.* at 414-18.

195. *Id.* at 417-18.

196. *See* Jamison v. Texas, 318 U.S. 413 (1943); Cox v. New Hampshire, 312 U.S. 569 (1941); Schneider v. State, 308 U.S. 147 (1939). *See generally* Kalven, *The Concept of the Public Forum*, 1965 Sup. Ct. Rev. 1.

197. Brown v. Louisiana, 383 U.S. 131 (1966).

198. Tinker v. Des Moines School Dist., 393 U.S. 503 (1969).

199. A full analysis would take into account the increasing refinement of the problems presented to the Court, which allowed it to "develop" themes arguably implicit in earlier cases without appearing to withdraw from those cases.

taining the appearance of political neutrality in the military,[200] educators evaluating the need for a nondisruptive teaching environment,[201] and so on. Thus, the new law of public forum speech distinguishes between political and bureaucratic decisionmakers, giving the latter a deference that is withheld from the former. Although this new law is consistent with the Marxist argument about the rise of administration, it does not fit comfortably with traditional doctrines that treat governmental actors as an undifferentiated group.[202]

The Court created an even greater tension when it added to its distinction between politics and bureaucracy the distinction between group and individual activity. Prison law provides the best example. Elizabeth Alexander has shown that the Court's decisions in *Procunier v. Martinez*[203] and *Jones v. North Carolina Prisoners' Union*[204] can be reconciled only on the ground that an individual produced the letters prison administrators censored in *Martinez*, while a group produced the pamphlets censored in *Jones*.[205] Yet, because the distinction between group and individual activity is difficult to mesh with standard approaches to first amendment law, the result in *Jones* is a decision whose restrictions on group activity are almost entirely formal; that is, they can be evaded by altering the manner but not the substance of prisoner activity.

Like race discrimination law, the constitutional law applicable directly to the public distribution of benefits shows an incoherence related to the difficulty of adapting traditional notions to the new role of the welfare bureaucracy. On the procedural side, the Supreme Court has firmly adopted the following flexible test to determine the procedures that can be used to alter the distribution of benefits:

> [I]dentification of the specific dictates of due process generally requires consideration of three distinct factors: First, the private interest that will be affected by the official action; second, the risk of an erroneous deprivation of such interest through the procedures used, and the probable value, if any, of additional or substitute procedural safeguards; and finally, the Government's interest, including the function involved and the fiscal and ad-

200. *See, e.g.,* Greer v. Spock, 424 U.S. 828, 839 (1976).
201. *See, e.g.,* Tinker v. Des Moines School Dist., 393 U.S. 503 (1969).
202. *See, e.g.,* Stone, *Fora Americana: Speech in Public Places*, 1974 SUP. CT. REV. 233. It is worth noting that this new law cannot be attributed entirely, as Stone sometimes appears to do, to the political conservatism of the Burger Court, since the basic idea was developed in *Tinker*, a Warren Court decision written by Justice Fortas.
203. 416 U.S. 396 (1974).
204. 433 U.S. 119 (1977).
205. Alexander, *The New Prison Administrators and the Court: New Directions in Prison Law*, 56 TEXAS L. REV. 963, 1000-03 (1978).

ministrative burdens that the additional or substitute procedural requirement would entail.[206]

Professor Mashaw has in turn identified difficulties with this test: the fuzziness of the criteria provides opportunity for manipulation, and process serves values other than efficiency, which is the sole concern of the Court's test.[207] As a component of the adaptation of public law to administration, however, the test can be understood. Its flexibility allows all but the most antediluvian bureaucracies to escape judicial scrutiny, and the reduction of value to efficiency is consistent with the market premises of the theory of the rule of law.[208] One must note, however, the shift in reasoning that has occurred. Earlier the Court had taken the adversary trial as its model of due process, and deviation was justified only in rare situations.[209] The current position is torn from any roots in established processes and allows procedures to be developed and justified in an ad hoc manner. Once again the Court has adopted an approach that implicitly distinguishes between what government previously did (when adversary trials were the model) and what it does now (when flexibility is the key), and has explicitly endorsed the flexibility sought by the administrators of contemporary public benefit programs.

The Court has drawn similar lines in other areas. For example, the rule of causation in section 1983 actions established in *Mt. Healthy City Board of Education v. Doyle*,[210] which the Court treated, probably erroneously, as constitutionally mandated, allows relief when the defendant fails to show that it would have acted as it did even absent impermissible reasons. Officials who receive adequate legal advice and know how to create a personnel file—the relatively more sophisticated officials—will find rare the occasions on which they are found liable. Another example is *Hutto v. Finney*,[211] in which the Court invalidated rules about indeterminate solitary confinement in the Arkansas prison system, but explicitly stated that the same rules might be constitutionally acceptable in a more modern prison system that did not have Ar-

206. Mathews v. Eldridge, 424 U.S. 319, 335 (1976).

207. Mashaw, *The Supreme Court's Due Process Calculus for Administrative Adjudication in* Mathews v. Eldridge*: Three Factors in Search of a Theory of Value*, 44 U. CHI. L. REV. 28 (1976).

208. The theory of the rule of law assumes that each person consults only his or her individual interest before acting and must therefore be restrained by government under appropriate circumstances. Similar consultation of self-interest alone is what defines action in a market.

209. *See, e.g.*, Goldberg v. Kelly, 397 U.S. 254 (1970) (due process requires an evidentiary hearing prior to termination of AFDC support, although not necessarily in the form of judicial trial).

210. 429 U.S. 274, 284-86 (1977).

211. 437 U.S. 678 (1978).

Texas Law Review Vol. 57:1307, 1979

kansas' history of brutality.[212]

A final example can be drawn from other areas of public law. The field of administrative law scholarship was created in the 1940s by a number of men whose retirements in the 1970s provoked a reconsideration of the nature of the field. The founders had been concerned with what they regarded as the questionable legitimacy of administrative agencies, whose decisionmakers were less subject to political control than might seem appropriate, and whose decisions were guided by claims to expertise that neither legislature nor court could easily evaluate. They established the legitimacy of agencies by guaranteeing that administrative decisions were made in a procedurally acceptable way—thus applying the realist synthesis to their field—and that judicial review would be available on questions of law.[213] Yet even as the founders developed their positions, "malaise in the administrative scheme"[214] set in. The malaise could be seen in the concern expressed about the failure of agencies to accomplish desired goals and in the widespread view of agencies as inexpert captives of their clientele.[215]

Dean James Freedman identified a number of factors supporting the uneasiness: a simplistic conception of separation of powers, an ambivalence about the enterprise of economic regulation, an overly idealistic belief in expertise, and a general overenthusiasm about the capacity of agencies to do good.[216] But there is more than this to the malaise among administrative law scholars. Their self-reflections contain a sense of the irrelevance of their endeavors. Like the realists before them, they have discovered that very little of the business of administrative agencies takes a form amenable to the statutory procedural framework or comes to the attention of the courts, and they have wondered, therefore, what they should study.[217] One popular response has been to argue that agency procedures are inextricably bound up with the substance of the agency's task—how the Veterans Administration behaves in processing applications for benefits necessarily differs from the Interstate Commerce Commission's procedure for setting rail-

212. *Id.* at 685-86.

213. The Administrative Procedure Act, 5 U.S.C. §§ 551-559, 700-706 (1976), and Crowell v. Benson, 285 U.S. 22, 42-48 (1932), express these answers. *See generally* Freedman, *Crisis and Legitimacy in the Administrative Process*, 27 STAN. L. REV. 1041 (1974); Verkuil, *The Emerging Concept of Administrative Procedure*, 78 COLUM. L. REV. 258, 261-93 (1978).

214. FTC v. Ruberoid Co., 343 U.S. 470, 482 (1952) (Jackson, J., dissenting).

215. The literature is collected in Freedman, *supra* note 213, at 1042-43 nn.7-11.

216. *Id.* at 1047-68.

217. *See, e.g.*, Gellhorn & Robinson, *Perspectives on Administrative Law*, 75 COLUM. L. REV. 771, 771-83 (1975); Rabin, *Administrative Law in Transition: A Discipline in Search of an Organizing Principle*, 72 NW. U.L. REV. 120, 127-35 (1977).

road rates.[218] The recommendation, then, is to be wary of generalization of law from agency to agency—ultimately, to eliminate the field by fragmenting it. More radically, Professor Rabin has suggested that administrative law be transformed into the study of the administration of the law in three generic areas—regulation, public management, and benefit distribution.[219] But now we can return to the lesson drawn from the nihilist challenge. As scholars examine the administration of public benefits, for example, they will soon discover that agencies distribute public benefits through a process of entirely discrete decisions. The unification of administrative law, then, is subject to the same defects that plague synthetic efforts in constitutional law; there is no law in the classic sense, only administration.

Professor Abram Chayes has developed some insights from the malaise of administrative law scholarship in one of the few stimulating articles on court procedure in recent years.[220] Professor Chayes is another scholar concerned with, but in this case approving of, the increasing importance of detailed, administrative-style action by judges. Professor Chayes discusses what he calls "public law litigation," classicly represented by the complex desegregation suit or the suit challenging a wide range of state prison practices as unconstitutional. He describes such litigation as follows:

> The party structure is sprawling and amorphous, subject to change over the course of litigation. The traditional adversary relationship is suffused and intermixed with negotiating and mediating processes at every point. The judge is the dominant figure in organizing and guiding the case, and he draws for support not only on the parties and their counsel, but on a wide range of outsiders—masters, experts, and oversight personnel. Most important, the trial judge has increasingly become the creator and manager of complex forms of ongoing relief, which have widespread effects on persons not before the court and require the judge's continuing involvement in administration and implementation.[221]

This type of lawsuit poses a serious problem for traditional conceptions of litigation, whose legitimacy had been established by either natural law or institutionalist arguments. Public law litigation does not resemble the traditional private lawsuit that formed the basis for the institutionalist arguments for judicial review.[222] Nor does the court's

218. Gellhorn & Robinson, *supra* note 217, at 783-97.
219. Rabin, *supra* note 217, at 135-45.
220. Chayes, *The Role of the Judge in Public Law Litigation*, 89 HARV. L. REV. 1281 (1976).
221. *Id.* at 1284.
222. *See id.* at 1285-1304.

Texas Law Review Vol. 57:1307, 1979

attention to the square footage and toilet facilities in jails fit well with natural law views; while standards of decency might be prescribed by natural law, it is odd to think that judges can rigorously deduce from it the precise content to be given those standards in concrete situations.

Professor Chayes attempted to justify public law litigation in a blend of institutionalist and natural law terms. He noted, for example, that the judge's professional tradition and career experience is likely to make him or her sensitive to the complexity of public policy choices, that courts can induce the parties to present the full range of information that a legislature might have, and that representation is flexible enough to guarantee participation even by those to whom a legislature might not respond.[223] He further suggested that public law litigation is primarily directed at the administration of the law by appointed officials and that the public law judge acts on behalf of those who "have no alternative access to the levers of power in the system."[224] But as Chayes acknowledged[225] and as commentators have recognized,[226] public law litigation cannot finally be reconciled with either tradition: it is too precise for natural law and too significant, particularly in its impact on state budgets, for institutional analysis.[227] Although Professor Chayes concluded by invoking "the deep and durable demand for justice in our society,"[228] his analysis of the process of public law litigation is fundamentally inconsistent with the view that justice can be achieved through the rule of law. In the end, students of administrative law and of public litigation come together with the nihilists: none can understand what the law is today in the universalistic terms established by the bourgeois theory of the rule of law; each reduces law to individualized decisions characterized by flexibility and discretion.

## V. Conclusion

The preceding section provides only an adumbration of what a Marxist interpretation of American public law would do. Both the theoretical framework and the illustrations require development of a sort that would be inappropriate in this essay. However, even this outline

223. *Id.* at 1307-09.
224. *Id.* at 1315.
225. *Id.*
226. Frug, *The Judicial Power of the Purse*, 126 U. PA. L. REV. 715 (1978). *See also* Nagel, *Separation of Powers and the Scope of Federal Equitable Remedies*, 30 STAN. L. REV. 661 (1978).
227. It should be noted, however, that the revival of institutionalism in Frug, *supra* note 226, and Nagel, *supra* note 226, has so far been a response to developments in remedial and not in substantive law.
228. Chayes, *supra* note 220, at 1316.

suggests directions for post-nihilist scholarship. We need not agree that nihilism describes more than a specific historical form that the law has taken. Thus, we could begin to explore the reasons, not just for the emergence of nihilism as a credible, even powerful, intellectual position, but also for the accuracy of the nihilist description of the law. I suggest that, at least as a working hypothesis, a Marxist approach will yield interesting insight. But in the end, a Marxist must be cautious. While believing that a Marxist analysis could be fruitful, he or she must acknowledge, for Marxist reasons, that it may well prove to be as sterile as traditional approaches, as long as the intellectual analysis is not connected to significant and organized efforts to supplant existing institutions.[229] That such efforts are desirable is, I believe, unquestionable; that they are likely to occur is an open question, the answer to which will determine, among other things, the utility of Marxist analysis of contemporary public law.

229. *See* P. ANDERSON, CONSIDERATIONS ON WESTERN MARXISM (1976).

# [15]
# The Future of Constitutional Law Scholarship

For over a decade constitutional law scholarship has been living off the remains of the Warren Court. Liberals nostalgic for the era of Supreme Court assistance in the promotion of their political programs grasp at anything that demonstrates the Court's present inclination to continue providing such assistance. Conservatives parade the bogey-man of "judicial activism"—such as invalidating the death penalty—as if the Court had not "deregulated" the field, in Professor Weisberg's apt phrase. The incarnation of Justice Lewis Powell, a very conservative judge, as a judicial moderate upon his retirement is symptomatic—and not a little embarrassing when it turned out that the views of his designated successor, who was attacked as an extreme conservative, were not that different from Powell's.

Of course people can delude themselves indefinitely, and scholarship about constitutional law that treats Warren Court decisions as canonical and later ones as aberrational may well persist. There are sociological reasons for that to occur as well. The legal academy is likely to remain dominated by liberal scholars, whose political inclinations will lead them to define their field in politically congenial ways. That's because the opportunity costs for conservatives who go into academic life are much higher than the opportunity costs for liberals: put bluntly, I'd have to take a substantial cut in pay to do the kind of legal practice that I would be inclined to do, but conservatives have to take substantial cuts in pay when they leave the kind of legal practice that they are inclined to do.

My utopian aspirations for the academy make me want to hope that reality will at some point intrude on constitutional law scholarship. What will happen when people realize that the Warren Court ended a while ago?

The most likely result is that the same kind of scholarship will be produced, with people simply switching sides. Liberals will start chastising the Supreme Court for failing to take serious account of the historical background of various constitutional provisions, for disingenuously dealing with precedents, for promoting its political agenda under the guise of enforcing the Constitution—all the things that conservatives have been attacking the Court for doing. And conservatives, few though they may be, will start saying that, although the Court's precise reasoning may have been somewhat inadequate, the result it reached can be defended along different lines.

This prospect is deeply depressing. Part of the problem is that the critiques of liberal decisions are so well-developed, and so obviously correct, that they can be deployed against *any* decision invalidating legislation. If conservatives were willing to follow through on their inconstant commitment to a populist majoritarianism, only one such critique would be available—that populist majoritarianism is inconsistent with the idea of constitutionalism. But the moment that they invalidate a statute—campaign finance regulation, affirmative action programs, legislation aimed at restricting the mobility of capital (plant-closing statutes)—conservatives are just as bad off as liberals, because everything they have said about liberals in the past can then be said about them.

There are already indications that this is going to happen. One would not have thought it possible for conservatives to rely on a worse historical understanding of the free exercise and establishment clauses than liberals have, but they have managed to apply their jurisprudence of original intent to the religion clauses in just that way. And Laurence Tribe would have no difficulty in agreeing with the assertion that television broadcasters and other commercial speakers are protected by the first amendment because we have to understand the purposes of the amendment on the right level of generality. Those who contend that affirmative action programs are unconstitutional sound like Ronald Dworkin in asserting that we have to interpret the equal protection clause in light of the concept of racial equality that it embodies, not in terms of the particular conceptions of equality held by its framers (who, after all, supported quite race-specific laws such as the Freedmen's Bureau statutes).

This prospect is depressing because it is not a lot of fun watching people shoot fish in barrels; indeed, one sometimes begins to develop sympathy both for the fish, who are doing the best they can in trying circumstances, and for their pursuers, who are doing the only thing they know how to do. In addition, it may be difficult to sustain the enterprise over the long run. We have already experienced the extrusion of certain subtopics from the field of constitutional scholarship: criminal procedure first, followed by a large part of the law of justiciability. I am told that many people already have abandoned teaching about the powers of Congress and federalism more generally. Oddly, the first two areas have been eliminated from the constitutional law course because there is too much law, while federalism may go because there is too little law about Congress's powers and too much law about the negative commerce clause and preemption. (You would have to be a pedagogical genius to be able to teach an introductory class the *CTS* case.)

If federalism were extruded from the constitutional law course, constitutional law as an academic field would consist of civil rights and civil liberties. (I haven't done the necessary research, but I do note that 1102 of the 1536 pages in the constitutional law casebook of which I am a co-author—about 72%—deal with those issues, and would bet that if one looked back a decade or two one would find that percentage substantially lower in the casebooks then in use.) But constitutional law isn't very interesting when the Court routinely upholds legislation; I suppose that is one of the reasons why *National League of Cities v. Usery* gave federalism as a field of study a shot in the arm, and why *Garcia v. San Antonio Metropolitan Transit Authority* is likely to deaden the field again. Given the likely composition of the Court in the future, civil rights and civil liberties cases will probably begin to resemble today's federalism cases—routinely upholding legislation. (There is one exception: the Justices, no fools about public relations, will occasionally uphold claims under the first amendment, to get the plaudits of the press that such decisions inevitably generate.) If that happens, constitutional scholarship focused on the Supreme Court will have to deal with presumptively uninteresting subjects—the cases.

Are there any alternatives to this grim picture?

One possibility is that constitutional law scholarship might turn away from its obsession with the Supreme Court. I think this is unlikely and perhaps even unwise.

Paul Brest and Sanford Levinson have been arguing for years, without substantial success, that constitutional law is made elsewhere than in the Supreme Court or even in the courts at all. The area of separation of powers seems to me a prime candidate for a study of constitutional law in which the courts figure not at all. (Do you think that your students are fairly equipped to write a memorandum to a conscientious Senator describing how the principle of ambition counteracting ambition applies to her consideration of a nominee for the Supreme Court?) Yet, the market is quite resistant to suggestions that *Youngstown, Chadha,* and the like are really not the best way to learn the constitutional law of separation of powers. Honestly, do you really think that you would assign and be capable of teaching from a constitutional law casebook that didn't include *Youngstown* as the heart of its presentation of separation of powers? At present I have no substantial thoughts on how the law of civil liberties and civil rights could be studied and written about without a focus on the Supreme Court, but I bet it could be done.

Perhaps, though, it should not be done. In recent years scholars of constitutional law have produced a substantial body of work in which the Supreme Court doesn't really play much of a role. I have in mind the application of moral philosophy to constitutional law. This body of work does not encourage one who thinks that lawyers should look elsewhere than the courts for enlightenment about constitutional law. The difficulty is that legal academics think that you can throw a little "equal concern and respect," a little Wittgenstein, a little whatever-else, into the pot, stir carefully, and come up with something that we should regard as real philosophy. This is the current version of what I once called the "lawyer as astrophysicist" assumption: We are people who have a generalized intelligence, and can absorb and utilize the products of any other discipline in which we happen to become interested. One has to read no more than the work of serious philosophers like Thomas Nagel in *The View from Nowhere* or Derek Parfit in *Reasons and Persons* to appreciate how embarrassingly amateurish our pseudo-philosophical efforts are.

What follows should perhaps be taken with some suspicion, given my preceding comments about the use of philosophy in recent constitutional scholarship. It may be that a useful terrain for constitutional scholarship would retain the focus on the Supreme Court, but begin to treat the cases as empirical phenomena rather than normative statements. This is, in my view, a job for intellectual historians, and maybe we will be as incompetent at intellectual history as we have been at philosophy. Still, I wonder who else might address a question like this one, which has puzzled me recently: How come the Supreme Court has become attracted to relatively formalistic analyses of separation of powers questions (but not entirely so, as *Commodities Futures Trading Commission v.*

*Schor* shows; shooting this particular fish involves making fun of the fact that *Schor* and *Bowsher v. Synar* were decided on the same day) when such formalism is not apparently as attractive elsewhere in the law? The project would involve trying to figure out the relationship between formalism-pragmatism and conservatism-liberalism (not meaning to suggest by this construction that the parallelism is accurate) in the present period.

The overall difficulty for constitutional law scholarship is that its producers, by our specialized training and our inclinations, are much better at dealing with Supreme Court cases than we are at doing anything else. Perhaps people with interdisciplinary training—in philosophy, political science, or history—will come up with some novel perspectives on constitutional law. Yet I note a structural impediment to the realization of that possibility: With rare exceptions, interdisciplinarians at or near the top of their other disciplines are unlikely to want to teach in a law school, preferring the company of those immersed in the other discipline. That means that, again with rare exceptions, people who do constitutional law scholarship and have interdisciplinary training or interests are unlikely to produce truly provocative work drawing on that training or interest.

In my view, the lines of analysis of the cases have just about played themselves out. Maybe the time has come to start doing something else. (Of course, I may be willing to say that because I have just published a book on constitutional theory that I unsurprisingly but undoubtedly erroneously regard as the last word on the subject, and maybe all that I mean is that the time has come for me to start doing something else.)

## CHARLES A. LOFGREN[9]

In view of the past fifty years of history under the Constitution, I find it difficult to think of many—if any—areas of American life *not* open to further examination by constitutional scholars. Certainly historians, whose domain is perhaps broader than that of their constitutional cousins in other disciplines, should greet the Bicentennial with renewed appreciation for Andrew McLaughlin's vision in 1935: "Constitutional history . . . , when viewed in its entirety, is of almost limitless extent, because to comprehend it fully one must have in mind social and industrial change and movement." Indeed, recent decades have suggested that McLaughlin

9. Roy P. Crocker Professor of American Politics and History, Claremont McKenna College, and member of the Graduate Faculty in History of the Claremont Colleges.

# PART FOUR

# PEDAGOGY

# [16]
# Elite Efforts to Restrict the Supply of Lawyers: A Comment on the Bok Report

Leaders of elite law schools periodically make efforts to maintain the position of their schools by restricting the supply of lawyers. They have urged that undergraduate degrees be required for admission to law school, that a three-year program rather than a shorter and cheaper one be required, and that proprietary law schools be driven out of business.[1] Traditionally the

1. Harry First, Competition in the Legal Education Industry (I), 53 N.Y.U. L. Rev. 311 (1978).

argument has been that the public interest is served by having better lawyers, and that these pedagogic changes will make lawyers better, though they will have the perhaps unfortunate side effect of restricting the supply of lawyers. Derek Bok's Report exemplifies a new genre in this tradition. Now the argument is that the public interest will be served directly by having fewer lawyers.

I wish to address two components of the argument: (1) "Overlawyering" for elite clients is a drag on the economy; (2) delegalization of many areas of life will make things easier for nonelite clients.

(1) Elite clients hire lawyers to facilitate the making of deals. Undoubtedly the deals could be made with less lawyering. But lawyers are needed to structure the deals to comply with public regulations designed in the main to keep one bunch of relatively well-to-do people from bilking another group of relatively well-to-do people. The lawyers structure the deals so that these public duties are performed at minimal costs; indeed, given the weakness of the regulations in the first place, the lawyers frequently can structure the deals to avoid compliance altogether.

Requiring that deals be structured in one way rather than another imposes a kind of tax on people who want to make deals. The tax, however, is paid to lawyers rather than to the treasury, and overlawyering drives home the recognition of who benefits from public regulation. One could resolve the problem of overlawyering by eliminating the regulations, letting the well-to-do bilk each other if they want, and imposing a modest but true tax on deals. This solution is both politically and ideologically impossible. Politically active segments of the well-to-do see themselves as more often potential bilkees than bilkers, and find it helpful to use the Treasury to bear the overhead costs of protecting themselves from their own foolishness. And public regulation helps conceal the fact that deals in our society are variations on cheating and swindling.[2] Ineffective regulation is especially useful, because it lets deals be made under the cloak of regulation which are no different from those made otherwise.

Overlawyering simply transfers income from the players—banks, entrepreneurs, and so on—to the lawyers. This is unlikely to have significant macroeconomic consequences unless lawyers save less than players or invest what they save differently. One player in a particular deal may have to sacrifice an engineer to pay the lawyer. But when the money gets to the lawyer and beyond, somewhere there will be a bank ready to make a deal that will let another player hire an extra engineer. I would have thought that, if lawyers' investment patterns differed from those of banks, it would be in favor of riskier Silicon Valley types of enterprises, which if true ought to please the engineers.[3]

Ordinarily one would think that elite clients would prefer less rather than more lawyering. The economy as a whole might not be affected, but the client would rather hire the extra engineer than see someone else do so. If the

2. Arthur Allen Leff, Swindling and Selling (New York: Free Press, 1976).

3. I would qualify this to the extent that lawyers' fees include overhead that is ultimately paid to secretaries and plumbers who save less of their income than lawyers do.

amount of lawyering exceeds what is required to comply with public regulations, there must be some explanation. Once clients accept a system in which they are charged by the hour, overlawyering is almost inevitable: The clients have imperfect information about the lawyers' activities, and over time they invest in human capital as "their" lawyers get to know their peculiar needs. But, even given uncertainty about how much time a particular job will take, the client does not necessarily accept the burdens of uncertainty by paying by the hour—unless (aha!) the supply of lawyers is limited.

Finally, clients promote a culture of overlawyering. Lawyers for elite clients work sixteen-hour days and through the night to get a document ready or a letter in the mail by 8:00 a.m. Unlike medical ones, real legal emergencies are rare. (That is why doctors carry beepers and lawyers, except for reasons of prestige, do not.) Partly the culture of overlawyering results from the "Kareem Abdul Jabbar" syndrome: The lawyer thinks, "Unless I work these incredible hours, I'll never get to be my generation's Joe Flom." The distorting effects of the syndrome on incentives and performance are well known. Partly the culture results from client demand. Clients are willing to sacrifice one engineer for the kick that comes from having the power to call up a senior partner at any hour and guarantee that the lives of several junior associates will be needlessly disrupted over the weekend.

As all this suggests, overlawyering for elite clients is of interest to sociologists. That the public interest would be served by reducing overlawyering seems to me questionable. And in any event it is unlikely that restricting the total supply of lawyers would have much effect on practice for elite clients.

(2) Delegalization of areas involving the working class would reduce the need for a certain kind of lawyer—the lawyer, rarely a graduate of an elite law school, who practices on his or her own or, as is increasingly common, who becomes the salaried employee of a chain like Hyatt Legal Services. Seen in this way the campaign for delegalization is just as direct as an attack on nonelite law schools as was the drive against proprietary ones.

Some argue that the delegalization actually creates new bureaucracies.[4] People who use the courts are in some ways acting politically to mobilize public force on their behalf. People who are shunted into the bureaucracies of "informal justice" become passive clients who end up in one way or another "cooled out" of their grievances. Further, the "rule of law" is one of our culture's primary symbols of value, and everyone has access to it at least in theory. Delegalization converts the "rule of law" into something like an expensive car, a thing of value available only to the well-to-do. It is of a piece with *Buckley v. Valeo*. Its proponents would be well advised to think twice about its consequences.

I find Bok's suggestions for reforming legal education largely unexceptionable. They are, more or less, exactly those proposals that have been on the agenda since the 1930s. In the circumstances one might wonder about the

4. See The Politics of Informal Justice, ed. Richard Abel, 2 vols. (New York: Academic Press, 1982).

relation between the specific illnesses that Bok identifies and the remedy he prescribes, since the remedy appears to be a universal cure-all for whatever ails elite law professors at the moment. One might also point out that the leaders of elite law schools have repeatedly crushed every effort to build serious empirical studies into their law schools and have thereby marginalized empirical inquiry in the law school world as a whole.[5] Perhaps they understand that serious empirical studies of the legal world would subvert their claims to elite status.

# [17]

# Scenes from the Metropolitan Underground: A Critical Perspective on the Status of Clinical Education

Despite the supportive talk one hears at meetings of the Association of American Law Schools, clinical education remains a marginal aspect of the law school curriculum. This essay will briefly describe the nature of that marginality, explain some of its sources, and discuss strategies that have been and might be used to overcome it. I must state at the outset my own perspective: I have taught only in the traditional classroom and in that sense I write from "the metropolis." But I suspect that because of the content of what I teach, students have a relatively untraditional experience. In that sense I write from "the underground." Finally, I strongly support the animating vision behind clinical education, although clinical education's response to marginality has distorted that vision.

Five or ten years ago clinical education was vulnerable rather than marginal. It was then a newly established activity subject to repeated attacks from which it narrowly escaped. Presently, firmly entrenched clinical programs repeatedly repulse similar challenges; nevertheless, most law professors consider them largely irrelevant to legal education. Clinical budgets have expanded and, although further growth may be unlikely, the present plateau represents a substantial investment in clinical education. Clinical instructors are often either on the tenure track or enjoy long-term contracts that provide the employment stability they desire.

The best analogy for clinical education is not that of a colonial outpost to the traditional classroom metropolis.[1] Rather, like the enclaves of Liechtenstein or Monaco, clinical education survives because it serves purposes that its more powerful neighbors find useful. Clinical education pacifies student demand for practical experience and social productivity. It also eases the conscience of liberal law professors who are uncomfortable because few of their students practice the public interest law that those professors consider important. But enclaves exist at their neighbors' suffrance as citizens of Goa recently discovered. Thus, marginality seems to describe best the status of clinical education.

Yet, some vulnerability remains. When faculties feel pressure to reduce budgets or to restrain rates of increase, they look first to, and often not beyond, the clinical curriculum.[2] The reason given is clinical education's unusually high cost. In making budgetary decisions, however, the relevant figure is not cost but the cost-benefit ratio. Yet, observing that clinical education is expensive says nothing about the cost-benefit ratio. Indeed, defenders of clinical education can make a good cost-benefit case, which explains why clinical education is less vulnerable than it was before. Vulnerability also results from the physical separation between the clinics and the traditional classrooms. Clinical instructors, even those on the tenure track, are not well-integrated into the faculty social network. Because of this lack of integration, tenure-track appointments and long-term contracts are less significant than they appear.[3] The impression of vulnerability is strengthened by the presumption of many faculty members that clinical programs contain more unnecessary fat than do traditional classes.[4] In my experience as a member of the nonclinical faculty, people identify the fat as the intellectual weakness of clinical education.

---

1. In colonies, missionaries and bureaucrats whose primary identity is tied to the metropolis carry out the tasks their superiors regard as necessary. Needless to say, clinicians do not see their role in that way.

2. These pressures seem likely to increase as the baby-boom wave crests in the next decade. That diminishing source of enrollment might be offset by increasing the percentage of people who deem law school an attractive post-graduate option and by expanding the range of eligible students by making concerted efforts to attract career-switchers.

3. Denial of tenure or nonrenewal of contracts occurs, or probably will occur, at only a slightly higher rate for clinical teachers than for traditional classroom teachers. Perhaps the tenure track or long-term contract for clinical instructors will become another version of the revolving door that exists in some places for minorities and women. The figures will remain steady, but the individuals occupying the positions may change.

4. There is, of course, a great deal of fat in the traditional curriculum, including courses like trusts and estates and future interests, which could be taught quickly and effectively with programmed materials.

The differences between clinical education and traditional classroom education expose the reasons for clinical education's marginal status. Those reasons relate to the perceived intellectual weakness of clinical education. I will identify some apparent differences, not in any particular order. First, clinical education deals with corporations or other imaginary entities like the entirely abstract plaintiff in a tort case.[5]

Second, clinical education concerns unstructured experiences — the confusion of everyday life before the interchange between lawyer and client formulates the legal issues. Traditional classroom education, however, incorporates highly structured experiences in two ways. The legal problems are presented in the cases as already defined by the lawyers. The student learns how to resolve that problem instead of how to define it in the first place. Furthermore, the traditional classroom is usually highly structured because the instructor knows exactly the result he or she wants to achieve. A clever instructor can subtly direct the discussion to predetermined conclusions.

Third, clinical education concerns primarily the poor; traditional education concerns primarily the rich. Only the rich can afford to litigate cases to the point that the issues are presented in a form that is useful for traditional instruction. Moreover, non-clinical instructors convey, not always consciously, the message that students will work, and ought to work, for the rich. By contrast, only the poor need legal assistance so desperately that they willingly accept what relatively untutored students can provide.

Fourth, clinical education, in at least some aspects, incorporates feelings; traditional education embodies reason. In the unstructured nature of the clinic, for example, the student attempts to discover exactly what happened to the client and takes part in settlement negotiations. The student interacts with adversaries. That kind of contact generates strong feelings, such as anger, a sense of inadequacy, submission, and suspicion of clients. In order to do the lawyer's job well, the clinical student must begin to appreciate the role that feelings play in legal practice. Traditional classroom instruction, on the other hand, seeks a detached analytical discussion of the legal issues raised by the cases.

There may be other differences between clinical education and traditional classroom education. However, a thread runs through these differences and probably the others as well. Clinical education concerns people, unstructured situations, and feelings, all of which in our culture are generally associated with being female.[6] Traditional education concerns abstractions, structure, and reason, all of which

5. *See* Gabel, *Reification in Legal Reasoning,* 3 RESEARCH IN L. & SOC. 25 (S. Spitzer ed. 1980). *See generally* J. NOONAN, PERSONS AND MASKS OF THE LAW (1976).

6. *See* Olsen, The Sex of Law (1984) (unpublished manuscript). Olsen explains that our thinking is structured into many dualistic categories — for example, rational/irrational, reason/emotion, power/sensitivity — which are sexualized. One half of the dualism is considered masculine and superior, the other half feminine and underprivileged. *See also* Kennedy, *The Political Significance of the Structure of the Law School Curriculum*, 14 SETON HALL L. REV. 1, 10 (1983).

are associated with being male. Those associations contribute greatly to the marginality of clinical legal education. The female characteristics make the men who dominate law schools extremely uncomfortable.

That discomfort is political and leads to an assertion of power based on false images of clinical and traditional classroom education. It seems as if the clinic works with people and feelings, whereas the classroom works with abstraction and reason. By falsely characterizing clinical and traditional classroom education in terms associated with gender hierarchy, those who dominate law faculties capitalize on the cultural loadings of the terms to maintain their positions.

One can invert the observations about clinical and traditional classroom education and illustrate the falsity of the characterization. When a clinical student meets a client, the student applies the norms of the adversary system to determine what the client wants and how to accomplish it. Applying those norms transforms the client into a client-type, an abstraction no less imaginary than Mrs. Palsgraf in the traditional classroom.[7] When a student in a traditional classroom discusses a case, the student learns that one technique of case manipulation is to draw into the discussion more and more of the actual circumstances in which the abstract plaintiff finds herself. Thus, the classroom only seems structured and the clinical experience only appears unstructured. In fact, clients and students enter the clinic with an enormous amount of cultural baggage that structures their interaction. Moreover, the classroom is always vulnerable to destabilization by a student or teacher who fails to play by the rules: students by reading newspapers, missing class, or knitting; teachers by expressing uncertainty about "the proper rule" governing the case under discussion.[8]

Of course, reason and analysis must guide students in the clinic in solving their client's legal problems. Similarly, feelings pervade the traditional classroom. Students dislike instructors who hide the ball, feel good about finding the ball before someone else does, resent — while often appreciating — a good job of manipulating the course of the discussion, or want to impress a special student of the opposite sex. The injustice of some cases makes students angry, other cases bore them to tears.[9] Teachers become angry at students bored by the

7. *See* Simon, *The Ideology of Advocacy: Procedural Justice and Professional Ethics,* 1978 WIS. L. REV. 29, 52-59.

8. The rich-poor opposition can also, with some strain, be inverted. The argument is that the poor do not enter clinics, nor do the rich pursue the litigation that gets into the casebooks, simply by virtue of their poverty or wealth. Not all, or even most, poor or rich people have their problems presented in the clinic or in the traditional classroom cases.

9. *See* Kennedy, *Legal Education as Training for Hierarchy,* in THE POLITICS OF LAW 43-44 (D. Kairys ed. 1982).

subject, fantasize about the students' sex lives,[10] and feel good when students understand the material. These feelings are systematically suppressed in the traditional classroom. Student and teacher alike know that they are not meant to show their feelings, and there are moments of high drama when anger or, less often, joy bursts through the crust. Students learn that they should transcend their initial untutored reactions of outrage caused by unjust results in order to understand how the apparent injustice is actually the reasonable result of rules that substantially promote justice. It should go without saying that the suppression of feeling in the traditional classroom, indeed the very denial of feeling, is a profoundly political act.

Understanding the marginality of clinical education as an assertion of the present form of gender hierarchy explains why clinical education has adapted to challenges as it has. There are two possible responses to marginality. Clinicians could say that clinical education is less female than it appears. This defensive posture claims that clinical education does just what traditional classroom education does. Clinicians could also deny the value of traditional classroom instruction; they could assert the positive value of femininity over the negative masculinity of the classroom. There are dangers associated with the defensive posture, and interesting methods for clinicians to take the offensive. Nevertheless, challenges of both types may be appropriate. In my experience, however, clinicians have too readily emphasized the defensive posture without recognizing its dangers and without vigorously pursuing the alternative. The question becomes one of strategic choice.

The defensive posture has failed for several reasons. Asserting that clinical education is as good as or better than traditional classroom education leads to the making of implausible claims. Because nobody really knows what good educational techniques are, the traditional faculty resort to student evaluations, and the evaluations from the clinics are, to put it bluntly, obviously unreliable. Students who are motivated to select a clinic over a large class are inclined to sympathize with the clinical instructor from the outset. They know that clinical education is vulnerable and they understandably shade their comments to avoid undermining the clinical faculty. Traditional faculty read clinical evaluations that uniformly praise each clinical instructor as the best teacher that has ever taught. This is simply implausible. Of course, comparing the experience of relatively personal clinical education with the experience of relatively impersonal classroom education leads one to conclude that students have a better experience in the typical clinical program. However, uniform rave reviews appear overstated because they imply that the processes of hiring clinical instructors work perfectly. Traditional instructors know that the processes of hiring classroom teachers are imperfect, and suspect that similar imperfections must plague clinical programs. The range of quality in clinical instruction is probably approx-

10. *See Towards an Erotics of Law Teaching,* Lizard, Jan. 7, 1984, at 5, col. 1.

imately the same as that in classroom instruction. Undoubtedly, the best clinical experience is better than the typical classroom experience, but similarly the best classroom experience is better than the typical clinical experience. The strongest plausible claim, which may not even overcome the cost concerns associated with clinical education, is that the median quality of teaching is higher in clinics than in traditional classrooms.

A second defensive position is to transform clinical education to make it resemble traditional education. If clinical education is weak because it concerns real people who are poor, this strategy would strengthen it by making clinics address the abstract problems of unreal people, through the use of simulation, tape recordings, or video equipment. Once that change occurs, however, clinical education becomes even more vulnerable. If clinical education only mimics classroom education but costs more, why expend resources on it? A clinic may propose a middle-income effort in tax accompanied by a seminar in tax policy and administration. Although the traditional faculty may enthusiastically support such a seminar, it is not obvious why a clinical instructor rather than a traditional instructor should offer it. In addition to offering the seminar, the traditional instructor would teach property, torts, or antitrust. Hiring a traditional instuctor produces the seminar plus a lot more; whereas hiring a clinical instructor, according to the defensive posture, produces only the seminar.

A third and related defense tries to combine teaching issues with publication. Because no one really knows what good teaching is, we use, but in the clinical context discount, student evaluations. Traditionalists also use, and properly so, writing and research as a surrogate for measuring teaching ability. A teacher who is actively engaged in the issues raised by a course is likely to provide a better education than a teacher who is not so engaged. Writing and research are good measures of active engagement. The clinical faculty offers in its defense a surrogate for publication: briefs as evidence of scholarship.[11] The clinician, if she is lucky, will have fine briefs in support of a position. The briefs do resemble the traditional faculty's writing except that the traditional faculty calls its pieces articles and overloads them with recapitulations of previous arguments and with footnotes. Once again the cost issue rears its ugly head. If, by all the measures we have available, clinical education is no better than traditional education, yet costs more, the defense is likely to fail.

An alternative strategy would be to attack traditional education at

11. Legal briefs are not, by definition, inadequate evidence of scholarly insight merely because they are partisan documents whose content is dictated by the needs of a client rather than by detached consideration of a problem. The usual example is the brief that systematically suppresses counterarguments. Such a brief is defective *as a brief*. And of course I reject the distinction between disinterested and partisan inquiry anyway.

its most vulnerable point: the use of writing and research as a surrogate measure of teaching contribution. Generally, research and writing is a good surrogate measure; it would be a tactical mistake for clinicians to deprecate the importance of writing and research. Rather, the traditional faculty is vulnerable because most of its writing and research demonstrates no useful engagement in the issues covered in the courses. Further, clinicians are better positioned to do useful intellectual work than is the traditional faculty. Clinicians could strengthen their position by capitalizing on the intellectual weaknesses of traditional education and on the strengths of the clinical experience.

Clinical education provides a tremendous opportunity for people to learn about the law in action, as it used to be called, rather than the law on the books. Students in clinics should observe the systematic methods by which institutions produce results that are perhaps consistent with the statutes but are nonetheless unsound policy. Clinicians can write about how bureaucracies transform legal rules into operational meaning, not about the proper interpretation of an obscure section of the Social Security Act.[12] Similarly, clinicians have excellent opportunities to see how people discover that their problems could be recharacterized as grievances and legal claims against others. Solid empirical evidence from the clinics about the process by which problems become legal claims could strengthen the theoretical literature on that process.[13] The criminal clinics could expose the effect on criminal defendants of inadequate representation that does not rise to the level of a constitutional violation.[14] Public-interest clinics could contribute to the scholarly examination of the process of public-interest representation, about which there is a substantial, but largely uninformed, critical literature.[15] They could examine how public-interest lawyers represent groups when the group has little financial control over the lawyer, thereby defining the role of client groups in public interest litigation. Although clinicians will be attracted to writing about the merits of their cases, they might be better off explaining how the cases emerged out of social movements into lawsuits, and what kinds of lawsuits resulted.

If studies like these came out of the clinics, the traditional faculty could hardly maintain that clinical education was just a more expensive method of teaching traditional law. Studies arising from the

12. *See, e.g.*, Simon, *Bureaucracy, Legality, and Class in the Welfare State*, 92 YALE L.J. 1198 (1983) (discussing experiences in legal services office).

13. *See* Bellow, *Turning Solutions Into Problems: The Legal Aid Experience*, 34 NLADA BRIEFCASE 106 (1977); Felstiner, Abel & Sarat, *The Emergence and Transformation of Disputes: Naming, Blaming, Claiming . . .*, 15 LAW & SOC. REV. 631, 632 (1980-81).

14. *See* Dickey, *The Lawyer and the Accuracy of the Presentence Report*, 43 FED. PROBATION, June 1979, ¶ 3, at 28, 33-36 (discussing, inter alia, the findings of an empirical study into the disclosure of erroneous pre-sentence reports by attorneys to their clients).

15. *See* Rohde, *Class Conflicts in Class Actions*, 34 STAN. L. REV. 1183 (1982) (footnotes providing a useful guide to the uninformed literature). *See also* Leleiko, *Love, Professional Responsibility, The Rule of Law, and Clinical Legal Education*, 29 CLEV. ST. L. REV. 641, 657 (1980) (analysis of clinical practice can lead to understanding of how laws are actually administered and enforced).

clinical experience would demonstrate that clinical education is both different from and better than traditional education, according to the very criteria that traditional classroom teachers themselves use to evaluate the worth of education. Publication of these studies would simultaneously reject the feminization of the clinical experience, affirm the importance of feminization of the entire curriculum, and reject the hierarchy that treats masculine activities as more valuable than feminine ones.

# [18]
# Evaluating Students as Preparation for the Practice of Law

For most lawyers, the practice of law is a collaborative enterprise.[1] Legal education should prepare students for the practice of law.[2] It would seem to follow that legal education should prepare students to do collaborative work.[3] Indeed, some aspects of legal education — notably, some forms of clinical legal education — do stress collaboration as an important aspect of the educational process.[4]

Clinical legal education is, on the whole, confined to second and third-year courses, whereas students are most powerfully socialized into the legal profession during the first year.[5] The incentive structures legal educators

---

I would like to thank Bruce Markell for his comments on this essay, and Elizabeth Brandt, Donald Berman, Naomi Cahn, Judith Frank, William Funk, Elizabeth Geltman, Gerald Hess, Kenneth Hirsch, Marina Hsieh, Jan M. Levine, Jessica Litman, Louis Lobenhofer, Gerald MacDonald, Eilis Magner, Bruce Markell, Michael Masinter, Ed Richards, Lauren Robel, Julie Shapiro, Stephen Sepinuck, J. Alexander Tanford, and Steve Zorn for the answers they provided to an "Internet" inquiry I posted. *See infra* note 4 (discussing this Internet inquiry).

1. According to the McCrate Committee, in 1988 only 46.2% of private practitioners, and only 33.2% of all lawyers, were sole practitioners, having declined from 64% and 46% in 1960. SECTION OF LEGAL EDUCATION AND PROFESSIONAL DEVELOPMENT, AM. BAR ASS'N, REPORT OF THE TASK FORCE ON LAW SCHOOLS AND THE PROFESSION: NARROWING THE GAP 33 (July 1992).

2. *Id.* at 3.

3. *See, e.g., id.* at 201 (stating that lawyers should develop "[s]ystems and procedures for . . . [c]ollaborating with other attorneys in the same office or other offices . . . .").

4. During the summer of 1994, I posted an inquiry to the "Lawprof" user group on the Internet for information about efforts to use evaluation systems that encouraged collaboration in first-year classes. [hereinafter Internet Query]. One respondent asked why encouraging collaboration was an important goal, given that when lawyers collaborate, they rarely do so as equals. Rather, as this respondent put it, "one of the group is ultimately reponsible for the product of the group, and has commensurate authority. . . . The partner/managing attorney/lead attorney has no counterpart in the collaborative exercises" described by other respondents. *Id.* In reply, another respondent described "a few situtations in which . . . training (or at least experience) in group dynamics helps: working with another law firm for a common client; consulting with peers/partners about a perplexing problem, and enlisting their support to provide the service to the client; working on law reform with state or federal bar committees or associations." *Id.*

5. For discussions of socialization in the first year, see ROBERT GRANFIELD, MAKING ELITE

create for first-year students, I believe, reinforce individualistic and meritocratic attitudes. Such attitudes are, in my view, intrinsically undesirable, and they are an impediment to becoming an effective lawyer.

The incentive structures used are, of course, our grading systems. For all that we encourage students to work together in study groups, when the time comes to evaluate them we split them apart, assigning grades on the basis of individualized and non-collaborative performances, primarily in time-limited examinations.[6] We encourage study groups because we think that collaborating to prepare for individualized examinations is an effective technique of stimulating learning. Would it be possible to design an evaluation system that provides stronger incentives for collaboration?

Our grading systems actually combine two perhaps incompatible goals. First, they provide the incentives we think may be needed, beyond the sheer desire to learn for knowledge's sake, to induce students to learn what we think they should. Second, they are tied to evaluation techniques that themselves provide an opportunity for students to learn. That is, a student who has gone through a well designed evaluation — a good examination, for example — will learn from that experience itself (and not just from the experience of preparing for the evaluation). Sometimes, though, an evaluation technique that provides a good learning experience may not provide the incentives we think appropriate.

In this essay, I report on and speculate about my failed attempts to develop an evaluation system that strongly encourages collaboration in a large first-year class.[7] I have developed a course called "Government Processes." The course attempts to introduce students to the different ways a legal system can respond to a perceived social problem. Using the problem of safety and health in the workplace,[8] the course examines the advantages and disadvantages of administrative regulation (the Occupational Safety and Health Act[9]), criminal regulation (prosecutions for maintaining unsafe

LAWYERS: VISIONS OF LAW AT HARVARD AND BEYOND (1992); ROBERT V. STOVER, MAKING IT AND BREAKING IT: THE FATE OF PUBLIC INTEREST COMMITMENT DURING LAW SCHOOL (1989).

6. I should note that I do *not* believe that time-limited examinations test for irrelevant skills, although they of course do not test for all the skills a lawyer should have. Much of the criticism I hear of time-limited examinations as "unrealistic" fails to appreciate the way in which lawyers come to have a "feel" for a problem, or to have implicit knowledge of a field or approach. My sense is that time-limited examinations are not a terrible way to help instill that feel and implicit knowledge.

7. It may be worth noting here that my Internet Query, *supra* note 4, indicates that my attempt appears to be unique. The exercises respondents described were primarily collaborative drafting exercises, which were ungraded (or pass-fail), with some other exercises in small classes. This may indicate that the effort is misguided, or that legal educators have failed to appreciate the importance of providing strong incentives to do collaborative work.

8. Other candidates for the problem the course addresses are environmental issues, housing, and racial and sexual harassment in the workplace. I chose workplace injury and disease because of my interest in questions concerning economic classes.

9. 29 U.S.C.A. §§ 651 *et. seq.* (1985).

conditions in the workplace), aggregative litigation (the asbestos cases), and market regulation (wage premiums for riskier jobs). The course has a heavy dose of economic and sociological material. It is offered as part of Georgetown University Law Center's "experimental curriculum,"[10] which is made available to one of the Law Center's four full-time sections of first-year students.[11] The section has approximately 125 students.

In designing the course, I believed that the "experiment" ought to go beyond changes in the substance of what students were taught. In particular, I believed that it would be educationally and professionally valuable for students to be given an incentive structure that strongly encouraged collaborative work. I therefore tried to design an examination system that would systematically allocate higher grades to those who worked collaboratively.

Collaboration can include pre-examination discussion of the materials, which occurs in study groups. In other courses, I encouraged that form of collaboration by distributing examination questions in advance. I informed students that, when they arrived in the examination room for their closed-book examination, they would be asked to answer three or four questions chosen at random on the morning of the examination from six or eight previously distributed questions.[12]

My experience with that examination technique was generally positive; students were indeed often better prepared for the examination than when questions were not distributed in advance. Further, the technique provided strong incentives for students to prepare as comprehensively as the potential questions allowed. Unfortunately, this method of examination had some serious drawbacks. The need for random selection on the morning of the examination created problems in administering the examination. All examination techniques incorporate some forms of arbitrariness,[13] but in this one

---

10. The other courses in the curriculum are: "Bargain, Liability, and Exchange" (combining elements of traditional torts and contracts courses), "Property in Time" (using aspects of property law as a vehicle for understanding the development of American legal theory), "Legal Justice" (introducing students to concepts of law and theories of substantive justice), "Process" (combining elements from traditional civil and criminal procedure courses), "Democracy and Coercion" (using topics from traditional criminal procedure and constitutional law courses as a vehicle for examining the normative and practical limits on private and public power), and a seminar that uses some contract doctrines and the issue of child abuse to examine the history of American legal thought.

11. The experimental section has been offered three times so far. Admitted students are asked whether they would like to be in the section, whether they would not mind if they were placed in the section, or whether they would prefer not to be in the section. So far the volunteers — those in the first group — have far exceeded the number of seats available. As the curriculum's novelty dissipates, that may change.

12. I emphasized the random selection to avoid student efforts to "game" the selection process by "figuring out" which of the questions were "better" than the others.

13. In-class examinations, for example, may arbitrarily reward students with better handwriting. Take-home examinations, if not carefully designed, may arbitrarily reward students who live closer to the law school than others.

the arbitrariness of rewarding people who could simply memorize more of the answers they and their study groups prepared was too close to the surface. And, perhaps most important, this technique consumes examination questions at an appalling rate.[14] For a new course at least, I found it impossible to think of enough potential questions to use this technique.

Another form of collaboration involves the submission of a joint work-product. By working together to prepare a paper — or an examination answer to be submitted jointly — students can clarify their thoughts in a focused context, can edit each others' work, and in general can (if all goes well) do better than each could do individually.

What sort of joint work-product, prepared under what constraints? The obvious answer to the first part of that question is, "A paper of some sort." The course content helped shape the constraints I devised. A substantial segment of the course dealt with problems of collective action: To what extent are the legislative and administrative processes affected by difficulties people with different resources and interests have in organizing themselves to affect those processes? How do groups go about making and enforcing decisions that affect everyone in the group? Such questions have become an important part of the scholarly literature in constitutional law, administrative law, and legislation, and — because lawyers are advisers to clients and participants in the legislative and administrative processes — they raise matters about which law students should think.

The constraints I designed could help students deepen their understanding of the problems of collective action we discussed in class. The idea was to set up a situation in which students attempting to develop strategies for collaboration would have to confront those problems. How, for example, would they deal with the free-rider — the student who initially agreed to contribute to the collaborative work but then failed to deliver, or failed to deliver a product that the others in the group found acceptable? I believed that the best I could do would be to stay away from the processes by which students developed their joint products. I would not, for example, prescribe the number of students who could participate in any single collective.

With that decision made, designing the rest of the evaluation system was straight-forward. On the first day of class, I announced to students that the examination in the course would be a take-home examination on which collaboration in the preparation of answers was permitted. All who submitted a single answer would receive the same grade.

This evaluation system foundered, at least in part, because it failed to

14. The Georgetown University Law Center's policy appropriately prohibits faculty members from using questions asked on earlier examinations. As a technical matter, that policy might not bar me from "reusing" the three or four questions that were *not* randomly selected. Nonetheless, designing a package of questions that covers the course materials makes that difficult.

ensure that some substantial portion of each student's grade would be reliably associated with that student's work alone.[15] My faculty colleagues thought it inappropriate to rest a final grade solely on joint work. In their view, some substantial part of each student's grade had to be based on work reliably associated with that student alone.[16]

Their reasons, which I confess still remain rather opaque to me, varied.[17] To several of my colleagues, a grade was in some essential sense a measure of a student's intrinsic understanding of the course material; allowing the grade to rest in substantial measure on collaborative work was incompatible with the "meaning" of a grade. To others, the student-teacher relation was in an important sense direct and one-to-one; allowing the grade to rest on collaborative work diffused the connection the teacher had to each student.[18] Still others believed that the system failed to provide strong enough incentives to learn the course materials; some students would free-ride

15. One of the major disadvantages of this design is that it proposed to base a student's entire grade on the collaborative project. Others have suggested that much of what I was interested in doing could be accomplished by predicating only a portion of the grade on the collaborative work. Typically, the suggestion is to base one-fourth of the grade on that work. I have not yet been persuaded, however, that doing so provides a large enough increment in the incentives to collaborate — beyond the incentives provided by having study groups, for example — to make the exercise worthwhile.

16. My Internet inquiry suggests that this view is widely held. Internet Query, *supra*, note 4. When people described incentive structures that, in my view, encourage collaboration only slightly more than the norm, they had the form of "a short paper or two, on which students can collaborate in groups of two to five, plus a final examination."

17. At one point during the discussions of my proposed evaluation technique, it was suggested that the ABA's *Standards for Approval of Law Schools* required the use of evaluation techniques that focused on the work done by individual students. Standard 304(b) provides: "The scholastic achievement of students shall be evaluated from the inception of their studies. As part of the testing of scholastic achievement, a written examination of suitable length and complexity shall be required in every course for which credit is given [with exceptions irrelevant here]." Am. Bar Ass'n Section of Legal Education & Admissions to the Bar, *Standards for Approval of Law Schools and Interpretations* S304 (1993). A 1975 interpretation of that standard states, "The examination should be by either written examination or term paper. The examination should not be an oral examination, nor should it be a progress report graded by fellow students. The intent of the Standard is to have a meaningful faculty assessment of *the* student's work product" *Id.* at I304 (emphasis added). The argument was that the use of the definite article in the final sentence of the 1975 interpretation required an evaluation based on each student's work alone. Had the question been "litigated," I seriously doubt that the use of the definite article could have borne the weight put upon it. The standard and the interpretation seem clearly aimed at ensuring that students produce written work of a relatively complex sort, which faculty members rather than others evaluate. My evaluation technique would have satisfied those requirements. Further, I doubt that an accrediting agency would interpret its standards to require quite so particularized an examination technique for *every* course in the law school. At most, I believe, the agency would require that individualized evaluation techniques predominate in the school's system.

18. I cannot resist the suggestion that this understanding of the student-teacher relation is the teacher's projection back on to our students of the strong fantasies we know our students entertain about our engagement with each and every one of them.

completely, while nearly all students would free-ride except with respect to a subset of the course materials.[19]

This concern was compounded when my colleagues and the students realized that the evaluation system gave stronger incentives to collaborate than they were comfortable with, and even more so when they realized that, under the rules of the evaluation system, the collaborative groups could be as large as the entire class.

Some students expressed discomfort with the idea of evaluation based on joint work. Some argued that they had developed a working style — the "lone wolf" approach — that made it difficult for them to collaborate, and that it would be unfair to adopt an evaluation system penalizing them. If, however, we are correct in believing that as a general matter students do better in whatever evaluation system we adopt — blind grading of in-class examinations, for example — if they participate in study groups than if they do not, the "lone wolves" are at a disadvantage no matter what. As indeed they should be, if one of the lawyers' skills we should be concerned about instilling in students is the ability to work cooperatively.

A significant variant of this objection was that some students found they had joined study groups that were not working as well as they could be. The best version of this argument is that the study group is helping its students prepare, but the group has just not "clicked" in a way that would make it appropriate to use the study group as a vehicle for doing joint work with a more significant impact on the students' grades than study groups usually have.[20]

As it happens, this argument is closely connected to one of the experimental curriculum's themes: the "base-line" problem, or the "action/inaction" distinction. At several points in the curriculum, we mount a sustained challenge to the view that the status quo — in this instance, the incentives that standard in-class examination techniques provide for getting into a "good" study group — is normatively correct.[21] So, the mere fact that stronger incentives to collaborative work "penalize" people who by mischance do not get into such a study group ought not be an argument against such incentives.[22] Few students saw the connection between the argument

19. That is, most groups were likely to divide the collaborative work up, and each student would concentrate almost exclusively on the portion assigned her by the group.

20. This objection had even more force the first time I tried to design an evaluation technique with strong incentives for collaborative work. My course was designed as a second semester course, but for scheduling reasons it was offered in the first semester. The chances of getting into a study group that did not "click" were of course greater in the first semester than in the second.

21. For a general challenge to this view, see CASS R. SUNSTEIN, THE PARTIAL CONSTITUTION (1993).

22. Of course, as I discuss below, there may be *other* objections to such incentive structures.

some of them were making and the critique of the "action/inaction" distinction that they had been learning.[23]

A more interesting objection was that the rules made it possible that everyone in the class would submit exactly the same answer.[24] Although few people understood that implication of the rules when they were announced, the recognition gradually grew as the semester went on. A number of students began to organize a "super-group," and apparently got about two-thirds of the class to commit to participating. Students who chose not to participate got increasingly anxious about the super-group. Eventually, their concerns made it impossible for me to use the evaluation technique I had proposed.

Before I announced my decision to revert to a standard in-class examination, I noted that students had indeed begun to think through the problems of collective action. They had not, however, faced up to what I was fairly confident was going to be the problem on which the super-group would founder. I begin with the latter.

Economists are familiar with the "market for lemons" problem.[25] Roughly, the problem arises in a market where sellers know more about the quality of each good being offered than do buyers. A person putting up a used car for sale knows whether it is a lemon or a good car. A prospective buyer does not. Suppose a seller offers a car for an average price. The prospective buyer ought to figure out that the car cannot be a "good" car, because it is underpriced for such a car. Then, however, sellers with good cars will not

---

23. If I had been willing to pursue the issue in even more depth than I did in class, I would have tried to help students see this connection. The class was already too concerned about the evaluation technique I proposed, however, and I am reasonably sure that the intellectual point would have been swamped by other concerns.

24. One colleague raised the objection that under the rules as I had stated them, students were not even barred from hiring an outside lawyer to write their answers for them. It was not clear to me that that was true, although it was true that in defining "collaboration" I had not explicitly ruled out the possibility of collaborating with someone not currently enrolled in the class. In the second iteration of my effort to encourage collaboration, some students did design a system in which money played a role, but they did not think of hiring outside counsel.

Several reasons probably account for the fact that students did not devise such a strategy of collaboration: (1) it is so far outside the ordinary rules for evaluation systems that they almost certainly thought it barred by the rules of even this one; (2) it has a strong aura of cheating about it; and (3) it would have been an extraordinarily dumb strategy. The time constraints students faced made it quite unlikely that they would be able to locate (and afford) a lawyer, or even a set of lawyers, who would be able to answer examination questions about the preemptive effect of federal pension law on state tort liability when a health insurer's failure to approve a medical procedure led to the insured party's death (a question based on Corcoran v. United Health Care, 965 F.2d 1321 (5th Cir. 1992)), *and* about the interpretation of state workers' compensation laws in connection with claims for compensation for illness caused by second-hand tobacco smoke (a question based on Palmer v. Del Webb's High Sierra, 838 P.2d 435 (Nev. 1992)), *and* about the relation between some excerpts by Duncan Kennedy and Mark Kelman.

25. For a basic presentation, see GEORGE AKERLOF, AN ECONOMIC THEORIST'S BOOK OF TALES 7-9 (1984) (explaining how the uncertainty in the quality of the product one buys results in a reduction of market size).

put their cars on the market, for they will never get the full value; prospective buyers will never believe that the car is worth what the seller asks.

In the examination setting, the market-for-lemons problem is similar. Consider a student who believes that she is the best student in the class. She should not participate in a large collaborative effort, because the collaboration is likely to *reduce* the quality of the answers she will submit. Further, if she makes her answers available to other students, the quality of *their* answers will improve, thereby reducing the gap between the best student's answers and those of her nearest competition.

The logic of what follows is straight-forward: the effort to organize a super-group unravels as every student realizes that the only people interested in participating in such a group are those who expect their individual performance to be below the average of all those in the group. Again roughly, students would conclude that only those who were truly worried about doing well on the examination were involved in the super-group. If they believed those concerns were likely to be correct, they would conclude that the super-group consisted primarily of those located in the bottom half of the class.

A less formal problem with the super-group should be noted as well. To the extent that participants in the group divided the work among themselves, really good answers were unlikely. Such answers have the striking insight, or make a point that only the best students understand. Precisely for that reason, other students will not see how good the insight is, and will fear that their colleague has gone off the deep end. Better, they will think, to take the safer course and give a routine, unexciting answer. The reciprocal problem is that of "group think."[26] Participants may develop a commitment to a quirky idea, convincing themselves that it is a deep insight when it really is not. The combination of group-think and rounding off the rough edges is likely to make large-scale collaborative answers worse than average.

The logic I have described is not iron-clad, for several reasons. First, and probably most important, students do not *know* that they are better than average, and those who believe they are will be uncertain about the quality of their judgment about their own ability.[27] That uncertainty meant that a larger-than-"appropriate" group was likely to form, and was likely to submit answers that were above some floor.[28] Second, although many students are strongly motivated by the prospect of ranking higher in the class than

26. *See* IRVING L. JANIS, VICTIMS OF GROUPTHINK (1972) (describing various problems inherent in group decisions by giving examples of several foreign-policy fiascoes).

27. Again, this uncertainty was compounded by the fact that I was offering the course in the first semester of the first year, when students had no reliable evidence about how a faculty member would assess their relative abilities.

28. My guess is that the answers would have been in the B to B− range, a slight bit above the historical curve on which I graded my first year class at that time.

others, other students are not. They may be misguided altruists,[29] willing to contribute their efforts to the improvement of their colleagues' grades.[30] Third, students who participated in the effort to construct the super-group might have suffered from the "sunk cost" fallacy: having put so much effort into creating the group, they may have thought it senseless to throw away that investment. Fourth, the time devoted to creating the super-group might have diverted students from other efforts to study the course materials, so that, even though they ultimately realized that the grades for the super-group were likely to be mediocre, at the point that realization hit home they may have had not other methods of preparing for the examination that would have made them better off.

Because I terminated the process before most students had begun to think through the problems with the super-group, the market-for-lemons problem apparently did not come to students' attention.[31] The super-group's organizers did understand other problems they would have to confront, however. These were the problems of defections and free-riders. The defection problem arises when a participant sees the answers she is committed to submitting and concludes that, with respect to some portion, she could improve the answer — perhaps by adding or deepening a point,[32] perhaps by clarifying the expression — and thereby gain an advantage over the others in the group.[33] The free-rider problem is obvious.

My judgment was that the market-for-lemons, free-rider, and defection problems were likely to generate substantial anxiety among prospective participants in a super-group. I thought it likely that, in the end, most students would participate in groups that were close to what I judged to be the optimal size of between five and ten participants. Given the qualifications I have mentioned, perhaps the super-group would have ended up somewhat larger,[34] and would have submitted an answer that was slightly

---

29. At least in its initial years, the experimental section appears to have attracted a disproportionate number of students with strong stated commitments to public interest law; for example, a disproportionate number of Georgetown's "Public Interest Law Scholars" have been in the experimental section.

30. I call them misguided because their efforts might improve their colleagues' grades but would not improve their colleagues' understanding of the course materials.

31. Perhaps it never would have, because it is a fairly subtle phenomenon. I should note, however, that the class had engaged in a bargaining exercise in which the "market for lemons" problem rapidly emerged and was explicitly identified by a student in the class (the person who, as it turned out, ended up getting the best grade in the class).

32. I can imagine a student calculating that it would make sense to divide his study and preparation time between the portion of the examination assigned by the group to him, and a "secret" portion on which he intends to supplement the group's answer.

33. As I understand it, the organizers of the super-group proposed to solve the defection problem by imposing severe time constraints on the distribution of the computer disk containing the group's answers.

34. I suspect that it would have ended up with around twenty participants.

better than the ones that would have been submitted by any set of smaller groups composed out of the participants in the super-group.

If those expectations had been realized, I believe the evaluation system I designed would have been a success. Its drawback was that the grades assigned to each member of a group could not be associated completely with the work done and understanding achieved by that member. As an incentive to learning, however, I believe the system would have worked well. Students would have gained a rather substantial understanding of the problems of collective action that were an important part of the course, based on their experience in putting the groups together and observing what happened to the super-group. And, to the extent that groups divided the work up and then recombined to discuss the work each member had done, each member would have developed an answer relating to one part of the course material of the sort ordinarily tested for, and would have thought seriously about answers relating to the rest of the course material. On the whole, the evaluation system still seems to me to achieve a reasonable balance between providing incentives to learn the course material and offering students some evaluation of their understanding of that material.

It was not to be, however. Student and faculty concern about my proposed system led me reluctantly to abandon it.

The next time I offered the course, I revised the design. Georgetown's large sections are divided into smaller groups for instruction in legal research and writing. At the semester's start, I announced that each of the eight legal research and writing sections would be responsible for revising one-eighth of the course materials. I also announced that students would *not* be graded on the quality of the revisions their sections submitted, but that one question on the examination would ask students to analyze how the small sections addressed some of the collective action problems the course dealt with.

Although not without its problems,[35] this revision was somewhat more successful in inducing students to think about the course materials. One group developed an ingenious market-like mechanism to allocate the

35. Two such problems deserve mention; my guess is that they both arose because, for whatever reasons, the chemistry in the class was not the best. (1) One persistent criticism of the course materials has been that they are too long; it seemed obvious to me that students had a comparative advantage over me in identifying what could be left out. Rather than regarding the assignment to revise the course materials as a method of eliciting a more focused "consumer" perspective, some students apparently resented the assignment because, as they saw it, they were being asked to do work that I or my research assistants ought to do. Some students also interpreted my statement that I would not take the quality of the revisions into account in grading to imply that I would not pay attention to the revisions. (2) According to the answers I received on the examination, some students simply did not believe that the quality of the revisions would not be taken into account in grading.

work.[36] More significantly, one student attempted to organize her small group, and then the class as a whole, to refuse to submit *any* revisions.

The collective action problems in getting the entire class to agree not to submit revisions defeated that attempt, in the limited sense that not every student signed on to the refusal. In another sense, however, the attempt was successful. It led to an awareness in the class that in fact no one had to submit anything. In the end, only about one-half the class actually turned in any revisions.

One important effect followed once it became clear that a substantial number of students had not turned in any revisions. That imposed a severe constraint on the question I could ask on the examination; indeed, in my view it dictated that only one question could possibly be asked.[37] That question was, "given the rules of the exercise, why did anyone turn in revisions?"[38] I received a generally thoughtful set of answers.[39]

---

36. Each student in the small group was asked to submit sealed "bids" indicating (a) how much she would pay to have someone else do her share of the revision, and (b) how much she would have to be paid to do the entire revision. (It is worth noting that we had discussed the "offer-asking" problem in pricing entitlements in class, and that students believed that this mechanism had some interesting connection to that problem.) The amounts students were willing to pay were added up, and the total was above the lowest amount for which a student was willing to do the revision. That student "won" the job, and the "bids" were pro-rated (that is, if the student doing the revision was willing to accept 75% of the total of the bids, each student had to pay 75% of what she had indicated she was willing to pay).

At some level, what is most interesting about this mechanism is that students found it acceptable. Two obvious difficulties occurred to me. (1) Why should the student doing the work accept anything less than the total of the bids? (2) In light of matters discussed in the text immediately following this footnote, why should the student committed to doing the work actually do it? There may be other difficulties.

37. I would have given an A on the question to any student who explained why the question I asked was the only one I could have asked. As I recall, one student came close to seeing the point.

38. I asked that question in a slightly different form: "One of your writing assignments was to revise a portion of the course materials. Because one of your classmates raised the issue for you (if for no other reason), the possibility of not doing the assignment was before each of you. Most of you completed the assignment nonetheless. Discuss the following comments.

> 1. The fact that most students completed the assignment demonstrates the inadequacies of a pure 'rational actor' model of human behavior. Completing the assignment was costly (at the least it took time away from other activities, and as I understand it at least one group's processes for determining who would do want involved monetary outlays). Yet, there were no obvious benefits to be gained from actually doing the assignment (aside from the minor ones associated with going over the material — as you would have anyway in preparing for this examination). A 'rational actor' doing a cost-benefit analysis ought to have concluded that completing the assignment was not rational.
>
> 2. The fact that most students completed the assignment demonstrates the power of a pure 'rational actor' model of human behavior. Without coordinated action, no one could be sure that (despite Tushnet's assurances) no sanctions would attach to any individual who did not complete the assignment by participating in a group that handed in the edited materials. And, without some alternative sanctioning mechanism, it was impossible to coordinate action.

39. By far the most interesting answers were those identifying the following issue: Unlike any other examination technique, this one made it impossible for students to resist the professor's

Unfortunately, I cannot use this method of encouraging collaboration again, because it will be apparent from the outset — as it was not when I announced the exercise — that no one has to turn anything in. So, from the outset, almost no one will devote any effort to collaboration on the project.[40]

Both of my efforts to develop an evaluation system that strongly encouraged collaboration foundered. The failure of my first attempt in particular may illuminate more than my pedagogic deficiencies. Its primary defect was this: under the rules of the system I designed, a student could receive a good grade without doing anything substantial to learn the course materials.

My colleagues and some students understood that defect to mean that the system failed to provide adequate incentives for students to learn the course materials. That understanding is itself defective, in my view. The conditional *could* in my characterization of the system's defect is crucial. As I have explained, I think it quite unlikely that more than a handful of students actually would have done so.[41] Why then did the proposal fail?

I believe that the answer combines two attitudes we — faculty and students — have about learning the law.[42] First, we believe that learning is an essentially individualized phenomenon. From the fact that, as we believe, the knowledge people have is inside the head of each one, we infer that people learn by figuring out how to get "stuff" — facts, arguments, ways of thinking — from "out there" into their heads. I have little doubt that this theory of learning is completely wrong-headed, so to speak. Perhaps more important, as a theory of learning it may actually impede our students' acquisition of the important professional skill of collaboration.

Second, we have internalized Oliver Wendell Holmes's "bad man" theory of law, transforming it into a theory of human nature. According to Holmes, "If you want to know the law and nothing else, you must look at it as a bad

demands, for even resistance was a form of complying with the technique's requirements. And, although students almost never actually resist, they ought to have the option of doing so.

40. I have considered a third iteration of the exercise, but it too has its drawbacks. That would involve distributing this essay at the beginning of the semester and inviting (or requiring) students to turn in an answer to the following question by mid-semester: "Design a *reusable* method of strongly encouraging collaboration through the examination system, and explain why it overcomes the difficulties identified in the essay distributed at the semester's beginning." I would decide which answer was best, and then use that method on the examination. The student or group of students that turned in the best answer would receive an upward adjustment in the final grade. (Once again, this method runs the risk that students would find the exercise an attempt to get them to do work that I ought to do.)

41. Once again, I would stress that the arbitrariness of all evaluation systems means that in any system a handful of students will receive good grades without doing much to learn the course materials. My judgment remains that the system I designed was at worst no worse than other systems with respect to arbitrariness in awarding good grades to students who did little to learn the course materials.

42. I use the term *attitudes* advisedly; they are not quite beliefs that we would fully defend when stated openly, but they are more than mere unthinking prejudices or assumptions.

man. . . ."[43] Students, we believe, are Holmes's bad people, who will in fact carefully calculate precisely what the rules allow and operate up to the rules' limits. Yet, as even my truncated quotation indicates, Holmes offered this theory as a jurisprudence, or as a pedagogical stance, not as an account of actual or ethical behavior.[44]

Perhaps the attitudes that underlie our approach to the mundane question of grading indicate the ethical stance we take toward students and each other. If so, I believe those attitudes deserve reexamination. If people do not actually behave as Holmes's bad people would, our attitudes towards students may miseducate them into thinking that all institutions — including law schools and law firms — should be designed with Holmes's assumption in mind.[45]

Articles about legal pedagogy rarely describe failures, and even more rarely attribute the failure to the author rather than to external forces (or worse, attribute it to the students who failed to appreciate the pedagogic ingenuity they were experiencing).[46] I therefore do not want to conclude without emphasizing that it could be that (a) I was wrong to believe that an evaluation system *should* be used to encourage collaboration, and (b) I was wrong to believe that one *could* be used, and (c) I designed a truly terrible system to do what a better system might properly have done.[47] And yet, I retain the perhaps utopian hope that someone will figure out how to do it. If she does, I believe that our students will be better prepared for the profession they are to enter.

---

43. Oliver Wendell Holmes, Jr., *The Path of the Law*, 10 HARV. L. REV. 457, 459 (1897).

44. It may be worth noting that there is some tension between the "bad person" view of law students, which generates the assumption that they will cheat, and the view that students would be inappropriately altruistic in sharing their work, which generated some of the concern over my first proposed evaluation technique. Holmes invited us to think about the bad person's perspective because he believed that the bad person was a self-interested utilitarian who would do whatever he or she could to advance his or her interests. Such a person will break the law, or in the present context cheat, if he or she can get away with it *and* if doing so advances self-interest. That, however, is not how altruists think. Perhaps the tension could be dissipated by the unrealistic assumption that bad people want to break the rules no matter what, that is, independent of the impact of rule-breaking on their well-being.

45. Without that assumption, of course, designing institutions that successfully address collective action problems is quite difficult. (With it, the design problem is simplified: all one must do is come up with a system of identifying and penalizing people who break the rules.) That, of course, was what I tried to induce students to think about through my evaluation system.

46. To cite an obscure source making this point, see Mark Tushnet, *On Being a Bad Law Teacher*, LIZARD (Conf. on Critical Legal Stud., Washington, D.C.), May 1987, at 22.

47. I put this qualification in the form that I have to indicate that, although it could be so, I remain unconvinced that it was so.

# [19]

# An Introduction (to Symposium: Academic Evaluations Focus)

Every few years Georgetown University Law Center's contract with our cafeteria operator expires. Each time students express dismay about the quality, variety, prices, and service in the cafeteria. They insist that the next contract be given to someone who will improve the cafeteria by installing a grill, training its workers to be more polite, adding more vegetarian food, and keep prices down. And each new contractor does indeed promise to do the job better. For a while students are happy, but eventually they find the food boring, the workers surly, and the prices high.

Students cannot be expected to observe how regular this pattern is, for they are present only for a three year period.[1] But those with a longer view can see it. And the fact that it is so regular suggests that the real problem is not what they focus on--limited offerings, high prices, and the like. Rather, the problem must be structural: There is something about the entire enterprise of attempting to operate a law school cafeteria that guarantees student dissatisfaction.[2]

So too, I think, with the subject of this symposium: law school grading and "the curve." In this introduction I place the articles that follow into my own framework. I admit at the outset that my framework is likely to be rather different from the ones the articles' authors would use. Still, I hope that my attempt to fit the articles into a particular point of view may help readers develop their own perspectives on them.

I suspect that every law school experiences the following: The institution starts out with some institutional grading practices. Grades are from A to F, or from 60 to 100, or Honors, Pass, and Fail; there is a suggested curve, or none at all; administrators monitor grading practices carefully, or they let faculty members alone. Students and faculty become dissatisfied. They say that the existing system draws artificial lines between equally able students; or that it fails to acknowledge real differences among students; or that the curve places students at a disadvantage in the job market; or that faculty members' grading practices vary widely, creating real issues of fairness. The institution responds by changing its existing practices.

For a while people are satisfied. Eventually, however, dissatisfaction builds, and the complaints are renewed: If the institution moved from a system with many gradations to one with fewer, the complaint is that the system does not acknowledge real differences among students; if it moved in the other direction, the complaint is that the new system has created artificial divisions; if the institution has adopted a grading curve, the complaint is that the curve artificially constrains accurate acknowledgment of differences among classes. Professor Sheppard's informal history of examination questions can be read to show how reforms generate their own problems, thereby provoking further innovation. What is striking about this, of course, is that the grading

---

1. Or, in the case of Georgetown's part-time students, for four or five years, during which they typically make less use of the cafeteria because of their schedules.

2. I wish I knew what it was. My guess is that it has something to do with the fact that only some students buy lunch at the cafeteria. This may reduce the possibility of making a profit from cafeteria sales to the point where some subsidy from the law school is required. But then students who do not use the cafeteria object to using their tuition money to subsidize students who do use it.

system Law School A adopts because it sees in the system a solution to its present problems is precisely the same system that is already causing difficulty at Law School B.

And, as with Georgetown's cafeteria problem, it seems likely that the difficulties with law school grading systems are structural. One way of putting the point is that proponents of grading reform typically offer what I would call technical--or, in my more pejorative moments, technocratic--solutions to the problems they identify.[3] In this symposium, the general form of the technical solution is clear: As Professors Downs and Levit put it, we need to "connect[] grading policies and pedagogical methods." Or, in Professor Glesner-Fines's words, "we must tailor our evaluation methods to match [our] instructional objectives."

This sounds fine. Who, after all, could defend a system in which evaluation methods were disconnected from instructional objectives? Under such conditions one would be evaluating something other than what you purport to be teaching. And that is decidedly peculiar. But I believe that the technical solution obscures the deeper structural problems that generate recurrent concern over grading. As Professors Feinman and Waire Post, among others, suggest, these problems are best understood as political, in the sense that they arise from the distribution of power in legal education.

More precisely, the problems arise from the fact that legal education as an institution combines authority and power. The nature of the authority is complex, that of the power is less so. Writing from position of a law school professor, I believe that we have authority because we know more about some things than our students, they know we do, and students and teachers all think it helpful for students to get to know some of the things we know. What we know is a complicated combination of facts about legal rules, a sense of what arguments work in the legal community as it is presently constituted, a sense of the dynamics of that community that gives us a feeling about what sorts of things might change the set of arguments that work: something that is barely captured by terms like *experience* and *judgment*. We communicate our experience and judgment in part by direct expression--lectures and the like--and in part by modeling the way in which the legal community as it is presently constituted, and as it might be changed, responds to different arguments.

If something like this is the nature of our authority, it is hardly surprising that we do not have well-developed instruments to evaluate how effectively we are doing our job. A large part of what we do involves socialization, which occurs over an extended period, and yet our evaluation systems ask for judgments every semester.

The difficulty is compounded, however, by the institutional power of legal education. Power does not reside in evaluation as such. As Professor Glesner-Fines indicates, evaluation systems can serve to motivate students, to communicate information to them about the areas in which they are strong and the areas in which they could usefully improve their performance, and the like. But grading's institutional functions go beyond that. Several articles in the symposium characterize grades as wealth the faculty distributes. Ms. Woodson's description of law firm hiring practices makes it clear that grades help students obtain--or, to pursue the metaphor, purchase--jobs. Our grading systems serve as gateways to the profession and as screens for potential employers to use.

3. The solutions' technical dimension is typically signaled by the degree to which the authors cite works by educational psychologists to support their proposals.

Another aspect of the power dimension of grading deserves more emphasis than it receives in this symposium, I think. It is, simply, that grades are a way in which faculty members exercise power over students. Professor Kissam's account of student conferences touches on this indirectly. Professor Waire Post disclaims the suggestion that faculty members distinguish between "female" and "male" handwriting styles in nominally anonymous grading systems, arguing instead that the norms against which we assess student performance are structured to favor the already powerful. And yet the mention of handwriting styles is significant in itself. Anonymous grading may allow law faculties to discriminate structurally, but less anonymous systems, including the kinds of face-to-face interactions Professor Kissam favors, provide opportunities for direct discrimination.

And there is more. I confess that I was made quite nervous by Professor Kissam's description of conferences and the physical layout of faculty offices, largely because it seems to me to overlook some fairly obvious questions about the gender dynamics of faculty-student interactions. The kinds of office arrangements Professor Kissam seems to favor are precisely those that increase the possibility of sexual harassment--or the possibility that behavior will be taken as harassing whatever its intent.[4]

Here then is the problem: Power pollutes authority. "Tailor[ing] our evaluation methods to [our] instructional objectives" would link our evaluation methods to our authority, but would disconnect them from our power. Some reform suggestions in the symposium point in the direction of separating authority from power. Professor Feinman's proposal, for example, can be understood as a method to reduce substantially the usefulness of in-school evaluations for external purposes. To the extent that grading systems involve exercises of power *by* faculty members, we could develop strong norms against their use as a tool of power, as we have tried to do with rules regarding sexual harassment. To the extent that grading systems reproduce structures of power by rewarding capabilities distributed differentially among our students, as Professor Waire Post suggests, we can reconsider the criteria we have for determining what is good work.

I personally favor most of the proposals along these lines made by the authors in this symposium. But it has to be said that at first glance the proposals have a strongly utopian tenor to them. The reason is clear as well: They run against the present preferences of important constituencies for legal educators.[5]

As several articles in the symposium make clear, important segments of law faculties think our power to certify and screen is normatively desirable, and of course we have an interest in preserving the power we exercise. More troubling, I think, is that

4. In referring to harassment, I do not mean to suggest that the only problem involves male faculty members harassing female students. I know of stories about male students engaging in behavior that I would characterize as harassing female faculty members, for example. And I know of female students who have "come on" to unreceptive male faculty members. (There is one category I have omitted in this catalogue because I have not heard stories about it, although I guess I am reasonably confident that there are examples there as well. I omit consideration of same-sex harassment for the same reason.)

5. In what follows I do not discuss preferences or demands from "external" constituencies such as the legal profession or university governing boards, because my sense of things is that the constraints they place on legal educators are much looser than we tend to think. For example, the profession could live with the elimination of grades as a screening device by substituting temporary employment by using the first years of employment as a try-out period--as the profession has already started to do.

some students like the existing systems of evaluation seen as power-exercises. These students, who seem to me fairly numerous, want us to certify them, to provide some seemingly objective and external confirmation of their own sense of themselves. Of course they would like to know that they are "grade A" sorts of people, but, I think, they sometimes take comfort in the fact that someone else has told them that they are merely mediocre, that the difficulty they are having in getting good jobs is what "people like you" deserve. Faculty certification depersonalizes what are apparently personal evaluations by objectifying them. But here too there is more. One does not have to be a thorough-going Freudian to believe that some part of all of us, deep down, actually likes to be subjected to the exercise of power by others. Students demand evaluation systems that rank them because some part of each student, deep down, does not mind being put at the bottom by someone else.

This then is a sketch of the structure that makes grading reform a seemingly endless task. On the first level we find a combination of power and authority. If we could divorce our authority from our power, we could probably develop evaluation systems that made sense. But there are structural obstacles to that divorce, lying in the complex combination of interest and psychodynamics I have described.

In light of this analysis, I propose to ask two questions about reform proposals of the sort offered in this symposium. Reformers tend to assume that we have already separated authority from power, and then ask, Would this proposal do a good job of evaluating those things with respect to which we have authority? My first question is a different one: Would adopting the proposal undermine the structure that makes it difficult to separate authority from power? I doubt that this question can be answered in the abstract, about generically described reform proposals. That concern generates my second question, addressed in part in Professor Waire Post's case study: Would the effort to adopt this proposal set in motion a political process that would make it easier to separate authority from power, even if the proposal is not adopted? Answering that question, of course, requires close attention to the circumstances in which a particular proposal is made. The articles in this symposium, I think, invite readers to reflect on their own circumstances with an eye to answering my two questions--and many others, of course.

# Name Index